pearson custom library
MUSIC

Ethnomusicology 50B
Hasse-Discover Jazz
UCLA

Ethnomusicology 50B

PEARSON

V092

Please visit our website at *www.pearsonlearningsolutions.com.*

Attention bookstores: For permission to return any unsold stock, contact us at *pe-uscustomreturns@pearson.com.*

Pearson Learning Solutions, 501 Boylston Street, Suite 900, Boston, MA 02116
A Pearson Education Company
www.pearsoned.com

ISBN 10: 1-256-60424-0
ISBN 13: 978-1-256-60424-2

Table of Contents

Free and Exploratory Jazz

by John Litweiler

TAKE NOTE

- Why was 1959 such a pivotal year in jazz history?
- What were the roots of free jazz?
- What were the innovations introduced by free jazz in melody, rhythm, harmony, and performance style?
- Who were the leading innovators in the free jazz movement?
- What role did cooperatives and independent performance spaces play in free jazz?

From Chapter 8 of *Discover Jazz*. First Edition. John Edward Hasse, Tad Lathrop. Copyright © 2012 by Pearson Education, Inc. All rights reserved.

1

HISTORICAL EVENTS   The 1960s   MUSICAL EVENTS

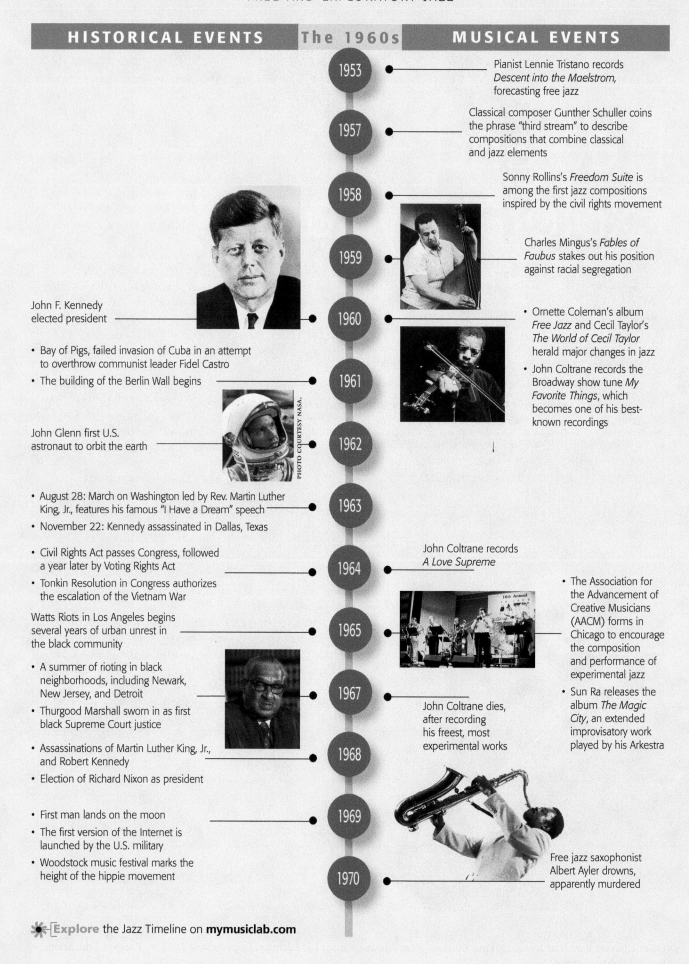

1953 — Pianist Lennie Tristano records *Descent into the Maelstrom*, forecasting free jazz

1957 — Classical composer Gunther Schuller coins the phrase "third stream" to describe compositions that combine classical and jazz elements

1958 — Sonny Rollins's *Freedom Suite* is among the first jazz compositions inspired by the civil rights movement

1959 — Charles Mingus's *Fables of Faubus* stakes out his position against racial segregation

John F. Kennedy elected president —— **1960**
- Ornette Coleman's album *Free Jazz* and Cecil Taylor's *The World of Cecil Taylor* herald major changes in jazz

- Bay of Pigs, failed invasion of Cuba in an attempt to overthrow communist leader Fidel Castro
- The building of the Berlin Wall begins —— **1961**
- John Coltrane records the Broadway show tune *My Favorite Things*, which becomes one of his best-known recordings

John Glenn first U.S. astronaut to orbit the earth —— **1962**

PHOTO COURTESY NASA.

- August 28: March on Washington led by Rev. Martin Luther King, Jr., features his famous "I Have a Dream" speech —— **1963**
- November 22: Kennedy assassinated in Dallas, Texas

- Civil Rights Act passes Congress, followed a year later by Voting Rights Act —— **1964** — John Coltrane records *A Love Supreme*
- Tonkin Resolution in Congress authorizes the escalation of the Vietnam War

Watts Riots in Los Angeles begins several years of urban unrest in the black community —— **1965**
- The Association for the Advancement of Creative Musicians (AACM) forms in Chicago to encourage the composition and performance of experimental jazz

- A summer of rioting in black neighborhoods, including Newark, New Jersey, and Detroit
- Thurgood Marshall sworn in as first black Supreme Court justice —— **1967** — John Coltrane dies, after recording his freest, most experimental works
- Sun Ra releases the album *The Magic City*, an extended improvisatory work played by his Arkestra

- Assassinations of Martin Luther King, Jr., and Robert Kennedy —— **1968**
- Election of Richard Nixon as president

- First man lands on the moon —— **1969**
- The first version of the Internet is launched by the U.S. military
- Woodstock music festival marks the height of the hippie movement

1970 — Free jazz saxophonist Albert Ayler drowns, apparently murdered

※ Explore the Jazz Timeline on **mymusiclab.com**

① 959: A Turning Point in Jazz History

Nineteen fifty-nine brought a turning point in jazz. The spring marked the deaths of three great swing era figures: saxophonist Lester Young, singer Billie Holiday, and soprano saxophonist-clarinetist Sidney Bechet. In that same season, the immensely popular Miles Davis Sextet disbanded, leaving two breakthrough albums in its wake: Davis's modal masterwork *Kind of Blue* and the supremely lyrical *Giant Steps* by Davis's departing tenor saxophonist, **John Coltrane**.

At the time, **Ornette Coleman** was still an obscure alto sax player, yet the three albums he recorded in California that year were as significant as those other key events. Two of the albums were by his own, carefully trained, pianoless quartet—*The Shape of Jazz to Come* and *Change of the Century*—and they announced a new era in jazz as surely as did Louis Armstrong's Hot Fives and Hot Sevens in 1926–27 or the first Charlie Parker-Dizzy Gillespie groups in 1945. And when the Coleman quartet played its first nightclub gig in New York City, in November 1959, it was the most combustible of all jazz debuts, igniting an explosion of exploratory creative activity by jazz musicians.

Of course, jazz musicians, those notorious nonconformists, have been explorers ever since New Orleans cornetist Buddy Bolden first played ragtime variations. But traditional jazz, swing, and bop improvisations were all based on the harmonic structures—the chord changes—of the songs the players played. Ornette Coleman's greatest innovation, on the other hand, was playing without fixed harmonic structures.

What Coleman did wasn't exactly unprecedented. A handful of musicians—among them, woodwind improviser Joe Maneri in Boston in the 1940s and alto saxophonist Joe Harriott in London in the 1950s—reportedly preceded Coleman in abandoning chord changes, though their early adventures weren't documented. Pianist Lennie Tristano's sextet created two notable recordings without preset chord changes in 1949, though the players instinctively imply conventional song form in the more successful piece, *Intuition*; more radical is Tristano's intense, atonal, overdubbed, aptly titled piano solo *Descent into the Maelstrom* (1953). As early as 1933 there were the strange, tumbling key changes of xylophonist-vibraphonist Red Norvo's *Dance of*

Ornette Coleman used the term harmolodic *for his approach to improvisation, which broke away from the chord-based soloing of bebop and mainstream jazz.* PHOTO COURTESY LEE TANNER

History & Culture

Trombonist Tyree Glenn and tenor saxophonist Chu Berry photographed by bassist Milt Hinton while on the road (ca. 1940). PHOTO COURTESY © MILTON J. HINTON PHOTOGRAPHIC COLLECTION.

Jazz: The Sound of Freedom

At the time jazz musicians began freeing themselves from traditional harmony, sound, and form, many turned the same impulse toward social issues, especially the burgeoning civil rights movement. The music and activism that resulted were only the latest manifestations of a desire for individual freedom—and with it, racial equality—that had long been present in jazz. "Jazz was not just a music," Sonny Rollins said. "It was a social force in this country, and it was talking about freedom and people . . . not having to worry about whether they were supposed to be white, black, and all this stuff."

Not that the racial discrimination coursing through the United States during the twentieth century wasn't also reflected in the world of jazz—and experienced firsthand by its musicians. From the start, the Octopus, and during the bebop era there were plenty of works pointing to a world beyond bop. *Dalvatore Sally*, by George Handy for the Boyd Raeburn band (1946); Ellington's atonal theme of *The Clothed Woman* (1948); *A Bird in Igor's Yard*, George Russell's bright fusion of classical composer Igor Stravinsky and bop saxophonist Charlie Parker, played by the Buddy DeFranco band (1949); early experiments by drummer Shelly Manne and reedman Jimmy Giuffre—these are especially noteworthy examples of musicians' stretching the boundaries of jazz. But these works were isolated experiments, even though most of the artists were repeat experimenters throughout their lives.

"The new music," "the new thing," "'outside' jazz," "free jazz"—there was never a universally accepted name, such as swing or bop, for the idiom that grew out of Coleman's innovations. Early journalists took to the term **free jazz**, partly because Coleman recorded an album titled *Free Jazz* (1960) and also because this music's freedom of expression came at a time of great social change.

The changes, in fact, were some of the most far-reaching of the twentieth century: freedom was in the air. The civil rights movement—a crystallization of African Americans' growing insistence on equal opportunity and the public's increasing awareness of the value and vitality of African American culture—was at its height, marked by the passing of the Civil Rights and Voting acts (1964–65). Among jazz musicians, the civil rights movement had a powerful

Watch the documentary on free jazz on mymusiclab.com

free jazz a style of jazz introduced in 1959 and developed in the 1960s and 1970s that relies on neither key nor chord progressions for improvisational structure.

prevailing social order guaranteed inequality of opportunity for black and white players: although black musicians may have played the first "jass" in New Orleans, it was a white group, the Original Dixieland Jazz Band, that first became famous.

For many years into the evolution of jazz, working conditions remained far from equal for white and black bands. In many parts of the United States, hotels and restaurants that served black customers were hard to find. And in some areas, particularly the South, black bands faced very real dangers. Cab Calloway recalled a 1931 gig in Virginia Beach, Virginia, in which the mostly white audience grew angry and "somebody shouted, 'Let's take this nigger out and lynch him.' And all this while I was trying to sing."

Integration onstage—pioneered in part by Benny Goodman's employment of a few major black musicians in his small combos—remained a rarity until the bebop era, when the increasing assertiveness of bop musicians began dovetailing with a free-thinking youth counterculture.

It was in the jazz realm that some of the earliest cracks in the wall of

discrimination appeared. From the beginning, the music attracted both black and white musicians and audiences; for many white listeners, racial prejudice began to crumble when they found themselves admiring black jazz players. And exchanges of ideas among musicians of both races were at the core of jazz evolution—in the 1920s, for example, virtually all of the white, Chicago-style musicians were powerfully influenced by Louis Armstrong, while in the 1930s the white Casa Loma Orchestra had a strong impact on black bands of the time.

The jazz world's advocacy of freedom and racial equality ultimately became more overt and direct. In 1950, Duke Ellington vowed that proceeds from his composition *Harlem* would be used to "stamp out segregation, discrimination, bigotry, and a variety of other intolerances." In the 1960s, calls for social liberation—whether in the form of songs such as Eddie Harris's *Freedom Jazz Dance* (1965) or even band names (**Charlie Haden**'s Liberation Music Orchestra)—became plentiful. Bassist Charles Mingus's 1960 tune *Original Faubus Fables* overtly called for "no more

Ku Klux Klan" and entreated, "Oh, Lord, don't let 'em shoot us ... stab us ... tar and feather us!" Saxophonist John Coltrane responded to the 1963 killing of four young girls in Birmingham, Alabama, by composing *Alabama*, its sound inspired by the cadences of the speech Martin Luther King, Jr., delivered at the memorial service. Drummer Max Roach issued the passionate 1960 album *We Insist! Freedom Now Suite*, and he remained a highly active vocal (as well as musical) advocate of civil rights.

Martin Luther King, Jr., himself recognized the connection between jazz and civil rights. "Much of the power of our Freedom Movement in the United States has come from this music," he remarked in his opening address at the 1964 Berlin Jazz Festival.

To many, the very idea of jazz became synonymous with freedom. "If jazz means anything," Ellington once wrote, "it is freedom of expression."

"Jazz," said Rollins, "has always been the music that had this kind of spirit."

—*Tad Lathrop and John Litweiler*

resonance. Louis Armstrong made headlines with his scalding criticism of President Eisenhower during the Little Rock, Arkansas, school integration crisis in 1957. There were civil rights inspired albums, including tenor saxophonist Sonny Rollins's *Freedom Suite* (1958), drummer Max Roach's *Freedom Now Suite* (1960), and drummer Art Blakey's *The Freedom Rider* (1961). And the free jazz musicians, mostly young and most black, were unanimous, often vocal, in their support of the struggle for social freedom.

👁 Watch the documentary on civil rights on **mymusiclab.com**

TAKE NOTE

- Why was 1959 such a pivotal year in jazz history?

Free Jazz Ancestors

Of the ancestors of free jazz, two offered especially powerful advances in technique and sensibility: composer-bassist Charles Mingus and composer Bob Graettinger.

Mingus based his music on chord changes and modes, but his passion was certainly a precedent for free jazz. Such Mingus works as *Pithecanthropus Erectus* (1956) and his *Tijuana Moods* album (1957) are volatile and full of complex activity and raw-edged playing, foreshadowing the sound of early 1960s groups with woodwind virtuoso **Eric Dolphy**; this is music that raises blisters. Along with beautiful melodies, he also composed the socially conscious pieces *Fables of Faubus* (1959), his musical assault on segregationist Arkansas governor Orval Faubus, and *Cry for Freedom (Prayer for Passive Resistance)* (1960). Of Mingus's big band works, quite the most important

As uncompromising in business as he was in music composition, bassist Charles Mingus made numerous career moves to counteract what he saw as restrictive commercialism in jazz. With drummer Max Roach, he ran a record label, Debut, in the early 1950s. In 1960 he and Roach organized Newport Rebels, an alternative to the mainstream Newport Jazz Festival. Such enterprises served as models for later musician-controlled record labels and organizations.

PHOTO COURTESY FRANK DRIGGS COLLECTION.

is his grand *Epitaph* suite (1962–89), encompassing decades of composition (including reconstruction by composer **Gunther Schuller**) and not performed until 1989, a decade after his death.

As for Graettinger, the works he composed for Stan Kenton's jazz orchestras bear only passing resemblance to any other jazz or twentieth-century classical music. His large-scale compositions sound like immense dreams. Graettinger's *City of Glass* (1950 version) and *This Modern World* (1951–53) are

atonal—without a harmonic foundation—and dense with polyphonic and polyrhythmic movement, lovely instrumental blendings, cold and bleak passages, blazing ensemble climaxes, and fugitive solo moments. These works are almost overwhelming in their complex, ever-changing activity; it's notable that every vivid, beautiful image evaporates.

> **TAKE NOTE**
>
> • What were the roots of free jazz?

Free Jazz Innovations

With all this diverse activity as a precedent, what was it about Coleman that made him such a powerful stimulus? And what is free jazz? To answer the second question first, there were four main areas of innovation in free jazz: sound, harmony, form, and rhythm. New conceptions of these four elements grew out of Coleman's early music.

Sonic Freedom

While early jazz and swing were rich with the personal sounds of expressive individuals, bebop's quest for virtuoso lyricism yielded a narrower range of sonorities. You hear this especially in brass instrumentalists. For instance, the smooth sound introduced by J. J. Johnson was pervasive among bop trombonists. In free jazz, on the other hand, the sonic range was unlimited. The emotive trombonist Roswell Rudd, a former Dixieland musician, brought back the rich intonation and slippery slides and blasts of swing, while such successors as George Lewis and Craig Harris went on to further exploit the trombone's power, range, and capacity for expression. Meanwhile, such trumpeters as the vividly dramatic **Lester Bowie** and the lyrical Leo Smith added new dimensions of humor and sweetness, fire and abstraction, and loud-soft contrasts. It's no accident that Leo Smith was once inspired by Joe Smith's (no relation) lyric trumpet accompaniments to Bessie Smith, or that Bowie was originally inspired by Louis Armstrong's epic solos; both Bowie and Leo Smith, like other free players, were returning to the quest for personal expression that was at the very root of jazz.

Coleman himself, for a time, played a white plastic alto saxophone, which had a rather dry sound

(((•—**Hear** a profile of Ornette Coleman on **mymusiclab.com**

atonal   composed without being based in traditional rules of harmonic relationships; for example, not in a key.

Trumpeter Lester Bowie explored free improvisation and "freak" sounds as a member of both the Association for the Advancement of Creative Musicians and the Art Ensemble of Chicago. PHOTO COURTESY MICHAEL WILDERMAN.

Harmonic Freedom

What startled listeners most when they first heard Ornette Coleman was the harmonic structure of his soloing. In swing and bebop solos, chord changes provided emotional shape and tension, and the harmonic tensions were almost inevitably resolved, creating a familiar pleasure for listeners. The singular quality of modal jazz was its reduced structural tension, for modal jazz had slower and subtler harmonic movement, especially in its early years.

Coleman had a third solution. "Before I met Ornette," said his bassist Charlie Haden, "I would sometimes feel to play not on the changes of the song; sometimes I would feel to play on the inspiration and the feeling of the song, and create a new chord structure to it in my solo. . . . And the first time I played with Ornette, he was doing that." Coleman recalled that when he taught his new music to his first quartet partners, Haden, trumpeter **Don Cherry**, and drummer Billy Higgins, "the most interesting part is: what do you play after you play the melody [theme]? That's where I won them over . . . finally I got them to where they could see how to express themselves without linking up to a definite maze."

that emphasized the crying quality in his melodies. His sound sometimes changed from phrase to phrase as he soloed ("I realized that you can play sharp or flat in tune," Coleman said). **Multiphonics**, or split tones (two or more notes at once), and **overtones** (notes higher than a horn's normal range) became commonplace in the music of Coltrane and **Albert Ayler** and later among the multitude of saxophonists whom they inspired. Instruments almost wholly new to jazz improvisation appeared from Africa, Asia, and the realm of classical music. The **Art Ensemble of Chicago** made a deliberate search for new sounds, adding hundreds of gongs, bells, whistles, and toys to the usual instrumentation. Oddly enough, although free jazz coincided with the development of the synthesizer, only bandleader **Sun Ra** and a handful of others created important work on the instrument. One of those others was trombonist George Lewis, who played duets with a computer he programmed to improvise music.

Years later, when world music and heavy metal rock were popular, the sounds the free jazz musicians made didn't seem quite as astonishing as they once had. On the other hand, Lester Bowie, later in his career, proposed forming a literally heavy-metal band—with sousaphones, bass saxophones, and steel drums.

---

multiphonics   two or more notes played at the same time by a single instrument.

overtones   harmonic overtones; in acoustics, secondary tones that are subdivisions of a fundamental tone or frequency; generated in stringed instruments by touching, rather than plucking, the string at points marking shorter segments of the string length that generates the main tone; also called harmonics.

Don Cherry played pocket trumpet in Ornette Coleman's quartet before recording as a leader. In later years Cherry attained renown as a pioneer in world music. PHOTO COURTESY FRANK DRIGGS COLLECTION.

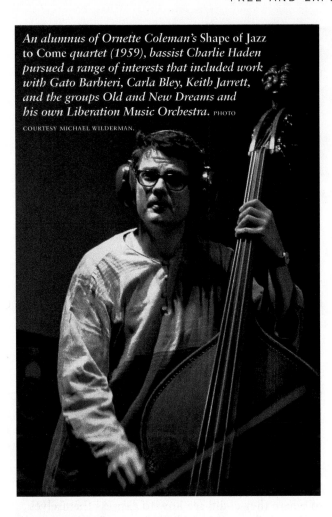

An alumnus of Ornette Coleman's Shape of Jazz to Come *quartet (1959), bassist Charlie Haden pursued a range of interests that included work with Gato Barbieri, Carla Bley, Keith Jarrett, and the groups Old and New Dreams and his own Liberation Music Orchestra.* PHOTO COURTESY MICHAEL WILDERMAN.

(1959) only the drummer of the Ornette Coleman Quartet kept time, while the trumpeter and saxophonist played the haunting melody in freely changing tempos and the bassist strummed spaced, arhythmic accents. And after the balladlike theme of *Beauty Is a Rare Thing* (1960) the Coleman quartet improvised together in freely moving lines with no fixed tempo or meter at all. Like free harmonic structure, free rhythmic structure was here.

Trumpeter Don Ellis's early combos played free-time pieces, and Jimmy Giuffre's trio created the daring *Free Fall* (1962), an album of free-time, "outside" improvisations. Ellis went on to compose big band scores using complex Indian rhythmic patterns, while four drummers—Sunny Murray, Andrew Cyrille, Milford Graves, and **Rashied Ali**—took the more radical step of abandoning fixed rhythm entirely, instead playing pure accent and momentum. What those drummers did was certainly revolutionary. And why not? Coleman's example was leading musicians to question the foundations of the entire jazz tradition.

Giuffre's and the drummers' explorations led to unaccompanied horn solos and free improvisation, which evolved largely in Chicago and England in the late 1960s. In free improvisation, soloists or groups (almost always small groups) of musicians improvised without themes, harmonic or rhythmic structures, or fixed forms.

Formal Freedom

Without chord changes, did Coleman's solos turn into chaos, as detractors once claimed? Quite the contrary: his music's formal unity was an important source of its power. He structured his solos by using fragments of melody, which he would alter and incorporate into virtually every phrase. This theme-based method was widely influential, though a good many alternatives followed. There were the free-association forms of Eric Dolphy; the cyclic forms of Coltrane; the grand architecture of pianist **Cecil Taylor**'s solos; the meticulously mounted lines of saxophonist Steve Lacy; the dramatic shapes of **Roscoe Mitchell** and Lester Bowie; the freely moving lyricism of saxophonist Fred Anderson—there were even vestiges of the classic building climax-anticlimax swing and bop form in the sonic adventures of tenor sax player Albert Ayler. Free jazz implied not freedom from form but freedom to choose form.

Rhythmic Freedom

Jazz had typically been played in $\frac{2}{4}$ and $\frac{4}{4}$ time, or occasionally in $\frac{3}{4}$ and $\frac{6}{4}$ meters, and the bassist and drummer marked the time. But in *Lonely Woman*

TAKE NOTE

* What were the innovations introduced by free jazz in melody, rhythm, harmony, and performance style?

Bandleader-trumpeter Don Ellis experimented with 12-tone rows, Indian additive rhythm, microtones, and other departures from standard European harmony and meter. His 1960s albums Electric Bath *and* Don Ellis at the Fillmore *were well suited for the progressive audiences of the era.* PHOTO COURTESY FRANK DRIGGS COLLECTION.

Style & Technique

How to Listen to Free Jazz

With many of the signposts for understanding standard jazz not applicable to free jazz, finding meaning in free jazz requires a shift of attention to different kinds of qualities.

You might apply a three-point approach to listening:

1. **Open listening.** At first, don't try to analyze or "make sense" of what you hear. Instead, focus on yourself: What are you feeling as you listen? What thoughts spring to your mind as you listen? How are you reacting to the music? Articulate answers to yourself (or in discussion) as precisely as you can. Then focus back on the music: how would you identify and describe some of the specific events and sounds that made you react as you did? This exercise should prompt an initial sense of engagement with the music.

2. **Listening for familiar characteristics.**

Melody: Listen for shapes, contours, and durations. Are small melodic building blocks (motifs) being used to create longer phrases? Notice whether phrases repeat. If there is minimal or no repetition, decide whether another kind of logic is driving melodic development.

Color and texture: Listen to the spectrum of tone colors you hear. Is there much variety? Inventory the tone colors used in the piece. Are they bright? dark?

woody? metallic? And listen for texture. Are there many instruments, creating a dense texture? Or are there only a few, leaving a sparse sound?

Voice, feel, and expression: You may hear more varied and unusual inflections and expressive devices in free jazz than in more traditional styles. Sounds may include those outside of an instrument's typical range or role. Blasts, squeals, squawks, whispers, murmurs are all part of the free jazz lexicon. You may even hear sound-producing devices—such as a car siren or bicycle horn—that are not normally considered musical instruments. Think about the expressiveness of what you hear and how you might describe it.

Musicians' roles, individual and collective: Pay attention to the relationships among players. Note whether there seems to be a leader and accompanist(s), a succession of different leaders, a "conversation" among equals, or some other arrangement of roles.

3. **Making sense of the unfamiliar.** In the areas of free jazz's greatest departures—form and harmony, for example—you need to reach beyond standard criteria for understanding.

Form: Chord progressions may not be present, so looking for an architecture based on them, with repetitions and variations, may not be relevant. You need to look for other elements on which form may be based. You might listen to changes in dynamics—soft sections and loud sections. Or you might listen to changes in texture, or

musicians' roles. There may be fragments of melody that repeat and transmute, or change in contour. The key is to recognize a larger architecture that emerges from the development of any of these elements over the length of the piece. It's conceivable, of course, that no overarching form may be discernible.

Harmony: The sense of movement in a free piece may not rely on resolution to a "home" chord (the tonic) the way traditional jazz or European tonal harmony does. But harmony may exist in the sense of chords forming, changing, sounding **consonant** (agreeably "in tune") or **dissonant** (discordant), and voiced closely (notes of the chord clustered close together) or openly (notes wide apart). Listen for tension and resolution, stasis versus motion, consonance versus dissonance, and change of mood.

Rhythm: In the absence of a repetitive, steady beat, or of any discernible rhythmic unity among musicians, look for patterns where you can find them and focus on how they may be repeating or developing. Focus your attention on one player, and notice not only the rhythm of the playing but also how it interlocks with (or ignores) surrounding rhythms. Attempt to discern rhythmic structure—unless there is none.

—*Tad Lathrop*

---

consonant notes or harmonies sounding agreeably "in tune"; the opposite of dissonant.

dissonant sounding discordant; the opposite of consonant.

Free Jazz Innovators

Coleman, Taylor, and Coltrane

The force behind Ornette Coleman's spearheading of free jazz came from the emotion in his music. He played without chord changes because it was in his nature to do so. "I think jazz should express more kinds of feelings than it has up to now," he said, and among his classic early pieces, *Peace* (1959), *Compassion* (1959), and *Sadness* (1962) convey the emotions of his song titles with a subtlety new to jazz. There is also the optimistic swagger of *Ramblin'* (1959), the electricity of *Free* (1959) and *Forerunner* (1959), the stark blues of *Lonely Woman* (1959), the sorrow of *Lorraine* (1959), the anger of *Kaleidoscope* (1960) and *Blues Connotation* (1960)—all shown in sharp relief. In his early solos he achieved rhythmic tension as acute as Charlie Parker's, though his own broken phrases are rhythmically simpler than Parker's. Like Parker's, Coleman's melodies are rich with blues; his angular

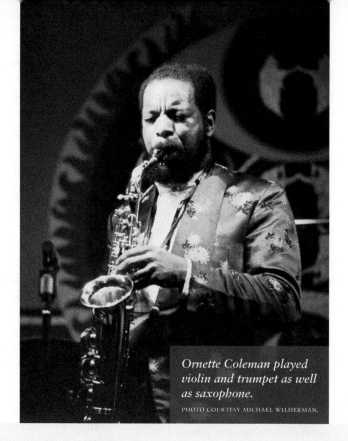

Ornette Coleman played violin and trumpet as well as saxophone.

PHOTO COURTESY MICHAEL WILDERMAN.

Listening Guide

CD II, Track 2/Download Track 26

RAMBLIN' • ORNETTE COLEMAN

Music: Ornette Coleman, 1959. Personnel: Don Cherry (cornet); Ornette Coleman (alto sax); Charlie Haden (bass); Billy Higgins (drums). Recorded October 8, 1959, in Hollywood. First issue: *Change of the Century*, Atlantic LP1327. Matrix no. 3874. Timing: 6:38.

Overview

It's only right that this masterpiece, with its blues and folk-music elements, is a loving reflection of America's frontier myth, for Coleman's discoveries opened the jazz frontier to possibilities that have been the main area of jazz development ever since 1959.

Key Features

- Improvisation: The first two phrases of Coleman's wonderfully flowing solo capture the jaunty feeling of the theme. They provide a motif that recurs in many subsequent lines, varied, embodied, or (as at 1:28) repeated.

In the fifth chorus a very blue sax phrase is mocked by a light, dancing phrase (1:58). This provides Coleman with new motif that leads to swaggering phrases. At 2:19 he moves into darker, bluer phrases that, by 2:30, morph back into the original optimistic mood. A long growl (2:27) foreshadows the end of this eight-chorus solo. Hear, especially, the beauty of Coleman's melodies.

Don Cherry's pocket trumpet solo offers four choruses of fine bop melodies. His form is almost classic, including (3:30) a climactic chorus centered on repeated notes.

Charlie Haden's simple, strummed bass solo (4:00) is derived from his vamp accompaniments to the horns. It sounds like variations on a nineteenth-century cowboy song of lonely, wide-open spaces. At 4:40 Haden strums a new melody that suggests a country fiddle song (*Old Joe Clark?*).

- Rhythm: A $\frac{4}{4}$ meter and an ideal medium-up tempo for inspiring improvisation with exhilarating swing.
- Harmony: Coleman's harmonic structure only irregularly matches the bass's blues changes, for it is essentially implied by his melodic lines. Cherry's solo follows Haden's chord changes more closely.
- Dynamics: The final contrast between fading bass and stabbing horns is a delightful surprise.
- Voice, feel, and expression: Coleman's sax sound ranges from light to full-bodied to (beginning at 0:58) mock-angry growls. The sound of Cherry's small trumpet is light, with a one-octave treble range. Haden's bass attack is especially aggressive.
- Musicians' roles: Traditional horn and rhythm-section roles, though without the customary support of a piano.

—John Litweiler

note choices and shifting keys added further tension, as did the accompanying interplay of harmonically ambiguous bass and drums. Coleman also explored **collective improvisation**—where every musician is free to improvise his part during a performance—most notably in the 40-minute *Free Jazz*, with eight musicians bandying lines back and forth over a fixed tempo—a kind of far-out Dixieland.

By the mid-1960s Coleman was also playing violin and trumpet, both with wild, spontaneous phrasing and unorthodox, self-taught technique. Over the years he retired from public performing several times, usually to compose. Few of his orchestral or chamber-music compositions have been performed; the best known is his *Skies of America* (1972) for symphony orchestra and improvisers. Following the mid-1970s, he played most often with his band Prime Time—which employed electric guitars and drums—in a hybrid jazz-rock idiom that he invented. These unique fusion-music adventures were rhythmically stimulating, but little of his latter-day music had anything like the power and

excitement of his early recordings on the Atlantic and Contemporary labels.

The commotion over Coleman at the start of the 1960s drew attention to two other highly advanced jazzmen: Eric Dolphy and Cecil Taylor. The almost human sounds—squawks, grunts, cries, blurts, mutters—of Dolphy's **bass clarinet** and Charles Mingus's bass in improvised mock arguments (*What Love*, 1960) were a fabulous spectacle, as was Dolphy's soaring, biting alto sax soloing (*Original Faubus Fables*, 1960): here at last was a passionate interpreter to match Mingus's own passion. Dolphy played with a full,

---

collective improvisation   spontaneous composition performed simultaneously by members of an ensemble.

bass clarinet   the lowest-pitched instrument in the clarinet family.

hambone   practice of using the human body as a rhythm instrument by using one's hands slapping against thighs, arms, chest, and other parts of the body.

TIME	SECTION	MELODY/INSTRUMENTATION
0:00	FIRST THEME, OPENING PHRASE	Four bars of horns, four bars of strummed bass vamp. This jaunty melody sets the feeling of *Ramblin'*. While the three-phrase theme resembles blues form, Coleman actually expands upon blues. So the initiating four-bar melody is answered by Haden's strummed bass chord, in a dancing **"hambone"** pattern derived from folk music.
0:09	SECOND THEME PHRASE	Two bars of horns, four bars of bass vamp. The down-turned phrases and abrupt, comic distortion of the melody suggest a realistic corrective to the optimism of the opening phrase.
0:15	THIRD THEME PHRASE	Two bars horns, four bars bass vamp. After this five-note return to optimism, the trumpet rides over the bass.
0:25	FIRST CHORUS	Follows the three-phrase form of the first, except that over the last bass vamp . . .
0:46	ALTO SAX SOLO	. . . Ornette Coleman begins his alto sax solo.
1:02		Alto solo continues over the bass's straight-ahead $\frac{4}{4}$ meter. For the rest of Coleman's solo, Haden alternates between 12-bar straightahead choruses on blues changes, and 16-bar choruses of strummed folk-dance variations.
2:56	TRUMPET SOLO	Drummer Billy Higgins switches to higher cymbals.
4:00	BASS SOLO	Higgins taps accompaniment on cymbal stand.
4:58	FIRST THEME, REPEATED ONCE	The band returns with the initial theme for two choruses.
5:43		Ending of the last theme phrase. Now both alto sax and trumpet ride in melodic counterpoint over the bass's cowboy-song strums. The bouncy horn melodies over the bass suggest a wagon train riding the prairie into the sunset. As the horns fade at 6:23, the strummed western song continues until . . .
6:28	CODA	. . . the final phrase. Horns and drums snap out the second (reality) phrase of the theme, for an irresolute conclusion. Perfect!

clear sound on all his horns—and on the flute—and employed wide harmonic leaps and dissonances that often sounded atonal, even though he maintained that "every note I play has some reference to the chords of the piece." In later years, he made many recordings with George Russell, Booker Little, Coltrane, Coleman, and others before his untimely death from diabetes at the age of 36.

Even before Coleman, Cecil Taylor was playing piano solos so dissonant and free they sounded atonal. Such classical composers as Béla Bartók and Igor Stravinsky influenced his music, as did Ellington and modern jazz pianists; a good introduction is his album *The World of Cecil Taylor* (1960). After that, turmoil grew in his highly complex solo forms, which often used fragmentary phrases to generate grand designs; he also composed knotty pieces with many mood changes and stops and starts. By the late 1960s, he was playing violently, as fast as humanly possible (and Taylor may be the most virtuosic of all jazz pianists), with dissonances crashing like thunder through the high ("astral" he called it), middle ("surface of the earth"), and low ("abyss") registers of the keyboard. He usually overpowered the horn soloists who played with him. He also improvised long, intense, unaccompanied pieces, full of detail, almost as demanding for the listener as for the performer; "To feel is the most terrifying thing in this society," he said. For an example of his playing of this era, listen to *Jitney No. 2* (JTSA Disc 5/Track 14). A lyrical side of his music subsequently grew in importance, especially in the 1980s. The most remarkable recording project built around a free jazz artist was Cecil Taylor in *Berlin '88*, a collection of 11 solo, duet,

Eric Dolphy's playing exuded warmth, humanity, and intelligence, notably in his innovative work on the bass clarinet. PHOTO COURTESY INSTITUTE OF JAZZ STUDIES, RUTGERS UNIVERSITY.

trio, and big band albums in which he was joined by a succession of excellent, mostly European players.

In subsequent decades, Taylor remained active while assuming a role—through teaching and performing—as a figurehead of experimental jazz. In 1990, he was recognized as a Jazz Master by the National Endowment for the Arts. Over the years, alumni of his college ensembles, at Antioch College and elsewhere, fanned out into the professional jazz community, promulgating his ideas.

John Coltrane was by far the most popular "outside" jazz artist, in large part because he had, according to Taylor, "great insight, a feeling for the hysteria of the times, and a conception that goes beyond that of his own horn." After 1960, Coltrane's solos became long, passionate conflicts in which he alternated lyrical playing with longer cycles that became progressively more

Cecil Taylor's stormy atonality drew on twentieth-century European music as well as jazz. PHOTO COURTESY MICHAEL WILDERMAN.

((•— **Hear** a profile of Cecil Taylor on **mymusiclab.com**

History & Culture

The Loft Scene

Each jazz era brought its characteristic venues. During the swing era, dancers flocked to ballrooms to hear big bands; after World War II, nightclubs, concert auditoriums, and outdoor festivals became the centers of jazz. The jazz recession of the early 1960s, coinciding with the emergence of a generation of free jazz musicians, pointed to a need for different kinds of performance settings—ones where adventurous musicians could ply their trade without the pressures imposed by more commercial nightclubs.

At the south end of Manhattan, where many of the most renowned "outside" musicians lived, the most daring music of the 1960s could be heard at coffee houses, little theaters, and especially in the large lofts where musicians maintained rehearsal spaces. Among the leading artists who conducted their early careers in these settings were pianist Cecil Taylor; saxophonists Albert Ayler, **Archie Shepp**, and Marion Brown; trumpeter Don Cherry; drummer Sunny Murray; and trombonist Roswell Rudd.

Lofts and other alternative venues offered informal surroundings, tended not to serve alcohol, and charged low admission prices. Attendees were typically young and liberal. Writer-poet LeRoi Jones noted in 1963 that "many serious young jazz listeners now seem more willing to go sit on the floor in a loft and hear good music than go to the formal clubs downtown and hear well-known chumps." Due in part to the close connection between artists and listeners fostered by the loft scene, the new music became the center of an underground community.

In the early 1970s, Ornette Coleman led his band in occasional concerts at his rehearsal space, Artists House, below his living quarters at 131 Prince Street. The veteran tenor saxophonist Sam Rivers and his wife, Bea, opened Studio Rivbea, 24 Bond Street, in 1971. Other jazz lofts followed, including several operated by musicians—Ladies' Fort (singer Joe Lee Wilson), Ali's Alley (drummer Rashied Ali), and the Brook (saxophonist Charles Tyler) were among them. The lofts provided key support for noncommercial musicians. When Edward Blackwell needed money for a kidney operation in 1973, fellow drummers Billy Higgins and Roger Blank organized benefit concerts, featuring a parade of top jazz artists, at Artists House. Several lofts joined forces to present festivals that competed with the annual Newport Jazz Festival in New York; the festivals showcased important musicians who had been excluded from the Newport bash.

Loft jazz wasn't confined to New York City; other centers included Philadelphia, Detroit, Chicago, Vancouver, and the San Francisco Bay Area. The roots of free improvisation, in fact, are traceable to the activities of drummer John Stevens and his cohorts in the 1960s at the aptly named Little Theatre in London.

What kind of music was played in the lofts? It wasn't always free jazz. Also heard were jazz veterans, now out of fashion at a time when nightclubs were few and their fare was limited. Ex-Basie arranger-tenorist Frank Foster led his Loud Minority big band in lofts, and a number of boppers such as Clifford Jordan, Sheila Jordan, Lee Konitz, and Hank Mobley alternated with a colorful variety of free players. Coleman and Konitz recorded albums at Artists House, saxophonists Tyler and Arthur Blythe recorded albums at

Saxophonist Sam Rivers and his wife, Bea, founded the Studio Rivbea loft. PHOTO COURTESY LEE TANNER.

the Brook, and five noted recordings from Studio Rivbea documented the 1977 Wildflowers festival that Rivers produced, which featured leading "liberated" musicians from California, Chicago, Philadelphia, and New York.

Most lofts disappeared after a few years. The longest lasting, Studio Rivbea, survived and even thrived until 1978, when a dispute with the landlord brought the music to an end. New York theaters and nightclubs were regularly presenting "outside" jazz by 1981, when Sam Rivers said, "Now there's not much need for loft spaces anymore except for rehearsals and for students." Since then, lofts have served as occasional concert spaces in New York and other principal cities, even as the audience for free jazz grew and small nightclubs, theaters, universities, and other venues emerged to accommodate musicians and listeners.

—*John Litweiler*

removed from the central harmony, leading to further cycles of multiphonics and overtone screams. These were terrifically intense solos, and much of Coltrane's tension derived from his harmonic straining against his pieces' modal non-structures. His tone was tender in his occasional ballad solos (as on the album *Ballads*, 1961–62) and iron-hard in his longer virtuoso pieces (*Traneing In*, 1957, and *Good Bait*, 1958). Sometimes he soloed on soprano saxophone for variety, as in his famous interpretation of the Rodgers and Hammerstein song *My Favorite Things* (1960; *JTSA* Disc 4/Track 10) from their musical *The Sound of Music*. Typical Coltrane quartet pieces featured extensive duets in which the powerful Elvin Jones played dense, multiple rhythms on a resonant drums-and-cymbals kit, creating huge waves of sound around the tenor saxophone.

After the spiritual turmoil of his album *A Love Supreme* (1964), Coltrane progressed to his greatest extremes of violent sound and harmony. The track *Acknowledgement* from that album is one of the best-known examples of his later style (*JTSA* Disc 5/Track 3). *Interstellar Space*, recorded shortly before his death in 1967, consists wholly of duets with drummer Rashied Ali. Coltrane recorded often, and he liked to encourage younger free jazz players; his quartets and quintets rivaled Miles Davis's quintet as the most popular jazz groups of the mid-1960s.

After Coltrane's death in 1967 his wife and final piano accompanist, Alice Coltrane, perceptively adapted his saxophone phrasing and forms to piano, harp, and organ. Her style resulted in highly ornate impressionism and her repertoire included blues-infused versions of traditional Hindu chants.

Born Alice McLeod in 1937, Alice had studied classical piano before becoming drawn to jazz. She backed mainstream guitarist Kenny Burrell and saxophonist Lucky Thompson in the early 1960s and, in 1966, replaced pianist McCoy Tyner in John Coltrane's group, offering up empathetic, harmonically ambiguous chordal accompaniments for his increasingly avant-garde soloing. From 1968 through the 1970s she issued a number of solo albums, including *Journey in Satchidananda*, echoing the spiritualism of her husband's

late work and paralleling the related efforts of such other John Coltrane protégés as **Pharoah Sanders** (whose 1969 *The Creator Has a Master Plan* is a fine, mesmerizing example of sensuous modal jazz). She retired from music in the late 1970s to commit herself to religious pursuits—while managing the John Coltrane estate—and founded the Vedantic Center, an ashram for the study of religions, in Los Angeles. She resurfaced in 2004 with the album *Translinear Light*, on which she was joined by her tenor and soprano saxophonist son Ravi Coltrane, sounding at times eerily like his father, and her altoist son Oran. Alice died in 2007, leaving a legacy of musical spirituality, along with her musical offspring to carry the family torch.

Jazz Underground

Controversy followed this music, far more and far longer than it did bop in the 1940s. Miles Davis's comment on first hearing Ornette Coleman is famous—"Hell, just listen to what he writes and how he plays. If you're talking psychologically, the man is all screwed up inside." A *Down Beat* reviewer called a Coltrane-Dolphy performance "a horrifying demonstration of what appears to be a growing anti-jazz

Saxophonist Archie Shepp (shown here in 1967) studied drums and played in R&B bands before emerging as a key free-jazz player via work with John Coltrane, Cecil Taylor, and others. His later work reflected his view of jazz as an expression of black culture and freedom. PHOTO COURTESY JAZZSIGN/LEBRECHT MUSIC & ARTS.

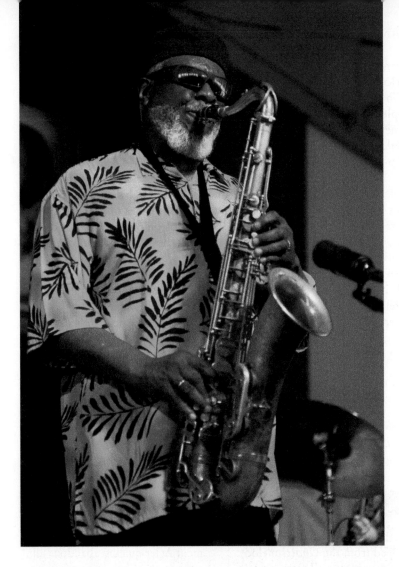

Pharoah Sanders's fat, raspy tenor saxophone sound brought him a modest degree of commercial success. His 1969 album Karma, *recorded with yodeling singer Leon Thomas, reached the pop charts. He is shown here at the New Orleans Jazz and Heritage Festival in 2007.*

All of this meant that Taylor and the younger free players found work only irregularly, and the music became an underground art in the 1960s. Coleman; his liberated, lyrical trumpeter Don Cherry; and especially Coltrane became father figures to a lively underground New York scene that included the dramatic tenor saxophonist-poet-playwright Archie Shepp, alto saxman Charles Tyler, tenor player Pharoah Sanders, trumpeter Bill Dixon, and pianist Paul Bley among others.

The new underground musicians, by and large, shared the social concerns and liberal attitudes of their jazz predecessors, and some—reflecting the era's social and political unrest—carried these attitudes further. "Outside" jazz musicians offered works that reflected uniquely African American experiences, while Coltrane's *Alabama* (1963) and Shepp's *The Funeral* (1963) and *Rufus* (1965) mourned victims of racist murders. Some young free musicians and audiences went on to favor black nationalism, violent revolution, and even Marxism, for which poet, author, and critic LeRoi Jones (later known as Amiri Baraka) was the most militant spokesperson on the jazz scene: "We want poems that kill!" he wrote.

Other Free Instrumentalists

Some players normally oriented toward chord changes, including tenor saxophonist Sonny Rollins, experimented with free playing. Even Miles Davis moved to Coleman-like freedom in his mid-1960s quintet, which had a remarkable rhythm section centered around the impulsive young drummer Tony Williams. Younger modal players, notably vibraphonist Bobby Hutcherson and pianist Andrew Hill, conducted several daring free jazz adventures. The change from "inside" to "outside" playing was permanent for some, including soprano saxman Steve Lacy. "It happened in gradual stages," he said. "There would be a moment here, a fifteen minutes there, a half hour there, an afternoon, an

trend," and jazz magazines were filled with columns about how "outside" jazz would destroy or save Western civilization.

At the same time that controversy was stalling the careers of free musicians, the 1960s rock-music industry was having a devastating effect on jazz. Motown Records artists, the Beatles, Bob Dylan, and other pop stars were winning over the young generation that had accounted for a large portion of the jazz audience. On a downswing from the height of modern jazz's popularity at the beginning of the 1960s, jazz clubs closed in cities all over the United States.

The remaining club and festival producers struggled with the new jazz economics by booking bop and swing acts that had already been dependable attractions. All of the leading jazz record companies, each with hundreds of titles in its catalog—Riverside, Savoy, Contemporary, Pacific Jazz, Blue Note, Prestige, Verve—scaled down operations drastically, went out of business, or were sold, usually to rock record tycoons. Significantly, the new Impulse! label, unlike its competitors, embraced new jazz wholeheartedly; it issued Coltrane albums about every three months and thrived.

evening, and then all the time." A highly influential artist, the prolific Lacy ranged from sweet melody to high overtone abstraction on his instrument, in contrast to the narrower soprano sax sounds employed by latter-day jazz traditionalists and newly emerging "fusion" players. Lacy and pianist Mal Waldron were unusual for their alternately free and bop-era repertoires.

Critics mocked free jazz as "outer-space music." But composer, bandleader, and poet Sun Ra might have considered that a compliment. "I've chosen intergalactic music, or it has chosen me," he said. "Intergalactic music concerns the music of the galaxies. . . . I'm actually painting pictures of infinity with my music. . . . The real aim of this music is to coordinate the minds of people into an intelligent reach for a better world, and an intelligent approach to the living future." Sun Ra's shows were always spectacles, with his Arkestra, as he called it, in vivid, glittering robes and space helmets, parading and

dancing through nightclubs and concert halls chanting "Next stop, Jupiter! Next stop, Jupiter!"

Sun Ra was among the first composers to work extensively with modal structures in the 1950s. His Arkestras employed exotic sounds, at least for jazz: oboe, piccolos, timpani, throbbing percussion, paired baritone saxes. By 1965 and *The Magic City*—a long, completely improvised piece—he was conducting spontaneous compositions by signaling his musicians to play in changing groupings. The climaxes of his shows were often his own extended solos on the synthesizer: dissonant, crashing, virtuosic; they were sustained explosions of sound. *A Call for All Demons* recorded in 1956 but not issued until its appearance on the album *Angels and Demons at Play* in 1965 is a good example of the Arkestra's sound (*JTSA* Disc 3/Track 13).

"It's late now for the world. And if I can help raise people to new plateaus of peace and understanding, I'll feel my life has been worth living as a spiritual artist," said Albert Ayler. The most radical free jazzman of the 1960s, he tried to reinvent the

((•—[Hear a profile of Sun Ra on **mymusiclab.com**

Listening Guide

((•—[Listen to *Ghosts: First Variation* by Albert Ayler on **mymusiclab.com**
CD II, Track 4/Download Track 28

GHOSTS: FIRST VARIATION • ALBERT AYLER

Music: Albert Ayler, 1964. Personnel: Albert Ayler (tenor saxophone); Gary Peacock (bass); Sunny Murray (drums). Recorded: July 10, 1964, New York. First issue: ESP-Disk 1002. Timing: 5:12.

Overview

The pure force and extremeness of Ayler's sound, with his high, overtone cries and split tones (multiphonics, or several notes at once), hits the unwary listener like a thunderbolt. *Ghosts*, the most popular of his songs, sounds at first like a children's nursery ditty—until it shifts to extraordinarily challenging free improvisation. "From simple melodies to complex textures to simplicity again" was how Ayler described his forms; this solo fits that description. Ayler's radical improvising style made him the most influential jazz saxophonist after Ornette Coleman and John Coltrane.

Key Features

- Improvisation: Ayler begins improvising in cyclic form in which each strain of theme

variations is further and further removed from the *Ghosts* melody. As he progresses, all references to the theme vanish altogether and his solo becomes a flow of pure sound in his horn's extreme ranges—overblown, honking, crying sounds that saxophone teachers traditionally teach students to avoid. Like Ayler's other mid-1960s solos, this is an adventure in pure sound.

- Rhythm: The 16-bar tenor sax theme is in the conventional meter of $\frac{4}{4}$; the rest of the performance is arhythmic. Before his variations progress very far, Ayler abandons the meter, and simply plays many notes very fast. Meanwhile the bass line has a much slower momentum while the drum line is a cymbal shimmer, with snare-drum raps that imply an intermediate momentum. The bassist and drummer are responding to the tenor sax lead rather than accompanying it in any standard sense.

- Harmony: After the theme statement Ayler quickly abandons all suggestion of harmonic structure. In fact, his imprecise pitch, the speed of his tenor sax lines, his overtone cries, and his split-multiphonics passages make the very idea of tonality irrelevant. The bassist, by contrast, is more conventionally atonal.
- Dynamics: Next to the extreme *fortissimos* of Ayler's tenor sax, the other instruments sound *piano* (soft) at the very most.
- Voice, feel, and expression: The work is an almost dizzying flight into the tenor saxophone's extreme ranges and techniques. Ayler's dominating presence yields excitement, energy, and exhilaration.
- Musicians' roles: The comparative simplicity of the bass and drum lines are the opposite of Ayler's complexity.

—John Litweiler

Sun Ra, born Herman Poole Blount, combined an outer-space mythos—he claimed to have been born on the planet Saturn—with over-the-top music and costumed big bands, variously known as the Solar Arkestra, the Intergalactic Research Arkestra, the Cosmo Drama Arkestra, or, often, just the Arkestra. PHOTO COURTESY JAMES F. QUINN.

TIME	SECTION/INSTRUMENTATION	MELODY
0:00	THEME, FIRST PHRASE	Ayler plays the first strain of the simple, diatonic theme unaccompanied, distorting some of the notes.
0:11	THEME, SECOND PHRASE	As Ayler plays the second strain, bassist Gary Peacock enters with a few out-of-tempo notes, quite unrelated to the melody. Sunny Murray, playing only on a cymbal and a snare drum, joins them.
0:21	BRIDGE	Instrumentation as in preceding phrases.
0:33	THEME, FINAL PHRASE	Ayler completes the thematic idea.
0:43	TENOR SAX SOLO	Ayler begins playing variations on the theme, adding rough, dissonant distortions and embellishments. He plays approximate notes rather than precise ones.
0:55		A second strain of theme variations, further from the melody.
1:06		Further strains of the theme variation . . .
1:17		. . . each of which is more distant, twisted.
1:23		Now the theme is scarcely a memory and the solo is pure sound. While Ayler does not play in a fixed tempo or meter, his momentum is fast and becomes faster as he progresses into atonality. His lines seems to career uncontrollably into multiphonics passages and high, wobbly overtones, but . . .
2:11		. . . with a fierce low honk for contrast, Ayler emphasizes his control of the solo. Approximate phrase lengths recurringly imply faint references to the theme until the end.
2:48	BASS SOLO	Gary Peacock's bass solo begins at a slower momentum, starting with spaced phrases, while the patter of Sunny Murray's snare drums and his ongoing cymbal sound provide background in a slightly faster momentum. As this solo progresses, the bass phrases become longer and busier (more notes), and the momentum become faster.
4:12	THEME	After all these adventures in atonality, Ayler returns playing a brief improvisatory melody in the bass register and then returns to the simple, diatonic theme (at 4:21), almost without variation or embellishment, over the atonal bass and arhythmic drums.

Listening Guide

BUSH MAGIC • ART ENSEMBLE OF CHICAGO

Music: Malachi Favors and Famoudou Don Moye, 1980. Personnel: Lester Bowie (trumpet); Roscoe Mitchell and Joseph Jarman (flute, wooden flute, piccolo, small percussion); Malachi Favors (first balafon, bass); Famoudou Don Moye (second balafon). Recorded May 5-6, 1980, live at the Amerika Haus, Munich, Germany. First issue: *Urban Bushmen* (ECM (G)1211/12). Timing: 5:06.

Overview

The most innovative and musically important free jazz group is the Art Ensemble of Chicago, formed in 1966. Its original members were together with few interruptions until Lester Bowie's death in 1999. For most of the AEC's history it was a quintet. Bowie was the most influential trumpeter since the mid-1950s, with a wide, mercurial emotional range and uniquely human expressive resources. Roscoe Mitchell created intense music on woodwinds and percussion, sometimes in very quiet sounds amid silence, sometimes in furiously violent alto or soprano sax solos. Joseph Jarman was capable of dizzying lyrical heights on woodwinds; the great Malachi Favors (a.k.a. Maghostut) created forceful bass lines; and Famoudou Don Moye added drama and rhythmic energy with his many percussion instruments. In the twenty-first century

Mitchell and Moye continued the Art Ensemble of Chicago.

Bush Magic is not a self-contained work but rather a quiet lull in an otherwise often dramatic, even exciting concert. It follows the concert's irresistibly catchy drum introduction by Moye. In its free jazz idiom, *Bush Magic* seems to move from emotional abstraction (the balafons) to subtle, complex feelings (the bass solo).

Key Features

- Improvisation: *Bush Magic* is wholly improvised, with no composed elements. It is almost wholly a **balafon** solo and a bass solo. Occasional percussion sounds accent, a held wooden-flute tone (1:11) and a piccolo (1:54) provide passing colors, then quiet trumpet tones appear (2:42).

  A lower balafon improvisation by Favors opens, and does not fade until 0:29. Meanwhile, Moye's high-register balafon solo becomes the foreground. Favors's bass solo begins in chords and becomes the group's foreground line.
- Rhythm: *Bush Magic* has no meter or fixed tempo. Nevertheless, very fast momentum arises from Moye's unbroken, many-noted balafon

solo. Favors's bass solo begins without tempo; after 4:11, momentum emerges and grows forceful.
- Melody: All improvised. The tiny notes of Moye's balafon solo only seem static, for close listening reveals a highly active line. The greater range and rhythmic variety of the bass solo yields a rich melodic line, mostly in long phrases.
- Harmony: Atonal or pan-tonal.
- Dynamics: A narrow range in the solos, with some quiet interjections by whistles, bells, horn sounds, percussion whacks, and a bicycle horn (3:26).
- Color and texture: *Bush Magic* is a relatively monochromatic lull in an otherwise mostly bright, multi-colored concert.
- Voice, feel, and expression: The balafon's treble range is small. By contrast, Favors's bass solo ranges high and low, in a true, unamplified sound, revealing fervent feeling.
- Musicians' roles: Moye and Favors solo, others comment quietly on their unusual instruments. This is worlds away from the standard horns-and-rhythm jazz combos.

—John Litweiler

TIME	INSTRUMENTATION	MUSICAL EVENT
0:00	LOWER-REGISTER BALAFON, PERCUSSION	A musical line begins on a fast rhythmic pattern.
0:16	HIGHER-REGISTER BALAFON; FLUTE (ENTERS AT APPROX 0:17); LIGHT PERCUSSION CONTINUES	A stream of tiny, very fast notes, with no rests; this stream of notes continues to 2:46.
2:33	BASS, ENTERS FOR THE FIRST TIME	The bassist (Favors) plays double-stops (chords) that now begin a foreground melodic line. Saxophone briefly comments at approx. 2:53.
3:05	BASS SOLO, WITH PERCUSSION ACCOMPANIMENT	The bassist solos alone.
3:52		Added tension enters the bass solo. A crucial phrase of up-bent tones, separated by space, appears. It leads to steady momentum after 4:11. By 4:30 the insistence of Favors's fast, undecorated line suggests emotional harshness, even anger, including demanding, repeated tones.
4:55	HORNS	Horns enter, announcing the end of the *Bush Magic* interlude. The concert's next episode (not heard here) begins with a comic march and soon moves into animated improvisations by the ensemble. Later in the concert Favors himself creates especially stark, forceful bass commentary to Bowie's ballad *New York Is Full of Lonely People*.

entire jazz tradition. The themes he composed—as in *Bells* and *Spirits Rejoice* (both 1965)—were like nineteenth-century pop songs, hymns, and bugle calls that sounded to writer Dan Morgenstern "like a Salvation Army band on LSD." Ayler played with a big tenor saxophone sound ("the biggest human sound I ever heard," critic Larry Kart said) and a wide, quavery vibrato. At fast tempos—and Ayler was another who played in the fastest tempos humanly possible—he did not play notes at all; rather, he approximated notes with distorted sounds, multiphonics, overtone screams, and wild, long, careening phrases. "It's a matter of following the sound . . . " said his brother and trumpeter Donald Ayler, "the pitches, the colors, you have to watch them move." Albert drowned, apparently murdered, in 1970; his own style became almost as influential as Coltrane's and Coleman's.

Terrifically fast tempos; dissonances and extreme sounds; and long, furious, exhilarating collective improvisations all characterized late-1960s New York free jazz—"energy music"—inspired by Coltrane, Ayler, Shepp, and Taylor. But energy music was emotionally narrow, even obsessive, compared to the music that was emerging in Chicago, where free jazz could be lyrical, soft as well as intense, simple as well as complex, composed as well as improvised, even swinging or humorous. The Chicagoans—members of the cooperative AACM (Association for the Advancement of Creative Musicians)—played in big bands led by veteran pianist-composer **Muhal Richard Abrams** as well as in small groups. One of them, the trio of altoist Roscoe Mitchell, trumpeter Lester Bowie, and bassist **Malachi Favors** (a.k.a. Maghostut) created musical lines that included "freak" sounds (bells, whistles, and

toys) and silences. In time they were joined by **Joseph Jarman**—who had achieved an unparalleled virtuosity in his alto saxophone's extreme ranges—and drummer Famoudou Don Moye, and they took the name the Art Ensemble of Chicago.

Like them, altoist **Anthony Braxton** explored free improvisation and unaccompanied soloing (his 1968 *For Alto Saxophone* album inspired a generation of horn players to play a cappella solos); like them, Braxton went on to master a number of different horns and became a prolific composer. More than the rest, he returned often to the bebop-era repertoire, with bop accompanists. To the early concept of free jazz—freedom from traditional harmonic, rhythmic, and formal restraints—the Chicagoans added a crucial element: freedom of choice. On his 1976 recording of Scott Joplin's *Maple Leaf Rag* (*JTSA* Disc 6/Track 1), Braxton along with fellow AACM member Muhal Richard Abrams on piano preserve the piece's essential spirit while playfully extending its melodic and harmonic roots.

Free Spaces

Where could the new musicians play? With nightclubs vanishing in Chicago, the AACM was formed to produce concerts by its member musicians. Churches, art galleries, high schools and colleges,

---

balafon West African tuned percussion instrument, played by hitting tone bars with mallets.

History & Culture

The Association for the Advancement of Creative Musicians (AACM).
PHOTO COURTESY MICHAEL WILDERMAN.

Jazz Cooperatives and Performance Spaces

The notion of musicians cooperating in business was a long-held one in jazz; members of early jazz bands often pooled income and shared responsibilities and decision making. But as jazz developed along less commercial lines, some musicians found it desirable to take more active steps to ensure their creative and economic survival. This inclination gave rise to jazz cooperatives—organizations formed for their members' mutual benefit.

In 1960, bassist Charles Mingus and drummers Max Roach and Jo Jones formed the **Jazz Artists Guild** to produce their own musical events. Though the Guild didn't last long, it planted an important seed: the idea that musician-run enterprises could work.

The Jazz Composers Guild, formed by trumpeter Bill Dixon in 1964, included a number of New York free jazz artists, among them Archie Shepp, Cecil Taylor, Sun Ra, and Paul and **Carla Bley**. The Guild produced weekly concerts in a New York City loft and sought to negotiate members' contracts with clubs

and record companies. Its efforts led to the formation of the **Jazz Composers Orchestra Association (JCOA)**, which lasted through much of the 1970s. The JCOA performed and recorded large-scale, big band compositions by its directors, composers Mike Mantler and Carla Bley, and other "outside" composers; its New Music Distribution Service distributed albums of free jazz produced by small labels, some of which were musician-owned.

There were other musicians' cooperatives, based outside New York. In 1961, pianist-composer Horace Tapscott formed the Union of God's Musicians and Artists Ascension (UGMAA) to produce concerts by his big band in Los Angeles. The **Association for the Advancement of Creative Musicians (AACM)**, the most successful cooperative, was founded in May 1956 and had its base in Chicago. Its longevity rested in part on its school, which produced the organization's later generations of musicians and teachers.

Inspired by the AACM, Oliver Lake, Julius Hemphill, and other St. Louis musicians formed the **Black Artists Group (BAG)**, which

was active at the turn of the 1970s; like the AACM, it emphasized the sharing of creative discoveries as a vital by-product of cooperation. In the 1980s, in Chicago, came a music lovers' cooperative, the all-volunteer Southend Musicworks, which produced a variety of jazz and even contemporary classical concerts.

Grants from the National Endowment for the Arts (founded in 1965), state arts councils, and private philanthropies helped support the teaching and performance programs of the AACM and its successors. In time, as free jazz found its way into a growing number of venues, and as the music gained favor with a younger generation of listeners, the need for cooperative efforts declined. And as individual musicians arrived at different levels of musical and popular success, the cooperative, all-for-one feeling often dissipated. Nevertheless, for a number of important modern jazz artists, participation in cooperatives marked a crucial stage of their careers.

—John Litweiler

A CLOSER LOOK

THE ART ENSEMBLE OF CHICAGO

The Art Ensemble of Chicago launched in 1966 and purveyed sonic explorations using the basic vehicle of trumpet, saxophones, drums, and bass. They also became known for embracing unusual instruments (including African instruments, bells, whistles, and musical toys). The Ensemble continued to perform together through trumpeter Lester Bowie's death in 1999.

✳ Explore on **mymusiclab.com**

Famoudou Don Moye •
Drums and Percussion

Moye preceded his tenure in the Art Ensemble with experiences that supported an adventurous approach to rhythm. Work with such forward-thinking musicians as guitarist Sonny Sharrock and saxophonist Pharoah Sanders, as well as involvement in African and Caribbean percussion, help extend his interests far beyond standard beat keeping—which fit ideally with the "free" aesthetic.

Roscoe Mitchell • Alto and Soprano Saxophone, Woodwinds, and Percussion

Mitchell emerged in mid-1960s Chicago as an especially imaginative improviser, as apt to use silence as sound in his solos. In the Art Ensemble of Chicago he brought variety, humor, and an unconventional, multi-instrumental voice to the group "discussions."

Lester Bowie • Trumpet

Bowie made "freak" sounds—blurts, smears, chuckles, squeals—an intrinsic part of the Art Ensemble sensibility. In so doing, Bowie played as strong a role as any of the other band members in casting the group's ensemble work as near "conversations"—at times a seeming convocation of voices from Maurice Sendak's *Where the Wild Things Are*.

PHOTO COURTESY FIN COSTELLO/REDFERNS/GETTY IMAGES.

Malachi Favors • Bass

Favors brought an earthy, swinging solidity to the Art Ensemble's free-ranging explorations. Like the other band members, he played more than one instrument: among them were the zither, banjo, and harmonica. But it was his rigorously honed bass technique—he had played bop with Dizzy Gillespie, Freddie Hubbard, and Andrew Hill before joining the AEC—that most distinguished his Art Ensemble role.

Joseph Jarman (not shown) • Flute, Saxophone, Wind Instruments, and Percussion

Jarman was an early member of the Association for the Advancement of Creative Musicians, the cooperative that spawned the Art Ensemble. Jarman's mastery of saxophone enabled him to play outside the instrument's standard register and timbre, and make audible his vast range of imagined unearthly sounds. He left the Art Ensemble in 1993, delved into Zen Buddhism, and later joined pianist Myra Melford and violinist Leroy Jenkins in the trio Equal Interest.

neighborhood taverns, a lodge hall, and a historic settlement house became concert sites for the AACM players, who booked, advertised, and sold tickets for concerts, then swept the floors and turned out the lights once the music was over. The AACM was not the first self-producing effort by musicians, but it lasted arguably the longest. For over three decades, beginning in the late 1960s, it ran a music school for inner-city youth; some excellent musicians, including saxophonists Douglas Ewart and Edward Wilkerson and trombonist George Lewis, were graduates.

In New York, jazz musicians and music lovers converted lofts in old factory buildings into concert sites; the best known of these were Artists House, owned by Ornette Coleman, and Studio Rivbea, operated by saxophonist Sam Rivers. In this respect, too, free jazz was revolutionary. Just as swing thrived primarily in ballrooms and bop in nightclubs, free jazz became a music of concert venues and performance spaces. And if free jazz began as underground experiments, in time it was featured at jazz festivals and major concert halls. Without a dominating figure such as Armstrong, Ellington, or Parker, free jazz took off in many different directions. Unlike leading postwar combos (the Modern Jazz Quartet, Horace Silver, Art Blakey, Miles Davis, Dave Brubeck, and Thelonious Monk), the most popular free jazz groups were only intermittently active—their members had too many other musical interests. So, for example, the members of the Art Ensemble of Chicago and the multisaxophone virtuosos of the **World Saxophone Quartet** (originally David Murray, Julius Hemphill, Hamiet Bluiett, and the brilliant, Dolphy-inspired Oliver Lake) also maintained individual careers as composers, sidemen, and leaders of small and large groups. (For an example of the World Saxophone Quartet's sound, listen to *Steppin'* [1981, *JTSA* Disc 6/Track 6].)

Similarly, the free jazz scene was geographically dispersed. New England and upstate New York (notably the Creative Music Studio, a school in Woodstock) were new-music centers, and handfuls of musicians sparked activity in Houston, Toronto, New Orleans, Detroit, and a number of other cities throughout North America. In San Francisco were the far-ranging ROVA Saxophone Quartet, which played works by its members and commissioned music by others. In Los Angeles

---

suite a musical work with multiple movements or major sections; examples are Tchaikovsky's *Nutcracker Suite*, Ellington and Strayhorn's *Far East Suite*, and Mary Lou Williams's *Zodiac Suite*.

two of Ornette Coleman's former associates—Bobby Bradford, a wonderful lyric trumpeter, and John Carter, who brought the clarinet back to jazz—formed a longtime team. Carter also composed a series of five **suites**—including *Castles of Ghana* (1985) and *Fields* (1988)—interpreting the historic black experience in the United States. Fred Anderson and Hal Russell, two pioneering free players, were catalysts in reviving the Chicago scene, beginning in the late 1970s: Anderson led bands and played endlessly creative, lyrical, blues-rich tenor sax, and the late multi-instrumentalist, composer, and teacher Russell led the freewheeling, often hilarious N-R-G Ensemble. None of the later AACM generations were much influenced by the innovations of the first generation, except for Anderson's protégés, especially saxophonist Douglas Ewart.

TAKE NOTE

- Who were the leading innovators in the free jazz movement?

Experimental Composers

One of the most radical departures of the era was undertaken in the traditional-jazz idiom by the Australian jazz and ragtime composer David Dallwitz. The subject of his *Ern Malley Suite* (1975) is a notorious down-under literary hoax. Imagine a singer like the young Billie Holiday warbling surreal lyrics ("Come, we will dance sedate quadrilles/A pallid polka or a yelping shimmy/Over these sunken sodden breeding-grounds! . . ./Culture, forsooth! Albert, get my gun") while a fine Dixieland band plays strange ragtime melodies.

"Outside" experiments came from the realm of

Anthony Braxton's compositions, titled with diagrams instead of words, reflected his interest in the mathematical aspects of music. PHOTO COURTESY VAL WILMER/DOWN BEAT ARCHIVES.

classical composition as well. In the 1950s, composer Gunther Schuller had conceived of "third stream" music, a fusion of the classical and jazz traditions. Two of his 1959–60 works are considered modern landmarks: *Abstraction* offers a string quartet playing an atonal piece in pyramid form with, at the apex, an unaccompanied Ornette Coleman alto solo; in the four *Variants on a Theme by Thelonious Monk (Criss Cross)*, improvisers including Coleman, Dolphy, and bassist Scott LaFaro enjoy interplay with each other and with a string quartet.

Performances by composer Carla Bley's big bands were often as entertaining and humorous as they were challenging. PHOTO COURTESY PHILIP RYALLS/REDFERNS/GETTY IMAGES.

Other classical composers, some encouraged by Schuller, contributed new works. They included Milton Babbitt's *All Set* (1958) and Krystof Penderecki's *Actions* (1971). The score of the 1997 opera *Amistad* by Anthony Davis included free jazz improvisers with the orchestra's symphonic musicians. Pianist-teacher Ran Blake advanced the third-stream idea to include the fusion of any ethnic and art-music traditions, whether improvised or composed.

Variations of the third-stream concept pop up in most extended pieces by free jazz artists, including Coleman. Carla Bley composed her "chronotransduction" *Escalator over the Hill* (1968–71) for a crowd of improvisers, singers, and reciters. For Charlie Haden's Liberation Music Orchestra, Bley's suites, such as *Dream Keeper* (1990), link Spanish and Latin American folk music with original pieces; her best scores for her own big bands, including *Spangled Banner Minor and Other Patriotic Songs* (1977), are notable for balancing distinctive elements and for a recurring whimsical humor. Cecil Taylor's large works for big band fuse composition and improvisation in grand polyphonic designs, as in *Alms/Tiergarten (Spree)* (1988). AACM artists, including Abrams, Jarman, Leroy Jenkins, Douglas Ewart, and **Henry Threadgill**, all composed large works. The largest is Anthony Braxton's *For Four Orchestras* (1978); among the most musically successful are Braxton's jazz-band scores and Leo Smith's *Return to My Native Land II* (1981).

Some other composers worked specifically within jazz traditions. The big band, octet, and saxophone ensemble scores of Julius Hemphill,

David Murray, and Edward Wilkerson (especially for his group Eight Bold Souls) gained vigor from Ellington sonorities and swing and bop phrasing. The potent trio Air (Henry Threadgill, woodwinds; Fred Hopkins, bass; Steve McCall, drums) created free interpretations of Scott Joplin rags as well as of Threadgill themes. In the 1980s Threadgill composed works—such as *Subject to Change* (1984) and *Theme from Thomas Cole* (1986)—with memorable melodies and countermelodies; rich harmonies; expressive soloing; and constant, ongoing, nervous activity for his sextet. As a composer, Roscoe Mitchell made some of the most far-reaching innovations of jazz form, including *Nonaah* (1976), originally a saxophone solo that he recomposed several times for wind and string ensembles. He created *L-R-G* (1978) for himself (woodwinds) and two brass instrumentalists (Leo Smith and George Lewis), in ever-mobile disparities; *The Maze* (1978), by contrast, contains the interactions of eight percussionists. In these works—Mitchell called them "sound collages"—form and musical line evolve from the unique sounds created by the performers.

Despite the artistic success of these big band and orchestra compositions, most were seldom performed because of the expense of paying so many musicians. Self-contained orchestras, including Sun Ra's Arkestra, whose members lived together in Philadelphia, or local phenomena like the AACM big band (Chicago) and Either/Orchestra (Boston) were rare. Needed were repertory ensembles dedicated to playing new music, just as the Lincoln

Issues

The Growing Role of Women in Jazz

Why has jazz music been dominated by male performers and composers through most of its history?

The jazz world, for all its sophistication and liberal-mindedness, proved to be largely male-dominated through most of its first century, leaving women underrepresented and underreported—particularly as instrumentalists.

Prior to the emergence of jazz, the most socially acceptable instrument for women was the piano, and

Influential pianist and composer Mary Lou Williams. PHOTO COURTESY FRANK DRIGGS COLLECTION.

the acceptable places to play it were the parlor and the church. Apart from signs of professional activity by women in ragtime—they composed music, demonstrated ragtime and pop sheet music at department stores, and played accompaniment in silent-movie theaters—there is scant evidence of working female jazz musicians in the early years of the twentieth century.

In the 1920s and 1930s, cutting contests and band battles further established jazz as a male-controlled enterprise. With rare exceptions, such as pianist Lil Hardin Armstrong, female jazz players were relegated to the sidelines. Women found themselves struggling against age-old strictures holding that while singing was suitably feminine, instruments that made them alter their facial expressions or stances were not "ladylike." A particularly challenging hurdle for women was gaining acceptance as drummers and as brass and reed players.

Excellent performances and the ability to survive the rigors of the road weren't enough to override the prevailing sentiment that women were too weak for such men's work. Consequently, musically committed women sometimes had to resort to extreme measures to secure opportunities to play. Trumpeter Valaida Snow, disgusted by her lack of acceptance in the United States, toured with Jack Carter's band in Shanghai from 1926 to 1928, eventually leading her own outfit in Europe from 1935 to 1940. Some women even cross-dressed, and one—Dorothy Tipton—masqueraded for 50 years as "Billy Tipton," passing as a male piano player and bandleader until her death in 1989.

In the 1940s, as jazz developed larger audiences and greater

Trumpeter and bandleader Valaida Snow. PHOTO COURTESY FRANK DRIGGS COLLECTION.

commercial potential, the contributions of women did increase—if they were vocalists. Audiences for big bands demanded female singers—or "fem chirpers," as *Down Beat* termed them. Both familiar and obscure white "chirpers" graced the magazine's covers, but the extraordinary talent and beauty of Billie Holiday, Ella Fitzgerald, and Sarah Vaughan were not deemed worthy of equivalent exposure during the same period. Also, fewer African American than white men were featured on covers or in photographs; ultimately this was noticed more than the absence of women, just as the issue of racial equality has tended to overshadow the subject of gender equality in jazz.

When the United States entered World War II, women took over the jobs vacated by soldiers—except in the music industry. Lacking opportunities to occupy the vacant chairs of musician inductees, women formed all-female groups, including the

International Sweethearts of Rhythm and Virgil Whyte's "All-Girl" Band, to tour the United States and perform in USO shows. Despite their excellent musicians, they were often viewed as mere novelty acts; most of them folded when men returned to civilian action.

Accounts of the rise of bebop after World War II have mostly ignored the contributions of women—for example, the impact of **Mary Lou Williams** as a mentor to bebop pioneers Charlie Parker, Thelonious Monk, Dizzy Gillespie, and Bud Powell. Male journalists gravitated toward the new sound emanating from Minton's Playhouse and New York City's 52nd Street nightclubs to fraternize with their male idols while many women musicians—wary of the encroaching drug lifestyle—stayed home. And so, as jazz became more "modern," women continued to be overlooked and underrecorded (unless under the aegis of Moses Asch, Leonard Feather, and a few other progressive record producers).

Significant change began to occur in the 1960s and 1970s, when colleges and conservatories began replacing big bands and jam sessions as the learning centers for jazz musicians. On the more level playing fields of academic institutions, women and men developed their skills together; men were exposed to the full range of women's musical abilities and developed an appreciation of and a natural rapport with their female colleagues.

Women became more prominent in jazz of the 1960s and 1970s, with such pianists as Joanne Brackeen, Carla Bley, and Toshiko Akiyoshi leading bands that

showcased their own compositions. Singer Betty Carter, for many years, led small groups that she shaped, with firm hand and solid arranging skills, into fitting vehicles for her idiosyncratic, highly improvisatory vocal approach. Such was the strength and effectiveness of her leadership that her band functioned as a "school" for young (mostly male) virtuosi.

By late in the century the climate for female jazz musicians had vastly improved: government grants were increasingly being awarded to subsidize their careers as performers and composers; changed attitudes stemming from the women's movement and the declining cachet of drug use among jazz musicians had made the atmosphere more conducive to interaction and collaboration between women and men.

Women built their own formal support systems and networks. In 1996, the Kennedy Center in Washington, DC, began holding an annual Mary Lou Williams Women in Jazz Festival as a forum for discussing gender-related problems in the business and as an opportunity for women to perform on the same stage. Musicians as dissimilar in style as pianists Geri Alien and Marian McPartland; as diverse as soprano saxophonist Jane

Ira Bloom and drummer Cindy Blackman; as powerful as the Maria Schneider Jazz Orchestra; and as multi-talented as singer-bassist Esperanza Spalding, have performed and informally jammed with new talent at the festival.

One of the highest-profile jazz musicians of the early 2000s was a woman. Pianist and singer Diana Krall's albums sold in the millions, an incredible achievement for a jazz performer. Krall's repertoire recalled the heyday of great jazz singers like Ella Fitzgerald and Sarah Vaughan, and Krall worked largely in the same mainstream idiom.

—*Ann K. Kuebler*

Composer and bandleader Toshiko Akiyoshi.
PHOTO COURTESY DOWN BEAT ARCHIVES.

Jazz and Classical Music: The Second Half of the Twentieth Century

In the first half of the century, most composers who adopted jazz—whether in America, France, or elsewhere—did so as outsiders seeking modernist energy in a musical idiom beyond their own cultural heritage. And none of their works invited improvisation. In the second half of the century, however, the most notable developments in concert-hall hybrids came from jazz musicians writing in extended musical forms that provided space for improvisation. Duke Ellington paved the way with his landmark *Black, Brown, and Beige* (1943), a multimovement "tone parallel to the history of the Negro in America," that premiered at Carnegie Hall. Ellington composed several other large-scale works, mixing notated and improvised music, such as *Harlem* (1950), commissioned by Arturo Toscanini and the NBC Symphony (though never played by them), and his and Billy Strayhorn's witty, swinging versions of Grieg's *Peer Gynt Suite* and Tchaikovsky's *Nutcracker Suite* (1960).

Inspired, in part, by Ellington's model, other jazz composers followed suit. Charles Mingus's masterpiece *The Black Saint and the Sinner Lady* (1963) lasts nearly 40 minutes, and combines written composition, extensive improvisation, and considerable editing and overdubbing overseen by the composer. At a time when Ellington was conceiving and performing a series of sacred concerts, Mary Lou Williams composed several jazz masses, most notably *Mary Lou's Mass* (1971). The renowned jazz musician, composer, and educator David Baker contributed such works as *Le Chat qui Peche*, for soprano, orchestra, and jazz quartet (1974); *Three Ethnic Dances*, a clarinet concerto (1992); and *Roots II* for piano trio (1992).

Gunther Schuller, the omnivorous composer, conductor, crossover French-horn player, and one time president of the New England Conservatory, acted as a figurehead among jazz musicians pursuing serious composition. In 1957, Schuller coined the term "third stream" to acknowledge and encourage compositions that blended genuine jazz elements and classical forms and techniques. Schuller's own works, such as *Transformation* (1957), *Seven Studies on Themes By Paul* Klee (1959), and *Abstraction* (also 1959), put his ideas into practice. Other important third stream composers included Ran Blake, Jimmy Guiffre, John Lewis, and George Russell.

In the 1980s and 1990s, jazz itself enjoyed a newly elevated status as a kind of classic music, and as a result, efforts to blend jazz and "classical" elements seemed less urgent. Yet such efforts continue in surprising, artistic, and ambitious ways. Perhaps the most prominent transformation of the impulse at the beginning of the twenty-first century could be found in the work of Wynton Marsalis, who wrote a series of works for Jazz at Lincoln Center. His *In This House, On This Morning* (1992) and his jazz oratorio *Blood on the Fields* (1997), which won a Pulitzer Prize, demonstrated the ongoing possibilities of extended, jazz-based concert music and its capacity to earn prestigious prizes and institutional support. So too does a series of pieces by the composer-reed player Paquito D'Rivera, a Guggenheim award winner, who has earned commissions from such groups as the National Symphony and the Turtle Island String Quartet and reinvigorated the Latin jazz tradition with fresh musical hybrids. Together, works by Marsalis and D'Rivera answer Dvořák's call beyond his wildest imaginings.

—*Jeffrey Magee*

Center and Smithsonian orchestras would focus on playing earlier jazz. In fact, for a time in the 1970s, trumpeter Mike Mantler maintained the Jazz Composers Orchestra as a workshop for New York composers. But most orchestral performances of jazz works were ad hoc, often resulting from grants by arts philanthropies. The largest arts funder, the National Endowment for the Arts, provided significant support for jazz composition in the 1970s and 1980s.

European jazz composers fared better than their U.S. counterparts. For over two decades, beginning in 1966, the Globe Unity Orchestra, comprising the best European free players, gathered almost annually to tour and debut new works by leader Alex Schlippenbach and other members. Bassist Barry Guy

Staying Free

In the twenty-first century a few major figures such as Ornette Coleman and Cecil Taylor remained attractions at jazz concerts. Pharoah Sanders, Henry Threadgill, and David Murray were among the prominent free jazz performers in mainstream nightclubs, concerts, and festivals. Communities of free jazz artists kept busy presenting concerts and nightclub gigs in Boston, the San Francisco Bay Area, Chicago, New York, London, and Berlin, among other hot spots. The leading U.S. festival devoted entirely to free jazz and free improvisation was the annual Vision Festival, in New York City, which offered veteran explorers from around the world and introduced bold young creators.

While the U.S. government encumbered visiting European artists with red tape, Canada had few such restrictions, so festivals such as those in Vancouver, British Columbia; Edmonton, Alberta; and Victoriaville, Quebec, annually presented international free jazz performers. Several European festivals, including the Total Music Meeting and Moers annual affairs (both in Germany), also showcased artists who played the new music.

U.S. radio coverage of experimental jazz, which had always been limited, became more so in the 1990s and 2000s. In keeping with that period's fashion for conservative playlists, a good many public radio stations eliminated innovative jazz entirely, leaving college and university stations to pick up the slack.

Buyers of jazz compact discs needed to be alert, because jazz albums tended to be yanked from the market a few months after release. The rock-music conglomerates that controlled most of the recording industry in the twenty-first century eliminated most jazz recording activity. On the other hand, some musicians made downloads of their work available on the Internet, while independent labels in the United States and Europe—such as Delmark, Intakt, Hat ART, and Emanem—released many albums, and many of their CDs remained available.

All of which served to underscore what had always been the case: the determined explorers at the frontiers of jazz are willing to do whatever it takes to expand the music's boundaries.

The experimental big bands led by composer Muhal Richard Abrams yielded future members of the AACM and the Art Ensemble of Chicago. PHOTO COURTESY BILL ABERNATHY/DOWN BEAT ARCHIVES.

formed and re-formed the London Jazz Composers Orchestra often, from 1970, to play his massive settings (including *Harmos*, 1989) for band and top British improvisers; the Italian Instabile Orchestra served as a similar showcase for Italian players.

Guy, who maintained dual careers as a jazz and classical musician, was one of a number of Europeans advancing the third-stream concept. Other successes included the fiery Brotherhood of Breath, 1970s South African exiles and English musicians who merged free jazz with black South African folk-pop; Pierre Dørge's New Jungle Orchestra (Denmark), fusing Ellington, free jazz, and West African music; and Willem Breuker's Kollektief (Holland), playing the leader's mad, satiric mélanges of jazz, classical, folk, and dance musics.

TAKE NOTE

- What role did cooperatives and independent performance spaces play in free jazz?

- Why was 1959 such a pivotal year in jazz history?

In 1959, saxophonist Ornette Coleman ignited an explosion of exploratory creative activity by jazz musicians. The musical idiom that emerged was given names such as "the new thing," "outside jazz," and "free jazz." Free jazz sought to remove all conventional ideas of melody, rhythm, harmony, and performance to allow for total individual expression.

- What were the roots of free jazz?

Free jazz emerged at a time of great social change. The passing of the Civil Rights and Voting Rights acts in the mid-1960s codified African Americans' insistence on racial equality, in itself manifesting a broader desire for personal freedom. Two important ancestors of free jazz were bassist Charles Mingus, who composed complex and challenging music, and composer Bob Graettinger, whose works for the Stan Kenton Orchestra incorporated atonality, polyrhythmic movement, and ever-changing activity.

- What were the innovations introduced by free jazz in melody, rhythm, harmony, and performance style?

In free jazz, melodies, rhythm, and harmony were freely improvised by each player. Musicians were encouraged to abandon preexisting or familiar riffs, harmonies, or rhythmic patterns. Performance style was assertive and uncompromising, taking bebop's anti-commercial stance to its logical conclusion. Free jazz was the most defiant attempt of jazz musicians to challenge their audience, rather than to aim for widespread success.

- Who were the leading innovators in the free jazz movement?

Although Ornette Coleman is considered the spiritual father of free jazz, the style was carried forward by a wide range of performers, including mainstreamers who embraced the new style (such as John Coltrane) and young innovators (pianist Cecil Taylor). Among the more adventurous were bandleader/keyboard player Sun Ra and saxophone players Albert Ayler and Anthony Braxton. The Art Ensemble of Chicago was an important ensemble that wed free jazz with an Afro-centric composition and performing style.

- What role did cooperatives and independent performance spaces play in free jazz?

The Chicago-based Association for the Advancement of Creative Musicians (AACM) and New York's Black Artist Group (BAG), among others, helped nurture the careers of young musicians, composers, and music promoters. Cooperatives enabled musicians to have a space in which to explore new musical formats. Alternative performance spaces similarly allowed for the new music to be heard, without having to be commercially successful.

DISCUSSION QUESTIONS

1. Identify several ways that 1959 was a turning point in the history of jazz.
2. Free jazz emerged in the 1960s. What else was going on in the 1960s that paralleled the revolution against jazz traditions?
3. Identify some of the major differences between free jazz and the jazz styles that preceded it.
4. Identify at least one way in which free jazz, as revolutionary as it was, can be said to be carrying on a jazz tradition.
5. Compare the roles of Louis Armstrong, Charlie Parker, and Ornette Coleman in their respective time periods and jazz movements.
6. Discuss the relationships between emerging popular music such as Motown and rock and the dwindling commercial prospects of free jazz.
7. Do you think free jazz musicians should have expected acceptance by a wide audience? Why or why not?
8. Why do you think there have been relatively few women instrumentalists in jazz? Discuss which instruments have had more female players and which instruments have had fewer. What are the differences?

KEY TERMS & KEY PEOPLE

Muhal Richard Abrams
Rashied Ali
Art Ensemble of Chicago
Association for the Advancement
    of Creative Musicians
    (AACM)
atonal
Albert Ayler
bass clarinet
Black Artists Group (BAG)
Carla Bley
Lester Bowie
Anthony Braxton

Don Cherry
Ornette Coleman
collective improvisation
John Coltrane
consonant
dissonant
Eric Dolphy
Malachi Favors
free jazz
Charlie Haden
Joseph Jarman
Jazz Artists Guild
Jazz Composers Orchestra
    Association (JCOA)

Roscoe Mitchell
multiphonics
overtone
Sun Ra
Pharoah Sanders
Gunther Schuller
Archie Shepp
Cecil Taylor
third stream
Henry Threadgill
Mary Lou Williams
World Saxophone Quartet

Mainstream Jazz

Mainstream Jazz

by Neil Tesser

TAKE NOTE

- What currents in American society influenced the development of jazz in the 1950s?
- Why was Miles Davis among the most important musicians of this period?
- How did hard bop develop in response to bebop and other styles?
- What distinguishes West Coast bop from other variants, and who were the key players in this style?
- What are the different saxophone styles of Dexter Gordon, Sonny Rollins, and John Coltrane?
- How were the musical approaches of composer-pianists Thelonious Monk and Dave Brubeck similar and how were they different?
- What is soul jazz and how does it differ from hard bop?
- How did earlier jazz traditions and groups grow and thrive during this period?
- What vocalists were important during the mainstream era?
- What other jazz styles were prominent during this time and how did they differ from the more dominant styles?

HISTORICAL EVENTS — The 1950s — MUSICAL EVENTS

PHOTO COURTESY DEPARTMENT OF DEFENSE.

1949 — The Lighthouse club opens just south of Los Angeles, becoming a center for West Coast/cool jazz

1950 — The new LP (long-playing) record finds acceptance and greatly extends the playing time of records, from 3 minutes per side to 25 minutes per side

Korean War — **1950–53**

1951 — Dave Brubeck forms his quartet, featuring saxophonist Paul Desmond.

1952 — Modern Jazz Quartet forms to play chamber jazz

• Polio vaccine introduced, helping to eradicate major childhood disease

• *Brown versus Board of Education* decision by the Supreme Court orders the end of segregated schools

1953 — Art Blakey and Horace Silver form the original Jazz Messengers, announcing the arrival of hard bop

1954 — The Clifford Brown (trumpet)-Max Roach (drums) Quintet debuts, with West Coast tenor sax player Harold Land; at the end of 1955, Sonny Rollins replaces Land

Rosa Parks refuses to "move to the back of the bus," a seminal event in the civil rights movement of the 1950s and 1960s — **1955**

1956 — Organist Jimmy Smith introduces soul jazz on a series of albums

Soviet Union launches first satellite, Sputnik, into outer space — **1957** — Elvis Presley sings *Hound Dog* on the *Ed Sullivan Show*, as rock and roll crowds jazz for the allegiance of young listeners

Arkansas Governor Orval Faubus employs the National Guard to keep Central High School in Little Rock from being desegregated; eventually, he relents under pressure from the federal government and the black students are allowed to attend

1958 — Thelonious Monk regains his cabaret card and begins playing at New York's Five Spot, reestablishing himself as a major jazz player

Alaska and Hawaii are admitted to the union as the 49th and 50th states

1959 — The album *Giant Steps*, considered one of John Coltrane's masterpieces, is released

1960 — Wes Montgomery's *The Incredible Jazz Guitar* introduces his distinct style to jazz fans

Now 87 percent of U.S. homes have television, drastically reducing radio listening

✳ Explore the Jazz Timeline on **mymusiclab.com**

33

he innovations of bebop—at first considered radical—eventually became jazz conventions. And as a growing number of up-and-coming players built on and reacted to those conventions, jazz entered what is perhaps its best-known phase. It was a time of maturation, a period in which jazz became firmly established and widely embraced as a distinct, deeply developed musical idiom. And it was a time dominated by jazz "giants"—musicians whose names even a casual observer of jazz history can't fail to recognize. **Art Blakey**, **John Coltrane**, **Bill Evans**, Herbie Hancock, **Charles Mingus**, the Modern Jazz Quartet, **Thelonious Monk**, **Wes Montgomery**, and **Horace Silver** are just a few of the players who either emerged or reached the peak of their artistry during the 1950s and 1960s and whose influence—and some of whose careers—stretched into the twenty-first century.

It's as difficult to imagine one stylistic description applying to all these musicians as it is to imagine a jazz world without any of them. Nonetheless, much of the music recorded during these years is now identified as **mainstream jazz**. The term emerged in the mid-1950s, and it came to embody the lyrical, cleanly structured music that predominated during that decade and remained central to the jazz experience through the remainder of the century. Within the mainstream, however, surged a number of musical currents—from cool jazz to hard bop and including such offshoots as chamber jazz and modal jazz—that were set in motion by the galvanic impact of bebop.

Miles Davis, whose influence dominated jazz in the second half of the twentieth century.

PHOTO COURTESY VERN SMITH/DOWN BEAT ARCHIVES.

Setting the Stage

American society in the 1950s is often described as a bridge between the rigors of World War II and the turbulent social changes of the 1960s. The decade witnessed widespread societal conformity but also technological advances in many areas, including aviation (jet aircraft), chemistry (plastics, Velcro), electronics (transistors, computers), aeronautics (the "space race"), and recording—when the **long-playing (LP) record** album replaced the 78 rpm records of previous decades. For the first time, musicians could record performances longer than about three minutes, which had been the limitation of the

---

mainstream jazz acoustic jazz as practiced in the 1950s and 1960s and preserved in the present day; some define mainstream jazz as including earlier classic jazz.

long-playing (LP) record a disc recording that plays back on a turntable moving at 33⅓ revolutions per minute (rpm); the principal music delivery medium from about 1950 through the 1980s, until it was replaced by the digital compact disc (CD).

older format. For jazz musicians, this new freedom provided the opportunity to record music that more closely reflected the live-concert setting, whereby lengthier improvisations helped define and advance the art.

Even as the fledgling idiom of rock and roll was taking flight, jazz maintained a strong and steady audience, largely because of the increasing importance of college life in America. Peacetime affluence allowed more people to send their children to college, where students sought out the cool and intellectual jazz sounds that had supplanted their parents' swing era dance bands. In addition, the GI Bill provided servicemen returning from World War II the opportunity to complete their education; many of these older students had developed a taste for jazz as popular music during the war. As the 1960s dawned, jazz musicians began to incorporate the earthy, bluesy sounds of the gospel church into what would eventually be known as "soul jazz," anticipating (perhaps subconsciously) the epochal struggle for civil rights that would peak during that decade.

TAKE NOTE

- What currents in American society influenced the development of jazz in the 1950s?

Miles Ahead

Miles Davis, more than any other musician, dominated the mainstream era. Although Davis had made his initial reputation working with Charlie Parker, not until the 1950s did he emerge as an innovator of enormous impact. During this period, he first showed the ability to synthesize emerging jazz sounds into coherent styles that others would embrace as new movements—an ability that would ultimately make Davis the most important jazz figure in the second half of the twentieth century in the minds of many.

Davis sometimes seemed to be doing it all with mirrors. On such tunes as *All of You* and *My Funny Valentine* (both first recorded in 1956, then burnished in repeated performances through the mid-1960s), Davis played introspective solos in a vulnerable, diffident trumpet voice, which boasted virtually none of bebop's trademark fireworks and clever one-upsmanship. Old-school trumpeters derided his technique, but Davis's style became the template for jazz expression among musicians and audiences for the next 20 years. The bands he assembled were small miracles: many of his musicians would brilliantly execute his concepts, exceeding what anyone expected of them, before going off on their own. Many never made music of the same

Watch the documentary on Miles Davis on
mymusiclab.com

quality again. Davis himself wrote relatively few songs, but time after time his recording of an old standard or a modern jazz tune became the definitive one, emulated by his contemporaries and successors. (Good examples include the Davis Quintet's 1956 versions of *Bye Bye Blackbird* and *'Round Midnight*.) And no jazz sound could have better mirrored the existentialist philosophy coloring Western society in the 1950s than Davis's lonely, emotionally naked sorties.

Davis often turned his back on his audience or left the bandstand entirely when not soloing (a practice immortalized in singer Eddie Jefferson's lyrics to one of Davis's best-known recordings, the 1959 track *So What*). And he turned his back on jazz entirely as the 1950s began, dropping out of sight and sound for the better part of two years to overcome the heroin habit he'd learned from Parker. But even in absentia, Davis wielded influence: the "cool school" inspired by his Nonet recordings became the "new sound of jazz." By the time Davis returned to the scene in 1953, "cool" had begun seeping up from the jazz underground to become the primary concern of American art, from film to fashion to literature to theater. From 1954 on, Davis's bands would brilliantly capture the hard bop style, but his own trumpet work never abandoned the hooded stance that characterized cool jazz.

TAKE NOTE

- Why was Miles Davis among the most important musicians of this period?

The Birth of Hard Bop

In the words of author Joe Goldberg, the cool breezes from the Pacific "went largely unnoticed by musicians in the East, except as an irritant." The cool school had offered its reaction to bebop, but in New York, Chicago, Philadelphia, and Detroit, the jazz of the 1950s derived primarily from bebop to become the style dubbed **hard bop**.

While such Miles Davis recordings as *Four* (1954) and *Walkin'* (1954) suggest the arrival of hard bop, the real parents were drummer Art Blakey and pianist Horace Silver. In the autumn of 1954, the two formed a cooperative quintet, the Jazz Messengers, and in 1955 they recorded a jubilee shout in the form of the 16-bar blues *The Preacher*, (*JTSA* Disc 3/Track 8) composed by Silver: as Goldberg put it, "The reaction to the reaction had taken place." To be sure, the hard boppers were responding to cool's constraints with

---

hard bop a post-bebop style marked by simpler chord progressions and earthy soulfulness, in contrast to the cool restraint of another post–bop style, cool jazz.

their explosive emotionalism. But they were also react-ing to the calcifications of bebop.

The hard bop musicians used much the same vocabulary and grammar as bebop, but they turned the language to somewhat different ends to suit the demands of a new decade. They relaxed the tempos that had often made bebop a breathtaking steeple-chase, and they simplified the knotty melodies that had delighted Parker and Dizzy Gillespie. In so doing, the hard bop players brought back an earthy soulfulness that had receded during the boppers' quest for more "serious" recognition.

This soulfulness had its roots in the ecstasy of church and gospel music, which provided the first listening experience for many black musicians, and which permeates such hard bop classics as pianist Bobby Timmons's *Moanin'*, recorded by the Jazz Messengers in 1958, and keyboardist Joe Zawinul's *Mercy, Mercy, Mercy*, recorded by **Cannonball Adderley** in 1966. The hard bop players dug even deeper into the blues than had their bebop predecessors, and minor-key melodies—such as Silver's *Señor Blues* (1956) and cornetist Nat Adderley's *Work Song* (1960; *JTSA* Disc 4/Track 8)—became increasingly popular. The hard boppers also made use of the new

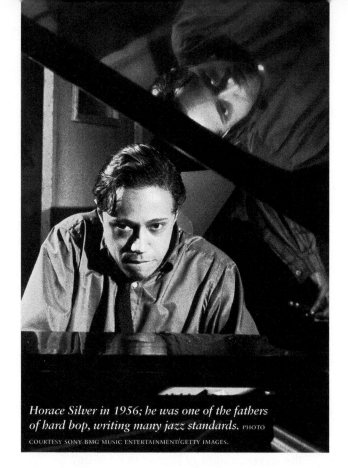

Horace Silver in 1956; he was one of the fathers of hard bop, writing many jazz standards. PHOTO COURTESY SONY BMG MUSIC ENTERTAINMENT/GETTY IMAGES.

long-playing (LP) record format to stretch out on extended solos, and the most important players went further still: they saw in the LP a chance to recon-ceive the jazz solo as a vehicle for large-scale thematic development.

The most important hard bop bands all developed under the guidance of bebop veterans: Davis, Blakey, drummer **Max Roach**, and Silver. In 1956, Silver left the Jazz Messengers to form a quintet concentrating on his own remarkable compositions. Many of these, such as *Doodin'* (1955), *Nica's Dream* (1956), *Sister Sadie* (1959), and *Song for My Father* (1964), have entrenched themselves in the mainstream repertoire. Meanwhile, Blakey assumed full command of the Jazz Messengers after Silver's departure and proved him-self a brilliant leader. The band epitomized hard bop until Blakey's death in 1990; the Messengers became jazz's answer to the Naval Academy, training a steady parade of new recruits to navigate the mainstream as leaders in their own right.

Horace Silver's post-Messengers career as a leader extended through the 1990s, during which he issued dozens of recordings. Like the Jazz Messengers, Silver's groups helped launch the careers of many important musicians, including saxophonists Joe Henderson and Junior Cook and trumpeters Art Farmer and

Art Blakey, 1955. Blakey nurtured upcoming talent in his long-running band the Jazz Messengers. PHOTO COURTESY BILL SPILKA/GETTY IMAGES.

[Watch] the video of *Build A New World* by Art Blakey on **mymusiclab.com**

Listening Guide

((•• **Listen** to *The Preacher* by Horace Silver and the Jazz Messengers on **mymusiclab.com**
CD II, Track 1/Download Track 25

THE PREACHER • HORACE SILVER AND THE JAZZ MESSENGERS

Music: Horace Silver, 1955. Personnel: Kenny Dorham (trumpet); Hank Mobley (tenor saxophone); Horace Silver (piano); Doug Watkins (bass); Art Blakey (drums). Recorded: February 6, 1955, in Hackensack, NJ. First issue: *Horace Silver Quintet Vol. 2*, Blue Note 5062 (10" LP). Timing: 4:20.

Overview

The Preacher embodies key qualities that Silver brought to post-bop jazz: a turn to soulfulness and earthiness, and a welcoming sense of music whose every note feels heartfelt and engaging. In it we hear gospel, blues, swing, and the seeds of rock and roll. Silver's accessibility and down-home emotionalism brought a joy and populism to jazz that contrasted with bebop's intellectualism and exclusiveness.

Key Features

- Form and structure: The chorus consists of four 4-bar phrases, reminiscent of gospel tunes. The first three phrases, A, A1, and A2 vary slightly, followed by a resolving phrase, B. Soloists improvise over the full 16-bar chorus.
- Rhythm: For the first two choruses, the beat saunters in half time ($\frac{2}{2}$). During the solos the time doubles to $\frac{4}{4}$, with the bass and drums leading the way, setting a more uptempo-feeling groove to support solos.
- Melody and harmony: The melody is simple compared to the convoluted lines used in bebop. The melody is accessible and singable. The harmony stays within the confines of standard gospel and blues tunes—nothing groundbreaking here.
- Improvisation: Three soloists, Kenny Dorham, Hank Mobley, and Horace Silver draw from bebop concepts but play them engagingly, making them accessible to non-jazz listeners.
- Color and texture: A prominent texture is provide by the trumpet and tenor sax playing in harmony on the melody.

—Tad Lathrop

TIME	FORM	INSTRUMENTATION	MELODY
0:00	CHORUS 1 HEAD	Band	The jubilant 16-bar melody launches straightaway, with trumpet and tenor saxophone in harmony backed by the three-piece rhythm section. (The tune slightly resembles the old-time standard *Bill Bailey, Won't You Come Home*, 1902.) The beat is ebullient, sauntering in counts of two. The melody unfolds in four phrases—in the form of A, A1, A2, B—posing a statement, varying it, and resolving conclusively.
0:23	CHORUS 2		The melody repeats.
0:44	CHORUS 3	Trumpet solo	Trumpeter Kenny Dorham ascends to a soaring F, holds it, and spills forward with jazz-blues phrasings mainly in eighth notes. The bass shifts from half notes to walking quarter notes, picking up the energy.
1:06	CHORUS 4		Trumpeter Dorham continues, repeating the opening figure of the first chorus and shooting up to an even higher F—heightening the excitement. He stays within the blues (rather than getting too "outside") and keeps the energy high.
1:27	CHORUS 5	Tenor sax solo	Hank Mobley's fat-sounding sax picks up Dorham's opening figure and launches into a solo that mixes blues ideas with irregular phrasings that draw from bebop.
1:48	CHORUS 6		Sax continues, now emphasizing straight-ahead bop lines until (2:04) ascending in half steps to a melodic curlicue of an ending.
2:09	CHORUS 7	Piano solo	Horace Silver enters with bluesy, rhythmic chording, shifting to single notes at 2:21.
2:30	CHORUS 8		Silver continues, establishing a downward-tumbling phrase (two-bars long) that he repeats at 2:33, 2:35, and 2:40, followed by a five-note figure (2:43) that he repeats lower and then truncates as he closes out the chorus.
2:50	CHORUS 9	Piano solo with backing	Silver continues with syncopated chordal statements that sax and trumpet "answer" with unison (an octave apart) blues riffs.
3:11	CHORUS 10		Silver keeps up his rhythmic chordal improvising as sax and trumpet continue their unison riffing.
3:31	CHORUS 11	Band	Head.
3:52	CHORUS 12		Head repeats.

History & Culture

New York Nights

"It was the same every night when we were closing at 4 a.m.," recalled Max Gordon, owner of the venerable Village Vanguard club in New York City. "There were always a few insomniacs and night prowlers left in the place who never wanted to go home."

Quite possibly, those night owls were still buzzing from the energy of a set by John Coltrane or Miles Davis or **Sonny Rollins**: the Vanguard, from the 1950s on, was the leading small venue for jazz, launching many an illustrious career and sustaining others that were already aloft. Jazz front-liners from Charles Mingus to Thelonious Monk regularly played there, and some immortalized the stints on LPs (notably Bill Evans's *Sunday at the Village Vanguard*, 1961, and several by Coltrane). Even Monday nights—typically off-nights in the club world—drew crowds, thanks to weekly sets by the Thad Jones-Mel Lewis Orchestra.

The Vanguard was smack in the middle of Greenwich Village, itself a focal point of live jazz following the demise of the 52nd Street nightclub strip in the late 1940s. The emergence of jazz in the Village reflected the growing interest in and identification with the music among college students, artists, and other cultured denizens of that neo-bohemian neighborhood.

Other downtown clubs that nurtured the latest jazz styles included the Five Spot, which booked such forward-looking players as Cecil Taylor and Ornette Coleman for lengthy residencies that helped their music develop; the Half Note, for

Pee Wee Russell, Muggsy Spanier, Miff Mole, and Joe Grauso, at Nick's Tavern, New York, New York (ca. June 1946). PHOTO COURTESY WILLIAM P. GOTTLIEB/WILLIAM P. GOTTLIEB COLLECTION/LIBRARY OF CONGRESS PRINTS & PHOTOGRAPHS DIVISION.

nearly 20 years a host to the likes of Charles Mingus, Lennie Tristano, and Coltrane; Slug's Saloon on East 3rd Street, where hard bop thrived in the hands of such proponents as Art Blakey, **Lee Morgan**, and Freddie Hubbard (and where Morgan was shot dead by his mistress on the night of February 19, 1972); and the Village Gate on Bleecker Street, another home of hard bop—and, like the Vanguard, a favored location for live recording sessions. Further uptown, at 1678 Broadway, the post-boppers could get a hearing at Birdland—a club named after their patron saint, Charlie "Bird" Parker.

But more traditional sounds also had their New York show spots, in both the Village and other parts of town. In the mid-1960s, such established stars as **Sarah Vaughan**, Louis Armstrong, Count Basie, and Lionel Hampton would occasionally take their acts to Basin Street East on 48th Street, and swing veterans Red Allen, Coleman Hawkins, and Roy Eldridge could sometimes be heard at the Metropole, on the western end of that same street. Meanwhile, Dixieland jazz enjoyed an extended life at Nick's, located on 7th Avenue in the heart of the Village.

Jazz may have livened up Boston, Chicago, Los Angeles, San Francisco, and other locales in the 1950s and 1960s. But the surging energy of New York made that town—and still makes the town—the jazz capital of the world.

—Tad Lathrop

Donald Byrd. Silver's music proved durable: it modeled a funky soul-and-jazz hybrid whose influence can be traced through the popular 1960s recordings of pianist Ramsey Lewis to the 1970s disco and jazz-funk tracks of Donald Byrd and jazz fusion of Weather Report and the Crusaders to the 1980s R&B-jazz fusion of David Sanborn and many others.

It was during his early development that Silver encountered the root sounds that he later brought to jazz. Silver's father had migrated to the United States from the Portuguese island colony of Cape Verde, off the coast of West Africa, where Portuguese, Caribbean, African, and Brazilian musical influences coalesced. The latter influence, and echoes of his father's jam sessions during Silver's youth, eventually inspired Silver's most popular tune, *Song for My Father*. But he also grew up on boogie-woogie, the blues, and **gospel music**, and he got an early start in mixing them into his own highly accessible brand of jazz. By the time he joined Blakey in the Jazz Messengers, Silver had toured and recorded at age 22 with Stan Getz, backed up Coleman Hawkins and Lester Young, and recorded his own tunes as a sideman and a leader. With 1955's *The Preacher*, recorded under the name Horace Silver and the Jazz Messengers, his funky, gospel-inflected signature sound was firmly in place.

The most brilliant of the hard bop bands was the one that bore the closest resemblance to bebop's fire. In 1954, Roach enlisted the startling young trumpeter **Clifford Brown**, creating one of the most respected partnerships in jazz history. (It was also one of the shortest lived: 30 months later, Brown died in a car crash that also killed the band's pianist, Bud Powell's younger brother Richie.) "Brownie" played with a honeyed tone, a sunny and exquisite lyricism, and a precision that challenged and at times eclipsed even the virtuosity of his idols, Dizzy Gillespie and Fats Navarro. Roach thought enough of Brown to grant him co-star status, and the Clifford Brown-Max Roach Quintet, with West Coast tenorman Harold Land, achieved overnight success with a sound typified by their take-no-prisoners romp on the bop favorite *Cherokee* (1955). The precocious genius Sonny Rollins replaced Land at the end of 1955, and for the next six months—until Brown's death—this

Drummer Max Roach, co-leader of the Brown-Roach Quintet. PHOTO COURTESY © HERMAN LEONARD PHOTOGRAPHY LLC.

band was fueled by the highest-octane front line in jazz.

Before joining the Brown-Roach Quintet, Rollins had participated in several memorable sessions led by Miles Davis, which produced the first recordings of the classic Rollins tunes *Airegin*, *Oleo*, and *Doxy* (all 1954). When Davis prepared to form his own hard bop band in 1955, he thought immediately of the tall, contemplative tenorist, whose playing had already begun to turn heads. But Rollins was unavailable, off in Chicago on the first of three celebrated hiatuses, so Davis turned instead to a relatively obscure saxophonist from Philadelphia, John Coltrane.

Their yin-yang collaboration—with Davis's progressively simpler solos set in bas-relief against Trane's increasingly complicated chromaticism—made this the most influential group of its time. With an unimpeachable rhythm section anchored by bassist Paul Chambers and drummer "Philly" Joe Jones, Davis turned out a series of album masterpieces

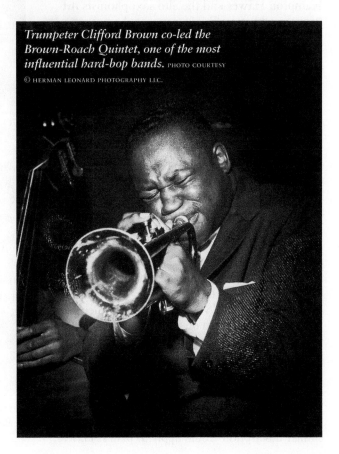

Trumpeter Clifford Brown co-led the Brown-Roach Quintet, one of the most influential hard-bop bands. PHOTO COURTESY © HERMAN LEONARD PHOTOGRAPHY LLC.

gospel music demonstrative African American religious music originating in the early twentieth-century United States, associated with Protestant denominations.

39

(*Workin'*, 1956; *'Round About Midnight*, 1955–56; and *Milestones*, 1958) that exemplified the hard bop style—and transcended it. For in the midst of this decidedly hard bop landscape stood the distinctly cool figure of Davis himself, turning the band into a bridge between the decade's two prevalent jazz idioms.

TAKE NOTE

- How did hard bop develop in response to bebop and other styles?

West Coast Bop

Although California was a hotbed of cool jazz, it also supported important musicians who had little to do with the style. But many of these musicians didn't fit the East Coast hard bop mold, either. Some of them—such as pianist Sonny Clark, trumpeter and flugelhornist Art Farmer, bassist Charles Mingus, tenor saxophonist Teddy Edwards, and drummer Shelly Manne—managed to consolidate key virtues of both schools: Clark, for instance, recorded with the cool-oriented Lighthouse All-Stars before moving to New York, where he worked with Sonny Rollins and led some of the era's most representative hard bop dates (such as *Cool Strutting*, 1958).

Other West Coasters—most notably pianist Hampton Hawes and the alto saxophonists **Art Pepper** and Sonny Criss—concocted a potent version of bebop. This music contrasted sharply with that of their cool compatriots, but it also differed from hard bop, which offered a somewhat relaxed adaptation of bop's frenzy; listening to the aptly named Pepper on such tracks as *Surf Ride* (featuring Hawes, from 1952) and the supersonic *Straight Life* (1954), most people have trouble believing the sessions took place anywhere near the Pacific Ocean. On the other hand, Pepper utilized certain "West Coast" devices to great effect, most notably the studied counterpoint that distinguished the quartet of baritone saxophonist Gerry Mulligan. But Pepper played it hot instead of cool: that same recording of *Straight Life* boasts a fast and furious bit of two-part invention for Pepper and tenor saxophonist Jack Montrose.

Pepper blurred the line further with *Art Pepper Meets the Rhythm Section*, the widely respected 1957 album on which he partnered with the rhythm section from the Miles Davis Quintet (pianist Red Garland, bassist Paul Chambers, and drummer "Philly" Joe Jones). By this time Pepper had arrived at one of the most compelling styles of the decade, a personal and deeply felt compendium of bebop, cool, California, and New York. A similar description would apply to pianist Hawes,

who—on the albums *Hampton Hawes Trio* (1955) and *Four* (1958)—proved himself one of the few pianists able to capture not only the virtuosity but also "the scorching intensity of Bud Powell's pianism," as music historian Ted Gioia put it. "He was, in his own words, the man with the 105-degree fever." Both Hawes (who died in 1977) and Pepper (who died in 1982) fought substance-abuse problems their entire adult lives.

Other than the members of Brubeck's and Mulligan's bands, the best-known West Coast jazzmen belonged at one time or another to the Lighthouse All-Stars, a loose-knit amalgam of players associated with the club called the Lighthouse. Just south of Los Angeles in Hermosa Beach, the Lighthouse was a restaurant down on its luck in 1949, when bassist Howard Rumsey convinced the owner to institute Sunday jam sessions. These sessions often displayed the bristling

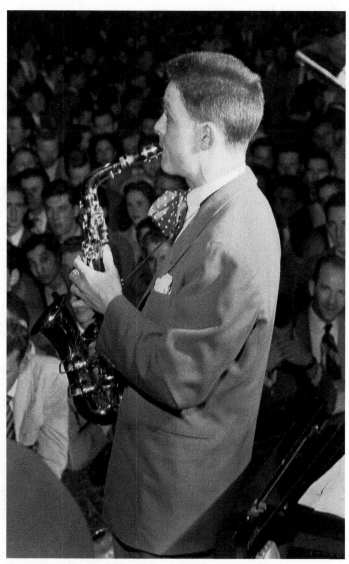

Art Pepper, 1948. Pepper would emerge as an important purveyor of West Coast bop in the 1950s. PHOTO COURTESY WILLIAM P. GOTTLIEB/
WILLIAM P. GOTTLIEB COLLECTION/LIBRARY OF CONGRESS PRINTS & PHOTOGRAPHS DIVISION.

● Style & Technique ●

Breaks and Fours

Jazz musicians have developed a number of common practices; two of the best known are breaks and fours. Both provide contrast and drama and allow the soloists to show off.

A break is a short solo passage by a single instrument or group of instruments—or, less commonly, a short period of complete silence. During a break the rhythm section lays out, but the meter, tempo, and beat remain intact and are ongoing. Breaks usually occur at the ends of sections, especially in the final phrase of a blues or a multi-strain composition.

The break serves a number of purposes: providing the soloist with a springboard into a solo; briefly changing the texture, which is typically otherwise constant; serving as a structural device to herald the next solo; and creating tension and excitement leading to the beginning of a new section. Breaks were found frequently in early jazz, and Jelly Roll Morton used them brilliantly in such recordings as *Black Bottom Stomp* and *Grandpa's Spells* (both 1926). By the 1940s, breaks had become less common, but Charlie Parker took a memorable one to set up his solo on his Dial recording of *Night in Tunisia* (1946). Other modern instances of breaks include John Coltrane's *Locomotion* (1957) and Stan Getz's *Night and Day* (1964).

Another venerable tradition in jazz performance is that of soloists' trading improvised phrases. Exchanging phrases of four measures is called playing fours, trading fours, or simply **fours**, while alternating phrases of eight bars is called **eights**, and so on. The length of these phrases is usually some equal subdivision of the tune's form. In playing a 12-bar blues, musicians could exchange complete *twelves*, two *sixes*, three *fours*, or four *threes*. In a 32-bar form, the phrases might be two, four, eight, or sixteen measures in length.

These exchanges most often follow a round of extended solos, affording the soloists space to build on what the previous soloists have played, revisit their own improvisational ideas, engage in friendly musical combat, and collect their thoughts between cyclical occurrences. The exchanges occur in a number of different settings, often between a solo instrumentalist and a drummer. They also frequently take place in a "round robin" of two or three instrumentalists in a small group setting, whereby a competition of improvisation ensues: for example, **Dexter Gordon** and Wardell Gray on *The Chase* (1947), Johnny Griffin and Eddie

*Big band drummer **Buddy Rich** (shown here in 1954), demonstrated dazzling technique when trading fours or taking long solos.* PHOTO COURTESY © HERMAN LEONARD PHOTOGRAPHY LLC.

"Lockjaw" Davis on *Blues Up and Down* (1961), and trombonists J. J. Johnson and Kai Winding on *It's All Right with Me* (1976). Sometimes a number of like instruments trade phrases, as the saxophones do on Woody Herman's *Four Brothers* (1947). Trading phrases—quite common in jam sessions—gives participants opportunities to express their personalities through concise statements.

—*David Baker*

---

fours trading fours: the jazz practice of showcasing a different soloist every four measures.

eights the jazz practice of showcasing a different soloist every eight measures, as in "trading eights."

energy associated with hard bop on the opposite coast; nonetheless, as the schedule expanded to every night of the week, the Lighthouse emerged as headquarters for such important cool jazz musicians as Shelly Manne and saxophonist Bud Shank, who led innovative groups that balanced composition with improvisation. Soon the club and its "house band," the Lighthouse All-Stars—which at various times included Shank, Manne, pianist Claude Williamson, tenor saxophonists Bob Cooper and Bill Perkins, and brass men Conte Candoli, Shorty Rogers, Frank Rosolino, and Jack Sheldon—came to embody West Coast jazz to most listeners.

Meanwhile, the cool trumpet voice of **Chet Baker**, one of the original West Coast stars, began a fadeout into the jazz background. Drugs took their toll on him, as they had on Pepper and Hawes.

TAKE NOTE

- What distinguishes West Coast bop from other variants, and who were the key players in this style?

Three Tenor Torchbearers: Gordon, Rollins, and Coltrane

The 1950s produced a number of important alto saxophonists—among them Cannonball Adderley, **Jackie McLean**, and Phil Woods. But the virtuosic genius of Charlie Parker remained an unmatchable benchmark for most alto players, so the spotlight shifted to the

tenor sax. The sound of bebop had belonged to trumpet and alto; the sound of hard bop was the tougher, more full-bodied sound of trumpet and tenor. In retrospect, the Sonny Rollins title *Tenor Madness* (1956), which paired Rollins with John Coltrane, could well describe the entire decade.

Both Rollins and Coltrane owed a huge debt to Dexter Gordon, the first important bebop tenorist, whose adaptability made him a vital voice in hard bop as well. Gordon fused the two streams of earlier jazz tenor playing, combining the huge sound and harmonic ingenuity of Coleman Hawkins with the light vibrato and quixotic grace of Lester Young; he also expanded upon Young's narrative abilities, playing solos that almost unfailingly told a story. (Excellent examples include *Dexter Rides Again* by Dexter Gordon and Wardell Gray (*JTSA* Disc 2/Track 15), *It's You or No One* from the Blue Note album *Doin' Allright* (1961), and his solo on Herbie Hancock's famous *Watermelon Man* (1962). Gordon's style fed two new streams, represented by Rollins and Coltrane, which then provided the primary inspiration for the next generation or three of jazz saxophonists.

Although he was four years younger than Coltrane, it was Rollins who first grabbed the attention of jazz cognoscenti, including Davis: in the section of Harlem in which he'd grown up, his neighbors included such towering figures as Hawkins, Monk, and Bud Powell, all of whom encouraged his interest in jazz. (As a teen, Rollins would wait on Hawkins's doorstep for the chance to see his first idol.) Rollins's first recordings with Powell in 1949—especially *Wail* and *Dance of the Infidels*—showed a youngster still mastering bebop's complexities but already possessing a distinct sound and innovative ideas. Before long, the intense young saxophonist had arrived at a style of unusually cogent thematic development, heard on such tunes as *I'll Remember April* (1956) with the Brown-Roach Quintet. Rollins's best improvisations—heard throughout the albums *Saxophone Colossus* (1956), *Sonny Rollins* (1957), *A Night at the Village Vanguard* (1956), and *The Bridge* (1962)—gracefully unfolded across multiple **choruses**. His solos sounded like spontaneous compositions rather than a series of fragments strung between harmonic signposts, and they set a new standard for jazz improvisation.

 Watch the documentary on John Coltrane on **mymusiclab.com**

chorus (1) in jazz, an iteration of a main theme; each time a jazz performer plays through, for example, a 12-bar blues or a 32-bar popular song, he or she is playing a chorus of that tune; (2) an improvised solo, as in "take a chorus"; (3) in a popular song, the main part of the song, which typically repeats, often preceded by its verse.

Sonny Rollins (right) playing with his early mentor Coleman Hawkins, 1963. PHOTO COURTESY LEE TANNER.

A CLOSER LOOK

COLTRANE FORMS HIS GROUP

John Coltrane's "classic" quartet came to fruition when Coltrane left the Miles Davis band in 1960 and struck out on his own as a leader. Coltrane's experiences in jazz up to that point were rich, and they included associations with Dizzy Gillespie, Charlie Parker, bluesman Earl Bostic, and famous groups led

✳ Explore on **mymusiclab.com**

by Miles Davis. This background, combined with his fervor for practicing and his spiritual exploration through music, spurred his and the quartet's innovative performances and recordings.

—*Jeff Rupert*

Jimmy Garrison • Bass

Jimmy Garrison had a depth of sound that anchored Coltrane's quartet. Coltrane had experimented with numerous bass players and settled on Garrison, whose rhythmic feel was in sync with the group. While he did not have the technique of some other bass players, his addition to the Coltrane group exemplified the importance of tone and feel in music.

McCoy Tyner • Piano

McCoy Tyner's "voice" in the quartet was crucial; his rhythmic approach was fierce, buoyant, and relentless, qualities embodied by the entire quartet. Tyner was an original soloist in jazz, relying somewhat on pentatonic techniques (five-note scales, as compared to eight-note scales), and quartal harmony; that is, harmony based on musical intervals of fourths, rather than thirds, which had been the basis for European harmony.

PHOTO COURTESY MICHAEL OCHS ARCHIVES/GETTY IMAGES.

Elvin Jones • Drums

Elvin Jones was the rhythmic center, or the heartbeat, of Coltrane's quartet. Jones's feel on the drums had an unrivaled buoyancy and propulsion. His conceptualization tended toward horizontal motion with vertical inflections, and he epitomized polyrhythmic (more than one rhythm at once) drumming, a West African carryover to jazz. Jones's physical strength enabled him to accompany Coltrane, who at this point would perform for hours without rest. Performances often consisted of one tune, with drum and sax duets in the middle.

John Coltrane • Saxophone

Although primarily a tenor saxophonist, Coltrane also played soprano. His approach was unique; at times his tone resembled an Eastern reed instrument (as exemplified on *India* from his album *Impressions*). Coltrane has been referred to as a "cosmopolitan" of religion. He studied Western and Eastern religious beliefs, all of which are embodied in his music. His jazz improvisation had an entirely different rhythmic approach than that of those who preceded him; at times he played so many notes that one critic referred to him as playing "sheets of sound." Equally, he could play a tender ballad or a driving blues. In all cases he had a unique and identifiable swing feel that created an uplifting air.

Listening Guide

CD I, Track 23/Download Track 23

GIANT STEPS • JOHN COLTRANE QUARTET

Music: John Coltrane, 1959. Personnel: John Coltrane (tenor sax, leader); Tommy Flanagan (piano); Paul Chambers (bass); Art Taylor (drums). Recorded May 5, 1959, in New York. First issue: Atlantic 1311. Timing: 4:47.

Overview

The title tune from Coltrane's breakthrough album, *Giant Steps* became a proving ground for the next two generations of jazz musicians. It consists of a rather simple melody, with only two notes per measure. But almost every note has a different chord attached to it; and these chords move through three keys, changing key as often as twice per measure. Taken at a blistering tempo, it remains one of the most challenging sets of chord changes ever designed for improvisation—an advanced study of harmonic interrelationships—requiring significant preparation in advance. (Coltrane had reportedly been working with these chords for nearly two years prior to the recording.) As an aside, consider the following: The 1930s Rodgers and Hart tune *Have You Met Miss Jones?* has a bridge with nearly the same changes, though a half step lower and at half the pace—making it a great warm-up for playing *Giant Steps*—and perhaps an inspiration for Coltrane's chord changes.

Key Features

- Form: The theme consists of a 16-bar melody that is then repeated, with a slight alteration in the last four measures.
- Rhythm: Much of the recording's propulsion comes from the pronounced use of evenly spaced eighth notes, as opposed to the "swinging" style of dotted eighths alternating with sixteenths.
- Improvisation: Coltrane takes one long solo (12 choruses) and then, after piano and bass, a shorter solo (two choruses) before restating the theme—a relatively unusual structure, previously used to strong effect by Sonny Rollins.
- For such a busy and forceful solo—and one that would become synonymous with Coltrane's early style—this improvisation features relatively little melodic novelty. Instead, it relies on Coltrane's ability to mix and match a handful of motifs to relentlessly explore the harmonic framework. Virtually all of these motifs are introduced within the first choruses of the solo.
- The song's difficulty is illustrated by the fact that seeing the sheet music for the first time at the recording studio, Tommy Flanagan—among the most accomplished post-bop pianists—could manage only a sparse, simple solo that all but ignores the rigorous harmony.
- Dynamics and texture: Variations in dynamics play no role in this performance. It succeeds entirely on speed and urgency, as opposed to gradations in volume or texture.

A nattily dressed Dexter Gordon.

PHOTO COURTESY MICHAEL OCHS ARCHIVES/GETTY IMAGES.

Coltrane's solos, on the other hand, seemed to burst directly from the horn rather than the head, even though they grew from his deep study of modern harmony; his first professional experience came in rhythm and blues bands, and the soulful passion of that music remained with him during his short life (he died in 1967, at the age of 40). Playing with Davis, Coltrane garnered a huge audience for his hell-for-leather style, which featured cyclonic, note-filled solos informed by a relentless appetite for harmonic permutations. Coltrane's albums with Davis, as well as his own *Blue Train* (1957) and *Soultrane* (1958), document the progression of his style, which became increasingly controversial: one reviewer criticized him as "anti-jazz," and Davis supposedly once told him, "Coltrane, you can't play everything at once!" The climax of these investigations came on his 1959 masterpiece, *Giant Steps*, the title track a tricky slalom of careening

- Usually, such concepts as "voice" and "expression" depend entirely on the musician's actual timbre. But here, the song and tempo also contribute to the instrumental voice: the yearning nature of Coltrane's sound gains extra power from the energy required to navigate the rapidly changing chords at fast tempo.
- The rhythm section is given little responsibility other than maintaining the speed of the performance and providing chordal mileposts for the tenor solo.

—Neil Tesser

TIME	SECTION	MELODY/INSTRUMENTATION
0:00	THEME STATEMENT	Standard quartet arrangement, except that rather than offering traditional "comp" rhythms, pianist Flanagan doubles the saxophone melody (using chords). Theme is restated in Chorus 2.
0:26	CHORUS 3	Coltrane begins his 12-chorus solo, introducing one of the dominant recurring motifs—call it figure A—an ascending four-note figure (at 0:30–0:32).
0:40	CHORUS 4	Coltrane begins this chorus with a single note held for almost five beats: a virtual eternity within the context of this swiftly moving solo. This contrasting trope—figure B—will also reoccur frequently.
0:43	CHORUS 4	Reappearance of figure A.
0:53	CHORUS 5	Intermittent use of figure A, from 0:53–0:59.
1:06	CHORUS 6	Variations on figure A reoccur at 1:06 and 1:10, and of figure B at 1:16–1:17 and 1:20.
1:46	CHORUS 9	Brief use of an ascending scalar figure introduces a new element and builds momentum.
2:26	CHORUS 12	Coltrane begins this chorus with a restatement of figure A.
2:52	CHORUS 14	As Coltrane concludes, drummer Art Taylor—most likely signaled by a visual cue from Coltrane—marks the solo's end with a series of rimshots that lead into Tommy Flanagan's piano solo.
2:55	CHORUS 14–16	Piano solo.
3:31	CHORUS 17	Pianist Flanagan plays chords, allowing bass line to be heard more clearly.
3:44	CHORUS 18–19	Second tenor sax solo (recapping elements of the first).
4:10	CHORUS 20–21	Restatement of theme.
4:35	CODA	Final flurry of notes against sustained final chord.

chords. Afterward, Coltrane set about assembling his own band, which by the end of 1961 had coalesced into his galvanic "classic quartet": McCoy Tyner (one of the period's most influential pianists), bassist Jimmy Garrison, and drummer Elvin Jones. The empathic interplay of the four reached a peak on *A Love Supreme* (1964; *JTSA* Disc 5/Track 3).

The track *Tenor Madness* (also from *Saxophone Colossus*) is the only on-disc meeting of Rollins and Coltrane, and it remains the perfect starting place to compare and contrast their styles. Both men benefited from Monk's tutelage, and their work under his name—on *Brilliant Corners* (1956) and *Monk with Coltrane* (1957), respectively—further illuminates their different approaches. Coltrane's music altered in the 1960s, and he became an iconic figure of the jazz avant-garde. Rollins also made significant changes, but not until the 1970s, when he unveiled a technique that was bluesier and far less refined than his music of the 1950s.

As for Dexter Gordon, his battle with narcotics addiction made him something of a shadow figure in the 1950s: he spent almost six years in jail and recorded only one album between 1951 and 1959. When he re-emerged in the 1960s, he showed that he had big enough ears to appreciate Coltrane and Rollins—and a small enough ego to adapt some of their innovations to his own style, as on *Both Sides of Midnight* (1967). This adaptability allowed Gordon to flourish throughout the 1960s and 1970s, and as an "elder statesman" in the 1980s, when he made his film debut in *Round Midnight* (and received an Academy Award nomination for best supporting actor).

TAKE NOTE

- What are the different saxophone styles of Dexter Gordon, Sonny Rollins, and John Coltrane?

Two Takes on the Piano

In the 1950s, most jazz fans would have considered Thelonious Monk and **Dave Brubeck** polar opposites. However, Monk and Brubeck played similar roles in their respective musical camps—that of the stubborn iconoclast, the exception that proves the rule. In his book *West Coast Jazz*, Ted Gioia offers an analysis of their unexpected similarities, pointing out that instead of the dominant 1950s piano style, characterized by hornlike single-note lines and sparse chords, "Brubeck and Monk brought out the intrinsically pianistic and orchestral qualities of the instrument. . . . Both began adopting more complex harmonic structures than their peers. . . . Both emphasized (almost to an extreme) the percussive nature of the piano . . . and focused as much on composing as on playing." And although both men were active in the 1940s, Brubeck and Monk—the second and fourth jazz musicians to appear on the cover of *Time* magazine—really wrote their legacies during the 1950s.

By far the most popular musician to emerge from California was pianist Dave Brubeck, a product of studies with classical composer Darius Milhaud and experiments in counterpoint and **atonality** in late-1940s San Francisco. Brubeck's first band was an octet that proved too esoteric for popular tastes, but subsequent trio recordings planted the seeds of a mass following that blossomed after the addition of alto saxophonist Paul Desmond made the Brubeck group a quartet. The contrast between Desmond's limpid elegance and Brubeck's weightier complexities, and the conversational improvisations that the pair generated on such recordings as *Over the Rainbow* (1952) and *You Go to My Head* (1952) carried particular appeal for the growing audience that approached jazz as a challenging intellectual experience. With an uncanny sense of where both technology and the public were headed, Brubeck began recording nightclub performances on 33⅓-rpm long-playing (LP) records, then

((∘• **Hear** Dave Brubeck describe how he composed *Blue Rondo à la Turk* on **mymusiclab.com**

---

atonal composed without being based in traditional rules of harmonic relationships; for example, not in a key.

The Dave Brubeck Quartet. From left to right: Paul Desmond (alto saxophone), Joe Dodge (drums), Dave Brubeck (piano), and Ron Crotty (bass). PHOTO COURTESY JOHN BROOK/DOWN BEAT ARCHIVES.

obtained bookings on college campuses and recorded those concerts as well—one of them, the album *Jazz Goes to College*, achieved commercial success in 1954.

Brubeck's popularity grew at a steady clip, but he refused to coast on his success, or on the West Coast phenomenon he nominally represented. He continued to develop his classically influenced compositions and to challenge himself and his listeners with unusual meters. This process culminated in his landmark 1959 album *Time Out*, featuring the famous *Take Five* (written by his saxophonist, Paul Desmond). *Time Out* was the first jazz album to sell a million copies—even though it was almost shelved by its label, Columbia, which thought it too "radical" for the record-buying public.

On the other hand, Monk's success in the 1950s represented a return to grace, as the jazz public began to rediscover his quirky compositions and one-of-a-kind piano style. This resulted from a combination of factors. In 1955 a fledgling jazz label, Riverside, decided to "rehabilitate" Monk's image with two albums designed to show him as less "far out" than generally believed: *Thelonious Monk Plays Duke Ellington* and a standards date, *The Unique Thelonious Monk* (a redundant title if ever there was one). Subsequent albums such as *Monk's Music* (1957) proved his stature, with Monk leading groups that mingled respected veterans with fiery newcomers; meanwhile, a few other musicians (most notably soprano saxophonist Steve Lacy) began to revisit his deceptively simple, elegantly constructed compositions and proselytize for them. In 1957 Monk regained his New York City cabaret card and took up residence at the Five Spot club, leading a quartet that featured the skyrocketing Coltrane and propelling himself into the jazz limelight; in 1959, his compositions were arranged for nonet for a famous concert at Town Hall (released on disc as *The Thelonious Monk Orchestra at Town Hall*). By the early 1960s, when Monk established his long-running quartet starring saxophonist Charlie Rouse, he was hailed as one of jazz's true geniuses. Monk tunes were still favorites decades later, having proved adaptable to a wide range of musical settings.

> ### TAKE NOTE
>
> - How were the musical approaches of composer-pianists Thelonious Monk and Dave Brubeck similar and how were they different?

Soul Jazz

As the 1950s drew to a close, one hard bop strain dominated all others. To be sure, the gospel-tinged but down-and-dirty sounds of "**soul jazz**"—simple, funky melodies, danceable rhythms, and plenty of the blues—had exerted a strong influence since the idiom

took shape. But now, inspired by the successes of Horace Silver's group and the remarkable keyboardist **Jimmy Smith**, jazz players began turning out one album after another on which they sought to parlay "the funk" into commercial success.

No one had a more important hand in this process than Smith, the Philadelphia pianist who started to play the electric organ in 1951. By 1956 he had mastered his driving, slashing, sophisticated combination of bebop and rhythm and blues. On his Blue Note Records debut, *A New Sound . . . A New Star* (volumes 1 and 2) and the follow-up *The Incredible Jimmy Smith*, all recorded in 1956, he established the model for the ultra-streamlined "**organ trio**" in jazz; it featured only a drummer, either a guitarist or saxophonist, and Smith himself, both hands and feet in constant motion on the organ's keyboards and pedals as he handled the chores of bassist, keyboard accompanist, and dynamic lead soloist. On subsequent albums, Smith was joined by a number of Blue Note hornmen in jam-session performances that fully exploited the new long-playing record format, with tracks that ran 15 minutes or more.

A similar format became a favorite of guitarist **Kenny Burrell** on such late-1950s "jam" albums as *All Day Long* (1957) and *Blue Lights* (1958). He had already worked on albums by Dizzy Gillespie, John Coltrane, and many of his colleagues from Detroit, which throughout the decade funneled jazz stars from its fertile, vibrant scene into New York. Burrell's mellow tone and easygoing style made him a leading guitarist of the time; in 1959, and then again decades later, he hooked up with Smith on such exceptional Blue Note dates as *Home Cookin'* (1958–59) and *The Master* (1993).

Smith's organ trio showcased the electric guitar to a degree not often heard in earlier jazz, paving the way for the success enjoyed by two other guitarists, Wes Montgomery and Grant Green. In his hometown of Indianapolis, Montgomery formed a trio with his brothers Buddy and Monk, but before long his virtuosity resulted in an extraordinarily successful solo career, best represented by his Riverside album *The Incredible Jazz Guitar* (1960). Montgomery played with a deep, soulful swing that gave his melodies unusual propulsion, and he was the first guitarist to improvise in octaves, a startling technique that at first

---

soul jazz a funky, bluesy style of jazz made popular in the 1950s and 1960s by such musicians as organist Jimmy Smith; guitarists Wes Montgomery, Kenny Burrell, and Grant Green; and saxophonist Cannonball Adderley.

organ trio a distinctive ensemble configuration consisting of electronic organ (usually a Hammond B-3), electric guitar or saxophone, and drums; introduced as part of the soul jazz and hard bop movements in the 1950s and 1960s primarily by organist Jimmy Smith.

Listening Guide

BLUE RONDO À LA TURK • THE DAVE BRUBECK QUARTET

Music: Dave Brubeck, 1959. Personnel: Paul Desmond (alto saxophone); Dave Brubeck (piano); Eugene Wright (bass); Joe Morello (drums). Recorded August 18, 1959, in New York. First issue: *Time Out*, Columbia CL 1397. Timing: 6:46.

Overview

Blue Rondo à la Turk is memorable for four reasons: its use of a meter ($\frac{9}{8}$) then virtually unknown in jazz; its incorporation of European rondo form; its unusual approach to the blues; and the contrasting playing styles of its two soloists.

Dave Brubeck considered himself as much a composer as a pianist, had long been incorporating classical-music forms in his compositions, and in the 1940s—under the influence of composer Darius Milhaud—Brubeck composed a piece he called *Rondo*. (In classical music, a **rondo** is a multisectional form—such as ABACA—with a repeating theme in the tonic or "home" key.) One of the most famous rondos in classical music was Mozart's "Rondo Alla Turca," the third movement of his Sonata no. 11 for piano, which had been inspired by a vogue for Turkish music, and Brubeck based *Blue Rondo à la Turk* loosely on Mozart's "Rondo Alla Turca." The incorporation of the European rondo form (and its use in the title) imbue this recording with aspects of third stream music—a blending of classical music and jazz.

In 1958, Brubeck's quartet traveled to the Middle East and India, and in Istanbul, Turkey, he heard street musicians playing in the unfamiliar meter of $\frac{9}{8}$—a rhythm from a folk dance called a *karşılama*. "I was on my way to a radio station to be interviewed in Turkey," said Brubeck in a Smithsonian oral history interview. "I was walking through the streets. There were street musicians playing in $\frac{9}{8}$." He repeated the rhythm over and over, and was inspired to build *Blue Rondo à la Turk* around the rhythm.

Blue Rondo was included in Brubeck's 1959 album *Time Out*, consisting entirely of pieces with unusual time signatures or meters. Defying the recording company's reluctance ("undanceable," an executive sniffed), *Time Out* became one of the best-selling jazz recordings ever. Two tunes from that album—*Blue Rondo à la Turk* and *Take Five* (in $\frac{5}{4}$ meter)—were issued in 1960, on opposite sides of a 45-rpm disc, selling an extraordinary million copies—highly unusual for a jazz recording.

Key Features

- Instrumentation: This recording exemplifies one of the most popular small ensembles in jazz: a quartet of piano, bass, drums, and saxophone (another common quartet consists of piano, bass, drums, and trumpet).
- Rhythm: The tempo is 140 beats per minute—what jazz musicians called "medium-up." What was highly unusual, even innovative, about the rhythm was its use of $\frac{9}{8}$ meter and the way the measures of $\frac{9}{8}$ were subdivided into rhythmic groupings. Whereas in classical music, works in $\frac{9}{8}$ rhythm were divided regularly into beats of 3+3+3, here the main theme features three measures subdivided 2+2+2+3—an irregular rhythm—followed by a measure subdivided 3+3+3. In the middle of the recording, the band alternates between $\frac{9}{8}$ and $\frac{4}{4}$, and then goes into eight choruses of straight $\frac{4}{4}$ rhythm. These large and small rhythmic shifts took considerable skill to perform and took audiences some getting used to.

- Style: The two soloists—Brubeck and Desmond—play in contrasting styles. Brubeck's firm piano playing—sometimes in block chords—tends to ground the performance, while Desmond's ethereal lines lift it skyward.
- Musicians' roles: The piano and bass take the lead not only in keeping the time but in switching time signatures from $\frac{4}{4}$ to $\frac{9}{8}$ and back and forth. Pianist Brubeck switches among four different roles: as sole presenter of the melody (for example, from 0:00 to 0:11 and 0:22 to 0:32); as co-presenter, with saxophonist Desmond, of the melody; as improvising soloist (3:52 to 5:32); and, from 2:13 to 3:51, as silent partner: during Desmond's solo, Brubeck stops playing completely.
- Form and structure: This recording features perhaps the most complex structure of any discussed in this text. Composer Brubeck has created a unique form that accentuates considerable contrast, juxtaposing the following: major- and minor-key melodies; exacting rapid-fire melodies with space for easy playing; a weighty piano lead with the airy alto sax sound of Paul Desmond; the non-danceable $\frac{9}{8}$ with a swinging $\frac{4}{4}$.
- Voice, feel, expression: A cool ambience is conveyed by Paul Desmond's airy, light Lester Young–like sound on alto saxophone. Although part of the piece is in blues form, there is very little blues tonality—blue notes, vocal-like slides and slurs—and the performance seems somewhat restrained emotionally in comparison with much jazz.

—John Edward Hasse

TIME	FORM	BARS	METER	MELODY/INSTRUMENTATION
0:00	A	8	$\frac{9}{8}$	Piano states main theme, built around a descending two-note figure in F major. At 0:05, bass joins piano: each measure, the bass plays four notes on the same pitch. Drummer plays few notes on cymbal.
0:11	A'	8		Sax enters to play a variation on the first four measures in A minor. Drums more active.
0:22	A	8		Sax drops out; piano plays main theme in F major. Drums now play continuously.
0:33	B	8		B theme (in A minor) is a variation of the A theme: built around repeating two-note figures, first ascending, then descending.
0:44	A	8		Sax and piano play main theme in F major in two-part harmony.
0:55	C	8		Piano, bass, drums alone.
1:07	A	8		Sax plays main theme in F major.
1:18	D	14		Percussive theme in A minor—played alternately by piano and sax—with longer notes than themes A or B.
1:38	E	8		From 1:38, no sax: piano plays thunderous chords. In key of A minor.
1:52	F	12	$\frac{4}{4}$ alternates with $\frac{9}{8}$	Now in F major. An ingenious transition from the preceding material to blues choruses that follow. Sax improvises two bars in $\frac{4}{4}$; sax drops out for two measures as piano plays A-section melody in $\frac{9}{8}$ meter. Bass walks during the $\frac{4}{4}$ measures; reverts to four unison notes per measure in $\frac{9}{8}$ passages.
2:13	G: IMPROVISED SOLOS	12	$\frac{4}{4}$	Piano drops out; sax plays solo over 12-bar blues progression. Walking bass defines the harmonic movement through the blues progression.
2:37		12		Second blues chorus: Desmond leaves space (rests) so that his solo line can breathe.
3:01		12		Third blues chorus.
3:26		12		Fourth blues chorus. Sax has built solo to climax, playing higher notes and blues inflections (3:25 and 3:36).
3:52	H: IMPROVISED SOLOS	12	$\frac{4}{4}$	Sax drops out; piano solo (12-bar blues): Brubeck transitions smoothly from the piano-less solo of Desmond by initially avoiding left-hand chords, instead playing single-note lines in his right hand. Walking bass continues.
4:16		12		Second blues chorus: By bar five (4:25), Brubeck has built to full chords.
4:43		12		Third blues chorus: He maintains the intensity of the previous chorus.
5:08		12		Fourth blues chorus: Brubeck returns to a single-note line to prepare for the transitional section with sax. He incorporates rests, which both serve to outline his phrases and draw attention to the playing of the bassist and drummer.
5:33	F	12	$\frac{4}{4}$ alternates with $\frac{9}{8}$	Band repeats material from 1:52 to 2:12, again ingeniously transitioning out of the blues into the main theme in $\frac{9}{8}$ meter.
5:54	A	8	$\frac{9}{8}$	The band restates the theme in F major. Sax is silent until 5:57.
6:03	D	14		In A minor, sax plays two bars with piano doubling the melody. Then piano plays two bars with no sax. This pattern repeats several times.
6:23	E	9		Sax drops out. Piece ends in A minor.

rondo a multisectional musical form, dating from the Baroque period, in which the principal theme alternates with other themes; for example ABACADA.

Issues

Jazz and Religion

Does jazz have a spiritual dimension?

At first glance, jazz and religion may seem as incompatible as gambling and God. Indeed, early on, jazz and the blues were often denounced as "the devil's music," regarded as disreputable by middle-class blacks and whites alike. Such attitudes took many years to soften. But jazz and religion have been connected in a number of ways—even beyond the obvious link between certain musicians' tastes and their formative experiences hearing church singing.

Early New Orleans jazz musicians performed such religious songs as *Glory, Sing On, In Gloryland* (*JTSA* Disc 1/Track 2), and *Down by the Riverside*. Still, in 1938, Louis Armstrong raised some eyebrows when he made swinging recordings of *Bye and Bye, When the Saints Go Marching In*, and other Negro spirituals.

Some jazz composers went to the spiritual well for inspiration. Duke Ellington composed the ravishing *Come Sunday* for his epic *Black, Brown, and Beige* (1943) and, commissioned by San Francisco's Grace Cathedral, wrote the controversial *Concert of Sacred Music* (1965). Two other sacred concerts followed (1968, 1973).

Bassist-composer Charles Mingus, inspired in part by his mother's visits to Methodist and Holiness churches, wrote *Wednesday Night Prayer Meeting* (1958) and *Better Git It in Your Soul* (1959; *JTSA* Disc 4/Track 5) —raucous, wailing pieces with hand-clapping, shouting, spontaneous bursts of emotion, and simultaneous improvisation. Gospel-influenced pieces such as Horace Silver's *The Preacher* (1955) and Cannonball Adderley's *Sermonette* (1956) echoed call-and-response patterns of down-home African American churches. Pianist Mary Lou Williams composed a

cantata, *Black Christ of the Andes* (1963), and three masses, and Django Reinhardt and Lalo Schifrin each wrote a jazz mass.

John Coltrane, after experiencing a religious awakening in 1957, composed and recorded a number of spiritual works that included *Amen* and *Dear Lord* (both 1965) and the mighty *A Love Supreme* (1964). "God," he wrote, "is gracious and merciful. His way is in love. . . . truly—a love supreme."

Beyond specific religiously inspired pieces, many people found jazz meaningful on a deep, spiritual basis. Perhaps echoing the ancient African integration of music, dance, ritual, religion, and daily life, jazz's "mysterious power to evoke ecstasy" and transcendence, as scholar Neil Leonard observed, made it magical or sacred to countless participants. No wonder many jazz adherents maintain such deep allegiance to the music.

—John Edward Hasse

---

made listeners think he'd gone back to overdub his solos. In the mid-1960s, he became one of the most popular jazz performers due to a series of albums with orchestra that emphasized his flowing sound (but not his brilliant solo constructions). Montgomery also formed a partnership with Jimmy Smith heard on *Jimmy & Wes: The Dynamic Duo* (1966) and *The Further Adventures of Jimmy and Wes* (1966), the latter including the track *King of the Road* (*JTSA* Disc 5/Track 6).

Green, meanwhile, came out of St. Louis with a ringing, shouting tone—tailor-made for soul jazz—and a powerfully direct style of soloing that placed him in great demand as a member of the Blue Note Records "stable": in 1961 alone, he served as either leader or sideman on 19 different record sessions, most notably on *Green Street* (1961). These three guitarists did much to make the instrument an increasingly strong

Wes Montgomery, one of the most significant and influential jazz guitarists, infused bop-blues phrasing with swinging energy. PHOTO COURTESY LEE TANNER.

History & Culture

Down Beat and the Jazz Magazines

Jazz magazines have come and gone with dizzying frequency. More than 800 jazz periodicals have been published in the United States and abroad, but most long ago ceased publication. At the end of jazz's first century, the best known included *Down Beat*, *Jazz Times*, and *Jazziz* (all in the United States); *Coda* (Canada); *Jazz Journal International* (United Kingdom); *Jazz magazine* and *Jazz hot* (France); *Orkester Journalen* (Sweden); *Musica Jazz* (Italy); and *Swing Journal* (Japan). In the early twenty-first century, several of them were no longer publishing. But others expanded with robust Internet sites, and newer entrants such as allaboutjazz.com redefined the notion of jazz coverage, combining journalism with multimedia programming and services for the jazz community. The Internet enabled a proliferation of other special-interest jazz information sites.

One of the jazz magazines, *Down Beat*, boasts a special place in jazz history. Of the English-language jazz magazines, it has survived the longest: since 1934. And along the way—through jazz's roller-coaster ride through changing sonic landscapes and jumps and dips in popularity—it stayed on track as the magazine that U.S. fans and musicians thought of first when seeking jazz information.

With its record and concert reviews, interviews, readers' polls, and educational features, *Down Beat* not only supported the efforts of working musicians but also inspired new generations to follow in the footsteps of their musical heroes.

The magazine helped launch the careers of some leading jazz writers, among them Dan Morgenstern, Nat Hentoff, and Gary Giddins. It also invited musicians to submit commentary, and many—including Jelly Roll Morton, Duke Ellington, Marian McPartland, Kenny Dorham, and Ornette Coleman—took them up on it, with sometimes controversial results. *Down Beat* ultimately codified musician participation in a feature called the Blindfold Test, in which musicians would listen to unidentified recordings and offer their critiques.

The magazine rose to popularity during the swing era, linking its fortunes with those of the big bands and players it advocated—including Duke Ellington, Benny Goodman, Woody Herman, and Jimmy Dorsey. When those fortunes began to sag, *Down Beat* was left seeking ways to maintain financial viability at a time when jazz—in its new bebop, cool, and experimental incarnations—was becoming a music of the devoted few rather than the general public.

Its answer, in part, was to focus on jazz education; by providing instructional articles, drawing attention to young talent in a "First Chorus" column, co-sponsoring instrumental clinics and music festivals, and conferring scholarships through its Student Music Awards, it would build its future readership. That approach took *Down Beat* into the 1960s and what some observers consider the magazine's heyday, as it was, to an extent, a heyday of mainstream jazz.

The arrival of the rock era and of magazines that chronicled its culture—*Rolling Stone*, for one—brought another turning point. With jazz eclipsed by the popularity of the Beatles, Jimi Hendrix, and other rock stars, the magazine faced the quandary of maintaining its strictly jazz focus or branching out and covering the many other new popular styles. It chose the latter route, and its decision to do so reflected what many jazz musicians were doing: drawing from increasingly varied musical sources for creative fuel and inspiration.

Down Beat later adapted to evolving technology, too, launching a Web site. The magazine's broadened content and expanded media reach were further indicators of the growing pluralism—and resilience—of jazz itself.

—*Tad Lathrop and John Edward Hasse*

COURTESY JOHN EDWARD HASSE.

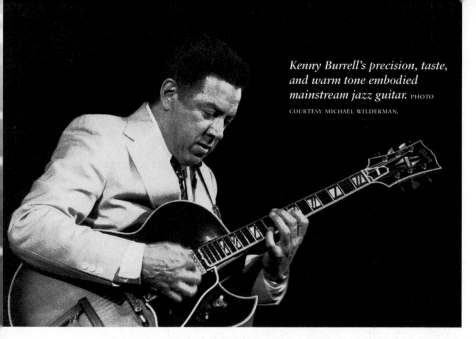

Kenny Burrell's precision, taste, and warm tone embodied mainstream jazz guitar. PHOTO COURTESY MICHAEL WILDERMAN.

in Ghana (1960), and Morgan's *The Sidewinder* (1964).

Morgan and Freddie Hubbard (his successor on trumpet in the Jazz Messengers) both came naturally to this idiom, having played a fair amount of "the funk" with Blakey. And both were able to transcend the rapidly accumulating soul-jazz clichés to create rich and lasting albums, including Morgan's *Search for the New Land* (1964), Hubbard's *Ready for Freddie* (1961) and *Breaking Point* (1964), and their 1965 face-off, the aptly titled *Night of the Cookers*.

Many of these albums starred pianist Herbie Hancock, for whom soul jazz held the greatest value. A child prodigy who performed with the Chicago Symphony at the age of 12, Hancock was a vital member of Miles Davis's progressive 1960s quintet. But on his own, Hancock showed a penchant for soul jazz, beginning with his Blue Note debut, *Takin' Off* (1962), an album that included *Watermelon Man*, which became a funk standard. A prolific and important composer, Hancock hit his stride on the 1965 album *Maiden Voyage*, a jazz exploration of the ocean's mysteries that remains a mainstream milestone.

presence in jazz during the 1960s, paralleling the rise of guitar-driven rock.

Around 1960, soul jazz became the preferred description for this branch of hard bop, after the term was applied to the recordings of alto saxophonist Cannonball Adderley. A technically brilliant and emotionally dynamic player, Adderley sported a brimming, almost fulsome tone and an impressive bag of expressive tricks. He and his younger brother, cornetist Nat, had moved in 1955 from their native Florida to New York, where jazz aficionados quickly discovered the white-hot talent beneath Cannonball's heavy drawl and country manner. After leaving Miles Davis's band in 1960, Cannonball founded a quintet with his brother; it also starred a noted Jazz Messengers alumnus in pianist and composer Bobby Timmons, and it quickly emerged as the most popular band on the hard bop scene. Prime examples of Adderley's soul jazz are present on the retrospective album *Phenix* (1975).

Even musicians whose main interests lay elsewhere—the progressive Charles Mingus, the darkly emotional alto saxophonist Jackie McLean, and Lee Morgan (a tough and even menacing presence on trumpet)—recorded famous examples of soul jazz. These include Mingus's *Better Git It in Your Soul* (1959; *JTSA* Disc 4/ Track 5), McLean's *Appointment*

Cannonball and Nat Adderley performing in Denmark, 1961. PHOTO COURTESY JP JAZZ ARCHIVE/ REDFERNS/GETTY IMAGES.

History & Culture

Jazz Festivals

The proliferation of jazz festivals—events showcasing multiple artists, sometimes over several days—occurred in tandem with the increasing perception of jazz as music to listen to rather than simply to dance, imbibe, or converse to.

Festivals offered audiences and musicians alike an alternative to cramped, noisy, smoky clubs. In often idyllic settings, listeners could enjoy a broad spectrum of artists playing a range of jazz styles—or different approaches to one style if the festival happened to focus on a particular theme.

For musicians, jazz festivals provided an important outlet. With hundreds of such gatherings presented around the globe every year, they added up to an international "circuit" that could keep bands on the road when nightclub gigs were hard to come by.

An International Jazz Congress was held in Chicago in 1926, but the festival idea didn't catch on until the presentation of the Festival Internationale du Jazz, held in Paris in 1949, which offered a wide range of U.S. and European performers. In years that followed, the Newport Jazz Festival (launched in 1954 and captured on film in the 1960 documentary *Jazz on a Summer's Day*) emerged as a leading stateside showcase, as did the Monterey Jazz Festival, founded in 1958 by disc jockey Jimmy Lyons and jazz critic Ralph Gleason. A half century later, continuing U.S. festivals included George Wein's Jazz Festival in New York, the Concord Jazz Festival in California, the still-active Monterey fest, the Chicago Jazz Festival, and the New Orleans Jazz and Heritage Festival.

COURTESY JOHN EDWARD HASSE.

Events also cropped up in other parts of the world, including nearly every European country.

Switzerland hosted one of the world's highest-profile yearly jazz events, the Montreux Jazz Festival (over time, mixing jazz with varied kinds of pop music); France drew visitors yearly to its Paris Jazz Festival; Germany staged festivals in Berlin, Köln, and Frankfurt; the Netherlands' North Sea Jazz Festival enjoyed a long run and gained a reputation as the world's largest jazz festival; the UK's offerings included an Edinburgh-based event; and Canada staged jazz fests all across the country, from Halifax and Montreal in the East to Victoria and Vancouver in the West.

Theme-based events included the Imatra Big Band Festival in Finland, the Festival of New Orleans Music in Switzerland, and the free-jazz Total Music Meeting in Germany.

Eventually, jazz festivals were being held in such far-flung places as St. Petersburg, Istanbul, Melbourne, Tokyo, Beijing, and even the islands of St. Lucia and Jamaica—proving that jazz had truly become a global art form.

—*Tad Lathrop*

In his early, pre-synthesizer years, Herbie Hancock penned such mainstream classics as Maiden Voyage *and* Dolphin Dance. *He is shown here in performance in 2004.*
PHOTO COURTESY MICHAEL WILDERMAN.

((•— **Hear** the Thad Jones-Mel Lewis Orchestra live at the Village Vanguard on **mymusiclab.com**

Soul jazz made dozens of converts, moving mainstream jazz further toward funk (and recapturing some of the audience that had turned to rock and roll). Pioneers and newcomers alike rubbed shoulders in the recording studios of Blue Note, Prestige, and Atlantic Records. Soul jazz even found its way into the relatively few big bands that established themselves during the 1960s as descendants of engines that powered the swing era.

In this sector, two important figures rose above the rest. Trumpeter and composer-arranger Thad Jones built upon his experience in the Count Basie Orchestra to add soul jazz to the big-band repertoire; the **Thad Jones-Mel Lewis Orchestra**, which began as a Monday night "**rehearsal band**" at New York's Village Vanguard, eventually set the standard for modern big band power. And saxophonist Oliver Nelson, who had worked for jump–band leader Louis Jordan in the early 1950s, offered imaginatively soulful renditions of his own tunes, notably on the album *The Blues and the Abstract Truth* (1961)—a perennial favorite led by its centerpiece, *Stolen Moments*.

TAKE NOTE

• What is soul jazz and how does it differ from hard bop?

---

rehearsal band group of musicians who meet to rehearse and play for each other rather than for the public.

Continuing Traditions

During this period, earlier jazz styles didn't just fold up and die. In fact, every previous idiom not only coexisted but also still thrived—and usually in the work of the musicians who had invented it. In 1955, such legends as Louis Armstrong and Earl Hines were still in early middle age, many of the swing giants maintained rigorous performing schedules, and the bebop rebels had just approached their prime. Jazz had yet to place Duke Ellington, Billie Holiday, Parker, and Gillespie on pedestals; fans were too busy checking out their latest records.

In fact, during the 1950s Ellington entered the second great arc of his storied career, during which his fame eclipsed even his previous success. This "comeback" began at the Newport Jazz Festival in 1956, where Paul Gonsalves's intense, 27-chorus tenor saxophone solo on Ellington's *Diminuendo in Blue* set the crowd (and then those who bought the *Ellington at Newport* album) on fire. From then until the end of his life (1974), Ellington and Billy Strayhorn spent increasing amounts of time on larger works, many of which are considered their greatest accomplishments: *Such Sweet Thunder* (1956–57), based on characters and themes from Shakespeare; Ellington's score for the film *Anatomy of a Murder* (1959); their *Far East Suite* (1966); and the *Second Sacred Concert* (1968).

In the work of other artists, the various eras of jazz flowed together, combining aspects of swing, bop, and

((•— **Listen** to *Isfahan* from Duke Ellington's *Far East Suite* (*JTSA* Disc 5/Track 7)

Cool jazz man Stan Getz got hotter as the 1950s unfolded.
PHOTO COURTESY DOWN BEAT ARCHIVES.

Billie Holiday, though past her prime, continued to work during the 1950s. Time had diminished her vocal range but seasoned her interpretative abilities. PHOTO COURTESY DOWN BEAT ARCHIVES.

((●• **Listen** to *I'll Remember April* by Errol Garner (*JTSA* Disc 3/Track 9)

cool into styles both unique and popular. Pianist **Erroll Garner**, for example, used an insistent left-hand pulse (à la the 1930s), angular bop syncopations, and richly chorded harmonies in creating perhaps the most popular jazz sound of the 1950s, heard on best-selling records (*Concert by the Sea*, 1955) and network-television variety shows. The song *Misty* (1954), for which Garner wrote the music, is one of the most performed 1950s-era compositions. The brilliant tenor saxophonist Stan Getz, previously associated with bebop and cool, reflected both schools in his spectacularly communicative style, at home in both the intimate setting of a quintet, as on *Stan Getz Plays* (1952–54), and the grand stage of orchestral strings, as on his 1961 collaboration with arranger Eddie Sauter, *Focus*.

TAKE NOTE

● How did earlier jazz traditions and groups grow and thrive during this period?

Vocalists of the Mainstream Era

The 1950s didn't launch many new vocalists, largely because so many of the "old" ones were still around—and in many cases sounding better than ever. The swing

Frank Sinatra and Ella Fitzgerald, both master song stylists. PHOTO COURTESY DOWN BEAT ARCHIVES.

era star Ella Fitzgerald reinvented herself not once but twice: in the 1940s she had become a terrific bop singer, and now she recorded a series of "songbook" albums celebrating the great American composers of popular music—including George and Ira Gershwin, Irving Berlin, Harold Arlen, Rodgers and Hart, and Cole Porter—that made her a national treasure. Sarah Vaughan, meanwhile, had to refashion herself only once: from the bebop rebel who scatted with Bird and Diz to a voluptuously swinging pop star who never lost her jazz roots. Yet when she placed her voice before a symphony orchestra—as on *Sarah Vaughan Sings George Gershwin* (1954–57)—she became the closest thing to an operatic diva jazz has ever known. (Listen to her version of *Wrap Your Troubles in Dreams*, *JTSA* Disc 4/Track 9). The work of Mel Tormé, the gifted wunderkind who had achieved fame in the 1940s, gained depth and chiseled his credentials as a great improviser on a par with Fitzgerald (as on *Mel Tormé Swings Shubert Alley*, 1960); the same could be said of **Anita O'Day,** who had created the mold for cool jazz singers as a member of Stan Kenton's band in the 1940s and, on such albums as *Pick Yourself Up* (1956), proved herself among the most intelligently swinging vocalists of the 1950s and 1960s. (Listen to early O'Day on *Let Me Off Uptown*, *JTSA* Disc 2/Track 11.)

Nat "King" Cole, best known as a pop singing star, was also an influential pre-bebop pianist and one of the great jazz singers. His rich baritone, liquid phrasing, excellent diction, warmth of tone, and superb musicianship won him a huge following among audiences, black and white, starting with his hip hit from 1943, *Straighten Up and Fly*

Jazz on Television

Television may have become a vast wasteland, as critics liked to point out, but jazz fans could occasionally find their music on the "box"—though it wasn't always easy. In television's early years, traditional jazz styles could be found on *Eddie Condon's Floor Show* (NBC and CBS, 1949–50), with such regulars as Wild Bill Davison and Pee Wee Russell; *Chicago Jazz*, featuring Art Van Damme and the Tailgate 7 (NBC, 1949); and *Adventures in Jazz* (CBS, 1949). The music was upbeat and accessible, and it usually stayed within the bounds of mainstream tastes—and racial preferences.

But at a time when segregation was still legal in much of the United States, television's increasing use of African American musicians in the 1950s helped chip away at the color line. Black jazz musicians not only performed on television but often did so in racially integrated groups. Well before the civil rights movement reached its peak, pianist Hazel Scott had her own network series (Dumont, 1950). What's more, television presented black musicians as artists, not just entertainers. On "The Sound of Miles Davis" (*The Robert Herridge Theater*, CBS, 1958), there was no shucking or jiving, no corny comedy bits; it was filmed with all the dignity and respect given to symphonic broadcasts. In the button-down Eisenhower era, *The Sound of Jazz* (CBS, 1959) enabled Americans to experience the work of such iconoclasts and nonconformists as Thelonious Monk and Lester Young.

Still, there was resistance to jazz on the part of some program sponsors. *The Nat "King" Cole Show* (NBC, 1956–57) featured **Ella Fitzgerald**, Billy Eckstine, and stars from Jazz at the Philharmonic, including Coleman Hawkins, Roy Eldridge, and **Oscar Peterson**, but the show was canceled due to sponsors' fears of alienating white southern viewers. Some shows got around such fears by appealing to a more highbrow, presumably more tolerant, audience. *Omnibus* (CBS and ABC, 1953–57), with host Alistair Cooke, is remembered for its sophisticated approach to classical and jazz music; on one broadcast it offered a reunion of the groundbreaking, racially integrated Benny Goodman Trio with Teddy Wilson and Gene Krupa.

Musicians Duke Ellington, Steve Allen, and Billy Taylor were instrumental in bringing jazz to a wider TV audience. Ellington was charming, articulate, and telegenic, as evidenced by his appearances on the *Bell Telephone Hour* (NBC, 1959 and 1967); *The U.S. Steel Hour* (CBS, 1957); and *Duke Ellington: Love You Madly* (National Educational Television [NET], 1967). On such shows, he achieved the rare balance of art and entertainment.

Pianist, composer, and comedian Steve Allen also managed to straddle the highbrow-middlebrow divide. *The Steve Allen Show* (NBC, 1956–58) featured jazz artists on a regular basis, including a memorable remote broadcast from Birdland by Count Basie's orchestra.

Pianist Billy Taylor became a mainstay jazz figure on TV, from

his musical-directorship of NET's first jazz series, *The Subject Is Jazz*, in 1958 to his ongoing role as arts correspondent for CBS's *Sunday Morning*.

When jazz wasn't the focal point its sound was used to evocative ends. Crime and detective shows used jazz music to suggest gritty realism or to convey a character's inner thoughts, notably on *Naked City* (ABC, 1958–63), with its theme by Billy May; *M Squad* (NBC, 1957–60) with music by Count Basie; *Asphalt Jungle* (ABC, 1961), for which Ellington wrote the opening music; and the highly successful jazz score by Henry Mancini for *Peter Gunn* (NBC and ABC, 1958–61).

In the late 1950s and early 1960s, network television largely ignored jazz, but things were different over at public television. NET—the precursor to the Public Broadcasting System (PBS)—didn't rely on ratings or sponsors, so it occasionally ventured into more modern, even avant-garde territory. Ralph J. Gleason's *Jazz Casual* series, for example, bravely devoted entire programs to performances by the quartets of John Coltrane (1964) and Charles Lloyd (1968). Another NET series, *Music U.S.A.*, presented a program titled "The Experimenters" with groups led by Charles Mingus and Cecil Taylor, including analysis and commentary by critic Martin Williams and novelist Ralph Ellison (1967). In tandem with America's rightward turn in the Reagan era of the 1980s, PBS programming became more conservative. But jazz continued to find airtime, notably in

Woody Herman on Cavalcade of Bands, *which ran from January 1950 to September 1951.* PHOTO COURTESY WILLIAM KAHN/ DOWN BEAT ARCHIVES.

alternative hip hop. In 2009, jazz was dropped and BET J was rebranded as Centric, a general-interest channel aimed at African American adults.

In 2001, PBS broadcast an ambitious 19-hour documentary miniseries titled *Jazz: A Film By Ken Burns*, featuring a narrative script written by Geoffrey C. Ward, historic film clips, and extensive interviews with prominent musicians, critics, and academics. The series stirred considerable controversy and criticism in jazz circles due to what some perceived as conservative bias and short shrift given to jazz after 1960. Five years later, PBS broadcast 12 episodes of a new series, *The Legends of Jazz*, hosted by Ramsey Lewis and featuring live studio performances and interviews.

As broadcast and cable outlets struggled with dwindling audiences, new and historic jazz television performances found a home on video-sharing Web sites such as YouTube, allowing collectors to post clips from off the air and from older video and film formats, many of which are commercially unavailable. YouTube and other such sites have been criticized and sued for failing to ensure that their online content adheres to copyright laws.

the series *American Masters* and *Great Performances*.

Meanwhile, jazz found an increasingly hospitable place on commercial cable television. BET on Jazz, backed by Robert Johnson's Black Entertainment Television, became the United States' most ambitious attempt to create a channel devoted solely to jazz music and its offshoots. However, at the close of the century it was still struggling to find an audience and sponsor. In an attempt to increase audience and market share, BET re-branded by changing the name of the channel to BET Jazz in 2002, then in 2006 to BET J as it shifted from jazz to R&B, neo soul, and

—*Larry Appelbaum*

Carmen McRae drew inspiration from Billie Holiday but established her own distinctive voice. Noted for the depth of feeling that she brought her performances, McRae remained active—as an actress as well as a singer—through the 1980s. PHOTO COURTESY JAMES J KRIEGSMANN/ DOWN BEAT ARCHIVES.

Francisco (1962), he made several jazz excursions, with such collaborators as Count Basie, Stan Getz, and pianist Bill Evans. In the 1990s and into the twenty-first century, his time-seasoned sound captured new jazz and pop fans.

Only a handful of vocalists really reflected the hard bop aesthetic in their music. Three of them sang together as (Dave) Lambert, (Jon) Hendricks, and (Annie) Ross; they perfected the art of vocalese, in which intricate lyrics are fitted to previously recorded improvised solos; highlights of their work include vocal versions of the Jazz Messengers' *Moanin'* (1959), Horace Silver's *Come On Home* (1961), and John Coltrane's *Mr. P.C.* (1961). **Carmen McRae** achieved her first success during the 1950s as well, eventually developing a gimlet edge to her singing that echoed the stance of such hornmen as Rollins, Davis, and Jackie McLean: *Carmen McRae Sings Lover Man and Other Billie Holiday Classics* (1961) is an homage to her idol, while her 1972 *Great American Songbook* remains the best snapshot of her piquant personality. Another bop-oriented singer, Betty Carter, first drew attention touring in 1948–51 with bandleader Lionel Hampton, who nicknamed her Betty Bebop. Carter's day wouldn't come till the 1970s and 1980s—it took audiences that long to catch up with her edgy, highly improvisatory style. But when recognition came, it happened in a big way: fans hailed her arranging and bandleading skills as well as her voice, and she gained additional respect for starting her own label, Bet-Car Records. The singer's talents are amply displayed on such albums as *I Can't Help It* (recorded in 1958–60), *Look What I Got* (1988), and *Feel the Fire* (1994).

The much-imitated Anita O'Day. PHOTO COURTESY PAUL J HOEFFLER/DOWN BEAT ARCHIVES.

Right. (Listen to Cole's *When I Grow Too Old to Dream, JTSA* Disc 3/Track 14.)

Even Frank Sinatra, en route to establishing himself as the century's symbol of American popular song, reverted to his big-band jazz upbringing, recording a fine album with Count Basie, a fair one with Duke Ellington, and delightful live dates with a quintet led by vibraphonist Red Norvo, heard on *Live in Australia 1959* ("rediscovered" by Blue Note Records in 1997). Sinatra's primary influence, Billie Holiday, continued to record throughout the 1950s. Her voice, ravaged by years of alcohol and heroin, had lost much of its luster, but hard times had also sharpened her interpretive skills; her many recordings in the 1950s featured noted mainstream instrumentalists, as heard on the album *Billie's Best* (1945–59).

Meanwhile, Sinatra passed part of Holiday's torch to the young Tony Bennett, who, like Sinatra, brought his jazz sensibility to a pop context. Although Bennett became primarily associated with such hit pop recordings as *I Left My Heart in San*

Jazz & the Arts

Jazz and Fiction

The impact of jazz on fiction is apparent in two types of writing: works that deal directly with jazz musicians and the jazz life, and works that appear to have been influenced or inspired by the aesthetics or spirit of jazz. In the imaginations of many twentieth-century writers, jazz symbolized liberation from bourgeois social conventions, an intense sense of living in the present moment, and living life dangerously on the edge. In effect, jazz served as a metaphorical frontier in the modern American literary mind.

The two most famous pieces of American fiction dealing with the life of a jazz musician are Dorothy Baker's 1938 novel *Young Man with a Horn* and James Baldwin's 1957 short story "Sonny's Blues." Both works established several conventions about the depiction of the jazz musician hero in fiction: In both books the character is a sensitive victim of dissipation caused by an uncaring, philistine, racist society. He is dedicated solely to his craft, to truth and beauty, and to a willingness to endure the pain necessary to bring that truth and beauty to the world. In short, both writers established the jazz musician as a highly romanticized figure, a martyr. Jazz is presented as an almost spiritual pursuit, a transcendent art, forced to exist in a low-life or pedestrian setting from which it draws its authenticity and vitality.

Preceding these two defining works were others of both artistic merit and cultural importance. Key books by African American writers include James Weldon Johnson's *The Autobiography of an Ex-Colored Man* (1912), a novel that chronicles the black sporting life and principally the world of ragtime, and Paul Laurence Dunbar's 1902 novel *The Sport of the Gods*, which envisions ragtime as a kind of morally degenerate music. There are vivid depictions of jazz or jazz-like music in many of the black novels of the Harlem Renaissance, including Claude McKay's *Banjo* (1929) and *Home to Harlem* (1928), Nella Larsen's *Quicksand* (1928) and *Passing* (1929), Wallace Thurman's *Infants of the Spring* (1932), and Jean Toomer's *Cane* (1923). Zora Neale Hurston's famous autobiographical essay, "How It Feels to Be Colored Me" (1928), contains one of the most famous depictions of jazz by a black writer of the era.

Literary writing about jazz became more varied and sophisticated as writers developed a deeper affinity with the creative processes and impulses of the jazz musician. Noted post-World War II works of fiction about jazz musicians include John A. Williams's *Night Song* (1961), William Melvin Kelley's *A Drop of Patience* (1965), Michael Ondaatje's *Coming Through Slaughter* (1976), John Clellon Holmes's *The Horn* (1958), Frank Conroy's *Body and Soul* (1993), Amiri Baraka's much-anthologized story "The Screamers" (1963), Bart Schneider's *Blue Bossa* (1998), and Rafi Zabor's award-winning *The Bee Comes Home* (1997). Another influential book dealing with jazz is Josef Skvorecky's two-novella *Bass Saxophone* (1977).

The two most significant American novels with a jazz sensibility are Jack Kerouac's *On the Road* (1957), the novel that defined the Beat movement of the 1950s, and Ralph Ellison's *Invisible Man* (1952). Although neither deals with jazz directly, both exhibit the flow and movement of jazz improvisation. Ellison was also one of the premier essayists on jazz.

Albert Murray's novels, *Train Whistle Guitar* (1998), *The Spyglass Tree* (1992), and *The Seven League Boots* (1997), have strong jazz and blues themes.

In children's literature, Christopher Paul Curtis's *Bud, Not Buddy* (1999) and Walter Dean Myers's *Harlem Summer* (2007) are about jazz during the 1920s and 1930s.

Whether romanticized, demonized, rendered realistically, or invoked as a metaphor, jazz proved a valuable means to various modern literary ends.

—*Gerald Early*

Another important hard bop singer, Mark Murphy, evoked the Beat writers with his cool baritone and ebullient phrasing on such albums as the 1961 *Rah*; his idiosyncratic phrasing continued to evolve into the twenty-first century.

TAKE NOTE

- What vocalists were important during the mainstream era?

Alternate Currents

While hard bop and cool jazz served as the borders of mainstream jazz, the music contained various other currents.

Chamber jazz offered an intimate alternative to big bands and busy combos; the Modern Jazz Quartet exemplified this sound but was hardly alone in making it popular. Taking as their model the hit 1940s recordings of Nat "King" Cole, Oscar Peterson and Ahmad Jamal each led piano-guitar-bass trios that had no drummer. The results couldn't have been more different. In New York, the Canadian-born Peterson floored audiences with his technical prowess, as on *The Lady Is a Tramp* from the remarkable 1957 live album *At the Concertgebouw*. But Jamal, on the recording *Chamber Music of the New Jazz* (1955), created airy, delicate textures in which the spaces between notes had all the impact of the notes themselves; these performances, recorded while he lived in Chicago, exerted a strong influence on Miles Davis.

In California, saxophonist Jimmy Giuffre—a former member of Woody Herman's Second Herd and a Lighthouse regular—spent the 1950s looking both backward and forward for new ideas. On the one hand, he immersed himself in the counterpoint of early New Orleans jazz; yet on Shelly Manne's *The Three*, in 1954, he joined in a trio that featured neither piano nor bass en route to "jazz with a non-pulsating beat," thus anticipating later hybrids of jazz and classical music. California drummer Chico Hamilton, on such albums as *Gongs East!* (1958) and *Man from Two Worlds* (1962–63), explored unusual and intimate textures with a quintet that featured flute and cello and helped shape the music of saxophonists Eric Dolphy and Charles Lloyd. Hamilton's description of the drums as "a very melodic . . . sensuous feminine instrument" suggests his ability to look beyond conventional strictures in his quest for greater freedom of expression.

In fact, "quest for freedom" would describe the stirrings all around mainstream jazz in the 1950s and 1960s. The idea of liberation took many forms, some of them quite subtle. After leaving Miles Davis's group in 1960, Bill Evans conceived a quietly radical trio that would free the piano, bass, and drums from their traditionally assigned roles—a highly democratic unit in which no one element dominated completely, thus allowing each man to steer the music at any given moment. Evans achieved this with drummer Paul

---

chamber jazz small-ensemble jazz intended for listening in concerts. The term is applied frequently to the music of the Modern Jazz Quartet, reflecting its intricacy, polish, precision, and formal presentation.

Oscar Peterson's keyboard virtuosity earned him legions of disciples. PHOTO COURTESY © HERMAN LEONARD PHOTOGRAPHY LLC.

Bill Evans brought new ideas to the piano-trio configuration. He is shown here in the mid-1970s. PHOTO COURTESY INSTITUTE FOR JAZZ STUDIES, RUTGERS UNIVERSITY.

Jazz & the Arts

Jazz and Visual Arts

Jazz inspired visual artists to explore primitivism and modernity, to construct racial and national identities, and to invent new styles. It embodied the natural, the exotic.

Realist painters found in jazz bistros a post-Victorian milieu that challenged gender, sexual, and racial boundaries. In Archibald J. Motley, Jr.'s, *Blues* (1929) and Reginald Marsh's *Tuesday Night at the Savoy Ballroom* (1930), the female figure and the dancers' intimacy exemplify taboo-breaking sensuality. Jazz was also associated with things African, as in Pablo Picasso's *Three Musicians* (1921), Fernand Leger's set and costume designs for the ballet *La Creation du Monde* (1923), and Arthur Dove's *Primitive Music* (1944).

Jazz was also a machine-age music of the city. While in New York, French painters Francis Picabia and Albert Gleizes incorporated jazz themes into their work—*Negro Song (Chanson Negre)* (1913) and *Composition (for "Le Jazz")* (1915), respectively—as an expression of modern U.S. culture, as did Otto Dix and George Grosz in Germany. Later, Stuart Davis captured New York's dynamism with jazz-inspired abstract color harmonies and dissonances in *Hot Still Scape for Six Colors— Seventh Avenue Style* (1940). Piet Mondrian merged jazz syncopation

Romare Bearden's Jammin' at the Savoy, *1980. Etching, 15½" × 23½".* ART COURTESY © ROMARE BEARDEN FOUNDATION/LICENSED BY VAGA, NEW YORK, NY.

with urban energy in *Broadway Boogie-Woogie* (1942–43). In Thomas Hart Benton's *Arts of the City* (1932), the saxophonist personified urban life. An African American perspective on jazz musicians and dancers is reflected in Aaron Douglas's *Song of the Towers* (1934), Romare Bearden's *Alto Composite* (1974), and David Driskell's *Jazz Singer* (1974).

Avant-garde artists equated jazz with creative revolution. Painters produced abstract works inspired by jazz recordings, as Arthur Dove did in *George Gershwin—Rhapsody in Blue, Part 1* (1927). Paris Dada artists in the 1920s considered jazz an unstructured anti-music or an alter ego, if you will, to their anti-art performances. French surrealists saw the music—with its convulsive rhythms and celebration of instinct, seen in Yves Tanguy's *Bar Americain* (1925)—as an example of psychic automatism. Improvisation served as a model for the collage cutouts of Henri Matisse's *Jazz* (1947) and helped inspire Jackson Pollock's drip painting method, exemplified *by Autumn Rhythm (No. 30)* (1950).

Images of jazz and the jazz musician, as in Jean-Michel Basquiat's *Discography II* (1983) and Larry Rivers's *Dick Schwartz, Umber Blues* (1987), have remained popular, guiding artists to create truly modern visual art.

—*Donna M. Cassidy*

Motian and the gifted but short-lived bassist Scott LaFaro, as heard on the 1961 recording *Sunday at the Village Vanguard*. Evans's exquisite lyricism and sonorous harmonies placed his music squarely in the mainstream, where his contemplative but energetic style greatly influenced the next three generations of pianists; these same qualities masked the revolutionary nature of his approach. His playing is beautifully illustrated in a performance filmed in 1975 of him playing the pop song *Up With the Lark*, featuring accompaniment by Eddie Gomez on bass.

---

avant-garde experimental, unconventional, cutting-edge.

Listening Guide

Listen to *So What* by Miles Davis Sextet on **mymusiclab.com**
CD I, Track 22/Download Track 22

SO WHAT • MILES DAVIS SEXTET

Music: Miles Davis, 1959. Personnel: Miles Davis (trumpet, leader); Cannonball Adderley (alto saxophone); John Coltrane (tenor saxophone); Bill Evans (piano); Paul Chambers (bass); Jimmy Cobb (drums). Recorded March 2, 1959, in New York. First issue: Columbia CL2126. Timing: 9:26.

Overview

Like the other four pieces on Miles Davis's 1959 album *Kind of Blue, So What* remains a cultural touchstone as well as a splendid and memorable musical experience. The entire album introduced the general public to a new organizing principle for jazz: modal improvisation. *So What*, the leadoff track and arguably the catchiest piece on the album, became a jazz standard, thanks to the original recording's evocation of "cool"; to the galvanic sax solos; and in part to the lyrics written and recorded later by vocalist Eddie Jefferson, which captured Davis's ambivalent public persona ("Miles Davis walked off the stage / *So what!*").

Key Features

- Melody: The melody of *So What* is almost comically simple. The entire melody consists of the same two-measure phrase, repeated 16 times (although it is transposed in measures 17–24). The melody updates the call-and-response technique found in field hollers, blues, and gospel, with Paul Chambers's bass stating the main line, answered every two measures by a two-note response.
- Form: A **rubato** (non-rhythmic) introduction by piano and bass precedes the 32-bar theme. This theme conforms to the traditional AABA structure, but is also novel in its simplicity. The first 16 measures essentially rest on one chord, followed by the bridge—which is nothing more than eight measures of the exact same melody, transposed up a half-step to a new harmonic center—and then a return to the initial chord.
- Blues feeling: Because the only harmonic movement is to the key one-half step up from the **tonic**—which here serves a function similar to that of the **subdominant** in the blues—the tune has a different form than the blues. But it still retains the emotional feel of a mid-tempo jazz blues.

Watch the video of Miles Davis's *So What* on **mymusiclab.com** for a comparison with this recorded performance.

Compare the video version of *So What* on **mymusiclab.com**

- Improvisation: The three main soloists present a striking variety of post-bop jazz solo styles: Davis, the spare, cool architect rebelling against bop's flurrying complexity; Coltrane, the fiery explorer, seeking new avenues for that complexity; and Adderley, the lyrical exponent of the soul jazz style that would grow especially popular in the 1960s.
- Davis's solo uses notes outlining chords as a unifying principle; he begins his solo outlining a D minor seventh chord, shifts to scalar melodies, and then returns to chord tones. Coltrane starts simply, but quickly launches into his famous "sheets of sound"; the tune's modal framework is quite congruent with his scalar approach. Adderley's solo incorporates both Davis's interest in chord tones and Coltrane's interest in

---

A much more blatant attack on convention than that of Bill Evans marks the work of Charles Mingus. Although his fluid and inventive technique raised the bar for jazz bassists, history remembers him mainly as a brilliant (if mercurial) bandleader—and the most important jazz composer after Duke Ellington. A self-professed descendent of Ellington and Monk, Mingus wrote the tenderest of ballads—among them his elegant threnody for Lester Young, *Goodbye Pork Pie Hat,* from the 1959 masterpiece *Mingus Ah Um*—as well as the most boisterous hard bop anthems (*Haitian Fight Song*, 1955, and *Hora Decubitis*, 1963). Some pieces, such as *The Clown* (from the 1957 album of the same name) combine jazz and poetry; on such

tunes as *Wednesday Night Prayer Meeting* (1959) and *Hog Callin' Blues* (1961), Mingus combined soul jazz and satire. Like Ellington, he envisioned jazz on a wider scale than did most of his contemporaries, then used the musical materials of the time—in this case, the sharply angled melodies and vibrant rhythms of hard bop—to realize his vision.

The blind visionary and multi-instrumentalist Roland Kirk created a quite different blend of jazz tradition with the freedom cry. In the mid-1960s, Kirk adopted the name Rahsaan, which he said had come

Watch *Up With the Lark* by Bill Evans on **mymusiclab.com**

---

rubato   freely; played expressively without adhering to a strict beat.

tonic   the root of a key.

subdominant   the fourth degree of the scale.

scales, but also includes examples of his irrepressible tunefulness.

- **Stylistic variety:** This piece, like the rest of *Kind of Blue*, belongs to both the past and its own future. It mostly contains familiar, mainstream elements, yet offers a path to improvisatory freedom, which would influence the avant-garde and progressive-jazz styles that supplanted bop in the 1960s.
- **Dynamics:** This track ranges from the pianissimo introduction to the full-throated cries of Adderley's alto. The theme statement itself, with the main melody carried by the bass, offers a radically different sound and texture than those found in most music of the day.

—*Neil Tesser*

TIME	SECTION	INSTRUMENTATION	MELODY
0:00	INTRO	Piano and bass	Piano and bass set a mysterious, out-of-tempo mood.
0:33	CHORUS 1 (THEME)	Bass lead, piano, horns	Bassist Paul Chambers presents the melody, with call-and-response replies from piano and then horns (0:50).
1:31	CHORUS 2	Trumpet	Davis begins two-chorus trumpet solo with notes from the D minor seventh chord. (2:01) He shifts to scalar movement, then, at the final A, returns to chord tones.
2:28	CHORUS 3		Davis starts the next chorus with notes outlining an A minor seventh chord—even though the key is D minor. This juxtaposition highlights the unique character of the underlying modal scale.
3:26	CHORUS 4	Tenor saxophone	Coltrane picks up on the last phrase of Davis's solo to start his own, then (3:40) returns to scalar movement. (4:08–4:19) Repeating a phrase hinted at earlier in the solo, Coltrane finds a motif that propels his solo into its second chorus.
4:19	CHORUS 5		This "propeller" motif bridges and unifies the two choruses of Coltrane's solo.
5:16	CHORUS 6*	Alto saxophone	After extensive use of scalar movement *and* larger intervals, Adderley "turns the time around" with a phrase that intersects the bridge and the last A section of his first chorus.
6:23	CHORUS 7*		Adderley lands on an idea—five notes on the beat—and repeats it.
7:06	CHORUS 8*	Piano	In the piano solo, the call-and-response pattern is reversed: the "response" (horn figure) moves to the front of each phrase, with Evans's piano "call" coming in response.
8:03			This unusual eight-bar insertion marks time until the theme returns.
8:15	THEME**	Bass lead, piano, horns	Bass plays main melody; piano and horns answer.
9:12	SLOW FADE**		

*In order to fit the accompanying CD I, choruses 6–8 are omitted. The full recording is on the mymusiclab.com download and also on *JTSA*.
**On the CD version the Theme begins at 5:16 and the Slow Fade starts at 6:13.

to him in a dream; another dream inspired him to resurrect two archaic reed instruments, the manzello and stritch. These he played simultaneously with his main instrument, the tenor saxophone—three horns at once, with Kirk using countermelodies to accompany himself and **circular-breathing** techniques to play for minutes at a time without stopping for a breath. His critics saw only a freak show, but Kirk's extraordinary musicianship (as on *The Inflated Tear*, 1968) allowed him to bridge genres and impart a great deal of Mingus-like humor and satire.

But as the 1950s closed, it was Miles Davis who once again shifted the mainstream in a new direction.

---

circular breathing technique used in playing wind instruments that permits continuous, unbroken phrasing.

Davis had already combined jazz and classical techniques on a series of Columbia albums, starting with *Miles Ahead* (1957), that reunited him with his *Birth of the Cool* (1949–50) colleague, arranger Gil Evans. These were really jazz concertos, as Evans's limpid, textured writing supported and engaged Davis's trumpet; on the famous *Sketches of Spain* (1959–60), Evans adapted a classical piece, *Concierto de Aranjuez*, penned by Joaquin Rodrigo in 1939.

With the 1959 landmark *Kind of Blue*, however, Davis instigated the most significant development in jazz since his creation of *The Cool*. On this album, he fully explored modal improvisation—which had shown up a year earlier on *Milestones* (1958)—instructing his band members to use preselected modes as the basis for their solos. These modes were specific scales named by the ancient Greeks, including but not limited to the standard major and minor; they replaced the chord progressions that had controlled jazz improvisation since bebop, liberating the soloists from bop's "tyranny of chords" and forcing them to look in new directions. (To further spark innovation, Davis presented this new musical puzzle to his players just a few hours before the recording session.) This new style was called **modal jazz**.

The aesthetic and commercial success of *Kind of Blue* pointed to new possibilities, specifically for musicians such as Jackie McLean—a fiery alto saxist who had never quite fit in as a hard bopper but who embraced the new freedom with such albums as *One Step Beyond* (1963). McLean's work—and that of his Blue Note Records colleagues vibraphonist Bobby Hutcherson, trombonist Grachan Moncur III, pianist Andrew Hill, and keyboardist Larry Young—widened the jazz mainstream considerably, incorporating the revolutionary spirit that would soon rock every aspect of the 1960s.

Davis himself found it impossible to stand pat. By 1964 he had completely rebuilt his quintet into a band that artfully dodged easy characterization—except for "Miles Davis's greatest band." Its brilliant balance of talents reached an acme on *Miles Smiles* (1966), in

performances that remained "mainstream" but reveled in looser song structures descended from Davis's modal music. The music pivoted on the elastic interplay between drummer Tony Williams (who joined Davis in 1963, at the age of 17) and pianist Herbie Hancock (only six years older than Williams). Ron Carter's malleable bass glued the rhythm section. And Wayne Shorter's elliptical solos presented a new model for modern tenor saxophonists, while his concise and memorable compositions—among them *Witch Hunt* and *Infant Eyes* (both 1965), *Footprints* and *Dolores* (1966), and *Pinocchio* (1967)—marked him as the most important writer since Monk and Mingus.

With this band, Davis sailed swiftly through the 1960s and 1970s, helping to pilot jazz through its most turbulent period in three decades. Others who made their marks in the 1950s and 1960s would be there as well, continuing to hone their skills and exploring new ways to apply them.

 Explore *Jazz Classics and Key Recordings* on **mymusiclab.com**

---

modal jazz a style of jazz developed in the late 1950s in which modal scales serve as the basis of improvisation.

TAKE NOTE

- What other jazz styles were prominent during this time and how did they differ from the more dominant styles?

TAKE NOTE

- What currents in American society influenced the development of jazz in the 1950s?

Although the 1950s are remembered as a decade when conformity and mainstream values flourished, there were also innovations in technology and race relations during the period. New, longer recording formats allowed jazz musicians to express themselves more fully. The building movement for civil rights was leading to a greater respect for African Americans and their art forms.

- Why was Miles Davis among the most important musicians of this period?

Miles Davis, more than any other musician, dominated the mainstream era. During this period, he first showed the ability to synthesize emerging jazz sounds into coherent styles that others would embrace as new movements—notably cool jazz and then modal jazz. He was also an expert bandleader and talent spotter, bringing to the fore such musicians as John Coltrane, Cannonball Adderley, and Bill Evans.

- How did hard bop develop in response to bebop and other styles?

Hard bop emerged in the mid-1950s. It featured more relaxed tempos, simpler melodies, and a more soulful emotionalism, with roots in the blues and gospel music, than did bebop. Some of the key proponents of hard bop were pianist Horace Silver and drummer/bandleader Art Blakey.

- What distinguishes West Coast bop from other variants, and who were the key players in this style?

In California, an offshoot of bebop developed that ran hotter than cool jazz but still carried forward some of its characteristics such as counterpoint. Saxophonist Art Pepper and pianist Hampton Hawes were innovators in this style.

- What are the different saxophone styles of Dexter Gordon, Sonny Rollins, and John Coltrane?

Where alto saxophone had typified the sound of bebop, the tougher, more full-bodied sound of tenor saxophone embodied hard bop, including Sonny Rollins and John Coltrane. Dexter Gordon, the first important bebop tenorist, combined the huge sound and harmonic ingenuity of Coleman Hawkins with the light vibrato and quixotic grace of Lester Young. Gordon's style fed two new streams, represented by Rollins and Coltrane. Rollins was the more intellectual, while Coltrane the more purely emotive player. Both extended the vocabulary of jazz performance.

- How were the musical approaches of composer-pianists Thelonious Monk and Dave Brubeck similar and how were they different?

Both were stubborn iconoclasts who emphasized the percussive and pianistic aspects of their instrument and focused as much on composing as performing. Monk continued to follow his own muse in the 1950s, but his music found a new audience that was more open to his quirky compositions and personality. Dave Brubeck, whose *Time Out* was the first jazz album to sell a million copies, brought jazz to a hip new audience of college students. His classically influenced compositions and experiments with unusual meters were typical of "third stream" experiments of the era.

- What is soul jazz and how does it differ from hard bop?

Soul jazz features both simple and funky melodies, danceable rhythms, and blues-gospel underpinnings. It grew out of hard bop's more aggressive style, but was more rooted in African American vernacular traditions, seeking a broader audience. Jimmy Smith brought elements of gospel organ into jazz and established the organ-trio format as a highly popular one for the music.

- How did earlier jazz traditions and groups grow and thrive during this period?

Almost all earlier forms of jazz continued to be performed during the 1950s, many by the styles' originators. Duke Ellington's career enjoyed a second renaissance, thanks to a successful appearance at the 1956 Newport Jazz Festival and Ellington's evolution as a composer. Such mainstream performers as pianist Erroll Garner created a listenable blend of jazz and pop styles to score major hits.

- What vocalists were important during the mainstream era?

Such mainstream singers as Frank Sinatra and Ella Fitzgerald set new standards for jazz vocalists. Fitzgerald was particularly influential through her series of *Songbook* albums, which featured the output of America's greatest popular song composers. The vocal trio Lambert, Hendricks, and Ross were among the few vocalists capable of matching the high-energy bebop style. Carmen McRae and Betty Carter emulated hard bop's phrasing and power in their singing.

- What other jazz styles were prominent during this time and how did they differ from the more dominant styles?

A search for artistic freedom and self-expression can be found in many of the alternate styles that emerged in the 1950s. Experiments ranged from Bill Evans's attempt to free the piano, bass, and drums from their traditional roles in his trio performances to bassist/bandleader Charles Mingus's blend of humor, social criticism, and soulful jazz in his compositions.

DISCUSSION QUESTIONS

1. What are the key differences between bebop, hard bop, cool jazz, and soul jazz?

2. Before you read this chapter, had you heard of any of the major mainstream musicians? Name some of the musicians associated with hard bop and soul jazz.

3. In the world of business, it is believed that concentrations of an industry in specific geographic regions can lead to high innovation and growth. Describe how that effect might apply to jazz and offer an example.

4. Describe some of the effects of evolving recording technology, such as the development of long-playing records, on the composition and performance of jazz.

5. Trace the line of influence in jazz trumpet playing, starting with New Orleans brass bands and Louis Armstrong and proceeding through swing, bop, cool jazz, hard bop, and modal jazz.

6. Discuss key players of the saxophone and how they influenced each other, starting from Coleman Hawkins and Lester Young and proceeding through bebop, cool jazz, hard bop, and modal jazz.

7. Trace the line of influence in jazz piano playing, starting with Jelly Roll Morton proceeding through swing, bop, cool jazz, hard bop, and modal jazz.

8. Bebop was a breakthrough style when it first emerged. What aspects of it were restrictive in ways that compelled musicians to seek alternative styles?

KEY TERMS & KEY PEOPLE

Cannonball Adderley
atonal
avant-garde
Chet Baker
Art Blakey
Clifford Brown
Dave Brubeck
Kenny Burrell
chamber jazz
chorus
John Coltrane
Miles Davis
Bill Evans

Ella Fitzgerald
fours
Erroll Garner
Dexter Gordon
gospel music
hard bop
mainstream jazz
Carmen McRae
Charles Mingus
modal jazz
Thelonious Monk
Wes Montgomery
Lee Morgan

Anita O'Day
Art Pepper
Oscar Peterson
Buddy Rich
Max Roach
Sonny Rollins
Horace Silver
Jimmy Smith
soul jazz
Thad Jones-Mel Lewis
  Orchestra
Sarah Vaughan

Bebop and Modern Jazz

From Chapter 6 of *Discover Jazz*. First Edition. John Edward Hasse, Tad Lathrop. Copyright © 2012 by Pearson Education, Inc. All rights reserved.

Bebop and Modern Jazz

by Bob Blumenthal

TAKE NOTE

- What musical movements began to replace big band jazz during the years following World War II?
- What is bebop and what roles did Charlie Parker and Dizzy Gillespie play in creating and popularizing it?
- Who were the early bebop pianists and how did they affect the growth of the musical style?
- What was cool jazz, who were its key proponents, and where did it develop?

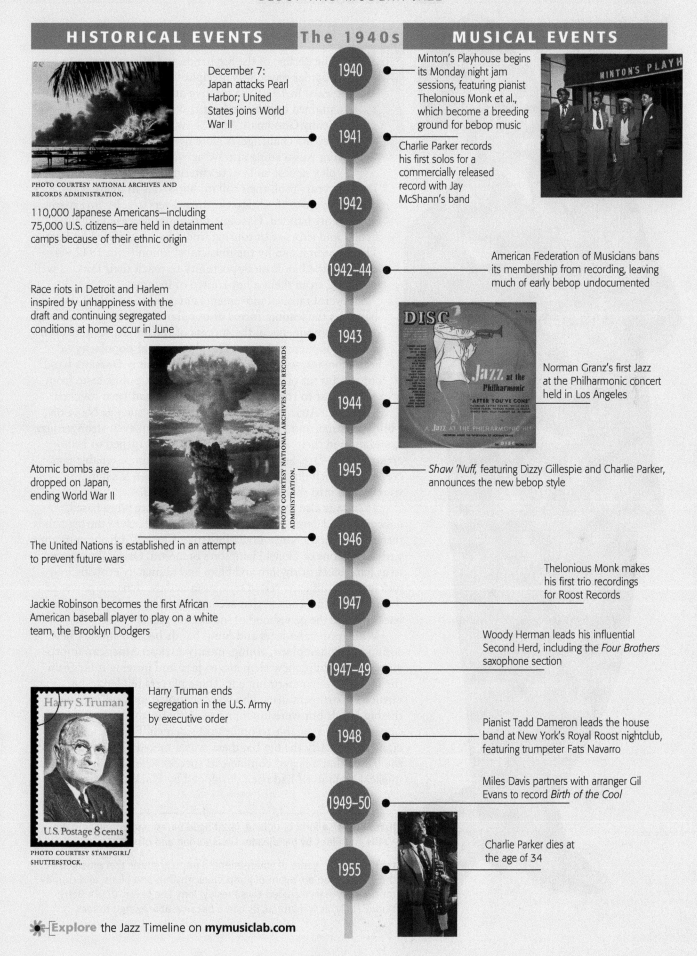

HISTORICAL EVENTS — The 1940s — MUSICAL EVENTS

1940

Minton's Playhouse begins its Monday night jam sessions, featuring pianist Thelonious Monk et al., which become a breeding ground for bebop music

December 7: Japan attacks Pearl Harbor; United States joins World War II

1941

Charlie Parker records his first solos for a commercially released record with Jay McShann's band

PHOTO COURTESY NATIONAL ARCHIVES AND RECORDS ADMINISTRATION.

110,000 Japanese Americans—including 75,000 U.S. citizens—are held in detainment camps because of their ethnic origin

1942

1942–44

American Federation of Musicians bans its membership from recording, leaving much of early bebop undocumented

Race riots in Detroit and Harlem inspired by unhappiness with the draft and continuing segregated conditions at home occur in June

1943

DISC

Jazz at the Philharmonic

"AFTER YOU'VE GONE"

A JAZZ AT THE PHILHARMONIC

Norman Granz's first Jazz at the Philharmonic concert held in Los Angeles

1944

PHOTO COURTESY NATIONAL ARCHIVES AND RECORDS ADMINISTRATION.

Atomic bombs are dropped on Japan, ending World War II

1945

Shaw 'Nuff, featuring Dizzy Gillespie and Charlie Parker, announces the new bebop style

1946

The United Nations is established in an attempt to prevent future wars

Thelonious Monk makes his first trio recordings for Roost Records

Jackie Robinson becomes the first African American baseball player to play on a white team, the Brooklyn Dodgers

1947

Woody Herman leads his influential Second Herd, including the *Four Brothers* saxophone section

1947–49

Harry S. Truman

Harry Truman ends segregation in the U.S. Army by executive order

1948

Pianist Tadd Dameron leads the house band at New York's Royal Roost nightclub, featuring trumpeter Fats Navarro

U.S. Postage 8 cents

1949–50

Miles Davis partners with arranger Gil Evans to record *Birth of the Cool*

PHOTO COURTESY STAMPGIRL/ SHUTTERSTOCK.

1955

Charlie Parker dies at the age of 34

✳ Explore the Jazz Timeline on **mymusiclab.com**

Trumpeter and bebop innovator Dizzy Gillespie. PHOTO COURTESY WILLIAM P. GOTTLIEB/WILLIAM P. GOTTLIEB COLLECTION/ LIBRARY OF CONGRESS PRINTS & PHOTOGRAPHS DIVISION.

The Postwar Jazz Scene

The decline of the big bands and of jazz's status as popular music was precipitous during the World War II years. In 1940, the creative and commercial success attained by the bands of Duke Ellington, Count Basie, Benny Goodman, Artie Shaw, and others appeared beyond challenge. A mere five years later the big band era was waning and swing was passé. In its place, complex new sounds were entering the jazz lexicon.

The war years took their toll on big bands in many ways. Key musicians were drafted into the armed services, leaving many bands short-handed. Gasoline rationing increased the difficulty and expense of touring (most bands traveled by bus). The recording ban by the musicians' union from 1942–44 deprived the bands an opportunity to reach their fans, as well as taking from them a key source of income.

Several musical movements emerged to supplant the big bands as the leading forms of popular music. Singers, already critical components in the success of the bands, became even greater commercial forces. The phenomenal popularity of Frank Sinatra, who rose to fame with Tommy Dorsey's band but soon went off on his own, helped shift public taste from a swing beat to romantic ballads. Sinatra had been touched by jazz, and African American singing stars such as Nat Cole, Billy Eckstine, and Ella Fitzgerald reflected an even stronger jazz foundation in their work; yet public taste had turned to lushly arranged pop fare. Soon, even singers with unimpeachable jazz credentials, including Sarah Vaughan and Dinah Washington, were pulled into these more placid pop waters.

There was also the strong tidal pull of a more blues-based, dance-oriented development that can be traced back to the big bands through alto saxophonist Louis Jordan (a Chick Webb alumnus) and various editions of Lionel Hampton's orchestra. Originally referred to as **jump blues** or rhythm and blues and ultimately evolving into **rock and roll**, this extroverted style sustained the dynamic power of the big bands in a context that accommodated a more pronounced backbeat and the new sound of the electric guitar.

While pop balladeers and jump bands became music's new commercial champions, young, mostly African American improvisers were adding new elements to jazz and moving it far from the realm of pop entertainment. These players tended to be virtuoso instrumentalists who were schooled in the discipline of the big bands but were unwilling to settle for the limited solo opportunities available to orchestral sidemen. For black musicians particularly the big band era was a mixed blessing: Most of the bands that enjoyed commercial success where white, while the musical form itself had been developed by blacks. Further, black

jump blues   a form of upbeat, jazz-tinged blues made popular in the 1940s and fifties by bandleader Louis Jordan and others.

rock and roll   genre of youth-oriented popular music that emerged in the 1950s as an amalgam of jump blues, rhythm and blues, and country music; early stars included Elvis Presley, Jerry Lee Lewis, Chuck Berry, Buddy Holly; as it matured, its name became abbreviated to rock.

musicians who had served in World War II experienced new opportunities (despite the segregation of the armed forces) and hoped that their service would inspire a recognition of the need for equal rights by society at large. Many were disappointed when they returned from the war to find that little had changed.

These forces helped push the younger generation of jazz players toward a more assertive mode of expression. The blues and popular song structures still served as the base of their creations, but these artists favored more complex and irregularly accented melodies, more sophisticated harmonic modulations, and faster tempos than those favored by the big bands. In effect, the young jazz players were establishing a new inner circle, an exclusive countercultural "club" that required virtuosity of musicians and an open-eared

History & Culture

From left to right: Thelonious Monk, Howard McGhee, Roy Eldridge, and Teddy Hill at Minton's Playhouse, New York, 1948. PHOTO COURTESY WILLIAM P. GOTTLIEB/WILLIAM P. GOTTLIEB COLLECTION/LIBRARY OF CONGRESS PRINTS & PHOTOGRAPHS DIVISION.

After Hours at Minton's

Jazz's modern era was nurtured in the clubs of Harlem, where musicians would go to try out new ideas—or simply to seek playing opportunities that the big bands did not provide—after completing club, theater, and ballroom gigs. The jam sessions that resulted, with musicians testing their limits and challenging others to keep up with the latest discoveries, have become legendary; the center of the legend was at 210 West 118th Street, where the former dining room of the Hotel Cecil was converted by M. Henry Minton into the Playhouse, a club we now know simply as Minton's.

The Playhouse opened in 1938 but attracted little attention until two years later, when saxophonist and bandleader Teddy Hill signed on to manage the room. Hill decided to institute more musician-friendly policies, including a Monday-night jam session that set the tone for the innovations that followed. The key to Minton's success was its house band, a quartet co-led by Hill's former drummer **Kenny Clarke** and trumpeter Joe Guy and including an iconoclastic young unknown, **Thelonious Monk**, on piano. As word spread about Monk's adventurous

harmonies and the daring rhythmic notions Clarke was adding from his drum kit, other musicians began frequenting Minton's to test their own new ideas. **Dizzy Gillespie**, another Teddy Hill alumnus, was a regular, and electric-guitar fountainhead Charlie Christian left an amplifier in the room so he could drop in as soon as his boss, Benny Goodman, was through for the night. Established stars, including Don Byas, Ben Webster, and Lester Young, often visited. Billie Holiday and **Charlie Parker** preferred Clark Monroe's Uptown House at

198 West 134th Street, which, as Barren Wilkins's Exclusive Club, had been the site of Duke Ellington's first steady New York job, in 1923; but they passed through Minton's as well. Some of the earliest evidence of the modern movement was captured at Minton's on a portable disc recorder by Columbia University student Jerry Newman, who documented Christian, Clarke, Gillespie, and Monk in full after-hours flight.

—Bob Blumenthal

attentiveness on the part of listeners. These performers would be the vanguard of a new musical style, which would come to be known as **bebop**.

Several heroes from the previous generation had paved the way for this new style. Tenor saxophonist Coleman Hawkins had exemplified the stream-of-consciousness creativity of the improvising soloist with his classic 1939 recording of *Body and Soul* and was among the first to demonstrate the feasibility of an instrumental soloist's playing for listeners rather than dancers—without singers or large orchestral accompaniment. As musicologist Scott DeVeaux has pointed out, Hawkins was *the* proto-bebopper: he was too proud to sing or otherwise try to please a mass audience and not inclined to lead a big band. Pianist Art Tatum, with his stupendous technique and harmonic knowledge, had revealed in such solo recordings as *Moonglow* (1934) and *Tea for Two* (1933) the complex potential of simple-seeming pop songs. The Count Basie band practiced a flowing,

((•— **Listen** to CD I, Track 14/Download Track 14, *Body and Soul* by Coleman Hawkins

---

bebop a style of jazz that emerged in the 1940s and established jazz as a music for listening rather than just dancing to; characterized by fast tempos, complex chord progressions, and virtuoso improvisation using multiple scales and altered tones; notable pioneers included Charlie Parker, Dizzy Gillespie, and Thelonious Monk.

liberating sense of tempo, while Basie's star soloist, Lester Young, introduced an oblique, floating approach that pointed soloists toward musical abstraction. Charlie Christian, the electric guitar innovator, reflected a similar attitude in his solos with Goodman, and Ellington's new star, Jimmie Blanton, was revealing the untapped potential of the string bass.

TAKE NOTE

- What musical movements began to replace big band jazz during the years following World War II?

Parker, Gillespie, and the Birth of Bebop

Even before the United States entered World War II, new ideas were developing among young players inspired by their innovative predecessors. The disciples fueled the evolutionary process by refining and sharing discoveries after hours in Harlem spots such as Minton's Playhouse and Monroe's Uptown House. Several players were central to this effort, but none more so than alto saxophonist Charlie Parker,

◉— **Watch** the documentary on Bebop on **mymusiclab.com**

Charlie Parker, Miles Davis, Allen Eager, and Kai Winding in New York, 1949. PHOTO COURTESY © HERMAN LEONARD PHOTOGRAPHY LLC.

Watch the documentary on Charlie Parker on
mymusiclab.com

ultimately known via his legend to even the non-jazz world as "Yardbird" or "Bird."

Parker was born in 1920 and grew up in the fertile musical environment of Kansas City. By 1941 and his initial recorded solos with Jay McShann's band, on such tracks as *Swingmatism* and *The Jumpin' Blues*, he was displaying a heady approach that merged the virtuosity of Tatum and the melodic daring of Young—topped off with a blues-rooted intensity uniquely his own. When Parker finally recorded as a solo artist, in 1945, he could draw upon additional big band experience with Earl "Fatha" Hines and Billy Eckstine and the ideas he had shared with such contemporaries as trumpeter John Birks "Dizzy" Gillespie, who had apprenticed in the big bands of Teddy Hill and Cab Calloway; drummer Kenny Clarke, another Teddy Hill alumnus who had been among the first to introduce complex polyrhythms behind soloists; and pianist-composer Thelonious Monk, whose work was filled with startling dissonance and rhythmic displacements. You can watch the dynamic interplay of Charlie Parker and Dizzy Gillespie performing *Hot House* in a rare 1952 TV appearance, on mymusiclab.com. Parker's solo demonstrates his complete mastery of the instrument and the bebop idiom. In the final chorus, Parker, Gillespie, and the drummer trade four-bar phrases.

This core group of innovators—particularly the charismatic Parker—first demonstrated their discoveries in jam sessions, then landed nightclub engagements on New York's 52nd Street, before the new music was disseminated widely through recordings. As a result, a slightly younger group of talented musicians had already rallied around Parker and Gillespie before the larger audience learned of their existence. Pianists Earl "Bud" Powell and Al Haig, trumpeter **Miles Davis**, trombonist J. J. Johnson, saxophonist Edward "Sonny" Stitt, and drummer **Max Roach** were among the most prominent of these disciples, and together they represented a loose yet identifiable modernist school.

The lack of recorded evidence of the experimenters' early efforts resulted from the 1942–44 ban on recording ordered by the American Federation of Musicians. When the musicians' union's ban ended in late 1944, the new music was poised to emerge from its period of incubation, and it spread quickly in the following year on a series of historic records issued under Gillespie's and Parker's names. Gillespie began 1945 by recording composer **Tadd Dameron**'s *Good Bait* and his own composition *Bebop*, which quickly

Watch the video *Hot House* by Charlie Parker and Dizzy Gillespie on **mymusiclab.com**

Fashions popularized by such boppers as Dizzy Gillespie and Thelonious Monk proved more than a rapidly passing fad; they spawned the berets-and-shades look associated with the beatnik counterculture of the 1950s. COURTESY JOHN EDWARD HASSE.

lent its name to the new style. Then Gillespie held two recording sessions—with Parker as a sideman—that introduced his pieces *Salt Peanuts* and *Groovin' High* as well as Gillespie and Parker's *Shaw 'Nuff*. Each of these recordings became modern classics. Parker's first session as a leader, which featured Miles Davis, Max Roach, and (on piano as well as trumpet) Gillespie, yielded its own classics: the blues themes *Now's the Time* and *Billie's Bounce* and the virtuosic variation on *Cherokee* called *Ko-Ko*.

Few recordings in jazz history proved as influential—and controversial—as these titles. Unsympathetic listeners disparaged the allegedly "thin" tones of the horn players, who had dispensed with the expressive vibrato of traditional soloists; lamented the irregular accents and dissonant harmonies such as the interval of the flatted fifth; and predicted that any music presenting such challenges to dancers had no future. Gillespie's former boss Cab Calloway had once called the trumpeter's more confounding experiments "Chinese music," and veterans as respected as Louis Armstrong attacked the new sounds in similar terms.

These reactions were further indicators of the uphill battle faced by the emerging modernists. Swing, as DeVeaux put it, had been "an integral part of the burgeoning entertainment industry. . . . All of the bebop musicians began their careers within this system. Their decision to break, or at least radically revise, their relationship to it was no casual act. Nor, given the realities of power in American society, could it hope to be entirely successful."

Not all of the older players rejected bebop. Ellington sax star Ben Webster loved to join the jam sessions at Minton's, pianist Mary Lou Williams became a mentor to the likes of Gillespie and Monk, and the harmonically audacious Coleman Hawkins

Listening Guide

((•● **Listen** to *Shaw 'Nuff* by Dizzy Gillespie and His All Star Quintet on **mymusiclab.com**
CD I, Track 18/Download Track 18

SHAW 'NUFF • DIZZY GILLESPIE AND HIS ALL STAR QUINTET

Music: Dizzy Gillespie and Charlie Parker, 1945. Personnel: Dizzy Gillespie (trumpet); Charlie Parker (alto sax); Al Haig (piano); Curly Russell (bass); Sid Catlett (drums). Recorded May 11, 1945, in New York. First issue: Guild 1002. Timing: 3:03.

Overview

Shaw 'Nuff is one of the first definitive modern jazz/bebop recordings. It contains several features that would become indicative of the style: unison melody lines by trumpet and alto saxophone, irregular rhythmic accents by both soloists and members of the rhythm section, trumpet and saxophone tones that place reduced emphasis on vibrato, and virtuosic improvisations—all at an accelerated tempo. The thematic choruses and solos are based on the harmonic progressions of Gershwin's *I Got Rhythm*, second only to the blues chorus as a preferred structure for improvisers, but these choruses are framed by an introduction/coda that adds a more uncommon structural element.

Key Features

- Improvisation: *Shaw 'Nuff* features rapid, technically dazzling improvising from its three soloists. Each plays a single chorus that displays great dexterity and variety.
- Rhythm: Both the written melodic material and the improvisations are filled with rapidly shifting accents that attack the symmetries of the form (see below) from a variety of angles, creating a headlong momentum that is sustained throughout the performance.
- Melody: Rather than building its theme exclusively in concise, symmetrical phrases, both the introduction/coda and the main melody of *Shaw 'Nuff* rely on complex melodic units of irregular length. Even the repetitive, riff-like sections of the theme employ these more jagged phrases.
- Harmony: While the underlying harmonic structure is taken from a popular standard, the soloists often expand upon this base by superimposing more complex **harmonic substitutions**.
- Sonority: By eliminating the vibrato that characterized earlier brass and reed soloists, Gillespie and Parker are able to execute their newly complex ideas with greater accuracy. This is particularly critical to the success of their unison passages.
- Musicians' roles: Among its other innovations, modern jazz marked a further liberation of the rhythm section, which is most evident in the support offered by the piano and drums. Both instruments place greater emphasis on spontaneous commentary: the piano through the replacement of sustained patterns with more spontaneous chords, and the drums by moving the primary time-keeping function to the ride cymbal and using tom-tom and bass drum for more diverse accents.
- Form and structure: The primary theme and solo choruses of *Shaw 'Nuff* employ the 32-bar, AABA chorus structure that is among the most common in popular music. This central form is surrounded, however, by a more harmonically static 16-bar section in AA'BC form that ends in a two-bar break that is omitted at the conclusion. Both Gillespie and Parker are credited as composers, and it is likely that one wrote the main theme while the other contributed the introduction/coda.

—*Bob Blumenthal*

TIME	SECTION	FORM	INSTRUMENTATION	MELODY	RHYTHM	HARMONY
0:00	INTRODUCTION		Piano, bass, drum, dominated by drum rolls on tom-toms		Static rhythm pattern.	
0:06	INTRODUCTION	AA'BC, 16 bars	Ensemble	Fanfare-like melody stated in unison by horns; ends with two-bar piano break.	$\frac{4}{4}$, sparsely stated with ride cymbal keeping the underlying beat.	Static harmony stated by rhythm section; bass plays repeated two-note figure.
0:20	MAIN MELODY	AABA, 32 bars	Ensemble	Rapid paced melody stated in unison by horns; phrases of irregular length throughout cut across the AABA structure.	$\frac{4}{4}$, ride cymbal states primary beat; rapidly shifting accents by pianist and drummer cut across the regular beat.	Based on *I Got Rhythm* chord changes.

TIME	SECTION	FORM	INSTRUMENTATION	MELODY	RHYTHM	HARMONY
0:33	MAIN MELODY	Bridge or B section	Ensemble	Stated in unison by horns; shorter contrasting phrases.		
0:40	MAIN MELODY	Return of A section	Ensemble	Stated in unison by horns.		
0:47	SOLO	AABA	Charlie Parker, alto saxophone	Parker begins with a relatively simple phrase, then quickly moves into more complex ideas.	Piano comping behind solo cuts across beat and symmetrical form.	At the bridge (1:01) Parker imposes substitute chord progression for four measures.
1:14	SOLO	AABA	Dizzy Gillespie, trumpet	Trumpet enters with a piercing glissando. Gillespie's solo is technically complex but with greater use of space and repeated phrasing than Parker's. The final eight bars (1:34) begin with repeated rapid triplets.		
1:41	SOLO	AABA	Al Haig, piano	Employs intricate phrases similar to those of Gillespie and Parker; however, Haig's bridge (1:55) hews more closely to the harmony, and his final eight bars (2:02) resolve into simpler ideas.	Walking bass emphasizes beat.	
2:09	MAIN MELODY	AABA, 32 bars	Ensemble	The opening ensemble passage is now played in reverse, beginning with a restatement of the theme.		
2:36	CODA		Piano, bass, drums with piano playing a repeated rhythmic pattern.		Return of initial static rhythm section.	
2:43	CODA	AA'BC, 16 bars	Ensemble	The unison introduction returns, but now the final two bars of solo piano have been omitted and replaced by a quiet piano **glissando**.		Static harmony stated by rhythm section; bass plays repeated two-note figure.

harmonic substitution   replacement of an established chord in a progression with an alternative to counter expectation and add interest.

glissando   a gliding slur or slide from one pitch to another.

Charlie "Bird" Parker playing at Birdland in 1949. The club's name was a nod to the alto saxophonist—and to his impact on the jazz world. PHOTO COURTESY © HERMAN LEONARD PHOTOGRAPHY LLC.

hired Monk and other young innovators as sidemen. Williams was particularly generous and supportive, opening her apartment as a spot for after-hours jam sessions, and encouraging Monk to continue to compose despite the fact that others in the young movement felt his playing was too eccentric. A new generation of musicians and non-dancing listeners—smaller than the audience that sustained the swing bands yet equally passionate—rallied to the modern sounds. The new fans responded to the music's restless energy and sophisticated virtuosity, and they identified with the countercultural trappings that already set the style's leading players apart. Jazz had been born outside the mainstream, and after the mass acceptance of the swing bands, bebop was returning the music to its niche of unconventionality. The new wave of players seemed intent on breaking rules both musical and nonmusical.

The most committed of the modern fans lived for each new Parker and Gillespie record, just as earlier

● **Issues** ●

Boppers versus Moldy Figs

Why did some older jazz fans resist the new bebop style?

Some people have a high need for the new and novel, others prefer the familiar, often leading to initial resistance to new artistic advances. The twentieth century alone is rife with conflicts over new styles, such as the famous 1913 Paris riot at the premiere of Stravinsky's modernist *Rite of Spring*, when the police had to be called in.

Bebop shared many commonalities with earlier jazz, but its dissimilarities attracted most of the attention and sparked a heated war of words. In 1946, the *Washington Post* described the strife as "an all-consuming holocaust." If that is an exaggeration, it was at least a fiery civil war—and sometimes not very civil.

On one side were the modernists—those who welcomed the innovations of Charlie Parker, Dizzy

Gillespie, and the other bop musicians. On the other side were proponents of either New Orleans-style traditional jazz, or swing music, or both—people who didn't understand, didn't like, or were threatened by the new style and much preferred the older, familiar music. The boppers derisively labeled them "moldy figs." Generational change was a big part of the clash: most of those attacking bebop were born in the 1890s or first decade of the twentieth century; those who promulgated it—musicians and critics—were mostly from the next generation, born in the 1910s and 1920s. Generational differences in—and struggles over—musical taste are, in fact, a recurring theme in American music.

The two jazz camps had their own adherents, detractors, sympathetic journalists, and nightclubs. Under the headline "Police Avert Clash of Dixieland and Re-bop," *Down Beat* reported in 1946 that New Orleans–style trombonist

George Brunis, performing on 52nd Street, decided to march across the street to where Dizzy Gillespie's bebop group was playing and have a battle of the bands, but the police intervened to break up what could have gotten out of hand. The *Washington Post* reported that New York City's famed 52nd Street tolerated "none of the Fundamentalists' Dixieland music and Greenwich Village, 'that little bit o' Basin Street in New York,' has squeezed out almost completely modern swing units."

On the traditionalist side, decrying the loss of the beat so prevalent in earlier jazz, concert violinist Sol Babitz wrote, "Such, alas, is the decay of jazz which started out by making everyone tap his foot because of the music and ends by asking you to tap your foot in spite of the music. . . . [Jazz is] coming to an onanistic end in the blind alley of New York where it has struck its head against a brick wall with an ominous 'bebop.'"

listeners had devoured the Armstrong Hot Fives and Hot Sevens and the Count Basie sides with Lester Young. Where the older disciples had copied the slang and mannerisms of Armstrong and Young, the new acolytes became similarly absorbed with their bop role models. Sporting Gillespie-inspired goatees, berets, and glasses was benign, but when Parker's heroin addiction became widely known and his followers mistakenly assumed that emulating this aspect of his lifestyle would allow them to produce music of similar brilliance, the hero worship had a far more destructive effect.

During his brief and often sensationalized lifetime, and to an even greater extent after his death in 1955 at the age of 34, Parker's music and life story evoked more passion—pro and con—than that of any of his contemporaries. Parker stood more clearly apart from previous jazz generations than did Gillespie, who was more of an accomplished entertainer—with his scat singing and onstage dancing—than the typical bopper. On the other hand, Parker was more approachable than the sometimes eccentric behaving pianist Thelonious Monk. Parker's music had a searing emotional quality that provided a fitting soundtrack to the drug and alcohol abuse, erratic behavior, and occasional hospitalizations that fueled his legend. Yet while Parker complained that many who came to hear him were only seeking a glimpse of "the world's greatest junkie, the supreme hipster," even his most casual fans were responding to a visceral intensity that gave jazz— and most particularly the blues sensibility so central to jazz—a contemporary immediacy. Together with the more commercial rhythm and blues players (including saxophone player Paul Williams who turned Parker's *Now's the Time* into the pop hit *The Hucklebuck* in 1948) and such raw urban-music innovators as Muddy Waters, Parker was taking the blues into the postwar era.

A writer named D. Leon Wolff castigated bebop:

Bop violates one of the major characteristics of good art— ease. The best that is done, written, said, or played ordinarily gives the effect of grace and fluidity. . . . But bop has carried frantic jazz to the ultimate.

Some of the harshest criticism came from jazz musicians playing earlier styles. Swing arranger-bandleader Fletcher Henderson charged that bebop was the most "phenomenal cruelty in all the world." "Mistakes—that's all re-bop is," Louis Armstrong told *Time* magazine. Armstrong did however, praise Gillespie: "I'd never play this bebop because I don't like it. Don't get me wrong; I think some of them cats who play it play real good, like Dizzy, especially."

Among those who welcomed and defended the new style was Barry Ulanov, the editor of *Metronome* magazine, who in his article "Feud for Thought," responded to the banning of bop by Los Angeles radio station KMPC:

Musically, men like Dizzy Gillespie are helping jazz to progress, are giving America's art greater harmonic depth, increasing its rhythmic and tonal resources. But as long as serious channels of information, such as a radio station and a leading newsmagazine [*Time*— quoted previously], misinform, mislead, distort and destroy, there will be no progress outside of the backrooms where the Dizzys make their rhythmic and harmonic explorations.

From the perspective of the twenty-first century, the word war may seem quaint, but while it lasted, it created a great deal of bad feeling. In retrospect, like many wars, it seems pointless. While bebop reigned as the progressive new music for some years, it did not vanquish the earlier styles to oblivion. Today, in major American cities, determined seekers can find all three styles being played—a victory not for one style or another, but rather for musical pluralism. SOURCE: BARRY ULANOV, "FEUD FOR THOUGHT," *METRONOME*.

—*John Edward Hasse*

Dizzy Gillespie wearing his trademark beret and horn-rimmed glasses.
PHOTO COURTESY WILLIAM P. GOTTLIEB/WILLIAM P. GOTTLIEB COLLECTION/LIBRARY OF CONGRESS PRINTS & PHOTOGRAPHS DIVISION.

Listening Guide

((•⫶ **Listen** to *Embraceable You (Take A)* by Charlie Parker Quintet on **mymusiclab.com** CD I, Track 16/Download Track 16

EMBRACEABLE YOU (TAKE A) • CHARLIE PARKER QUINTET

Music: George Gershwin, 1930. Personnel: Charlie Parker (alto saxophone); Miles Davis (trumpet); Duke Jordan (piano); Tommy Potter (bass); Max Roach (drums). Recorded October 28, 1947, in New York. First issue: Dial 1024. Timing: 3:48.

Overview

The nickname "Bird" proves apropos as Charlie Parker pilots his alto saxophone on astoundingly rapid, darting flights of melodic exploration in this recording that captures the bebop pioneer at peak form. Working with his most famous quintet, which included the young trumpeter Miles Davis and the innovative drummer Max Roach, Parker recorded a number of tracks between October and December of 1947, *Embraceable You* being one of the earliest. Recently released from Camarillo State Hospital, where he had undergone treatment for drug addiction, Parker brought to the recording a renewed vitality.

While most bravura bebop performances rely on fast tempos, *Embraceable You* is a ballad. Yet Parker defied convention—which would typically dictate a slower, smoldering, ruminative approach to soloing—and instead used the slow pace as a wide-open platform for highly varied, sometimes hummingbird-fast melodic forays. The detail, precision, structural rigor, and sheer innovation of Parker's improvisations are testimony to the genius (there's no other word) that enabled such virtuosity at so young an age and without formal training. (But not without serious woodshedding: "I put quite a bit of study into the horn, that's true," Parker said in a 1954 interview. "I used to put in at least 11 to 15 hours a day. . . . I did that for over a period of three to four years.")

Miles Davis, on the other hand, had absorbed some formal training—at the Juilliard School of Music—and (though not necessarily as a consequence) his solo on the track is in stark contrast to Parker's. Davis is the reserved, cool foil to Parker's acrobatic, extroverted front man. Already, with his dry tone, vibrato-free delivery, and pensive stance, Davis is foreshadowing the cool jazz that he would help introduce in 1949 with his *Birth of the Cool* recordings and all but define in 1959 with his *Kind of Blue*. Although Parker dominates this recording, it's clear in retrospect that he is marking the pinnacle of a period style while Davis, less visible in the shadows, already holds a key to the future.

At the same recording session, a second take (Take B) of this performance was made that gives insights into how Parker shaped his solos in different renditions of the same piece. You can hear that second take on the download set of music that accompanies this book and follow an online listening guide on mymusiclab.com.

Key Features

- Improvisation: With melody entirely improvised, the tune encompasses Parker's 64 bars of soloing and Davis's 40. Parker builds his solo, in part, on a six-note figure that he echoes periodically.
- Accompaniment and rhythm: The rhythm section—pianist Duke Jordan, bassist Tommy Potter, and drummer Max Roach—provide solid, straightforward, and unobtrusive support as they leave the spotlight to the soloists. The meter is in **cut time**, moving in relaxed half notes.
- Melody and style: Parker chooses to not play Gershwin's melody at all, departing from tradition even more markedly than Coleman Hawkins did on *Body and Soul*

when Hawkins played only the first few bars of the original melody. Here, Parker's solo is a compact lexicon of bebop conventions, both melodic and rhythmic. Parker continually displaces his phrasing, starting and ending at unexpected points, which maximizes the listener's sense of uncertainty and surprise. He alters the velocity of his melodies. He offers endless variation of shape and contour, interweaving scalar melodies linked via **chromatic**, **passing**, and **neighbor tones** with harmony-outlining (or altering) **arpeggios**. He makes substantial melodic use of notes outside the base scale, including the flatted and sharped fifth and ninth. Accents are frequently on offbeats.

- Harmony: Based on George Gershwin's composition, the harmony hews to a major-key progression in the key of F, which Parker and company freely alter and embellish with substitute harmonies.

—Tad Lathrop

((•⫶ **Listen** to *Embraceable You* Take B on **mymusiclab.com**

cut time a meter emphasizing two beats per measure.

chromatic related to half steps, as opposed to diatonic and modal, which refer to arrangements of whole and half steps.

passing tone a note that connects two stable tones.

neighbor tone a note a step above or a step below another note.

arpeggio the notes of a chord played sequentially rather then simultaneously.

TIME	FORM	INSTRUMENTATION	MELODY
0:00	INTRODUCTION	Piano	Pianist Duke Jordan sets the mood with a four-bar intro previewing the first chords of the tune in F. The feeling is warm and intimate.
0:13	CHORUS 1	Alto sax	Charlie Parker ignores the written melody and begins improvising immediately with a six-note figure similar to the opening of the standard tune *As Time Goes By* (and possibly a direct quote of a 1939 song titled *A Table in a Corner*). He reworks the figure three times before (0:27) using it as the springboard for an extended phrase ending on a segment of the figure. (He's using the figure as a structural device for melodic development.) His next phrase (0:31) picks up where the last left off, but lower, and spills forward in a continuing, snaking path that closes the chorus characteristically on an arpeggio using altered (non-scale) notes resolving to the unexpected note D.
0:42	CHORUS 2		Entering before the **downbeat**, and now in double time, Parker hurtles forward, ascending and descending, before halving the time in bars two and three and ending (0:45) with a three-note figure of A, low A, B-natural. He repeats this start-fast-then-relax approach on the next four-bar phrase (0:48), punctuating it (0:55) with a complex chromatic flourish. A third phrase (0:57) revisits the opening figure at 1:00, then extends a bar past the expected fourth-bar (bar 12 of the chorus) ending. For the last two bars (1:07) he begins the next chorus unexpectedly ahead of schedule . . .
1:11	CHORUS 3		. . . playing through the downbeat and pausing in the first bar, then resuming (1:13) with an ornamented passage ending on a paraphrase of the opening figure (1:15), which he echoes, first higher (1:19), then lower (1:22). From the flitting gesture of a bird alighting on a branch (1:24–1:27), Parker slows down for an ascending phrase over a G minor chord climaxing with a high descending eighth-note figure (1:30) outlining a D-flat chord rather then the underlying C7 of the accompaniment.* He resolves to the home chord with three ascending iterations of a four-, then five-note arpeggiated motif. A final-bar descending cascade of sixteenth notes leads to . . .
1:41	CHORUS 4		. . . a pause on the note B-flat, then (1:43) lifting off to more flights of convoluted, corkscrewing, up-and-down melody, broken by brief stop-offs on a D-flat note (1:45) and an A (1:49). A slowed-down phrase rises to yet another iteration of the original figure (1:52), repeated with a lowered first note (1:54), then lowered further to—surprise!—a new motif, repeated a half-step lower (1:58); then it's raised back to—another surprise!—an extended resolving phrase that lands "home" on the third of the F scale (2:04). Parker transitions out with several more "afterthought" flourishes.
2:11	CHORUS 5	Trumpet	Taking a much different approach, Miles Davis stays mostly with the beat and plays less-busy melodies that could be sung. He emphasizes economy, playing fewer notes but choosing those that define (and maximize the feeling of) the tune's harmonic motion (2:18, 2:23, 2:32), which he connects via passing strings of melody. Davis sounds downright minimalist compared to Parker's gregarious, ostentatious, note-packed displays.
2:42	CHORUS 6		Davis continues in the same vein, while Parker makes occasional background musical comments. (At 3:02 Davis plays, and fluffs, a three-note figure that implies D-flat major—reminiscent of Parker's idea at 1:30.) This chorus extends for an additional eight bars (3:12–3:28) as Davis closes out his solo, ending with octave jumps from Fˈ to F.
3:29	CODA	Band	Parker joins Davis in a harmonized coda lasting four bars, with a melody that suggests—but doesn't exactly replicate—the closing phrase of the original song.

*This characteristic Bird (and bop) practice involves making melodies out of altered (flatted or sharped) notes of the underlying scale or chord (the C7 chord in this example). At times these melodies may match the regular (unaltered) scale tones of a separate key (D-flat major in this example), making for two keys being implied simultaneously—the technical term for which is **polytonality**.

---

downbeat the first beat of a measure; can also refer to the first beat of a tune.

polytonality two or more keys played simultaneously.

Style & Technique

Old Chords, New Melodies

Many of the compositions created by bop-era musicians were **contrafacts**: new melodies written to the harmonic structures—what musicians call the chord changes (or simply "the **changes**")—of preexisting songs.

The practice is as old as jazz itself. It could be argued that every 12-bar blues is this type of "contrafact"; but the technique was applied to popular song forms as well, by some of the greatest jazz composers. Duke Ellington made use of the final harmonic sequence of the classic composition *Tiger Rag* (the "hold that tiger" strain) often in the early days of his orchestra, in such pieces as *The Creeper* (1928)

and *High Life* (1929), and built *In a Mellotone* (1940) on the chords of *Rose Room*, while his collaborator Billy Strayhorn's immortal *Take the "A" Train* (1941) borrows harmonies from *Exactly Like You*. Such appropriations were hardly confined to Ellington's circle; witness the Kansas City staple *Moten Swing*, written in 1932 on the changes of the pop song *You're Driving Me Crazy*.

With the arrival of the modern-jazz era, the creation of such contrafacts grew exponentially. In a sense, using a familiar harmonic sequence simply verified the continuity between the new jazz and earlier styles, while also underscoring the melodic, rhythmic, and (through the addition or **substitution** of more

complex **passing chords**) harmonic distinctions that the modernists had introduced. It was also an economic strategy to reap financial benefits from these new creations. While an improvised solo could not serve as the basis for generating earnings, at least the crafting of a new melody over chords that (like solos) enjoyed no copyright protection provided a source of royalties. Some record companies, determined to solidify their own profits and avoid payments to established composers, even insisted that musicians record original material with the label acting as publisher—a practice that generated even more contrafacts.

It did not take long for *I Got Rhythm* (1930) to become the jazz world's favorite harmonic sequence

For most of the decade (1945–55) during which he reigned as the acknowledged leader of the boppers, Parker's working life involved leading a combo—usually a quintet in which his alto saxophone was joined by trumpet, piano, bass, and drums—on recording sessions or in club and concert performances. Parker had played for dancers during his years of big band apprenticeship, yet his new ideas were better suited for listeners. This shift to jazz as listening music not only helped the nightclubs that were now the centers of instrumental music performance but also sustained a growing number of independent jazz labels that could not marshall the production budgets required for recording larger ensembles. (Coleman Hawkins and Lester Young had anticipated the shift to combos, club work, and independent jazz labels before and during the war years.)

The lineup of Parker's best-known group—with Miles Davis on trumpet, Duke Jordan on piano, Tommy Potter on bass, and Max Roach on drums—was ideal for expressing the premium the new music placed on speed of thought and execution. Parker recorded with these musicians for both the Dial and Savoy companies in 1947 and 1948, and the resulting

performances, including *Scrapple from the Apple*, *Bird Gets the Worm*, and *Dexterity*, redefined the sound and textures of small-group playing. The shift in Parker's performing venues during these years—from the after-hours Harlem spots to the nightclubs on and around 52nd Street (which ultimately included a room named Birdland in Parker's honor) and finally to the bohemian haunts of Greenwich Village—also reflected the broader route this new style of jazz was traveling,

---

contrafact a composition that superimposes a new melody on a preexisting chord progression; employed extensively in the bebop era, notably in the writing of new melodies to the chords of *I Got Rhythm* and *Indiana*.

changes the arrangement of chords—the chord progression—that defines a tune; "*Rhythm* changes," for example, is jazz shorthand for "the chords of *I Got Rhythm*."

[chord] substitution replacement of a chord that is standard or written with another to create musical interest; most often applied to transitory chords such as the dominant seventh.

passing chord transitional chord that connects stable chords; chord that conveys a sense of irresolution and tension, resolved by movement to another chord.

after the blues, and for Charlie Parker to become the king of the *Rhythm* remakers. The harmonic motion of the Gershwin classic was ideal for jazz improvisation, and Parker mined it constantly with such new-melody reworkings as *Red Cross* (1944), *Anthropology* (1946), *Cheers* (1947), *Dexterity* (1947), *Chasin' the Bird* (1947), *Ah-Leu-Cha* (1948), *Steeplechase* (1948), and *Kim* (1952). Sometimes he worked variations into the practice, as on *Constellation* (1948) and *Merry Go Round* (1948), in which the primary themes are built on the main chordal scheme of *Honeysuckle Rose* and the second theme (or bridge) is based on the bridge of *I Got Rhythm*. Parker liked to play compositions based on other songs as well: Tadd Dameron's *Hot House* (1945), Miles Davis's *Donna Lee* (1947), and Benny Harris's *Ornithology* (1946), based on *What Is This*

Thing Called Love?, *Indiana*, and *How High the Moon*, respectively.

When it came to such contrafacts, virtually everybody was doing it in the 1940s and 1950s. That is why such classic compositions of the period as Thelonious Monk's *Rhythm-a-ning* (1941), **Bud Powell**'s *Wail* (1946), and Sonny Rollins's *Oleo* (1954)—not to mention Duke Ellington's *Cotton Tail* (1940) and Lester Young's *Lester Leaps In* (1939)—can claim *I Got Rhythm* as a common point of origin.

—*Bob Blumenthal*

COURTESY JOHN EDWARD HASSE.

COURTESY JOHN EDWARD HASSE.

out of the black community to the precincts of the educated (primarily white) audience.

Parker was not confined exclusively to combos and clubs, however; a significant portion of his recorded legacy reveals that the new music was already functioning elsewhere. In addition to the triumphant recordings of *Ornithology*, *Yardbird Suite*, and the Gillespie composition *A Night in Tunisia*, all from 1946, some of the key products of Parker's stay in California between 1945 and 1947 include recorded performances with Jazz at the Philharmonic, a forum in which he and Gillespie demonstrated, to listeners who had open ears and minds, that their approach was perfectly compatible with that of predecessors Roy Eldridge, Coleman Hawkins, and Lester Young. When **Norman Granz**, the producer of Jazz at the Philharmonic (JATP), expanded upon the success of recordings from the concerts to create his own jazz label Clef in 1946, Parker was included on one of the first releases, *Slow Drag*, a JATP jam. Several of the saxophonist's studio projects under Granz's supervision announced even more far-reaching aspects of the new music.

Granz began by recording Parker with Machito's Afro-Cubans, the orchestra fronted by vocalist

Frank Raul "Machito" Grillo. Under the musical direction of Machito's brother-in-law, multi-instrumentalist Mario Bauzá, the Afro-Cubans had successfully merged Latin American rhythms and forms with big band concepts. Dizzy Gillespie, who had been introduced to Latin rhythms by Bauzá while both were members of the Cab Calloway trumpet section, had established himself as the prime champion of this Latin-jazz fusion by featuring Cuban conga drummer Chano Pozo on *Manteca* (*JTSA* Disc 2/Track 13) and *Cubana Be/Cubana Bop* in 1947. This stylistic conjunction continued to develop in the years before Parker's death: **Stan Kenton** paid tribute in a piece entitled *Machito* (1947); Latin bandleaders including Tito Puente and Tito Rodriguez followed Machito's lead and made frequent room for guest jazz soloists; and popular jazz combos of the early 1950s—led by pianist George Shearing and vibraphonist Cal Tjader—returned the compliment by incorporating Latin percussionists.

History & Culture

Swing Street

It was called "Swing Street" and "the street that never slept." In its nightclub heyday—which lasted roughly from 1933 to the late 1940s—the stretch of Manhattan's 52nd Street that ran between 5th and 7th avenues served as a vibrant center of jazz activity.

Clubs such as the Onyx, the Famous Door, and the Three Deuces lit the street in neon. Over time, they also cast light on the changing face of jazz. In the late 1930s, a walk past a club marquee and downstairs into a basement would plunge a visitor into a crowded, smoke-filled setting alive with the sound of swing. Ten years later, that same descent would immerse the clubgoer in the hyperkinetic energy of bebop.

The Street offered a grab bag of options for fan and player alike. On any given night, a jazz seeker could snake from one brownstone to another and catch sets by Art Tatum, Coleman Hawkins, and Billie Holiday. The musicians themselves would hop from club to club,

finishing up their regular shows and then rushing across the street or a couple of doors away to sit in with other bands. With new ideas and players circulating freely, tested for durability in late-night "**cutting sessions**," 52nd Street became a hothouse of innovation and evolving styles.

It was on the Street that many musicians heard sax innovator Charlie Parker for the first time, when he would drop in unannounced to jam. "Everybody just flipped," clarinetist Tony Scott recalled. Parker's influence would course through the Street's echoing basements and on into future jazz.

The clubs were numerous, and each had its own mini-history. There was the Onyx, one of the Street's earliest jazz venues, where in 1933 one could hear Tatum and the swing quintet Spirits of Rhythm; two years later, audiences could catch the sextet of violinist-singer Stuff Smith, who had a novelty hit in 1936 with *I'se a Muggin'*. By the mid-1940s Dizzy Gillespie was there, playing virtuosic bop trumpet with a group that included bassist Oscar Pettiford and drummer Max Roach. Across the street was the Famous Door, which played host, over the years, to the likes of Count Basie's big band, Gillespie, Lester Young, Ben Webster, and Jack Teagarden.

Another club, the Hickory House, opened its doors in 1934. By 1936 it was showcasing one of 52nd Street's first racially

mixed groups, led by clarinetist Joe Marsala and featuring Red Allen on trumpet. Marsala seemingly couldn't leave: he played at the Hickory House off and on through 1945.

At the Club Downbeat, featured acts included Holiday, guitarist Tiny Grimes and his group, and Hawkins, who worked there with Thelonious Monk in 1944, at around the same time Gillespie was bringing bop to the Onyx.

Gillespie also played the Three Deuces. And in 1947 young trumpeter Miles Davis could be heard there, earning his stripes in a quintet led by saxophone sensation Parker and propelled by Max Roach.

Kelly's Stable was the site, in 1939, of Hawkins's debut engagement after an extended stay in Europe. Hawkins's classic Bluebird recording of *Body and Soul* was a product of his Stable stint. Nat Cole, Holiday, and Hot Lips Page were others heard there.

Two doors down from the Onyx was Jimmy Ryan's, a site that specialized in traditional jazz: Page, Allen, Earl Hines, Sidney Bechet, and Bob Wilber played there. The club outlasted the Street itself, closing in 1962.

After World War II, the Street's jazz began to slip away, drawn to clubs in other parts of town—clubs such as Bop City, the Royal Roost, Birdland, and Greenwich Village's Cafe Society and the Village Vanguard. Strip joints and pockets of vice replaced it. Several decades later, following its transformation into a gray stretch of nondescript office buildings, the "street that never slept" finally turned out the lights for good.

—*Tad Lathrop*

cutting session a jam session featuring informal competition among soloists.

52nd Street, New York City, 1948. PHOTO COURTESY WILLIAM P. GOTTLIEB/WILLIAM P. GOTTLIEB COLLECTION/LIBRARY OF CONGRESS PRINTS & PHOTOGRAPHS DIVISION.

History & Culture

Big Bands in the Modern Era

A combination of changing economics and changing tastes may have brought a close to the big band era, but it hardly extinguished all big bands. In addition to the ongoing enterprises of jazz's orchestral Olympians, Duke Ellington and Count Basie, a number of newer large ensembles emerged as jazz entered the modern era.

Unfortunately, the two big bands that became known as the incubators of the modern era were victims of the 1942–44 recording ban. These were the Earl Hines Orchestra of 1943, which included Dizzy Gillespie, Charlie Parker, and Sarah Vaughan, and the first edition of the band formed by Hines vocalist Billy Eckstine, which featured Gillespie, Parker, and Vaughan as well as such other leading modernists as trumpeter Fats Navarro, tenor saxophonists Gene Ammons and Dexter Gordon, and drummer Art Blakey. By the time Eckstine's band recorded, Gillespie and Parker had moved on.

The big band was a natural setting for Gillespie's virtuosic trumpet and extroverted showmanship, however; and in the latter half of the 1940s he led an orchestra of his own. The compositions *Things to Come* (1946), *Cool Breeze* (1947), and others demonstrated that the innovations heard most frequently in combos could also be applied to larger ensembles, while *Algo Bueno* (1947) and the two-part *Cubana Be/Cubana Bop* (1947) revealed the potential in merging jazz with Afro-Cuban music.

Modern ideas also drove what came to be known as the First and Second Herds of veteran bandleader Woody Herman—especially the 1947–49 Second Herd, which bore

COURTESY JOHN EDWARD HASSE.

the strong influence of both Parker and (in the sound of its *Four Brothers* sax section) Lester Young.

Another variety of modernism was purveyed by the bands of Stan Kenton, who used Jimmie Lunceford as the initial model for his band, yet by the end of the 1940s was the exemplar of all things "progressive." There was much pretense in Kenton's music (particularly in his constant recasting of 1943's *Artistry in Rhythm*), but much innovation as well, beginning with his use of bassist Eddie Safranski and the Kai Winding–led trombone section on such performances as *Collaboration* and *Minor Riff* (both 1947). Early-1950s editions featured the challenging scores of Bob Graettinger (*City of Class*, 1951) and Bill Russo (*23 Degrees North, 82 Degrees West*, 1952; *JTSA* Disc 3/ Track 5). By that time, trumpeter

Billy Eckstine. PHOTO COURTESY DOWN BEAT ARCHIVES.

Shorty Rogers, saxophonist **Gerry Mulligan** (who wrote the influential *Young Blood* [1952] but did not play in the band), and others had introduced ideas into Kenton's orbit that would also prove to be forerunners of "cool" jazz. Ultimately, however, the economics of bandleading proved prohibitive. By 1950, Gillespie had disbanded, Herman and Kenton only toured for parts of each year, and even Count Basie was temporarily reduced to leading a combo. Only Duke Ellington, in a class of his own as always, remained on the road, the exception that proved the rule that big bands had become an unaffordable luxury.

—*Bob Blumenthal*

History & Culture

Jazz at the Philharmonic was the first "live" jazz album ever released.
COURTESY BENCAR ARCHIVES.

Norman Granz, 1947. PHOTO COURTESY WILLIAM P. GOTTLIEB/ WILLIAM P. GOTTLIEB COLLECTION/LIBRARY OF CONGRESS PRINTS & PHOTOGRAPHS DIVISION.

Norman Granz and Jazz at the Philharmonic

Along with the annual Carnegie Hall concerts that Duke Ellington embarked on in 1943, producer Norman Granz's Jazz at the Philharmonic concert series was among the gathering indications that jazz could find a new home in formal settings that typically hosted symphony orchestras and classical soloists. Not that JATP, as it quickly became known, confined itself to the esoteric aspects of the music. The concerts were organized jam sessions, loose and extroverted and frequently derided for the solo displays of such regulars as tenor saxophonists Illinois Jacquet and Flip Phillips that approached the exhibitionism of rhythm and blues. In honoring Granz's preference for the spontaneous, JATP drove home the point that all "serious" music was not necessarily committed to manuscript paper; and at its best, as in the 1946 concert that produced Charlie Parker's solo on *Lady Be Good*, JATP presented informal cross-generational summit meetings in which such young innovators as Parker and Dizzy Gillespie could stand shoulder-to-shoulder with such influential elders as Lester Young and Roy Eldridge.

JATP's 1944 debut concert at Hollywood's Philharmonic Auditorium had been organized by Granz to raise funds for Mexican American defendants in a murder case, and the producer's commitment to civil rights was further demonstrated by his insistence that integration take place both onstage and in the audience at all JATP concerts. The 1944 debut was also recorded, later appearing on 12-inch, 78-rpm records. These became the first commercially issued live jazz recordings, and their popularity made JATP an international concert phenomenon and Granz the first acknowledged jazz impresario. He continued to present JATP through 1957, generally with vocalist Ella Fitzgerald and the trio of pianist Oscar Peterson as the centerpieces of the star-heavy packages.

Granz also excelled as a recording executive and personal manager. He owned the labels successively known as Clef, Norgran, and Verve, which dominated independent jazz production throughout the 1950s by presenting Fitzgerald, **Stan Getz**, Gillespie, Billie Holiday, Parker, Peterson, Art Tatum, Young, and other stars. After selling Verve in 1960, Granz returned to recording with his Pablo label in 1973, where Basie, Fitzgerald, Peterson, and guitarist Joe Pass all found a home. Granz also personally oversaw the careers of Fitzgerald and Peterson and enjoyed a productive if less exclusive business relationship with Duke Ellington.

—Bob Blumenthal

Issues

The Jazz Musician as Outsider

Why are jazz musicians often perceived as being "outsiders" who shun the values of mainstream American life?

Part of the reason jazz music was controversial from the beginning was that the occupation of jazz musician challenged notions of middle-class respectability and normative behavior. Late hours, uncertain employment, and an often-itinerant work life—not to mention jazz's early associations with New Orleans sporting houses, scandalous dancing, drinking, and nightlife—led some parents to ask, "Would you want your daughter to marry a jazz musician?"

Sociologist Howard S. Becker has argued that jazz musicians, at least at mid-century, constituted a deviant subculture—deemed unorthodox by more conventional members of society—but nonetheless one that was stable and long lasting. Jazz musicians segregated themselves musically and felt a conflict with the non-musicians who hired them, and with people (musicians or not) outside of jazz, who were often thought to be "square"—the opposite of hip. Signs of the isolation of the jazz community, wrote Alan P. Merriam in *The Anthropology of Music*, included "special language, greeting rituals, titles, and dress; folk plots in stories which are traded among members; a lack of race prejudice. . . ."

Until the latter part of the twentieth century, few jazz musicians learned their craft in school; the image of the jazz musician as outsider was stoked by the fact that jazz existed largely outside of respectable institutions such as schools, colleges, and churches. The temptations and abuse of alcohol were ever-present for players whose main living was in nightclubs and dancehalls, where booze was easily consumed, as symbolized by the 1931 death from alcoholism of the brilliant cornetist Bix Beiderbecke, at the age of 28.

Drug use became part of jazz's public image—sometimes in good humor, as in Cab Calloway's signature song, *Minnie the Moocher* (1931), a light-hearted story of an opium smoker. Marijuana, popular among some jazz musicians, was memorialized in Don Redman's *Chant of the Weed* (1931) and the song *Reefer Man* (1932). Though hidden from the public, Louis Armstrong smoked weed, he said, every day of his adult life. Drummer Gene Krupa's 1943 arrest for possession of two marijuana cigarettes—he was given a three-month jail sentence—helped further a connection in the public's mind between jazz and drugs.

In the 1940s, the image of the jazz musician as abnormal ratcheted up considerably when Charlie Parker and Billie Holiday underwent well-publicized arrests and prison terms for heroin addiction. "Dope, heroin abuse, really got to be a major problem during the bebop era, especially in the late forties, and a lotta guys died from it," recalled trumpeter Dizzy Gillespie in his autobiography, *To Be or Not to Bop*. In the 1950s, a range of other musicians—Miles Davis, John Coltrane, Stan Getz, Ray Nance, Art Pepper, Bill Evans, and many others—would struggle with drug addiction, strengthening the image of jazz musicians as deviant outsiders.

Jazz musicians often actively cultivated the image of outsider, as it was their artistic prerogative to stand apart from, or outside, the main culture. Often jazz players looked down on other kinds of music, creating the word "corny" to refer to non-jazz sweet pop music. Their stance as outsiders helped them to develop unconventional, highly personal ways of playing and improvising, even speaking and dressing. Indeed, innovation and creativity are often linked with "outsider" behavior; in the creative arts generally, high creativity and deviant behavior have often gone together, from Vincent van Gogh to Jack Kerouac, William Burroughs, and Andy Warhol. During the 1950s, as part of a countercultural literary movement dubbed "the Beat generation," writers such as Kerouac and Lawrence Ferlinghetti embraced jazz and held poetry readings with live jazz, reinforcing the image of the jazz musicians as oddball "beatniks" or outsiders.

The stereotyping of the jazz musician as outsider would ultimately be challenged, if not shattered, by the rise of Wynton Marsalis, in the 1990s and the 2000s, as an immaculately attired, eloquent, powerful cultural figure who was equally at home teaching in an inner-city school, hosting his own show on PBS television, lobbying on Capitol Hill, or performing at the White House. But the image of the outsider jazz artist would last a very long time.

—*John Edward Hasse*

Granz also recorded Parker with a string section, fulfilling one of the saxophonist's lifelong ambitions and inspiring a small but steady stream of similar performances from soloists with the artistic or commercial clout to merit such lavish treatment. Parker was extremely proud of his work with strings, especially his stunning interpretation of the standard *Just Friends* (1949), and the *Charlie Parker with Strings* recordings (1949) were easily his most popular.

Parker's diehard fans were able to preserve many of his more typical quintet performances, because his music was broadcast frequently from nightclubs on radio "remotes" and could be saved through the new home-recording technology. Fans made their own copies of these "**airchecks**" as well as in-person dubs of concerts, club sets, and even informal rehearsals and jam sessions. This activity generated an astounding number of unauthorized Parker recordings, which began surfacing before his death and continued to emerge over the decades. These multiple versions of the same stable of bebop compositions, together with many alternate studio **takes** saved by the labels for which Parker recorded, testify to his inexhaustible creativity. Several location recordings are masterpieces, such as the 1953 Massey Hall concert in Toronto in which Parker, Gillespie, Powell, Roach, and bassist Charles Mingus held something of a bebop summit. Even the rough and unpolished snippets of Parker's alto preserved elsewhere, with ensembles and solos by other band members omitted to save precious tape or discs, include brilliant improvisations and reinforce Parker's status as a cult figure.

Parker's image as a self-destructive outsider established an unfortunate stereotype for his musical generation. This romantic notion of the doomed jazz genius done in by his or her addictions actually predates Parker and can be traced back at least as far as the 1920s cornetist Bix Beiderbecke. Still, the identification of jazz with drug abuse grew stronger in the 1940s, boosted by Gene Krupa's and Lester Young's marijuana-related run-ins with the authorities, Parker's erratic behavior leading to his commitment in California's Camarillo State Hospital, and Billie Holiday's imprisonment for heroin possession. Frank Sinatra's portrait of fictional drummer Frankie Machine in *The Man with the Golden Arm* (1955) plus later movie biographies of Holiday and Parker contributed to an environment in which extramusical notoriety often

overshadowed artistic achievement. Notwithstanding the distortions and racial double standards that fed such sensational depictions of many great musicians, there is no denying that substance abuse was a particularly devastating scourge in the jazz world during this period and interrupted the careers of many prominent musicians. For such innovators as baritone saxophonist Serge Chaloff, tenor saxophonist Wardell Gray, and trumpeter Theodore "Fats" Navarro, as well as Parker and Holiday, these addictions would prove fatal before the 1950s ended.

TAKE NOTE

- What is bebop and what roles did Charlie Parker and Dizzy Gillespie play in creating and popularizing it?

Piano Modernists

Even in the face of such problems, players in the 1940s and early 1950s generated a vast quantity of great music, beginning with the work of those who formed Parker's immediate circle as his style took hold. Much of the most interesting music came from the era's pianists. Bud Powell—the musician who best transferred

Pianist, composer, and bandleader Tadd Dameron.
PHOTO COURTESY WILLIAM P. GOTTLIEB/
WILLIAM P. GOTTLIEB COLLECTION/
LIBRARY OF CONGRESS PRINTS &
PHOTOGRAPHS DIVISION.

---

aircheck a recording made from a radio broadcast by the station for its own purposes; sometimes, years later, they were issued.

take in a recording session, one run-through; several takes may be required in order to achieve an acceptable rendition.

the speed and complexity of Parker's alto playing to the piano—worked with Parker only infrequently, yet he defined the standard for modern piano in several early trio, solo, and quintet recordings and became, arguably, the most influential modernist after Parker. Powell was at best an erratic presence. Psychiatric problems that had apparently been caused or exacerbated by a police beating in 1945 led to lengthy incarcerations, during which Powell underwent shock treatments that left the pianist even more disoriented and withdrawn. The toll taken on Powell's technique became increasingly audible in his playing; yet the pianist's initial recordings between 1947 and 1951, including *Dance of the Infidels, Tempus Fugit, Parisian Thoroughfare, Indiana* (*JTSA* Disc 2/Track 17), and *Un Poco Loco*, capture some of the era's most brilliant and completely realized music.

Tadd Dameron also played piano but is primarily remembered as one of the era's most gifted

Piano modernist Bud Powell. PHOTO COURTESY © HERMAN LEONARD PHOTOGRAPHY LLC.

bandleaders and composers (*Good Bait*, 1944; *Hot House*, 1945; *Our Delight*, 1946; *If You Could See Me Now*, 1946). During his period of greatest activity, 1947–49, Dameron led a significant band at the Royal Roost on 52nd Street. His featured trumpeter was Fats Navarro, whose melodic gifts and balanced technique were easier for other trumpeters to emulate than those of the more virtuosic Gillespie. Prior to his death in 1950, Navarro made several important studio recordings with Dameron (*The Squirrel*, 1947, and *Lady Bird* [*JTSA* Disc 2/Track 21], 1948) and Powell (*Bouncing with Bud* and *52nd Street Theme*, 1949), as well as aircheck recordings with Dameron and Parker, that continue to enhance his legend.

The late 1940s marked the first recordings by a third important pianist-composer, one who had

The melodic trumpet style of Fats Navarro (left, shown with Illinois Jacquet) was easier to emulate than that of the more virtuosic Dizzy Gillespie. PHOTO COURTESY DOWN BEAT ARCHIVES.

Listening Guide

(((•))) **Listen** to *Misterioso* by Thelonious Monk Quartet on **mymusiclab.com**
CD I, Track 19/Download Track 19

MISTERIOSO • THELONIOUS MONK QUARTET

Music: Thelonious Monk, 1948.
Personnel: Thelonious Monk (piano);
Milt Jackson (vibraphone); John Simmons
(bass); Shadow Wilson (drums). Recorded
July 2, 1948, in New York. First issue:
Blue Note 560. Timing: 2:47.

Overview

Misterioso employs the most common
of jazz structures, the 12-bar blues,
to new and audacious ends. Unlike
much of the new music of its period,
it sets aside the more obvious signs
of virtuosity for equally refined uses
of sonority, rhythmic displacement,
and melodic development, together
with a more consistent emphasis on
harmonic dissonance. The angular
nature of the theme, the more brazen
ensemble sound, and the tensions of
the rhythms (which sometimes seem
to lurch yet always swing) define
the personality of composer/pianist
Thelonious Monk, as distinctive a
musical presence as jazz has known.

Key Features

- Melody: *Misterioso* employs
  simple melodic ideas to complex
  effect. For most of its length,
  the melody uses the interval of
  a sixth in a see-saw pattern that
  has sometimes been described
  as "walking sixths." The sixths
  are taken through the standard
  harmonic structure of the blues,
  leading at the end of the chorus to
  a single minor seventh (the "blue"
  seventh), creating an unresolved
  feeling that carries dramatic
  tension.
- Harmony: Monk makes extensive use of dissonance, both in
  his own solo lines and the chords
  with which he accompanies Milt
  Jackson's vibraphone solo.
- Rhythm: Monk is masterful in the
  way he employs slight adjustments
  of his phrases, anticipating or
  delaying his attack to constantly
  surprising effect.

- Tempo: While a medium-slow
  tempo is employed for most of the
  performance, it is doubled excit-
  ingly in the final theme chorus.
- Color and texture: Both Monk
  and Jackson use the sustaining
  qualities of their instruments in
  a manner that extends the drama
  and harmonic resonance of the
  performance.
- Stylistic variety: There is great
  contrast in the approach of the two
  soloists, with Jackson more technically fluent while Monk is deliberate. At the same time, both display
  an unquestioned affinity for the
  emotional terrain of the blues.
- Form and structure: With the
  exception of the four-bar introduction, the entire performance consists of standard blues choruses;
  yet Monk has taken great pains
  to ensure variety through changes
  in texture and rhythmic emphasis,
  creating a complex totality rivaling

Thelonious Monk at Minton's, 1949. PHOTO COURTESY WILLIAM P. GOTTLIEB/ WILLIAM P. GOTTLIEB COLLECTION/ LIBRARY OF CONGRESS PRINTS & PHOTOGRAPHS DIVISION.

mentored Powell at Minton's and collaborated actively with Parker and Gillespie in
defining the modern jazz vocabulary. It took
far longer, though, for the public and even
many musicians to see beyond Thelonious
Monk's personal idiosyncrasies and hear
beyond the passing dissonances of his bold,
unpredictable creations. Wearing dark glasses
and a variety of distinctive hats and given to
occasional cryptic pronouncements, Monk
was an ideal candidate for the role of jazz's
leading eccentric, earning him the nickname
of "the high priest of bebop." From his
first recordings as a leader in 1947 until he
began his influential series of albums for the
Riverside label eight years later, Monk was
a man ahead of his time, valued, if at all, for
his quirky yet undeniably fascinating compositions (*Misterioso, Evidence, 'Round [About]
Midnight, Little Rootie Tootie*) but frequently
challenged regarding his percussive, jarring
keyboard attack. It did not help that Monk

such earlier blues classics as Duke Ellington's *Ko-Ko*.

An alternate take of *Misterioso* exists, and was first issued on Blue Note 1509. It reduces the length of the piano solo to one chorus and retains the original unison for the final theme statement, while featuring different improvisations by Jackson and Monk.

—*Bob Blumenthal*

TIME	FORM	INSTRUMENTATION	MELODY
0:00	INTRODUCTION	Piano solo	Monk states the two-bar phrase that is the final resolution of the melody twice as an introduction. The phrase ends on a minor seventh, creating an unresolved feeling after the walking sixths. This introductory section announces the two melodic/harmonic ideas—the major sixth and minor seventh—that provide the substance of the composition.
0:11	THEME	Full quartet	The full quartet, in unison, plays the melody, which is a four-note see-saw pattern played in sixths, thus creating an echo effect. The phrase, one measure in length, is modulated through the form and harmonic progressions of the 12-bar blues, with a melodic adjustment at the end of bar eight (0:34) and the climactic minor seventh at bar 12 (0:43).
0:46	CHORUS 1	Vibraphone with piano, bass, drums	Milt Jackson begins his vibraphone solo by anticipating the beginning of the next chorus. Jackson's solo lasts one chorus, with Monk's support limited to the minor seventh phrase at the end of the melody while the drummer and bassist play in the medium-slow $\frac{4}{4}$ tempo of the performance.
1:22	CHORUS 2-3	Piano with bass and drums	Monk plays two solo choruses on piano, which include such techniques as descending **whole tone scales**, parallel octaves (2:02), and a frequent return to the minor seventh that has taken on a defining character for the composition. His unexpected accents and use of space gain added impact against the steady support of bassist Simmons and drummer Wilson.
2:39	THEME	Full Quartet	The theme returns, but now Wilson is playing in double time and, while Jackson states the melody, Monk is creating further tension by playing only one or two notes in each bar, while varying the placement of those notes from bar to bar. In the eighth bar of the restatement (3:02), Monk rejoins Jackson in **unison**, the tempo slows, and as the final note is sounded (3:14), Monk adds a concluding whole tone scale.

had taken a drug rap for one of his musician friends, losing, in the process, the "cabaret card" license that was required for performers seeking work in New York establishments where alcohol was served. For years, Monk did much of his playing in his West Side apartment, where young musicians, including tenor saxophonist Sonny Rollins and pianist Randy Weston, would come for intensive tutorials. Monk's day would arrive in the late 1950s. But during the period he helped inaugurate, Monk's brilliant recordings were widely ignored, and he remained a prophet without honor.

Another pianist and bandleader often considered as "far out" as Monk had a more immediate impact. While still in his native Chicago, **Lennie Tristano** developed a personal philosophy of improvisation and began attracting students. He spent hours learning classic recorded performances of Armstrong, Eldridge, Young, and others by ear. His work showed off his strong melodic imagination, while he downplayed more traditional piano techniques, such as the use of tone color and a rhythmically active accompaniment. The style was best captured in a series of 1949 recordings—including *Wow* (*JTSA* Disc 2/Track 24)—in which Tristano was joined by his two leading disciples, alto saxophonist Lee Konitz and tenor saxophonist Warne Marsh. Two of these performances—*Digression* and *Intuition*—were totally improvised and are now viewed as harbingers of the free-jazz movement that emerged a decade later. While Tristano's influence was significant,

whole tone   a whole step.

whole tone scale   scale consisting only of whole steps; in jazz improvisation, especially applicable to the augmented chord.

unison   simultaneous playing of the same pitch or melody by different voices.

Watch the video of *Blue Monk* by Thelonious Monk on **mymusiclab.com**

'Round Midnight

'Round Midnight (also known as *'Round About Midnight*), with music by Thelonious Monk and Cootie Williams and lyrics by Bernie Hanighen, is one of the most enduring compositions to come out of the modern-jazz era. In the decades since its birth, there have been more than 1,400 recordings of this remarkable piece by such diverse artists as Miles Davis, Wes Montgomery, Ella Fitzgerald, Bobby McFerrin and Chick Corea, Cecil Taylor, the Art Ensemble of Chicago, Sun Ra, June Christy, Laurindo Almeida, Linda Ronstadt, Eydie Gorme, Eileen Farrell, the Kronos Quartet, and virtually every major modern-jazz instrumentalist and singer.

'Round Midnight dates from 1944, when it was first recorded by trumpeter Williams. Like so many other works by Monk, it stands successfully as a composition with or without improvisational embellishment; unlike the great majority of jazz pieces, it is almost always presented with the written introduction and coda intact.

The piece was the focal point of collegial reciprocity between Monk and Dizzy Gillespie, whom Monk introduced to the harmonic and compositional potential of the half-diminished chord (also known as the minor sixth chord) with the sixth in the bass. In turn, the introduction of *'Round Midnight* drew from Gillespie's use of the chord in the ending of his own *I Can't Get Started* (recorded in 1945). The coda of *'Round Midnight* is, again, Gillespie's invention, based loosely on the chord changes to the bridge of Gillespie's *Con Alma* (1954). The half-diminished chord, which Gillespie also used in *Woody 'n' You* (1944) and other tunes, and which composer Tadd Dameron used so prominently in *Hot House* (1945), seems to hold a special fascination for both jazz and art-music composers and performers. Few classically trained musicians escape a discussion of this so-called Tristan chord, so named because of its prominence in the Tristan theme of Richard Wagner's opera *Tristan und Isolde*.

The body of *'Round Midnight* is beautifully structured, with a perfect balance between chordal and scalar lines, rising and falling phrases, constantly unfolding sequences, and the illusion of inevitability of resolution without a hint of predictability. Its two main themes are among the most alluring, haunting, and memorable in jazz literature—romantic without being sentimental or maudlin, tender but with muscularity and sinew, and capable of capturing both heart and mind.

The piece is one of a very few works by jazz composers (Ellington excepted) that have become popular successes as well as jazz standards. It's one of two works of Monk's that have become titles of successful movies: *Straight, No Chaser* (a biographical documentary) and *'Round Midnight* (a fictional story of a jazz musician who is a loose composite of Lester Young and Bud Powell). In the minds of many, *'Round Midnight* is Monk's magnum opus.

—*David Baker*

particularly in Europe thanks to Konitz's recordings and appearances, it might have been more keenly felt had the pianist not made teaching his priority from 1951 until his death in 1978.

Tristano's systematic methods and dispassionate approach—perhaps reinforced by the fact that he and his circle were white rather than African American—made his work appear to be a more cerebral or "progressive" alternative to bebop. In fact, Tristano was one of Parker's most individualistic disciples, the creator of a music that could not have existed without bebop and the harmonic discoveries of Art Tatum as primary sources. Then again, with rare exceptions (such as Erroll Garner, a pianist who rose to popularity with a merger of swing and modern elements, or young classicists such as cornetist Ruby Braff and clarinetist Bob Wilber, who played in more traditional styles with older players), it is hard to identify any young musicians from the period who were not working from a bebop foundation.

TAKE NOTE

- Who were the early bebop pianists and how did they affect the growth of the musical style?

Metronome All-Stars Billy Bauer (guitar), Eddie Safranski (bass), Charlie Parker, and Lennie Tristano, 1949. PHOTO COURTESY © HERMAN LEONARD PHOTOGRAPHY LLC.

Cool Jazz and the West Coast Scene

Also based on bop, although often viewed as independent of it, was the music that came to be known as "**cool**" or "**West Coast**" **jazz**. As it gained popularity and turned briefly into a marketable commodity, cool jazz became identified with lighter, vibrato-free lines (similar in this respect to Tristano's music); the use of flute, French horn, tuba, and other instruments that were uncommon in earlier jazz styles; and a greater emphasis on counterpoint and other supposedly classical techniques. The style was identified with California, even if such leading cool lights as Stan Getz, Gerry Mulligan, and Shorty Rogers had grown up on the East Coast. One of the most popular figures, **Dave Brubeck**, would cross over into popular, mainstream success with his work of

the late 1950s and early 1960s. Cool was also taken by many to be the exclusive domain of white musicians, even though the leader of the recordings that mark the style's emergence was Miles Davis, and the ensemble most deeply immersed in European influences was the **Modern Jazz Quartet**. Once again, nomenclature disguised evolutionary continuity, because cool jazz was as rooted in the Kansas City continuum of Count Basie, Lester Young, and Charlie Parker as it was in any alternative geographical or cultural soil.

A primary source for the light, floating sounds of cool jazz was the dance orchestra led in the 1940s by pianist **Claude Thornhill**, which employed symphonic

---

cool jazz   a style of jazz developed in the late 1940s and 1950s, in part a reaction to bebop; notable for its understatement, restraint, lighter vibrato-free lines, use of counterpoint, and use of atypical jazz instruments such as the French horn, tuba, and flute.

West Coast jazz   the collective name for jazz that emerged from Los Angeles and San Francisco in the 1950s and 1960s, generating much of what became known as cool jazz, but also offering experiments in instrumentation, composition, and counterpoint by such musicians as Dave Brubeck, Gerry Mulligan, and Jimmy Giuffre.

Stan Getz (ca. 1955). PHOTO COURTESY BOB WILLOUGHBY/REDFERNS/ GETTY IMAGES.

The rich, understated sound of pianist Claude Thornhill's orchestra (here with Lee Konitz, back row, third from the left, on alto sax), shaped in part by arranger Gil Evans, offered a moody alternative to the high energy of bop and helped pave the way for the cool jazz movement.

PHOTO COURTESY WILLIAM P. GOTTLIEB/WILLIAM P. GOTTLIEB COLLECTION/ LIBRARY OF CONGRESS PRINTS & PHOTOGRAPHS DIVISION.

brass and woodwinds in addition to the more standard big band instruments. **Gil Evans**, Thornhill's primary arranger beginning in 1941, was fascinated by the colors these additional instruments placed at his disposal and began employing them to obtain a range of impressionistic tonal effects. Evans was influenced by a movement that some called **third stream**, an attempt to wed classical technique and instrumentation with a jazz sensibility. While admiring classical tonalities, he embraced the new sounds of the modern-jazz combo.

In 1947, Evans orchestrated the Parker recordings *Yardbird Suite* and *Donna Lee* and the Parker-Gillespie collaboration *Anthropology* for Thornhill as features for the band's distinctive new alto sax soloist, Tristano student Lee Konitz. Evans also began sharing ideas around this time with younger musicians from the Parker quintet such as Miles Davis and future Modern Jazz Quartet leader John Lewis, as well as composers Gerry Mulligan, John Carisi, and George Russell. Their interaction produced the

---

third stream compositions blending jazz elements with classical forms and techniques; term coined in 1957 by composer Gunther Schuller.

short-lived but seminal Miles Davis Nonet, a compact version of the Thornhill band featuring the solos of Davis, Konitz, and Mulligan and the writing of Evans (*Boplicity*), Mulligan (*Jeru*), Lewis (*Move*), and Carisi (*Israel*).

The Davis Nonet obtained only one booking, in the fall of 1948, but it managed to record on three later occasions, and the dozen titles it produced—which were later collectively named *Birth of the Cool*—had a powerful impact. Their influence extended most directly to the work of Milton "Shorty" Rogers, a young trumpet player and arranger who made similar use of a midsize ensemble in recordings by his Giants group (*Popo* [*JTSA* Disc 3/Track 3] and *Didi*) that began to appear in 1951. Rogers also drew heavily on the riff-based example of the Count Basie band and the surface restraint of Lester Young, whose influence on young soloists predated Parker's and was still widely felt. The "cool" that Rogers represented echoed jazz's most emphatically swinging sources, as did the playing of a favorite Rogers collaborator, alto saxophonist Art Pepper.

Like many other former big band sidemen adjusting to shifts in the music industry, Rogers found a new outlet for his playing and writing in

A CLOSER LOOK

Miles Davis's 1949–1950 recordings later released as *Birth of the Cool* employed a nine-piece group whose approach marked a distinct shift, in color and texture as well as in performance style, from the bebop style that preceded it. French horn and tuba, unusual instruments in jazz, were included in the nonet. The

✳ Explore on **mymusiclab.com**

musicians and the arranger (Gil Evans) brought in "classical" orchestral techniques. The result was an understated "cool" mix of jazz expressiveness delivered with an orchestral sheen.

Kai Winding • Trombone

Trombonist Kai Winding played on this recording session, but J. J. Johnson played trombone on some of the other sessions for this album. Both were considered to be great trombonists in jazz, and recorded together (*The Great Kai and J. J.*, 1960). The *Birth of the Cool* is a testament to racial integration reaching greater acceptance by the late 1940s and early 1950s.

Miles Davis • Organizer and Trumpet

Davis spearheaded the innovation of a new style. His association with the Charlie Parker Quintet (1945–1948) revealed a trumpet style completely different from that of Dizzy Gillespie, the main force in bebop trumpet playing. Early on, Davis's style embodied an understated and introspective approach within the bebop idiom.

The Rhythm Section

This rhythm section comprised piano (Al Haig), bass (Joe Shulman), and drums (Max Roach). The drummer Max Roach is not pictured here, but the drums can be seen behind the baffle (a moveable wall used in recording studios). This rhythm section's approach was very similar to the bebop style but with less volume and fewer accents. The drive and forward momentum of the rhythm section was deceptively concealed by the serene nature of the performance.

PHOTO COURTESY FRANK DRIGGS COLLECTION.

Bill Barber • Tuba
Junior Collins • French Horn

Unlike its role in early jazz, the tuba was used here for color instead of playing a bass line. Behind the tuba in this photograph is a French horn (an unusual choice for the jazz band), which was also used experimentally in jazz. The arranger Gil Evans had experience with these instruments from his earlier work with Claude Thornhill's band. The wind instruments for the *Birth of the Cool* band were arranged in pairs, high and low: trumpet and trombone, alto and baritone sax, and French horn and tuba.

Gerry Mulligan • Baritone Sax

In addition to performing as a soloist and playing section parts on this record date, Gerry Mulligan arranged five of the twelve pieces on the *Birth of the Cool* sessions. Aside from being less intense than bebop, the "cool" movement revisited counterpoint, which was an element of New Orleans jazz. As a compositional practice, counterpoint reached its zenith in the works of Bach. Counterpoint is a property of polyphony, whose antithesis is homophony (a single melody over chords), which characterizes a lot of the swing era big band music.

Lee Konitz • Alto Sax

Miles Davis's original consideration for this chair was Charlie Parker's contemporary and perhaps disciple, Sonny Stitt. However, Gerry Mulligan believed that Stitt's allegiance to the style of Charlie Parker would overshadow the originality and focus of the recording session. Mulligan instead recommended Lee Konitz as a fresh alternative, whose light alto saxophone sound (unlike Charlie Parker's) harkened back to that of Lester Young. Most saxophonists (including Gerry Mulligan) of the cool era were profoundly influenced by Young's saxophone tone.

the Hollywood studios, where music for films and television began to take on a jazz flavor. (As time went on, studio work for the film, television, and advertising industries—as well as for popular-music recordings—would become a key source of income for some jazz musicians.)

The movie industry's growing infatuation with jazz scores was only the latest of Hollywood's interactions with jazz, which had long included the use of jazz as subject matter for dramatic, musical, and comedic films. But racial discrimination had prevailed in Hollywood, helping to explain the predominance of white jazz musicians in California (although

Chet Baker, performing at the club Jazzhouse Montmartre, in Copenhagen, February 1983.
PHOTO COURTESY JAZZSIGN/LEBRECHT MUSIC & ARTS.

Listening Guide

((•— **Listen** to *Boplicity* by Miles Davis Nonet on **mymusiclab.com**
CD I, Track 20/Download Track 20

BOPLICITY • MILES DAVIS NONET

Music: Miles Davis, 1949. Personnel: Miles Davis (trumpet); J. J. Johnson (trombone); Sandy Siegelstein (French horn); Bill Barber (tuba); Lee Konitz (alto saxophone); Gerry Mulligan (baritone saxophone); John Lewis (piano); Nelson Boyd (bass); Kenny Clarke (drums); Gil Evans (arranger). Recorded: April 22, 1949, in New York. First issue: Capitol 57-60011. Timing: 3:03.

Overview

Boplicity, one of the dozen tracks recorded in 1949–50 by the Miles Davis Nonet and compiled several years later into the influential album *Birth of the Cool*, melded divergent ideas as well as interesting personalities. In its tightly knit ensemble passages interwoven with brief solos, the Nonet joined improvisatory jazz with a more arranged, orchestral approach. Davis's ensemble fused the cool, airy, but understated sound of the earlier Claude Thornhill orchestra (employing some of its players) with the more active, syncopated melodies of bebop. It brought together musicians who themselves combined disparate inclinations—toward "classical" compositional techniques on the one hand and jazz expressive qualities on the other. Most notably, on the people side, it partnered Miles

Davis with Thornhill's former arranger Gil Evans, a collaboration that some years later yielded such orchestral jazz masterworks as *Porgy and Bess* and *Sketches of Spain*. In *Boplicity*, the Davis-penned melody is colored and thickened by Evans's orchestration.

Key Features

- Style: Bebop's angularity, syncopation, and swing combine with impressionistic orchestral color to yield an early example of cool jazz.
- Form and structure: An AABA melody stated at the outset becomes obscured as composed passages and solo statements unfold, returning to a final full-band recapitulation of A at 2:40.
- Improvisation: Rather than dominating, the ad-libbed segments are nestled within constructs of fixed composition. Soloists must have their "say" within strictly limited durations.
- Melody and harmony: The angular melody is less a singable "tune" than a string of characteristic bebop devices: eighth-note lines varied with rests, triplets (0:02), syncopation (0:04), and double-time embellishments (0:08), following the underlying chord

progression but including altered notes (0:04, 0:07, 0:13). The harmonic progression proceeds simply, in the key of F major, through the two A sections, and in the B section it departs into a progression in descending half steps from C minor, leading back to the A section. The progression is conventional, yet the ensemble writing adds color and complexity.
- Color and texture: Instrumentation is a pared-down version of Claude Thornhill's orchestra, including the French horn and tuba that were common in European chamber music but were rare in mid-century jazz ensembles. The texture is thick and rich, with tight ensemble harmony on the melody line, yet smooth and fluid. At points, space opens up for individual soloists.
- Voice, feel, and expression: Note the horns' chordal swells (0:13, 0:27), the melodic accents on offbeats (0:34–35), and the tight rendering of sixteenth-note embellishments (0:06, 0:29), all of which contribute to expressiveness and a feeling of swing.
- Pulse: The $\frac{4}{4}$ pulse is subdued.

—Tad Lathrop

African American veterans such as Benny Carter and Harry "Sweets" Edison were quietly cracking barriers in the segregated system).

Not all the white musicians who ventured west sought studio work. Gerry Mulligan wrote the influential *Young Blood* for the Stan Kenton band when he relocated to Los Angeles in 1952, but the move also led him to form a quartet for appearances at a nightclub called the Haig. The group featured an inspired blend of Mulligan's virtuosic playing of the baritone saxophone and the fragile, lyrical trumpet of **Chet Baker**, a self-taught newcomer who had impressed no less a figure than Parker himself.

Mulligan and Baker would frequently improvise simultaneously, a practice that harkened back to early New Orleans music yet took on a modern feeling that was enhanced by the absence of a piano in the quartet's rhythm section. The lean, witty Mulligan sound proved as definitive of West Coast cool as that of any band's, and it turned both Mulligan and Baker into international stars.

Watch the video of *Indiana* by Gerry Mulligan on **mymusiclab.com**

comping playing chordal accompaniment for a soloist.

TIME	SECTION	FORM	INSTRUMENTATION	MELODY
0:00	HEAD (CHORUS 1)	32 bars: A (0:00) A (0:14) B (0:28) A (0:42)	Trumpet leads full ensemble	Without an intro, the swinging melody begins, fully harmonized. Listen to the final chord of each A section: it sounds unresolved, intentionally, due to the addition of a note (B-natural) from outside the tune's key signature (F major). Notice the bass line, which occasionally departs from walking (keeping time) to join the melody (0:54).
0:57	CHORUS 2	AA	Baritone sax solo with piano accompaniment	Gerry Mulligan solos over two A sections as the horns drop out and John Lewis provides punchy chordal backing on piano. Mulligan's melodies follow the bop conventions of linear "swing" eighth notes broken up by occasional rests (1:08, 1:11) and dressed up with sixteenth-note figures (1:09, 1:21).
1:25		Extended B	Ensemble minus trumpet; trumpet returns at 1:36 for solo	The texture changes as the ensemble re-enters (minus trumpet) with a six-bar flowing unison melody that soon sprouts a spinoff line (1:36) led by Davis on trumpet. For the next four bars (1:36 to 1:43), Davis solos in the foreground backed by the ensemble in a composed passage.
1:43		A	Ensemble	The passage seems to spill over into the next section—a new, robust-sounding melody variation by the ensemble, loosely referencing the harmony of the A section.
1:57	CHORUS 3	AA	Ensemble; trumpet solo begins on the second bar	The ensemble continues into the first bar of chorus 3, which plays out over variations on the A-section chord progression. Davis begins his solo in bar two, soloing with bebop eighth-note phrases and a showy sixteenth note-passage (2:08), as he's accompanied by horn-ensemble countermelodies and then (2:12) by **comping** on the piano. After a pause, Davis continues (2:18) with a Charlie Parkerish anticipation of the downbeat, proceeding through four bars of swinging arpeggiated and scalar lines connected by chromatic passing tones and embellishments.
2:26		B	Piano with ensemble	In the B section, John Lewis's piano emerges from the background with a spare two-note syncopation that develops into a long phrase. He pauses, then (2:35) plays a second phrase in the bop style of the preceding soloists. Drummer Kenny Clarke switches to brushes to achieve a softer sound under the pianist.
2:40		A (extended from eight to nine bars)	Ensemble	As the drummer returns to playing his instrument with drumsticks, the ensemble returns for a final statement of A. They hold the last note (2:54 to 2:57) for an extra measure, making this section nine, instead of eight, bars.

Jazz & the Arts

Jazz and Film

Explore the Viewing Guide for *St. Louis Blues* on **mymusiclab.com**

They grew up together. At the same time in the late nineteenth century that audiences were first paying to see images projected on a screen, musicians in New Orleans were beginning to stir up a musical gumbo we now call jazz. Both movies and jazz started out as scandalous, "low" entertainment but quickly won huge popular followings; today they are regularly hailed as art. From the outset, however, jazz and the movies have both been typically American, typically romantic means of expression in which artists and audiences alike have explored their dreams and aspirations.

The two art forms interacted from the beginning. Musicians improvised in theaters while customers watched such "silent films" as *The Jazz Bandits* (1920) and *Children of Jazz* (1923). By 1927, key jazzmen like Duke Ellington and Bix Beiderbecke were creating groundbreaking work. In that same year the movies first began to talk, appropriately in a film called *The Jazz Singer*. Two years later, Ellington was playing a serious composer and bandleader in Dudley Murphy's 19-minute short, *Black and Tan*.

The dignity afforded Ellington in *Black and Tan* was not typical of the film industry's treatment of jazz musicians, however. Also in 1929, director Murphy cast Bessie Smith in *St. Louis Blues* as an abused, gin-swilling woman who sings not because she is an artist like Ellington but simply because her man has left her. Jazz musicians fared much better if they happened to be white, like Paul Whiteman, who regally presided over the bizarre revue *The King of Jazz* (1930).

In the 1930s jazz artists of color were more likely to appear in short subjects or even cartoons than in full-length features. Eubie Blake played the piano, Nina Mae McKinney sang, and the Nicholas Brothers danced their hearts out in the nine-minute *Pie, Pie, Blackbird* (1932). Louis Armstrong played a cannibal in a 1932 Betty Boop cartoon, and Cab Calloway was cast as an animated dancing walrus in another short feature with Ms. Boop. In the full-length films *Check and Double Check* (1932), *The Big Broadcast* (1932), and *King of Burlesque* (1935), artists such as Ellington, Calloway, and Fats Waller were carefully segregated in brief segments that could easily be edited out for people who were unnerved by the sight of black men.

Jazz in the movies probably came of age in the 1940s. Films with all-black casts—among them *Cabin in the Sky* (1943) and *Stormy Weather* (1943)—offered great performances by Ellington, Armstrong, Calloway, Waller, and singer Lena Horne.

COURTESY FRANK DRIGGS COLLECTION.

Interracial casts appeared in *Birth of the Blues* (1941), inspired by the Original Dixieland Jazz Band, and *Syncopation* (1942), which cast the great cornetist and jazz writer Rex Stewart as a character based on cornetist King Oliver. Audiences were given behind-the-scenes dramas about the immensely popular swing bands in *Orchestra Wives* (1942) and *The Fabulous Dorseys* (1947). *Jivin' in Be-Bop* (1947) served as a vehicle for Dizzy Gillespie and his orchestra, and *Rhythm in a Riff* (1946) featured the early bebop band of Billy Eckstine. In 1948's *A Song Is Born*, jazz was portrayed as an art form with a history (albeit a history so willfully misconceived that it emphasized Spanish explorers and ignored the slave trade).

Some filmmakers found jazz to be useful as a sign of corruption and criminality. In Frank Capra's *It's a Wonderful Life* (1946) the jazz that plays in bars and nightclubs signifies the decadence of "Pottersville," the nightmare alternative to the small-town paradise of Bedford Falls. In *The Wild One* (1953) a gang of motorcyclists in

black leather listen not to rock and roll but to big band music that suggests Stan Kenton. And in *The Rat Race* (1960) a group of talented jazz musicians steal Tony Curtis's saxophones and flutes at a fake audition.

After jazz ceased to be a popular music in the 1950s, it was most likely to be heard in nostalgic biopics about bandleaders from the swing era (among them, *The Benny Goodman Story*, *The Glenn Miller Story*, and *The Five Pennies*); in grainy, "independent films" like *Shadows* (1960) and *The Connection* (1961); or in such documentaries as *Jazz on a Summer's Day* (1960) and *The Last of the Blue Devils* (1974). Jazz also became a musical flavor of choice in movie

soundtracks, most memorably in *A Streetcar Named Desire* (1951), *Man with the Golden Arm* (1955), and *The Pawnbroker* (1964), not to mention *Anatomy of a Murder* (1959), with its great score by Duke Ellington and Billy Strayhorn. In the 1970s, Hollywood tried valiantly to make hit movies focusing on jazz with *Lady Sings the Blues* (1972) and *New York, New York* (1977). A decade later, the ambitious biographical jazz films *'Round Midnight* (1986) and *Bird* (1988) drew even smaller audiences.

At the end of the twentieth century, the most revealing treatment of jazz could be found in such documentaries as *Thelonious Monk: Straight, No Chaser* (1988), *Let's Get Lost* (the 1988 film about the life of Chet Baker), and *A Great Day in Harlem* (1995). But filmgoers could hear bits and pieces of jazz in many Hollywood films, especially in scenes establishing emotional intimacy. Although jazz had become an art music, in the movies it was still very much the music of romance.

—*Krin Gabbard*

COURTESY FRANK DRIGGS COLLECTION.

Some of the new West Coast sounds emerging from California actually *were* created by musicians with roots west of the Mississippi. Saxophonist and clarinetist Jimmy Giuffre, a Texan, had gained early fame as the composer of *Four Brothers* (1947; *JTSA* Disc 2/Track 19) for Woody Herman's Second Herd (a bebop-oriented follow-up to the swing-heavy band Woody Herman's Herd). After studying advanced compositional techniques, Giuffre began to explore more compact, folkish themes in his intimate Jimmy Giuffre 3, a band that eliminated drums and even, in one unusual clarinet-trombone-guitar configuration, bass. The Giuffre 3 featured the gentle abstractions of guitarist Jim Hall, who had made his debut in the quintet of former Mulligan drummer Chico Hamilton. With its emphasis on flute, cello, and atmospheric percussion, the Hamilton quintet established two Los Angeles natives, Hamilton and woodwind master Buddy Collette, among the leading figures in the cool style.

Beyond the Cool

The Modern Jazz Quartet, which was based in New York, made many of the same inroads with college and concert-hall listeners. The MJQ had originated as the rhythm section in Dizzy Gillespie's 1946 big band, where it comprised pianist John Lewis, vibraphonist Milt Jackson, bassist Ray Brown, and drummer Kenny Clarke. Shortly after it began performing as a unit in 1952, with Percy Heath in place of Brown and (beginning in 1955) Connie Kay in place of Clarke, the MJQ cultivated a veneer of chamber-music propriety in such recordings as *Vendome* (1952), *Django* (1954; *JTSA* Disc 3/Track 7), and *Milano* (1954). The members often appeared in tuxedos and played compositions that recalled Baroque fugues. Yet the jazz bona fides of Jackson, one of the music's most exceptional blues and ballad players, and the rest of the MJQ could not be denied. They were cool jazz modernists forthright enough in their playing to also connect with the hard bop style that emerged around the time of Charlie Parker's death.

This cool/hard dichotomy was increasingly the rule as jazz continued to evolve. In this regard, no musician exemplifies the frustrations of drawing

Watch the video of *The Golden Striker* by the Modern Jazz Quartet on **mymusiclab.com**

Hear a profile of John Lewis on **mymusiclab.com**

stylistic boundaries more vividly than Miles Davis. First an important member of the Parker quintet, then the harbinger of cool with his nine-piece band, Davis also laid the groundwork for the bluesy, percussion-driven hard bop style in *Dig, Walkin'*, and other of his early 1950s recordings. These investigations of a more assertive and emotional style would hardly exhaust the trumpeter's curiosity or temper the innovations he introduced subsequently. More than any of his peers, more than even his mentors Parker and Gillespie, Davis demonstrated that, as modern jazz came of age, it remained a miraculous engine for change.

TAKE NOTE

- What was cool jazz, who were its key proponents, and where did it develop?

Explore Jazz Classics and Key Recordings on **mymusiclab.com**

The Modern Jazz Quartet (clockwise from upper left): drummer Connie Kay, pianist John Lewis, vibraphonist Milt Jackson, and bassist Percy Heath. PHOTO COURTESY JAMES J KRIEGSMANN/DOWN BEAT ARCHIVES.

Jazz & the Arts

Jazz Poetry

For more than three quarters of the twentieth century, poets responded both to jazz and to jazz musicians. While the term "jazz poetry" tends to conjure stereotypical images from the 1950s (coffee houses, black berets, and the like), the complex history of jazz-related poetry offers a far more diverse collection of poetic styles and sensibilities.

The earliest published jazz poems were written by white writers, such as Carl Sandburg, whose *Jazz Fantasia* (1920) was one of the first to appear in print. Many of his contemporaries, including e.e. cummings and Vachel Lindsay, associated racial and sexual anxieties with jazz; much of the poetry from the 1920s displayed an ignorance of the jazz aesthetic. In 1926, however, Langston Hughes published *The Weary Blues*, a collection of poems that, for the first time, embraced jazz as an art form integral to American and African American culture. Hughes published prolifically, including two exceptional jazz-related poetry collections, *Montage of a Dream Deferred* (1951) and *Ask Your Mama: 12 Moods for Jazz* (1961). Although several writers from the 1930s and 1940s made substantial contributions to jazz poetry—chiefly Sterling Brown and Melvin Tolson—Hughes's achievements outweigh the efforts of any other writer from the first half of the century.

The popularity of bebop generated a stunning number of jazz poems, particularly among Beat poets. In 1957 Lawrence Ferlinghetti and Kenneth Rexroth performed their work with a jazz band in San Francisco, spurring a series of live poetry-read-to-jazz

The Story of Jazz
narrated by LANGSTON HUGHES
with Documentary Recordings
WRITTEN BY LANGSTON HUGHES, AUTHOR OF "THE FIRST BOOK OF JAZZ" PUBLISHED BY FRANKLIN WATTS, INC.
FJ 7312 FOLKWAYS RECORDS & SERVICE CORP., N.Y.

Poet Langston Hughes created The Story of Jazz *for Folkways Records as an introduction to the musical style for young listeners.*
COURTESY BENCAR ARCHIVES.

performances and recordings by such writers as Kenneth Patchen and Jack Kerouac. Ultimately, most of the writers and musicians had great reservations about these performances, and the fad virtually died out by the end of that decade. Since then a number of poets—most notably Amiri Baraka (LeRoi Jones) and Jayne Cortez—have more successfully integrated their work with jazz musicians. The 1970s group the Last Poets fused poetry with black pop—and laid the groundwork for 1990s rap music and hip-hop.

Although poets have celebrated hundreds of jazz musicians, two saxophonists dominate the list: Charlie Parker and John Coltrane. Poets in the late 1950s—mainly white writers from the West Coast—repeatedly found inspiration in Parker's artistic innovations as well as his self-destructive lifestyle. Many of these homages conferred a godlike status on Parker and, in doing so, lost the humanity of the man; against the barrage of bad verse, Bob Kaufman

worked diligently to make words sound like jazz and best captured some of Parker's magnetism. In the late 1960s, African American poets began to identify Coltrane's music with the black civil rights movement. Major voices from that time—including Don L. Lee (Haki Madhubuti), Baraka, Sonia Sanchez, and Larry Neal—invoked Coltrane's sound as a direct political commentary on race.

Compared to the work from the 1950s and 1960s, jazz poems after 1970 were rather quiet in tone and strongly narrative, but the number of jazz poems rose exponentially. Some of the major voices included Al Young, Hayden Carruth, Sherley Anne Williams, Akua Lezli Hope, Yusef Komunyakaa, and William Matthews. The growing volume of activity—combined with increasing critical interest in jazz-related literature after 1990—suggests that poets will continue to explore the unlimited associations between poetry and jazz as long as the music survives.

—*Sascha Feinstein*

TAKE NOTE

- What musical movements began to replace big band jazz during the years following World War II?

Several musical movements emerged to supplant the big bands as the leading forms of popular music. Vocalists broke away from the big bands to enjoy success on their own, singing popular ballads and songs. A more blues-based, dance-oriented music was developing, originally called jump blues. Exemplified by the small group led by saxophonist/vocalist Louis Jordan, this dynamic style wed the power of the big bands with a pronounced backbeat and the new sound of the electric guitar. Finally, a new style of jazz was on the horizon that would change all of the rules: bebop.

- What is bebop and what roles did Charlie Parker and Dizzy Gillespie play in creating and popularizing it?

Bebop was developed, following the decline of big band swing music, mostly by younger, African American improvisers. They favored complex and irregularly accented melodies, more sophisticated harmonies, and faster tempos than those of the big bands. A standard practice of bebop was to write and improvise new melodies to preexisting songs, and devise interesting-sounding substitutions for some of the underlying chords. Saxophonist Charlie Parker was known for his lightning-fast playing and rich musical imagination; he became the model for dozens of future boppers. Dizzy Gillespie, with his outstanding compositional skills and sense of showmanship, was a prime spokesperson for the movement and helped spread its popularity.

- Who were the early bebop pianists and how did they affect the growth of the musical style?

Thelonious Monk was among the best-known of the original bebop pianists. His angular compositions and percussive piano playing helped define the bebop style. Bud Powell was another important pianist, although personal problems shortened his playing career. Lennie Tristano was a more melodic, cerebral pianist than Monk, and had a strong impact on the growth of West Coast cool.

- What was cool jazz, who were its key proponents, and where did it develop?

A school of jazz arose on the West Coast and came to be known as "cool jazz." Arranger Gil Evans shared ideas with Parker associate Miles Davis and others, yielding the important cool jazz recording *Birth of the Cool*. Saxophonist Gerry Mulligan participated in that recording, and his baritone sax work, often in association with trumpeter Chet Baker, helped popularize the new style. The Modern Jazz Quartet took cool in a classical direction, using sophisticated compositions to create chamber jazz.

DISCUSSION QUESTIONS

1. Had you heard bebop before reading this chapter and listening to the selections? If so, in what contexts had you heard it? What were your impressions of it? What did it remind you of? Do you feel differently about it now? How?

2. What factors led musicians of the early 1940s away from commercial popular music and toward more individualized and experimental music?

3. Do you think the names "bop" and "bebop" served the music well? Why or why not?

4. Describe some of the important differences between bebop and swing music.

5. Why do you think that bebop created such vehement negative reactions among some jazz musicians and listeners?

6. How would you compare and contrast Dizzy Gillespie and Charlie Parker?

7. The image of the jazz musician as a doomed genius was fed by Charlie Parker. What other instances of this image have you seen? Have there been some in later musical eras? How has the image been promoted in movies? In literature?

KEY TERMS & KEY PEOPLE

arpeggio	Miles Davis	Charlie Parker
Chet Baker	downbeat	passing tone
bebop	Gil Evans	polytonality
Dave Brubeck	Stan Getz	Bud Powell
changes	Dizzy Gillespie	Max Roach
[chord] substitution	glissando	rock and roll
chromatic	Norman Granz	Shorty Rogers
Kenny Clarke	jump blues	third stream
comping	Stan Kenton	Claude Thornhill
contrafact	Modern Jazz Quartet	Lennie Tristano
cool jazz	Thelonious Monk	unison
cut time	Gerry Mulligan	West Coast jazz
Tadd Dameron	neighbor tone	whole tone

Fusion Jazz

Fusion Jazz

by Stephen F. Pond

TAKE NOTE

- What is fusion jazz and how does it compare to other jazz styles?
- What were some of the early forms of fusion jazz?
- What were some of the key fusion bands of the early 1970s, and how did their styles differ?
- How did fusion jazz become more commercial by fusing with R&B music?
- How has fusion continued to develop and who are some current performers?

HISTORICAL EVENTS	The 1970s	MUSICAL EVENTS

1967

Gary Burton Quartet, featuring guitarist Larry Coryell, records *Duster*, an early example of jazz-rock fusion

- First Earth Day celebration is held
- May: A demonstration against the Vietnam War ends with the massacre of several students at Kent State University by members of the Ohio National Guard

PHOTO COURTESY NASA.

1970

Miles Davis's *Bitches Brew* launches jazz-rock-funk fusion

1971

- John McLaughlin's Mahavishnu Orchestra brings together world music, rock, and jazz influences
- Weather Report, co-led by Wayne Shorter and Joe Zawinul, releases its first album
- Keyboard player Chick Corea forms the band Return to Forever

The Watergate crisis begins with a secret break-in at Democratic National Headquarters by members of Richard Nixon's campaign staff

1972

Roe versus Wade establishes the right for women to have a legal abortion

1973

Herbie Hancock achieves mainstream success with his group Headhunters, playing a jazz-funk-electronic fusion

Richard Nixon resigns as president amid the Watergate scandal

1974

The Vietnam War ends with the fall of Saigon

PHOTO COURTESY DEPARTMENT OF DEFENSE.

1975

Miles Davis "retires" and doesn't return to performing until 1981

Microsoft Corporation is established by Bill Gates and Paul Allen

1976

Breezin' is a top pop hit for guitarist George Benson

1977

Camp David Peace Accords between Israel and Egypt are brokered by President Jimmy Carter

1978

Iran hostage crisis begins with the taking of 63 Americans at the American Embassy in Tehran

1979

Joni Mitchell releases *Mingus*, her tribute to the great jazz bassist/bandleader with whom she collaborated for this album

Explore the Jazz Timeline on **mymusiclab.com**

105

Jazz musicians in the 1960s explored breaking down the boundaries of meter, structure, and harmony, but a significant number also branched out to experiment with expressive elements associated with other musical styles. They used these elements to expand their expressive palettes, while leaving their core jazz identities intact. Another set of players sought to graft their jazz styles to other popular styles in more fundamental ways. By the 1970s, many jazz musicians were turning to rock, soul, funk, avant-garde, classical music, and a variety of non-Western musics in search of new approaches to harmony and rhythm, new production methods, and new audiences. These fusions of jazz with other musical styles also brought jazz back to the popular music audience in a way that had not been seen since the swing era.

Fusion jazz expanded the diversity of musical styles that could be considered jazz. In fact, although we can talk about fusion as a musical movement, trying to pin it down stylistically can be difficult. Rather than a *style*, fusion jazz emerged (and continues today) as an *approach* to music making, one in which jazz musicians both embraced jazz's recent past and distanced themselves from it.

Defining Fusion Jazz

Since the mid-1970s, the term fusion jazz has encompassed a variety of approaches and styles. Some of the more well-known fusion styles are as follows:

- Music played in rock's straight dance groove rather than jazz's swing rhythm (**Mahavishnu Orchestra**, **Return to Forever**)
- Funk/dance-pop inspired players that make heavy use of synthesizers (**Herbie Hancock**, **Weather Report**, George Benson)
- Groups like Blood, Sweat and Tears that feature a jazz horn section with a rock lead singer and rhythm section
- Hybrids of instrumental jazz and pop, like the very popular music played by Kenny G
- New age/impressionistic players like **Pat Metheny**
- World music fusions that might incorporate South Indian elements (**John McLaughlin** with Shakti), Afro-Brazilian ones (Oregon, Weather Report), or Spanish flamenco (**Al Di Meola** with Paco de Lucia)

It's difficult, and maybe impossible, to locate a set of stylistic principles that weaves these diverse strands together into a single fabric. Yet all of them thread through music that has been labeled fusion.

Another way to think about fusion jazz (or any kind of music) is to consider how the music is marketed to its consumers. Who listens to it and ultimately buys it? Prior to the late 1960s, the jazz press rarely mentioned rock performers, and popular music magazines rarely mentioned jazz

Guitarist John McLaughlin with his twin-neck electric guitar (ca. 1974).
PHOTO COURTESY SONY BMG MUSIC ENTERTAINMENT/ GETTY IMAGES.

---

fusion jazz   a mixture of different musical styles; introduced in the 1960s as a term for the blend of jazz with rock and funk pioneered by Miles Davis, Weather Report, and others.

musicians. By 1970, that segregation was breaking down. Around the same time, a similar eclecticism showed up in the rise of free format (free-form) FM radio, a precursor to today's independent college radio, in which fiercely independent deejays routinely served up what they deemed best from widely diverse fare. Record labels also began cross-marketing the same music to several audiences at once—and to all these audiences as newly integrated. Together, free-form radio and cross-marketing confronted the fiction that people listen to only one type of music. (Students in surveys rarely claim to like only one type of music, although they sometimes do claim to *hate* one or two styles.)

The same can be said for the musicians themselves. As **Miles Davis**'s mid-1980s bassist and collaborator Marcus Miller commented, "It's just music, and the lines dividing these things aren't as thick as people think. . . . Musicians coming from urban situations are exposed to all these kinds of music at one time, in equal amounts." The multiplicity of tastes Miller described in the 1980s was equally true in the 1960s. For many musicians of that era, it seemed a natural outcome to incorporate elements from any and all of these musical exposures.

A working definition of fusion jazz, then, is two-pronged: the music resulting from musicians' attempts to extend jazz's traditional aesthetics of adventure and improvisation, borrowing from a range of other music styles; and the drawing together of jazz audiences with others formerly beyond jazz's reach.

TAKE NOTE

• What is fusion jazz and how does it compare to other jazz styles?

Foreshadowing Fusion

Early Mixes

Many of the jazz styles explored in this book can be linked to certain historical eras. Bebop, for example, emerged in the 1940s, and it makes sense to examine bebop in the context of the era's musical, social, and economic forces, and as a continuing presence in jazz since then. Fusion jazz can also be discussed in this way as a response to these same trends in the 1960s and 1970s. But fusing in jazz—jazz musicians incorporating elements from outside jazz—has a long history, and though it proved a highlight of jazz activity in the 1960s and 1970s, it continues to this day.

Jazz has always drawn on other popular musical styles as a basis for its own repertory. From its earliest days, to "jazz" a blues or military march meant

to play a popular tune in the vocabulary of jazz, and bebop players of the 1940s routinely used popular music as fodder for creative reworking. At various times, as in the case of the **western swing** played by Bob Wills and the Texas Playboys, musicians outside of jazz returned the favor. Wills played country and western songs in a modified big band format, blending the lilt and sway of the "territory" big band to his core "country" instruments of fiddle and steel guitar and a homespun vocal delivery. Beginning in the mid-1940s, **jump blues** was a hard-driving, small-group swing style, one of the styles that collectively came to be coined "rhythm and blues" (R&B), exemplified by tenor saxophonist Louis Jordan (*Choo Choo Ch-Boogie*, 1946) and by vocalist Big Joe Turner. Other jazz hybrids abound. Afro-Caribbean and Afro-Brazilian musics, for example, have never been far from jazz's core, a fact explored and highlighted in the **mambo**, **Cubop**, and **bossa nova** styles of the twentieth century's middle decades. In fact, hybridizing—fusing—is a long-standing practice in jazz.

Rock, Funk, and the Climate for Fusion

As the 1960s unfolded, rhythm and blues and rock and roll took on new identities. Soul (especially the polished, pop soul of Motown Records) incorporated more sophisticated lyrics and a wider range of orchestration and recording techniques than its jump blues and **doo-wop** predecessors. Rock recordings paralleled and, as in the case of the Beatles' mid-decade LPs, intensified these changes (*Revolver*, 1966, and *Sgt. Pepper's Lonely Hearts Club Band*, 1967). Rock guitarists embraced the practice of distorting their

---

western swing   a mixture of jazz and country music, popularized in the 1930s by Bob Wills and His Texas Playboys and, later, Asleep at the Wheel.

jump blues   a form of upbeat, jazz-tinged blues made popular in the 1940s and 1950s by bandleader Louis Jordan and others.

mambo   (Bantu) a highly syncopated instrumental genre created by Cuban bandleader Pérez Prado and first performed by him in Mexico; a dance style highly popular in the 1950s that was a precursor to salsa.

Cubop   from "Cuban" plus "bebop"; Afro-Latin-flavored bebop, pioneered in the 1940s by Cuban trumpeter-arranger Mario Bauzá; later known simply as "Latin jazz."

bossa nova   Portuguese for "new tendency"; a syncopated, sensuous musical style refined from the samba and introduced in the late 1950s in Rio de Janeiro, Brazil.

doo-wop   popular vocal music of the 1950s and 1960s, in which a lead singer was backed by harmony vocalists. A style of rhythm and blues, doo-wop was often sung a cappella (without instrumental accompaniment).

instruments' sounds, using fuzz-tones, amplifier feedback, wah-wah effects, and other add-ons to extend the timbres that had been so important to their blues forebears' style.

Guitarist **Jimi Hendrix,** whose virtuosity seemed to announce a new expressive universe, became a towering influence for rock musicians as much through his stunningly creative use of controlled noise as through his inventive note choices or his high-velocity melodic runs. Live rock performances by such late 1960s/early 1970s groups as Cream featured extended guitar solos. Borrowing licks, songs, and—perhaps most importantly—sounds from T-Bone Walker, Muddy Waters, Albert King, and other urban blues guitarists of the 1940s and 1950s, Cream often played whole sets consisting of a single, extended song—even over a single, cycling riff.

At about the same time, soul artist James Brown introduced a new style that featured stripped-down, raw-edged vocals, punctuating a tight matrix of sounds from his big band in a driving funky rhythm (*Papa's Got a Brand New Bag*, 1965). Grounding the groove on the bass guitar and the bass's pronounced arrival on the **downbeat** (the "one" of the bar), Brown spread the rest of the groove throughout the band, the musicians—even horn players—playing as percussively as possible, making each sound an essential part of a groove matrix. Other groups, notably Sly and the

Family Stone, would soon pick up the groove-matrix technique, the foundation of an increasingly pervasive style that became known as **funk.**

Playing extended solos over riffs or over short, repeating song forms has a long history in jazz, too. Territory bands during the swing era famously mastered the riff tune (as in Count Basie's *One O'Clock Jump*, 1937; Disc I, Track 12/Download Track 12). Paul Gonsalves's 27-chorus blues solo on Ellington's *Diminuendo and Crescendo in Blue* at the 1956 Newport Jazz Festival brought the normally staid audience to its feet, demonstrating the ability of a mere 12 bars, repeated many times, to build creative tension to the frenzy point. John Coltrane used modal vamps in such pieces as *My Favorite Things* (1960, issued 1961) and *Acknowledgement* from *A Love Supreme* (1964, issued 1965; *JTSA* Disc 5/Track 3) to provide surprisingly flexible frameworks for his extended solos.

With modal playing and with the free jazz movement, jazz musicians were finding routes outside of the normal approaches to harmony that had driven Western music for four centuries and that also had provided the chord progressions for bebop. Given rock's and soul's attentiveness to timbre and groove, described previously, and given jazz's readiness to wander from harmonies that were beginning to seem predictable and confining, a closer encounter between rock, soul, and jazz seemed to beckon. Each style offered creative openings to the others.

The way rock musicians were packaged offered an additional area for jazz adaptation: fusion jazz musicians largely adopted the rock model of a self-contained band with a stable set of musicians. To be sure, some prominent jazz group personnel had remained steady—the Modern Jazz Quartet, the Dave Brubeck Quartet, the second "great" Miles Davis Quintet, and the John Coltrane Quintet of the mid-1960s are examples of this—but the most common organization for jazz musicians entailed a shifting constellation of players (**sidemen**) orbiting a lead musician. In this environment, a three-month tour would seem an oasis of stability. Fusion jazz groups, in contrast, tended to assume a group identity (thus, "Weather Report," not the "Wayne Shorter-Joe Zawinul Quintet." This relative stability added

COURTESY DAVE JASEN.

downbeat   (1) the first beat of a tune; (2) the first beat of a measure.

funk   a style of late–twentieth century African American popular dance music, evolved from rhythm and blues and soul music, with a strongly accented first beat in each bar and highly refined syncopated rhythm—or groove—expressed throughout the ensemble.

sideman   an accompanying or supporting musician, in contrast to the leader; a member of a backup band.

impetus, as we will see, to a later trend within the fusion movement that favored intricate compositions over the bebop-derived structure of playing a sequence of solo choruses over a popular song's chord progression, the approach that had held sway for some 30 years.

Early Fusions

Fusion began to emerge in the mid- to late 1960s, although its labeling as such didn't occur right away. Fusion was first hinted at in the experiments of a number of groups on both the rock and jazz sides. In the **progressive rock (prog rock)** movement, for example, there were echoes of hard bop and avant-garde jazz, and of avant-gardism in Western art music. The Soft Machine, formed in England in 1966; the Los Angeles-based Mothers of Invention (especially in 1967–71), led by Frank Zappa; and the Beatles were among the rock-based groups that made use of word play, **musique concrète** techniques ("found" sounds edited to express musical ideas), electronic instruments (including the theremin and other early synthesizers), and atonality and extreme dissonance as expressive tools. All of these also were part of the avant-garde's stock in trade.

Rock also drew on jazz traditions to extend its range. A number of groups grafted big band horn sections onto their basic rock-combo instrumentation. These included Blood, Sweat & Tears (formed in 1967), Chicago Transit Authority (1967, later shortened to Chicago), and Tower of Power (formed in 1967). Still others flirted with jazz by inserting hard bop elements into their rock-based sound. Van Morrison's 1968 album *Astral Weeks*, for example, sported top-notch jazz players, and his 1970 track *Moondance*, from the album of the same name, would become a jazz staple.

The Jimi Hendrix Experience took influence from jazz, in the interplay between Hendrix's and drummer Mitch Mitchell's improvisations, in Mitchell's drumming style generally, and in songs that overtly addressed jazz, wrapped in Hendrix's signature guitar style (*Third Stone from the Sun* and *Up from the Skies*, both 1967).

Larry Coryell (left) pioneered a mixture of jazz and rock, starting with the Free Spirits and then the Count's Rock Band, in 1966–67. The Gary Burton (right) album Duster *featured Coryell's brittle guitar work.* PHOTO COURTESY DOWN BEAT ARCHIVES.

At about the same time, young jazz musicians, who had grown up listening also to rock and soul, saw exciting potential in melding all the parts of their musical personalities. Flutist Jeremy Steig, for example, played with jazz avant-gardist Paul Bley and folk-blues-rock singer Richie Havens before forming Jeremy and the Satyrs in 1967, a group whose first album was heavily marketed to the rock audience. Fusion jazz guitarist **Larry Coryell** later recalled loving the Rolling Stones as well as Wes Montgomery: "We wanted people to know we [were] very much part of the contemporary scene, but at the same time we had worked our butts off [to master jazz]." Arriving in New York in 1965, Coryell met other like-minded young musicians, forming the Free Spirits (1966) with a line-up that included drummer Bob Moses. The Free Spirits' promising blend of jazz improvisation and the emerging **psychedelic rock** sound was undercut by amateurish lyrics, and the group did not survive. By the next year, Coryell had hooked up with vibraphonist **Gary Burton**.

Burton, arriving on the jazz scene as a teenage prodigy, quickly established a formidable reputation, working with pianist George Shearing, who had blended a cool jazz style with Afro-Cuban rhythms; the Stan Getz Quartet; and his own projects. In 1967, Burton formed a quartet, recording *Duster* with Coryell, bassist Steve Swallow, and drummer Roy

---

progressive rock (prog rock)   rock music characterized by structural complexity and instrumental virtuosity.
musique concrète   (French) musical composition created by recording and manipulating natural sounds; pioneered in 1948 by the French composer Pierre Schaeffer.

psychedelic rock   a style forged in the late 1960s with an aesthetic influenced by the hallucinogenic experience induced by mind-altering drugs such as LSD; notable practitioners included the Grateful Dead and Jefferson Airplane.

Listening Guide

Listen to *Miles Runs the Voodoo Down* (Single Version) by Miles Davis on **mymusiclab.com**
CD I, Track 24/Download Track 24

MILES RUNS THE VOODOO DOWN (SINGLE VERSION) • MILES DAVIS

Music: Miles Davis, 1969. Personnel: Miles Davis (trumpet); Wayne Shorter (soprano saxophone); Bennie Maupin (bass clarinet); Chick Corea (electric piano, right channel); Josef Zawinul (electric piano, left channel); John McLaughlin (electric guitar); Dave Holland (electric bass); Harvey Brooks (electric bass); Don Alias (Charles Donald Alias, drums, left channel), Jack DeJohnette (drums, right channel), Jumma Santos (credited as "Jim Riley," shaker). Recorded: August 20, 1969, in New York. First issue: Original 14:04 version issued on the album *Bitches Brew*, Columbia P 26 CBS 66236. First issue of this radio promotion version: *Bitches Brew: The Singles*, Columbia CSK 41598, 1998. Timing: 2:49.

Overview

Harmonically, this song is constructed of a vamp on a single modal scale; there are no chord changes at all. The laid-back tempo and static harmony would seem to be a recipe for a boring performance, yet *Miles Runs the Voodoo Down* conveys a sense of

mounting tension. Three elements, all building gradually, contribute to the excitement: volume, register, and texture. The texture—the density of notes at a particular moment—begins sparely and gradually becomes a bubbling cauldron of activity. This slow but sure shift is mirrored in an equally protracted crescendo overall. An instrument's "high-ness" or "low-ness" within the instrument's range of possible pitches is its **register**. Here, Davis's trumpet solo uses a gradual shift from his trumpet's low to high registers and back again, creating the sense of an "arch." But at key moments, Davis breaks the continuity with a startlingly high note, using the element of surprise to add tension overall.

This recording is one of several single-length tracks that Columbia Records sent to radio deejays as a promotion. Although shorn of four-fifths of the original length, this version captures Davis's approach to improvisation as well as his emphasis

of groove over the harmony as a compositional foundation.

Key Features

- Drums and bass: Don Alias (drums, left channel) and Harvey Brooks (bass) take primary responsibility for establishing the basic groove, allowing drummer Jack DeJohnette (right channel), Dave Holland (bass, beginning at 0:42), and guitarist John McLaughlin to add interesting flourishes and fills along the way.
- Electric pianos (**Chick Corea**, right channel; **Josef Zawinul**, left channel) play mostly jabbing tightly clustered chords to add texture.
- Wayne Shorter, who plays on the original version of the recording, is not heard on this shortened one.
- Shadings on the chart indicate growing loudness and density of instrumental texture.

—Steven F. Pond

Haynes. The album is frequently cited as one of the first important jazz-rock recordings, although the acoustic bass, clean guitar sound, and relative absence of bass drum in the mix undermine the rock side of the equation. By the second album, *Lofty Fake Anagram* (1967, now with Bob Moses on drums), the two styles were more evenly balanced.

By the 1968, the fusion circuitry was there. Someone had to connect it; that someone was trumpeter Miles Davis, who always seemed to be restlessly seeking a new sound.

Miles Davis: Fusion Pioneer

Miles Davis incorporated rock and funk elements into his music over a period of years. For decades, the classic harmonic progressions of blues and

popular songs had formed the backbone of jazz. While bebop players extended the harmonic vocabulary, they continued to base their music on pop standards. In the late 1950s, Davis had challenged bebop-era harmonic progressions, with his turn to modal playing in the soundtrack for the Louis Malle film *Ascenseur pour l'Échafaud* (*Elevator to the Gallows*, recorded 1957 and released 1958), *Milestones* (1958), and his landmark 1959 album, *Kind of Blue*. Having re-formed his group with stunning young players—saxophonist Wayne Shorter, pianist Herbie Hancock, bassist Ron Carter, and drummer **Tony Williams**—he pushed further away from jazz's harmonic past in 1965. This second "classic" quintet, with Davis at the helm, seemed to brush aside the very notion of chord progressions, relying instead on the ability to sense and react to

Watch the video of *Children's Songs* by Gary Burton and Chick Corea on **mymusiclab.com**

register the range of the pitch spectrum, from low to high, available to an instrument or voice.

TIME	INSTRUMENTATION	MUSICAL EVENT
0:00	DRUMS, BASS, CONGA	Quiet, sparse groove; the "moan" sound is supplied by the conga player, rubbing its head with his thumb. The combination is vaguely portentous.
0:14	PLUS GUITAR	Guitar joins in, with jarring dissonance.
0:20		Dramatic cymbal flourish. Second drummer continues basic groove.
0:24	PLUS BASS CLARINET	Bass clarinet trills in lowest register (these will continue intermittently).
0:27		Guitar chords simulate a **vamp** borrowed from soul music, but of a kind more variable than in soul.
0:34	TRUMPET SOLO	Davis's solo begins on a long, low, wavering pitch, drenched in echo.
0:44-0:52		Davis hovers near the bottom of the trumpet's range, his echo-y notes allowed to die off in the distance.
0:54		Sudden interjection in the horn's high register; two drummers and second bassist become subtly but perceptibly "busier."
0:55-1:26		Davis's sudden high note elongates into a descending gesture, coming to rest again near the bottom of the trumpet's range, amid the bass clarinet's trilling.
1:26		Davis renews his solo, now in the middle register, perceptibly louder. Electric pianos jump in more aggressively with cluster-style chords.
1:41		Davis's notes, already higher, are now more clipped and percussive. Drums are more active, more cymbal-drenched.
1:46-1:53		Another sudden, high, and loud trumpet interjection that winds down in a short descent. Guitar "soul vamp" chords are high on the neck of the guitar, drums are more active with fills.
2:02-2:16		Davis plays a long, stuttering **glissando** that uses echo to build force and tension to a climax point (2:07) before descending to a resting point.
2:22-2:50	Ensemble	With the rhythm section boiling underneath, the guitar and electric pianos are playing high and loud; Davis hits a glass-shattering high note and ends in a dense stream of notes as the recording fades out.

each others' changes in tempo, melody, and timbre. These changes were all set against a regular beat stated by Ron Carter's insistent walking bass line.

A further innovation in Davis's playing occurred in 1968, when he emphasized the groove as an organizing core. Expressive tension could be created by establishing a groove and stacking others on it (related in principle to stacking riffs in the swing days) or by allowing one groove to morph into a new one, or by moving out of a regular-time feel altogether. By this time, Davis's music and stage persona were taking on some of the dance orientation, colorful tone, and flamboyant style of rock and funk. For Davis, the musical attractions of rock had to do with its timbres and rhythms; rock's cultural attractions had to do with its embrace of youth-oriented, countercultural expressivity.

Simultaneously, Davis mined rock's amplified, distorted, and electronic sounds for new creative pathways. *Stuff* on *Miles in the Sky* (1968) features Herbie Hancock, now on electric piano, and Ron Carter on electric bass, with Tony Williams providing a groove that hovers between rock and soul. This extended jam on a single chord challenged jazz fans used to their heroes "running the changes." Noted rock critic Lester Bangs greeted Davis's 1969 album *In a Silent Way*, with this effusive endorsement: "There is a new music in the air, a total art which knows no boundaries or categories." Bangs recognized that Davis's music was not exactly rock but it was "nothing stereotyped as jazz either." Davis's other albums of this period—*Bitches Brew* (1969, issued 1970), and *A Tribute to*

⊙ [Watch the video of *Directions* by Miles Davis on **mymusiclab.com**

vamp   a brief chord pattern, repeated an indeterminate number of times, used as filler and most commonly to introduce a piece.

glissando   sliding upwards or downwards between two pitches.

"Miles wants you." When musicians got that call, they answered. It was like being anointed. PHOTO COURTESY ANDY FREEBERG.

Jack Johnson (1970, issued 1971)—made it clear that he was seriously committed to the jazz-rock hybrid. Taken together, they trace Davis's growing fascination with electric instruments and the possibilities of groove.

Bitches Brew stands as the moment when rock, jazz, and funk collided and fused, as a *fait accompli*. The double album sold more than 300,000 copies during its first year, an astounding success for jazz—jazz albums routinely sold in the 3,000 to 5,000 range at the time, and sales of 15,000 copies were considered a hit. With an expanded group featuring heavily amplified and distorted electric guitar, electric bass, up to three electric keyboards, bass clarinet and soprano saxophone alternating with the more conventional tenor saxophone, Afro-Caribbean percussion, and drums, *Bitches Brew* created a molten environment over which Davis's trumpet soared—now altered with echo and wah-wah effects. Beyond this reframing of the sound, Davis and his long-time producer, Teo Macero, embraced the pop industry's use of post-production recording techniques, particularly splice editing and multitrack recording. Moments that had been recorded for one take might be found in an entirely different one, or a guitar solo might be shortened and grafted elsewhere. This material was then presented as a series of extended jams, rather than as individual "songs" as had appeared on jazz albums in the past.

Receiving the endorsement of so towering a jazz figure as Miles Davis meant that jazz and rock

musicians could pursue each others' idioms at will. For others more nostalgic for the "old" Miles, his new turn was confusing and off-putting. Despite (or perhaps partly because of) his rising sales numbers, the jazz mainstreamers cried foul, accusing Davis of pandering to the youthful audience that had come so completely to dominate the music scene.

In today's world it may be impossible to appreciate the unprecedented impact of youth on American society in the 1960s and early 1970s. Using 1972 music industry data, Steve Chapple and Reebee Garofalo reported that "[a]bout 80 percent of recorded music is rock music." During the Kennedy years, marketers began to stress youthfulness ("Now it's Pepsi, for those who think young," 1961), and the youth demographic drove the advertising mill in the mid-1960s (the "Pepsi generation" in 1963). By the early 1970s, youth dominated the advertising landscape. Coca Cola's television advertising suggested a love-in ("I'd like to teach the world to sing in perfect harmony," 1971); youth seemed to offer a tired world a transformative future.

Jazz, though, was the soundtrack for an earlier time. A generation of jazz musicians had seen their youth appeal erode as they and their audiences aged. Now, in the generation-gap atmosphere embodied in the slogan "Don't trust anyone over thirty," Davis was performing at the Fillmore East, Fillmore West, and other major rock venues. His shift away from the standard songbook and his renunciation of traditional harmony, along with his embrace of loud and distorted sound, and of the popular music industry's production and marketing techniques, prompted astonishment and anger in some corners. For some critics, these moves amounted to a renunciation of jazz, which could only be explained as Davis's chasing the big sales and notoriety that the rock world could confer. This argument was strengthened by Davis's obvious relishment of his enhanced wealth and fame.

Jazz magazines found that they now had to find a way to accommodate popular music. *Down Beat*, the leading jazz magazine since 1934, added "jazz-blues-rock" to its masthead, beginning with the July 22, 1971, issue, bringing in young music writers Gary Giddins to review jazz and Alan Heineman to review rock, with fusion up for grabs.

TAKE NOTE

- What were some of the early forms of fusion jazz?

Fusion in the Early 1970s

Several key groups, notably **Lifetime**, the Mahavishnu Orchestra, Weather Report, Return to Forever, and the **Headhunters**, spun off from Davis's *Bitches Brew* ensemble. While they by no means account for the majority of fusion activity in the 1970s, they do illustrate several streams of development as the decade progressed.

Lifetime

As a teenager in Boston, drummer Tony Williams had played in avant-garde jazz settings. He had also played in several hard-bop organ trios, and had later been a fan of the Beatles. In the mid-1960s, a

time when resentment ran high among jazz musicians over what they saw as a connection between rock's ascendance and their own shrinking audiences, Williams's attraction to popular music seemed odd to some. After all, he sat in the drum chair in one of the preeminent jazz combos of the age. Undaunted, Williams pestered Miles Davis to listen to rock throughout his tenure in Davis's quintet, and Williams encouraged Davis's gradual move to electronic and amplified instruments. In 1969, just prior to *Bitches Brew*, Williams left Davis to form his own band, Lifetime, with Larry Young (a.k.a. Khalid Yasin; organ) and John McLaughlin (electric guitar), later joined on bass and vocals by Jack Bruce, formerly of the blues-rock supergroup Cream. Young,

History & Culture

Offspring of *Bitches Brew*

The recording sessions that yielded *Bitches Brew* (issued 1970) and all

but one track of *Big Fun* (issued 1974) spanned nearly half a year: August 19, 1969, to March 3, 1970. Almost all of the musicians who played on those sessions went on

to perform in important fusion jazz ensembles or to back key fusion headliners. This family tree shows the major players and the groups that they went on to form or join.

*aka Khalid Yasid

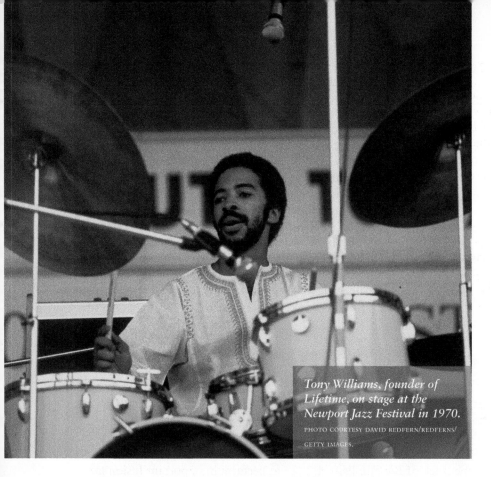

Tony Williams, founder of Lifetime, on stage at the Newport Jazz Festival in 1970.
PHOTO COURTESY DAVID REDFERN/REDFERNS/ GETTY IMAGES.

style of the French guitarist Django Reinhardt at an early age, and as a young man became enamored of the harmonic approaches of both Thelonious Monk and John Coltrane. His early career included stints in hard bop organ trios and in the hard-edged blues revival band the Graham Bond Organization, where he first encountered future Cream bassist Jack Bruce. It was Tony Williams who brought McLaughlin to the attention of Miles Davis. Davis invited McLaughlin into the recording sessions that produced *Bitches Brew* and invited McLaughlin to join his band permanently. McLaughlin, however, had already committed himself to Tony Williams and Lifetime. Far from acting jilted, Davis encouraged McLaughlin to form his own band when it became clear that Lifetime was destined to fold.

The band that McLaughlin formed, the Mahavishnu Orchestra, helped establish fusion's image as stunningly virtuosic (among its fans) and slightly pretentious (among its detractors). McLaughlin, using a guitar with two necks (allowing him to alternate between a traditional six-string and a twelve-string instrument), brought all of his interests into play. He unleashed rock's creative use of distortion combined with Coltrane-esque melodies of dense, complex note groupings; his harmonies included Coltrane's **modalism** and extreme dissonance, coupled with a penchant for lightning fast, **flamenco**-styled runs. His bandmates matched McLaughlin's abilities and intensity, especially Czech synthesizer keyboardist Jan Hammer, electric violinist Jerry Goodman, and Panama-born Billy Cobham, an ambidextrous speed-wizard on the drums. Audiences gaped at the Mahavishnu Orchestra's impossibly fast, crystalline runs and penchant for challenging, odd meters. *Celestial Terrestrial Commuters* (*JTSA* Disc 5/Track 11), in $\frac{19}{8}$ time, demonstrates all of these qualities.

(((•— Hear John McLaughlin discuss the influence of John Coltrane on his music on **mymusiclab.com**

modal jazz   a style of jazz developed in the late 1950s and 1960s in which modal scales serve as the basis of improvisation.

flamenco   (Spanish) a body of dance and music—guitar playing, singing, and percussion—from Andalusia in southern Spain.

supported by McLaughlin's agile, forceful, and imaginative approach to improvisation, had found a way to graft John Coltrane's advancements in harmony, dense clusters of melodic notes, and fearless give-and-take among brilliant equals (reminiscent of the John Coltrane-Elvin Jones relationship). The result pushed beyond anything resembling the blues organ grooves of a decade before. The group's potential for fame floundered, through a combination of lackluster promotion, substandard recording quality, and a tendency toward bombastic lyrics. Nevertheless, Lifetime brought together Williams's attraction to rock and avant-gardist experimentation, his decade at the top of the jazz world, and his background with organ trios. Lifetime also adapted the rock concept of the supergroup to fusion jazz.

Mahavishnu Orchestra

John McLaughlin split his time between Lifetime and the Miles Davis ensemble before forming the Mahavishnu Orchestra, the band he became most known for. McLaughlin had been part of the coterie of young English blues fanatics whose ranks eventually swelled the leading British Invasion bands of the 1960s, such as the Rolling Stones, the Yardbirds, Cream, and Led Zeppelin. But he also drank deep from the wells of jazz and flamenco music. McLaughlin dedicated himself to learning the

Fans also paid attention to McLaughlin's spiritual attraction to Eastern religious philosophies and Hindustani music. Eventually the group splintered, riven by fractious personality conflicts and musical disagreements. McLaughlin configured a short-lived second Mahavishnu Orchestra, and then pursued a more overt amalgamation of jazz with Indian music with a new group, Shakti.

Beginning in 1971, McLaughlin had studied South Indian music at the University of Connecticut, and had commissioned an acoustic guitar fitted with drone strings to simulate the similar strings on a North Indian **sitar** or south Indian **veena**. While at Connecticut, McLaughlin jammed with leading North Indian (Hindustani) and South Indian (Carnatic) musicians, eventually forming Shakti, a fusion of jazz with both Indian traditions. (The aesthetic gulf that Hindustani **tabla** drummer Zakir Hussain and Carnatic mridangam drummer Ramnad Raghavan traversed was as broad as the gulf either faced with McLaughlin.) Through both the Mahavishnu Orchestra and Shakti, John McLaughlin provided visionary leadership in the harmonic, metric, and stylistic expansion of jazz.

Weather Report

By 1970, saxophonist Wayne Shorter had moved on from the Miles Davis Quintet. Shorter had been a driving force in the quintet for the better part of a decade, providing a signature saxophone role while also contributing compositions for some of Davis's most significant albums (*E.S.P.*, *Footprints*, *Nefertiti*). Keyboardist Joe Zawinul had recorded with Davis on *In a Silent Way*, *Bitches Brew*, and *Big Fun*, although, as a member of Cannonball Adderley's group for a decade, he had not toured with Davis. When Ron Carter left the Miles Davis Quintet in 1968, Davis hired Czech bassist Miroslav Vitous to fill in. Zawinul recalled, "As it happened, Miles and Miroslav couldn't get it together. . . . [Vitous] called Wayne and Wayne called me. We had a meeting." They formed Weather Report, which, after an initial bit of personnel

((•● Hear a profile of Joe Zawinul on **mymusiclab.com**

shuffling, included Zawinul, Shorter, Vitous, and a succession of drummers and Afro-Brazilian percussionists (some of whom went on to other key fusion groups or became sought-after **session players**). Throughout Weather Report's decade-and-a-half run, Zawinul's embrace of the **synthesizer** keyboard, coupled with changes in the bass chair, fueled a remarkable evolution in Weather Report's sound. The bass role begun by Vitous, primarily an acoustic bass player, shifted to a far funkier direction with Alphonso Johnson on electric bass (1974–76).

Then the group took a major leap into new expressive territory, sparked by Johnson's replacement, **Jaco Pastorius** (1976–81), the self-proclaimed "greatest bass player in the world." Pastorius's bold inventiveness on the fretless electric bass proved as influential as Jimi Hendrix had been on guitar. Beyond his startling technique, a penchant for playing countermelodies, and a virtuosic use of a variety of **harmonic overtones** lay his mastery of distortion effects (all Hendrix trademarks). For his part, Zawinul, ambidextrous and able to play intricate lines on two instruments simultaneously, began to add multiple synthesizer keyboards to his arsenal. Weather Report's music emphasized an architecture of successive **grooves**, energized with layers of timbre: Afro-Brazilian percussion interlocking with virtuosic improvisational drumming, Pastorius's everywhere-at-once bass playing, and multi-voiced synthesizers providing a landscape over which Shorter could dip and soar.

Return to Forever

Like Weather Report and Herbie Hancock's group Headhunters, Chick Corea's band Return to Forever (RTF) explored the new frontier of the synthesizer and Africa-diasporic percussion. By the time RTF was formed in 1971, 30-year-old Corea had spent a decade playing hard bop, Latin jazz, and avant-garde jazz at the top professional level (*Matrix*; *JTSA* Disc 5/Track 9).

◉ Watch the video of *Boogie Woogie Waltz* by Weather Report on **mymusiclab.com**

---

session player   a musician who plays in recording studios.

synthesizer   a sound production device that blends waveforms to create new sounds; the device stores the sounds, which are playable via a keyboard or other controller.

harmonic overtones   in acoustics, secondary tones that are subdivisions of a fundamental tone or frequency; generated in stringed instruments by touching, rather than plucking, the string at points marking shorter segments of the string length that generates the main tone.

groove   the rhythmic architecture, or *feel*, of a tune, especially in late twentieth-century popular dance music and *funk*.

---

sitar   Indian stringed instrument consisting of a resonating gourd and a long neck supporting seven principal strings, plus 12 to 20 sympathetic strings.

veena   (also *vina*) Indian stringed instrument with a resonating gourd and a long neck supporting four melody strings and three drone strings.

tabla   a pair of drums of North India, played with the fingers, palms, and hands.

A CLOSER LOOK

Weather Report, founded in 1971, thrived under the leadership of former Miles Davis sidemen Josef Zawinul (keyboard) and Wayne Shorter (saxophone). A procession of sidemen—drummers, percussionists, and bassists—passed through their ranks. Yet the band remained at the forefront of fusion jazz, known by most listeners for their 1977 album *Heavy Weather*, and its track *Birdland*.

 Explore on **mymusiclab.com**

Joe Zawinul • Leader
Joe Zawinul was an Austrian pianist and composer who moved to the United States in 1959 and became well-known through his work with Cannonball Adderley and Miles Davis. He then co-founded the band Weather Report in 1971. This was a jazz-rock-fusion group that was highly influential in its time and enjoyed considerable commercial success.

Manolo Badrena • Percussion
Central to Weather Report's sound was the inclusion of multiple percussion for added timbral variety and color. Those who provided this over time included master percussionists Airto Moreira and Dom Um Romão. Manolo Badrena joined the group in time to record *Heavy Weather* (1977), the album for which the group may be best known.

Jaco Pastorius • Bass Guitar
Pastorius, as well as Miroslav Vitous—the original Weather Report bassist—was able to switch among a variety of roles including walking bass lines (playing on all four beats), repetitive funk bass figures, extended unaccompanied solos, and non-repetitive, interactive playing. Pastorius was an enormously influential musician to many players in the 1970s and 1980s. His unprecedented virtuosity and ability to produce a singing tone and unique sounds from the electric bass made him a much-emulated figure among other bass players.

PHOTO COURTESY ANDREW PUTLER/REDFERNS/GETTY IMAGES.

Wayne Shorter • Tenor Sax and Soprano Sax
Wayne Shorter became known as a saxophonist and composer through his work with drummer Art Blakey in the early 1960s, with trumpeter Miles Davis in the mid- to late 1960s, and also through his work with Weather Report in the 1970s and later. In the context of this group, he changed his style to one that featured sparsely placed bursts of short notes, as opposed to his earlier fluid melodic statements. To put it another way, he became more of an ensemble improviser than the jazz soloist in the strict sense that he was before.

Alex Acuña • Drums
Weather Report was a group that did not always assign its members the traditional roles for their instruments. In that sense, the drummer not only kept time, but also could interact with the rest of the band on a more "melodic" level in long, collectively improvised sections where the focus could constantly be shifting from one instrument to another (as opposed to the strict solo-accompaniment paradigm of earlier jazz styles). Alex Acuña was one of the many drummers who played this role in the group. Peter Erskine and Alphonse Mouzon were two others.

Chick Corea, leading keyboardist, bandleader, and composer.
PHOTO COURTESY MICHAEL WILDERMAN.

listener to keep their rhythmic bearings is extreme. Corea also developed a fondness for what might be called "extreme juxtaposition." Blistering along at a loud and ferocious pace, the texture suddenly and jarringly shifts to a quiet, extremely fast, yet crystal-clear flamenco melody played in unison by Corea on synthesizer and by Di Meola on muted guitar strings—then quickly shifts back to the earlier heavy-metal texture as if nothing had happened. Woven into this compositional approach was Corea's increasing inclusion of grand, orchestral effects, made possible with synthesizer technology that rapidly expanded his timbral palette, and of stunningly fast, virtuosic solos by the members of the group. The overall effect was comparable to that of the Mahavishnu Orchestra, to whom Return to Forever was often compared.

During this time, he was a member of the expanded Miles Davis ensemble that recorded *Filles de Kilimanjaro*, *In a Silent Way*, and *Bitches Brew*. After leaving Davis in 1970 Corea formed the avant-garde group Circle and acted as Stan Getz's musical director. While playing with Getz, Corea formed Return to Forever, the two groups sharing some members. Return to Forever embraced Corea's attractions, in more-or-less equal measure, to post-bebop jazz, Afro-Brazilian music, the prog rock movement, Spanish flamenco, and synthesizer-driven avant-gardism. Soon eschewing the saxophone and auxiliary percussionists in the line-up, RTF gestured more solidly toward a fusion of jazz and rock, with the addition of rock guitarist Bill Connors. In 1974 Al Di Meola, a 19-year-old guitar phenomenon, replaced Connors. Corea brought to the group a harmonic sense derived from the impressionistic chords of Bill Evans and Herbie Hancock, but couched in a deep awareness of Afro-Cuban and Afro-Brazilian rhythms. Beyond this, he and Di Meola shared a fondness for flamenco, which provided many opportunities to dive into stunningly quick and accurate melodic runs.

Corea, along with Joe Zawinul and Wayne Shorter of Weather Report, emerged as an important composer. Corea's songs *500 Miles High* and *Spain* have become jazz standards (both from the 1972 album *Light as a Feather*). *Spain* showcases a chorus of notes grouped in a dizzying array of short syncopated bursts that somehow, in the aggregate, fit within an overall regular pulse. The challenge to both performer and

Headhunters

Pianist Herbie Hancock left Miles Davis gradually through the late 1960s and early 1970s, continuing to record with him on occasion. Hancock had enjoyed a robust recording career even during his tenure with Davis, beginning with the 1962 album (*Takin' Off*) that produced the hit *Watermelon Man*—and spawned over 170 cover versions to date. Later, while transitioning out of the Miles Davis Quintet, Hancock provided the soundtrack for a Bill Cosby animated show, *Hey, Hey, Hey, It's Fat Albert* (1969), which spun off a successful R&B-styled big band album (*Fat Albert Rotunda*, 1969). Buoyed by the album's success and expecting more just like it, the Warner Brothers label put Hancock on contract. In an abrupt shift from the cute animation soundtrack, Hancock, now known as Mwandishi (a Swahili word for "composer") formed a sextet. The new group, often dressed in traditional African garb, emphasized free improvisation, accompanied by synthesizer soundscapes provided

Watch the documentary on Herbie Hancock on **mymusiclab.com**

Listening Guide

(((•□ **Listen** to *Birdland* by Weather Report on
mymusiclab.com
CD II, Track 5/Download Track 29

BIRDLAND • WEATHER REPORT

Music: Josef Zawinul, 1976. Personnel: Joe Zawinul (synthesizer, piano, voice); Wayne Shorter (soprano and tenor saxophones); Jaco Pastorius (electric bass, voice); Alex Acuña (drums); Manolo Badrena (percussion). Recorded October 1976, in Hollywood. First issue: *Heavy Weather*, Columbia CK 34418. Timing: 5:59.

Overview

Birdland is one of the best-known examples of mid-1970s jazz-rock-pop-funk fusion. The band behind it, Weather Report, started out as a jazz supergroup fronted by Josef Zawinul (keyboards, composer) and Wayne Shorter (saxophones). Personnel changed over several albums until young electric bassist Jaco Pastorius and percussionists Alex Acuña and Manolo Badrena were brought in for the album *Heavy Weather*, generating what many consider to be the band's defining sound. The introduction of the virtuosic Pastorius was a key to the success of both the album and its first track, *Birdland*.

The tune represents an evolution of Zawinul's R&B-jazz sensibility, first established with his 1967 hit song *Mercy, Mercy, Mercy*, now electrified, polished, and liberated from strict song form.

Birdland is a musical tribute to the famous New York nightclub named after 1940s saxophonist Charlie "Bird" Parker—and to jazz itself. Zawinul once said, "Birdland was the most important place in my entire life. . . . I had a concept for this album to go back to those good old days when stuff was happening in New York. I wanted to show some of the feeling happening in those days, man . . . Exactly like when I used to come down the stairs at 2 o'clock and Count Basie or Duke used to be working there."

Key Features

* Improvisation: Less soloing is featured than is typical in jazz. The piece is primarily a fixed composition, with space provided for several understated solos by keyboardist Zawinul (2:36) and saxophonist Shorter (3:07). Improvisations use **paraphrase** (keyboard, 5:12), **formulaic** (keyboard, 5:44), and motivic (saxophone, 3:38) approaches.
* Stylistic variety: The tune blends sounds from the blues (0:18), funk (1:47), gospel (2:02), and swing era big bands (2:02).
* Harmony: Unlike the complex harmonies of many older jazz pieces, the framework of *Birdland* rests on one tonal center, or chord. It's a blues chord: a major chord with a minor seventh. But the movement of "voices" and rhythms in the orbit of that central tonality is varied and complex.
* Rhythm: The overall feeling is upbeat, energetic, and exciting, propelled by powerful rock-style rhythm and drumming as aggressive as that found in 1970s rock and funk. The meter (beat) is in fours.
* Form and structure: An overarching ABA' form lays out a series of smaller themes (see Listening Guide grid). Section A presents four different themes, surrounded by periods of rest and transition. Section B encompasses a two-part interlude with synthesizer and saxophone solos. Section A' reiterates the first part in more condensed form, and includes a synthesizer solo over the final theme.
* Color and texture: Electric instrumentation—synthesizer, electric bass—matches the colors and textures of 1970s pop and rock. Thin sounds (acoustic piano) contrast with fat, rich tones (electric bass). Electronic sounds contrast with acoustic ones. Textures change throughout: sections of spare instrumentation (1:01) contrast with the full band (3:59). The changes appropriately match the tune's rich variety of themes.
* Voice, feel, and expression: One of the most distinctive voices is that of the bassist, Jaco Pastorius.

by member Patrick Gleeson. Despite critical enthusiasm, audiences dwindled. Adding to the problem, for Hancock, was the loss of young, hip, black faces in the audience; Hancock despaired over jazz's loss of relevance to its original black constituency. The group lasted only three years.

By 1973, Hancock was growing increasingly attracted to the funk of James Brown and Sly and the Family Stone. He was intrigued by black popular music on two counts. Playing a concert with the Pointer Sisters, a popular vocal quartet, Hancock was floored by the frenzied rapport between the singers and their audience; a recent convert to Nichiren Buddhism, Hancock saw their music as inclusive and populist. Musically, he was slightly mystified by Sly's and Brown's funk: he knew he could play

(((•□ **Hear** a feature on Headhunters by Herbie Hancock on **mymusiclab.com**

paraphrase improvisation   quoting another tune in an improvisation.

formulaic improvisation   creating solos by manipulating, at the speed of thought, musical formulae or patterns that one has worked out and internalized.

He alternates popping, smartly articulated phrases with slurring, almost weeping-sounding statements in a style he pioneered. Wayne Shorter, too, is easily identifiable due both to his sound on soprano saxophone and the seeming ease with which he can dispense complicated flurries of melodic material.

- Musicians' roles: The tune combines a tight group sound with plenty of opportunity for individuals to shine. The electric bass plays a prominent role, providing melodies that at times are in the foreground (0:18) and at other times blend and interact with other melodies (0:42).

—*Tad Lathrop*

TIME	FORM	MELODY/INSTRUMENTATION
0:00	INTRODUCTION	Introductory phrases, each with seven notes consisting of two similar stepwise **motifs**.
0:18	SECTION A, THEME A	Bass and percussion enter, providing a brisk syncopated beat. The melody played on electric bass over the intro phrase, moves quickly and mostly stepwise, with a bluesy sound (repeated at 3:35).
0:42	SECTION A, THEME B	The full band enters powerfully. The melody moves mostly stepwise in motifs of three notes (long-short-short); it is supported by a contrasting countermelody on bass. Saxophone and synthesizer simulate the sound of a big band horn section.
1:02	SECTION A, THEME C	A new melody is introduced on piano, with two phrases of seven notes each, played with a stabbing rhythmic quality. In contrast, long, slurring notes are played on the bass (1:19).
1:32	INTERLUDE	Saxophone re-enters, playing the opening melodic phrases (see 0:00), "answered" by the piano. Saxophone sustains a high note.
1:47		The bass trades sharp, punctuated sounds with the piano, ending on a sustained low note.
1:59	SECTION A, THEME D	All instruments join in an upbeat, joyful chorus, with two brief three-note motifs, followed by a long note leading to a bouncy four-note phrase.
2:36	SECTION B: SYNTHESIZER SOLO	A long, low note on synthesizer note introduces a synthesizer solo, played on low-sounding notes (the lower register).
3:07	SECTION B: SAXOPHONE	Descending chords support a solo by the saxophonist, who seems to dart around the cascading chords with flurries of phrases.
3:35	SECTION A': THEME A	The bass repeats the first theme (see 0:18), and is joined by the saxophone.
3:59	SECTION A': THEME B	Repetition of the first full-band entrance (at 0:42).
4:12	SECTION A': THEME C	Repetition of punchy melodies on piano.
4:23	SECTION A': THEME D	Restatement of the earlier upbeat chorus (with a wordless vocal added at 4:35) supports a final synthesizer solo.

the notes but wanted to understand funk more deeply. For his next album, *Head Hunters* (1973), Hancock retained reed player **Bennie Maupin** from his Mwandishi and *Bitches Brew* days as part of a new band, the Headhunters. The balance of the new lineup focused on young, hip players versed in both jazz and funk. *Head Hunters* relentlessly explored funk's dance groove while providing room for extended improvisation on reeds (Maupin, on soprano and tenor saxophones and bass clarinet) and keyboards (Hancock, on piano, electric piano, and a variety of synthesizers). The album drew fire from critics who challenged whether it was jazz at all, but it became the first platinum-certified (million-selling) album on *Billboard* magazine's newly created Jazz Album chart category. (Previously, jazz recordings had been charted as popular music or rhythm and blues.) A follow-up, *Thrust*, continued both the sales success and critical consternation.

Hancock would continue to draw critical fire and praise. He helped to kick-start a "neo-bop" movement with V.S.O.P., a reunion band of the mid-1960s

---

motif (motive)   a brief pattern of notes; typically the building blocks of longer phrases.

Listening Guide

Listen to *Watermelon Man* by Herbie Hancock and the Headhunters on **mymusiclab.com**
CD II, Track 6/Download Track 30

WATERMELON MAN • HERBIE HANCOCK AND THE HEADHUNTERS

Music: Herbie Hancock, 1962. Personnel: Herbie Hancock (Fender Rhodes electric piano, Hohner D6 clavinet, ARP Odyssey synthesizer, ARP Soloist synthesizer); Bennie Maupin (soprano saxophone); Paul Jackson (electric bass); Harvey Mason (drums); Bill Summers (beer bottle *hindewhu*, tambourine, congas, *shekere*). Recorded September, 1973, in San Francisco. First issue: *Head Hunters*, Columbia KC32731. Timing: 6:29.

Overview

Hancock combines four elements, all distinct, to create a recording that invites contemplation of something lost but remembered. These elements are a musical reference to Africa, a funky bass line, jazz harmonies, and an echo effect. The interlocking whistle-and-voice segment that opens and closes the piece are recreations of a central African tradition (*hindewhu*), performed by percussionist Bill Summers. As the *hindewhu* fades out, it becomes more and more drenched in echo: the African reference is a memory, a dream. Ebbing away, the sound of Africa remembered is soon replaced by the echo-less, funky bass groove; we are jolted back to the present. The spare, plucking accompaniment and almost nonexistent tenor sax melody lead to a sharply punctuated set of descending chords on the electric piano, re-setting the form (1:44). These chords recall Hancock's post-bebop jazz history, and serve to remind us of jazz's central place in the mix. African *hindewhu*, an echo-drenched fade-out, jazz harmonies, and funky bass—each of these conveys something specific (African cultural memory, loss, jazz, and black youth) in ways that suggest possible interpretations but leave Hancock's intention slightly indistinct and vaporous.

Key Features

- The overall dynamics of the piece are restrained, even quiet. The percussive-sounding **clavinet** sounds like barely plucked, muted guitar strings. The overall texture is sparse.
- The tempo is slow and relaxed, but slightly faster than a typical ballad.
- Improvisation is kept to a minimum in this recording.

—Steven F. Pond

TIME	SECTION	MELODY/INSTRUMENTATION
0:00	INTRODUCTION: "AFRICA REMEMBERED"	*Hindewhu* entrance.
0:14		Second *hindewhu* track.
0:26		Third *hindewhu* track.
0:33		Fourth *hindewhu* track, including handclaps. Echo begins to elongate as *hindewhu* fades out.
0:45		Bass entrance establishes the groove.
0:58		Drums join the groove as *hindewhu* continues to fade out.
1:18	FIRST CHORUS	Clavinet seems to add another layer to the groove, but it's also outlining the song melody.
1:44		With punches by the Fender Rhodes electric piano, the tenor sax discretely plays the close to the blues melody.
2:04		The section ends. Melody fragment by "guitar" is doubled by the saxophone (2:09).
2:30	SECOND CHORUS	Saxophone now plays melody more clearly, but still quietly, almost tentatively.
2:40		The drums' "dry" sound—with resonating heads removed—add to the overall sense of dynamic restraint. Without the resonant echo, the drum's "bigness" becomes ambiguous.
3:25	THIRD CHORUS	Saxophone plays clearest statement of the melody yet, slightly louder and more assertively. The piano chords return, but this time opening a new section, based on a new bass vamp.
4:08	FUNK INTERLUDE	The group plays louder and punchier.
4:17		Ramping up the energy, the sax offers improvisational commentary on the repeated "electric guitar" melody fragment.
4:37	CODA	The climax being reached, the bass-drums-clavinet groove returns.
5:00		As the groove continues, it is joined by the *hindewhu* layers, the full complement now heard as an interactive complex.
5:26	ECHO-DRENCHED FADE OUT	As the *hindewhu* tracks build, the echo becomes more pronounced. The sound gradually becomes indistinct and fades out.

History & Culture

The Soul-Funk Connection

In addition to the jazz figures who explored R&B, soul, and funk, several key artists whose careers are more closely associated with R&B have incorporated jazz into their work, further demonstrating the permeable borders between jazz and black popular music. Here are a few prominent examples:

- James Brown remains the single most important figure in the development of funk, and he holds a seminal position in rhythm and blues of the 1950s and soul of the 1960s. In his memoir, Brown relates that he fundamentally saw his roots as being in jazz, not the urban blues of B. B. King and others.
- Maurice White gained journeyman experience as a session drummer behind jazz saxophonist Sonny Stitt and jazz pianist Ramsey Lewis prior to forming the funk-pop supergroup Earth, Wind & Fire.
- Robert "Kool" Bell and his brother Ronald (later known as Khalis Bayyan) grew up in

a jazz-loving household and formed the Jazziacs. In the 1970s, they emerged as the R&B/funk/disco powerhouse Kool and the Gang.
- Producer-songwriter Quincy Jones's career has crossed many genres. He has produced some of the most significant recordings in black popular music (including Michael Jackson's landmark *Thriller*, 1982, the best-selling album of all time) and has collected an astounding 27 Grammy awards as of this writing. His early career included stints with Lionel Hampton and Dizzy Gillespie, and he has frequently returned to his jazz roots.

As funk and R&B records gained extensive play in dance clubs in the 1970s, spawning the disco phenomenon, certain fusion recordings found their way onto deejays' turntables. Brazilian keyboardist Eumir Deodato's 1972 adaptation of *Also Sprach Zarathustra* (the Richard Strauss orchestral prelude included in the soundtrack for the Stanley Kubrick film *2001: A Space Odyssey*),

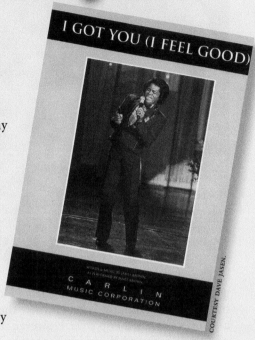

I GOT YOU (I FEEL GOOD)

CARLIN MUSIC CORPORATION

COURTESY DAVE JASEN.

Herbie Hancock's *Chameleon* (1973), guitarist George Benson's *Breezin'* (1976), and flugelhorn player Chuck Mangione's *Feels So Good* (1977) became widespread disco favorites. So popular did these recordings become on the disco circuit that, to critics, the artists' jazz credibility suffered.

—*Steven F. Pond*

Miles Davis Quintet substituting Freddie Hubbard (and later Wynton Marsalis) on trumpet, a move that gained critical approval. His forays into funk and **hip hop** had jazz traditionalists gnashing their teeth, but Hancock went on to silence this criticism with masterful acoustic jazz recordings such as *Gershwin's World* (1998) and *River* (2007), a collection of **Joni Mitchell**'s songs.

---

clavinet an electronic keyboard with a distinctive staccato, guitar-like sound; used notably for the main riff in Stevie Wonder's 1972 hit *Superstition*.

hip hop a largely African American popular music characterized by talk-sung rhymes over funk-derived beats.

TAKE NOTE

- What were some of the key fusion bands of the early 1970s, and how did their styles differ?

R&B Fusion

By now it should be clear that fusion artists looked beyond rock music for influence. Another important, if underreported, strain stemmed from rhythm and blues and its derivatives: soul, Motown, and funk. Just as important, this fusion style owed much to the "soul jazz" and other hard bop jazz styles of a decade or so before. The Jazz Crusaders (dropping the "Jazz" from their name in 1971) are an example of this trend. The

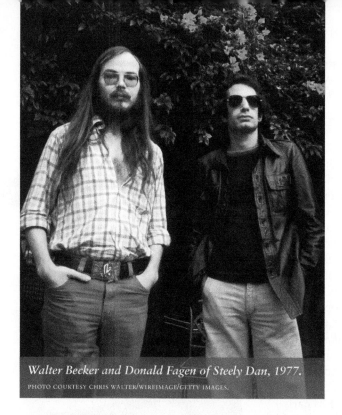

Walter Becker and Donald Fagen of Steely Dan, 1977.
PHOTO COURTESY CHRIS WALTER/WIREIMAGE/GETTY IMAGES.

group's members were originally from Houston, Texas, but then settled in Los Angeles, where they played in a mainstream hard bop style. However, the addition of electric bass and electric guitar marked a shift in a funkier direction. Their signature sound stemmed from a simple variation on the standard bebop procedure of trumpet and alto saxophone playing the "head" melody in unison: now the unison melody was carried by the tenor saxophone and trombone, with the funky rhythm section boiling underneath. Along with a group of other local musicians—including saxophonist Tom Scott, post-bebop alto saxophonist Phil Woods, and drummers Harvey Mason (based in Los Angeles) and Steve Gadd (based in New York)—they formed a critical mass of "first call" recording session players who turned up on each others' albums as well as on rock and R&B recordings. For example, they formed the musical core for the rock band Steely Dan's mid-1970s albums *Katy Lied* (1975, featuring Woods, and members of **the Crusaders**), and *Aja* (1977, with Woods, the Crusaders, and Wayne Shorter). Jazz musicians have long been favored as sidemen for pop music recording sessions, and now this coterie of fusion jazz players found themselves in high demand.

The R&B and funk flavors of fusion maintained an audience, and the musicians to entertain them, on into the next decades. Bassists proved especially able frontmen in this realm—due in part to their technical proficiency inspired by the likes of Jaco Pastorius and their use of the overtly rhythmic **slap-bass** technique pioneered by Larry Graham of Sly and the Family Stone, Marcus Miller (sideman to many, including Miles Davis), and other bassists. Miller, Stanley Clarke

(of Return to Forever), Alphonso Johnson (of Weather Report), and Gordon Edwards (myriad pop, funk, soul, and Latin sessions) all spearheaded either solo careers or notable group efforts. Guitarists, too, gravitated toward funk-laden fusion. Blues-based 1960s guitar "hero" Jeff Beck embraced the kind of popping, stop-on-a-dime rhythmic precision heard on Stevie Wonder's hit *Superstition*—among other sounds—for his own electric, and electrifying, brand of fusion. Los Angeles session guitarist Larry Carlton fronted his own albums of astoundingly fluid and melodically inventive soloing over tightly rendered pop-funk rhythm, for decade after decade. The northern California blues player Robben Ford, who replaced him in the Crusaders and in singer Joni Mitchell's backup band, also expanded into fusion (backed by Los Angeles session players the Yellowjackets) before delving back into his trademark state-of-the-art electric blues (with a jazz edge).

Of the bands that purveyed R&B-jazz into the 1980s, 1990s, and 2000s, Pieces of a Dream—essentially a rhythm section (drums, bass, and keyboard) supplemented by assorted instrumentalists and sometimes vocalists—proved prolific. Also popular were saxophone-led Spyro Gyra, the keyboard-based Jeff Lorber Fusion, and, through the 1980s, the Brecker Brothers.

Polishing and Popularizing Fusion

The idea of building a "stable" of key session musicians held appeal for record labels. Producer Creed Taylor, a key figure in the important 1960s jazz labels Impulse! and Verve (with credits including the classic *The Girl from Ipanema*, 1963 [CD II, Track 10/Download Track 34]) founded his own CTI label (Creed Taylor International). With CTI, Taylor built a label identity showcasing top jazz performers with accessible "easy-listening" arrangements, high-quality sound production, glossy album art, and a core group of "first call" session players, who frequently appeared on each other's albums. Prominent among these were tenor saxophonist Grover Washington, Jr., alto saxophonist David Sanborn, keyboardist-arranger-composer Bob James, and guitarist-singer George Benson. Likewise, GRP Records—the brainchild of composer-keyboardist Dave Grusin and producer Larry Rosen—built its own sound, frequently using studio professionals to back up featured artists.

At the same time, the Crusaders and others maintained their independence, preferring to work as independent contractors. Nevertheless, they and their

---

slap bass   an acoustic bass technique made by pulling and releasing the strings sharply against the fingerboard, producing loud snapping, popping sounds; on the electric bass produced by slapping the thumb down on a lower string and plucking a higher string with the fore- and middle fingers.

Jazz versus Fusion

Was fusion music the "path of the sell-out" or an invigorating new direction for jazz?

From the start, critics, historians, and musicians have fiercely debated in print over fusion's place in jazz, indeed whether it can be considered jazz at all. Assessing the state of jazz on the first day of the 1980s, journalist-producer Leonard Feather wondered publicly if "slickly packaged fusion sounds" topping the charts could be considered jazz. "Virtually every jazz critic the world over would answer all three questions in a resounding negative." Historian Grover Sales exemplified the contempt that an outspoken purist faction held for fusion. In his 1984 book *Jazz: America's Classical Music*, Sales sniffed, "Some bored rock artists had been gravitating toward jazz, while some jazz players dallied with rock to recapture their dwindling audience."

In the 1990s, the critique turned venomous. Peter Watrous, assessing Wayne Shorter's career, commented in 1995, "Like his peers who inhabit jazz's loftier realms—Herbie Hancock, Ornette Coleman, Sonny Rollins—[Shorter] has spent the last quarter century flashing bits of his grand talent, then finding the nearest drain down which to dump the rest." Watrous laid the blame at the feet of Miles Davis, calling Shorter's artistic slide evidence of the "Miles Davis Curse." To Watrous, Davis's former

sidemen pursued fame at the expense of their art. Critic Stanley Crouch, in an assessment titled "Play the Right Thing," amplified the venomous characterization of Miles Davis's turn to fusion as "rapaciously commercial."

Davis never tried to justify his artistic decisions to his audience or his critics. Nonetheless, he did argue that his 1980s and 1990s recordings—which showed funk, R&B, and hip hop influences—were his attempt to reach a contemporary audience for artistic as well as commercial reasons. Davis noted that this was the music of the young, urban audience, and he wanted his music to be equally relevant to them as these popular forms. Through his entire career, he had repudiated the idea of "jazz" representing a static style that had to be preserved for future generations, but rather was a style to be explored and expanded as musical times changed.

Another response to such a toxic critical atmosphere has been to play up fusion's connections to jazz's history of high-art aspirations. Stuart Nicholson, whose *Jazz-Rock: A History*, is one of the few large-scale studies of this music, proposed *two* separate jazz subgenres. After complaining that "people doing the defining wanted jazz to be what it used to be, not what it is," he went on to distinguish jazz-rock from fusion "and its latter-day equivalents, variously marketed as smooth jazz, quiet storm, lite-jazz, hot tub jazz, or yuppie jazz." Guitarist Pat Metheny

famously raged, on a blog post, over smooth-jazz saxophonist Kenny G's temerity in deciding to overdub himself onto Louis Armstrong's vocal recording of *What a Wonderful World.* Metheny wrote, "Kenny G has created a new low point in modern culture—something that we all should be totally embarrassed about—and afraid of."

Despite these controversies, fusion musicians have continued to follow their tastes. Herbie Hancock, Chick Corea, Pat Metheny, John McLaughlin, and many others have played a variety of musics—from bebop to fusion, to avant-garde, to funk, to flamenco—as the spirit moves them and as opportunities present themselves. Herbie Hancock, when asked if his 1976 reunion concert with V.S.O.P. (the Miles Davis Quintet with Freddie Hubbard substituting for Davis), was a repudiation of fusion jazz, commented, "Not at all. I mean, neither was doing the *Head Hunters* thing a move away from doing acoustic stuff." He continued, "I think that our society kind of supports the idea that you can only do one thing, and the fact of the matter is human beings can do many things. But in most cases we never get to find that out. Because if we find one thing that we can do, we have a tendency to rest on our laurels and enter a holding pattern there, because it's safe."

—*Steven F. Pond*

label-bound counterparts established such powerfully consistent "sounds" that the labels eventually suffered from a certain generic quality, ultimately to their artistic cost. By the late 1970s and early 1980s their aggregate sound was fostering a new, smooth, "quiet storm" or "smooth jazz" style that critics lamented as

no longer jazz even as it proved the most commercially successful "jazz" style.

So successful was smooth jazz that 30 years later it still thrived. From its first minting through its worldwide circulation in the twenty-first century, smooth jazz soothed audiences—and sometimes infuriated jazz purists who deemed it safe and simplistic—in a range of flavors. Some of them included the R&B tinge of the group Pieces of a Dream and their stylistic kin. Saxophonist David Sanborn plied a distinctive and highly polished update of the early rough-hewn R&B sax style of King Curtis (also audible in the sound of Bruce Springsteen's sax player Clarence Clemons) to great success. Soprano saxophonist Kenny G (born Kenneth Gorelick), while playing a decidedly smoother sax style in mellower musical settings than Sanborn, nevertheless shared some stylistic traits, including a distinctive "cry" gesture, often at the ends of phrases. Kenny G's pop-oriented style yielded album sales in the millions, dwarfing the yield of the typical jazz recording and prompting heated criticism from jazz purists. One of G's highest-profile critics, guitarist Pat Metheny, has himself issued sounds described by some as smooth jazz, while Los Angeles session guitarist Lee Ritenour (sometimes with his group Fourplay) comfortably rode the smooth jazz airwaves through most of his career. Not jazz per se, the vocalist Sade and her group nonetheless demonstrated the kind of commercial success attainable by jazz-influenced players when focused on simplicity, groove, color, and mood.

dyad two notes.

Listening Guide

CD II, Track 7/Download Track 31

BRIGHT SIZE LIFE • PAT METHENY

Music: Pat Metheny, 1975. Personnel: Pat Metheny (electric guitar); Jaco Pastorius (fretless electric bass); Bob Moses (drums). Recorded December, 1975, in Ludwigsburg, Federal Republic of Germany. First issue: *Bright Size Life*, ECM 1073. Timing: 4:43.

Overview

This recording captures ascending talents, and points the way toward later stellar developments. At the time of this recording, Metheny was making a name for himself as a guitar prodigy. Enrolling and then teaching at Boston's Berklee School of Music, he had found himself in the Gary Burton Quartet—all before his 20th birthday. Metheny was already developing his signature sound—a dark, midrange-heavy tone, with a pronounced delay effect (he now uses two digital delay devices), and very little distortion. The resulting sound was somewhat like guitarist Wes Montgomery's, but slightly smoothed over and glossy. The trio of Metheny, Pastorius, and Moses had been gigging around Boston when they made this recording in the German studio of Manfred Eicher. Eicher, whose ECM label was already setting a standard for high recording quality because of his fanaticism for clean, clear sound, was intensely selective about the artists he would record. Eicher's endorsement added luster to Metheny's fledgling reputation; this recording helped propel Metheny (and Pastorius) into jazz's top ranks.

Pastorius reveals the stunning skills that would soon cause electric bass players everywhere to re-learn their art, much the same effect Jimi Hendrix had had on electric guitar players nearly a decade before. Pastorius displays the penchant for countermelody, lightning runs, and bold use of chords—especially **dyads**, two-note chords that he plays in a bending gesture (called "bent dyad" in the chart). Added to these, he favors harmonic overtones (lightly touching the string to produce a higher, ringing note; for example, Pastorius's second note is a dyad of overtones), and other techniques that caused jaws to drop.

Moses's prodding drum style feeds rhythmic ideas throughout, in this three-way conversation. Even so, Moses has lamented that this recording does not capture the group's live sound.

Key Features

- The form is AABA, and it follows the bebop tradition of head melody/solo choruses/out-chorus. The rising, sawtooth-shaped melody is used as an organizing element.
- The rhythm, especially the drum pattern, suggests either a funk or an Afro-Caribbean angularity (a "Latin feel") without referencing a specific tradition. Moses consistently heads for a funky feel in each bridge (the B section of the AABA form). However, the high, resonant tuning of his drums and his cymbal-laden playing style underscore the trio's jazz sound. (Compare Moses's sound to Harvey Mason's tuning and playing style on Herbie Hancock's *Watermelon Man*.) Metheny would later live for a while in Brazil, soaking up Afro-Brazilian traditional and popular music idioms.
- Metheny's soloing style foregrounds clean, clear groups of notes, sometimes with subtle bends. This sometimes lends a "folk" sensibility, although he does not reference any folk song material directly. At the same time, his solo gestures derive from the single-note lines of earlier jazz guitarists Charlie Christian, Wes Montgomery, and Tal Farlow, whom he cites as influences.
- Pastorius, in the perceptive words of Stuart Nicholson, "regarded the electric bass as an electronic instrument rather than an amplified acoustic one, in the way Jimi Hendrix revolutionized the electric guitar."

—Steven F. Pond

- How did fusion jazz become more commercial by fusing with R&B music?

Later Fusions

Guitarist Pat Metheny is one artist who garnered both acclaim and raised eyebrows in the 1970s and 1980s. A onetime teenaged prodigy, Metheny, with his principal collaborator, keyboardist Lyle Mays, combined formidable technique and harmonic sophistication with a smoothed-out, gentle guitar sound and a penchant for nostalgic images of Americana in his playing and album art (for example, *American Garage*, 1979, issued 1980). Metheny was influenced by a variety of sources, blending elements of folk, rock, bossa nova, and other samba-based Brazilian music with avant-gardist elements from his jazz heroes, Ornette Coleman and John Coltrane. Among his innovations, Metheny experimented extensively with alternate guitar tunings—and

sixteenth note a note value representing one-sixteenth the duration of a whole note; notated as ♪.

TIME	SECTION	MELODY
0:00	FIRST CHORUS (HEAD MELODY): A	The sawtooth-shaped melody makes its first appearance. Bass and drums play sparingly, giving the guitar the first moment in the sun.
0:12	A	Second A of AABA form.
0:26	B (BRIDGE)	Drummer Moses turns to funky texture, which he will vary at each subsequent bridge.
0:36	A	The return of the sawtooth melody is the final A of the AABA form.
0:48	SECOND CHORUS	Guitar solo: Metheny starts his solo with a rising sequential figure. Once he arrives in a satisfying hand position, he will hover there.
1:10		Pastorius's figures become busier, and his tone becomes sharper.
1:17		Listen for Pastorius's bent dyad, one of his signature figures.
1:25		Moses's drumming gathers in density; Metheny's figures glide over the denser texture of bass and drums.
1:33	THIRD CHORUS	Metheny continues his solo.
1:35		Metheny's approach to the solo is to alternate double-time, sequential figures with sparser moments, as if to catch his breath.
1:56	BRIDGE	Metheny reinforces Moses's samba-based, funky drum pattern.
2:07		Metheny finishes the solo with sparse, high ringing notes.
2:18	FOURTH CHORUS	Pastorius solo: Pastorius's approach is almost entirely melodic. He plays a start-and-stop melody in a high register, allowing the tone to linger.
2:41	BRIDGE	Waiting for Moses's funk theme to get established, Pastorius then plays ascending double-time figures. His tone becomes more brittle.
2:55		Pastorius finishes the form with a cross-rhythm gesture, diving to the lowest reaches of the instrument. The solo's narrative arc is high-to-low and sparse-to-dense-to-moderately dense, letting both the high notes at the beginning and the low notes at the end resonate and recede.
3:04	FIFTH CHORUS	Pastorius continues his solo, reprising the cross-rhythms of before, abruptly shifting to an ascending figure of grouped **sixteenth notes**—a deceptively simple harmonic gesture difficult to execute.
3:15		Pastorius combines several techniques almost simultaneously: a spacious melodic line, interspersed with flashes of dense sixteenth notes, and a harmonic overtone for color.
3:26	BRIDGE	Pastorius uses the bent dyad repeatedly, working it as a solo idea, as opposed to a momentary accompaniment gesture.
3:40		Moses's playing is its most active, foregrounding cymbals and angular drum accents, helping build a sense of impending climax.
3:49	OUT CHORUS	The drums quiet down, as the sawtooth gesture, played in octaves by Metheny and Pastorius, signals that this will be the culminating chorus.
4:35	ENDING	As if reining in a galloping horse, the action suddenly slows and dies out in a satisfying major chord.

with alternate guitars. He commissioned, for example, a three-necked, 42-stringed guitar instrument from Canadian luthier Linda Mazur (*Quartet*, 1996). By 2010, he was exploring more new territory, as he toured and recorded playing an orchestrion—a giant set-up of mechanically triggered acoustic and acousto-electric instruments (*Orchestrion*, 2010).

Singer-songwriter Joni Mitchell, one of the leading voices in rock music's post-Beatles creative surge of the 1970s, brought many jazz fusion musicians into her stage and recording projects during the 1970s and 1980s. Her albums traced a trajectory of ever-deeper commitment to jazz exploration, yet she never abandoned the poetic voice that had made her a star in the folk-rock mold. Rather, the contemplative interiority in each of the two idioms clearly appealed to her. Her final album of the 1970s was a collaboration with jazz bassist Charles Mingus as he was fighting a losing battle against Lou Gehrig's disease (amyotrophic lateral sclerosis). The album, *Mingus* (1979), included Herbie Hancock and members of Weather Report, prominently featuring Jaco Pastorius on electric bass. Although Mingus supplied six new melodies for the album, and Mitchell re-worked his tribute to Lester Young, *Goodbye, Pork Pie Hat*, Mitchell and the other musicians resisted the temptation to produce a "Mingus" sound. Mitchell's lyrics achieve sophisticated word painting. Describing an encounter with a Las Vegas tourist who's impossibly lucky (*Dry Cleaner from Des Moines*), Mitchell (as Mingus) marvels, "He got three oranges/Three lemons/Three cherries/Three plums/I'm losing my taste for fruit/Watching the dry cleaner do it/Like Midas in a polyester suit." Elsewhere (*A Chair in the Sky*), she becomes Mingus floating into and out of consciousness, peering out from his Manhattan hospital room window "the rain slammed hard as bars" and trapped by dual ravages of disease and medication: "Daydreamin' drugs the pain of living/Processions of missing/Lovers and friends/Fade in and they fade out again/In these daydreams of rebirth." Throughout the album, Mitchell extends her penchant for inventive guitar tunings, resulting in fresh, quirky harmonies. Pastorius and Wayne Shorter (soprano saxophone) weave a *pas-de-deux*, with short bursts of melodic saxophone commentary amid Pastorius's characteristically angular, everywhere-at-once bass playing.

> **TAKE NOTE**
>
> • How has fusion continued to develop and who are some current performers?

Conclusion

Fusion, as an approach to playing jazz, has continued. In 1985, Miles Davis, with bassist-producer Marcus Miller, created the R&B-laced *Tutu*. Likewise, Herbie Hancock has regularly confounded jazz purists (and purists of other varieties generally), breezily traversing from techno-funk (*Future Shock*, 1983) to the inclusion of hip hop (*Dis Is da Drum*, 1995) and to *Gershwin's World* (1998)—the latter ranging from post-bebop jazz juxtaposed with African and Afro-Caribbean drumming, to an orchestral arrangement of Gershwin's *Lullaby*, to a piano concerto movement by Maurice Ravel, to a stride piano cutting-contest piece performed as a duo with Chick Corea.

Pat Metheny in 1984. PHOTO COURTESY HULTON ARCHIVE/GETTY IMAGES.

sampling (1) the use of a "sampled" section or piece of a preexisting recording in a new recording; (2) digitally recording a singer, instrument, or other sound to use as a "voice" in a synthesizer.

freestyle the improvisational style of hip hop.

MC; MCing rapper; rapping.

acid jazz a style of jazz fusion combining elements of jazz, funk, and hip hop, especially looped beat samples from earlier jazz.

History & Culture

Hip Hop and Jazz

The connections between hip hop and jazz are deeper and more integral than many are aware. The instrumentation and approaches of the two styles may seem totally different, yet hip hop can be seen as a generational extension of jazz, the two styles have idiomatic similarities, and both are part of the continuum of African American musical conception.

There are three key areas where jazz and hip hop overlap: sampling and quotation, rhythmic displacement; and improvisation.

Sampling: Just as jazz musicians borrow or **sample** melodies and quotations from other songs in their solos, hip hop artists also sample melodies and snippets from songs. The main difference is that hip hop artists sample the actual recording of the song, enabled by sampling technology. It is similar to the visual art technique of "pastiche."

Rhythmic displacement: This is used in hip hop as it is used in jazz. The swing feel of jazz musicians is a characteristic of playing "behind the beat." Musicians lay back while playing a musical line to create a bouncing pulse in the music. Hip hop artists use the same technique to create rhythmic interest in their music. They play "behind the beat" in their vocal delivery or in the track to give an underlying bounce to the rhythm. The main difference between hip hop and jazz in this area is that jazz emphasizes beats two and four where hip hop emphasizes "the one."

Improvisation: The improvisational form of hip hop is known as **freestyle**. The art of **MCing** actually began with freestyling but became a written form early in its development. Rhyming from the "top of the dome" (head) is the hallmark of freestyling and is very similar to improvising jazz in approach and

method. Phrases and ideas are woven together spontaneously over a rhythm and MCs seek to create a meaningful statement.

Their histories are similar as well. Many critics of jazz over the decades wrote off the new movements in the music, as in the case of bebop and free jazz. Critics of hip hop have also been unfavorable to the art form and have underestimated the influence and importance of hip hop's artistic impact.

Fusions of hip hop with jazz have produced intriguing results, bringing jazz textures and recognizable "quotes" to hip hop's sonic collages. An **acid jazz** movement of the 1980s grew from nightclub deejays sampling hard bop grooves; by the 1990s some hip hop groups were sampling jazz snippets. In 1993 the jazz-rap group US3 found popular success with the track *Cantaloop (Trip Fantasia)*, which sampled Herbie Hancock music. The group A Tribe Called Quest sampled Cannonball Adderley, Roy Ayers, and Les McCann for their 1990 album *People's Instinctive Travels and the Paths of Rhythm*. Digable Planets' 1993 hit *Rebirth of Slick (Cool Like Dat)* sampled both Art Blakey and the Jazz Messengers and soul singer James Brown's backup band. Guru, of the hip hop duo Gang Starr, went further by employing a live jazz band rather than jazz samples, especially on his albums *Jazzmatazz Vol. 1–4* (1993–1997). Other notable hip hop integrators of jazz included the Roots and De La Soul.

Jazz musicians have turned to hip hop for ways to extend their creativity—and, in some cases, audiences. Miles Davis's final studio

Hip hop/jazz fusion group the Roots in concert. PHOTO COURTESY MICHAEL JACKSON.

album, *Doo-Bop* (1991), was a jazz-rap project. Saxophonists Greg Osby and Branford Marsalis released albums that incorporated rap elements (Marsalis's 1994 disc *Buckshot LeFonque* featured producer DJ Premier on turntables, beats, and drum programming). M-Base founder Steve Coleman drew on hip hop (among other sounds) for a number of albums in the 1990s.

More recently, pianist Jason Moran achieved interesting results recording a piano version of *Planet Rock* (2002), achieving melodic atonality by copying the rap-vocal cadences on the original tune recorded by Afrika Bambaataa in 1982.

Trumpeter Roy Hargrove sought to merge elements of hip hop (and soul and R&B) with bop in albums with his collective RH Factor (*Hard Groove*, 2003, and *Distractions*, 2006), while in *Def Jazz* (2005), he rendered smooth jazz versions of hit tracks from the hip hop record label Def Jam. Pianist Robert Glasper maintained parallel involvements in hip hop and jazz and showcased both in his 2009 album *Double Booked*.

His ability to achieve a ruminative jazz expressiveness against a tight funk drumbeat can be heard in the track *Downtime* (2009).

—*William E. Smith and Tad Lathrop*

In the meantime, a younger generation of performers, eclectic in their musical backgrounds and catholic in their interests, have extended fusion's tendency toward hyphenation: acid jazz (Digable Planets, US3), jazz-house (Jamiroquoi, St. Germain), jazz-rap (the Roots, Black Science Orchestra), newgrass (Bèla Fleck and the Flecktones, Nickel Creek), free-funk (Ornette Coleman's Prime Time), M-Base (Steve Coleman, Greg Osby, Cassandra Wilson), and many more styles claim jazz parentage and listenership.

Fusion jazz experienced a heyday from the mid-1960s to the mid-1980s, but to bracket that time as "the fusion years" would be as much a disservice to a historical understanding as it would be to describe the 1940s as "the bebop years," as if that music hasn't continued to the present day. Fusing—hybridizing—has been a feature of jazz since day one; "the fusion years" merely refers to a time of increased attention to this hybridization. Fusion responds to musicians' exposure to, and investment in, a widening variety of musical influences. Beyond this, fusion, like jazz generally, responds to developments in audience demographics, music technology, the music industry, and political life. All of these factors continue to change and evolve, and fusion jazz continues to reflect these changes. From the moment it began to be called *fusion* jazz, critics disparaged the music as a kind of anti-jazz. Rather, fusion continues a line of engagement with popular and other music styles that has characterized jazz since the beginning.

 Explore Jazz Classics and Key Recordings on **mymusiclab.com**

TAKE NOTE

- **What is fusion jazz and how does it compare to other jazz styles?**

Fusion jazz attempts to extend jazz's traditional aesthetics of adventure and improvisation, using elements borrowed from a range of other music styles. One of the main sources of inspiration was the popularity of rock music, particularly rock rhythms and electronic instrumentation.

- **What were some of the early forms of fusion jazz?**

Precursors of fusion included western swing and jump blues from the 1940s and 1950s, and experimenting rock musicians from the Beatles, Jimi Hendrix, and Cream to Blood, Sweat and Tears. Miles Davis's experiments with electronic instrumentation, inspired by rock musicians such as guitarist Jimi Hendrix, yielded two important albums in 1969 and 1970: *In a Silent Way* and *Bitches Brew.*

- **What were some of the key fusion bands of the early 1970s, and how did their styles differ?**

Weather Report emphasized grooves, layers of timbre, and funk or Afro-Brazilian percussion; pianist Chick Corea's Return to Forever purveyed dense, aggressive rock; pianist Herbie Hancock's Headhunters favored funk; drummer Tony Williams's Lifetime pursued rock and avant-gardist experimentation; and guitarist John McLaughlin's Mahavishnu Orchestra combined rock energy with modalism, impossibly fast runs and challenging, odd meters.

- **How did fusion jazz become more commercial by fusing with R&B music?**

The Jazz Crusaders and a group of widely recorded session players developed a funkier, R&B-inflected approach to jazz that grew in popularity through the many hit records that these musicians played on. Players of R&B-jazz into the 1980s, 1990s, and 2000s included Pieces of a Dream, Spyro Gyra, Jeff Lorber Fusion, and, through the 1980s, the Brecker Brothers.

- **How has fusion continued to develop and who are some current performers?**

Smooth jazz—a brand of rhythm and blues fusion featuring a light funk rhythm combined with blues- and soul-styled soloing—achieved popularity during the late 1970s and early 1980s. Guitarist Pat Metheny is among the most successful of the more recent fusion artists. Other blends of jazz and popular music included hip hop/jazz fusions, notably acid jazz.

DISCUSSION QUESTIONS

1. Identify some of the forces and impulses—aesthetic, social, economic—that may have attracted jazz musicians to rock ideas in the 1960s and 1970s.

2. Do you think rock musicians were as attracted to jazz music? Why or why not?

3. Think back through the history of rock—jump blues, rockabilly, rock and roll, Beatles pop, British blues, Jimi Hendrix, guitar heroes, psychedelic rock, progressive rock in the 1970s, punk rock, heavy metal, jam bands, electronica, noise pop—and identify points of convergence with jazz. Which movements and musicians have had elements of jazz? And what were those elements?

4. How would you explain the differences between rock, jazz, and classical music to someone with very little knowledge about them?

5. Discuss the impact of Miles Davis on jazz-rock fusion. Then discuss Davis's impact throughout the history of jazz.

6. What were the key differences between the fusion bands Weather Report, Mahavishnu Orchestra, and Return to Forever?

7. Make an argument for the legitimacy of fusion music as a form of jazz. How would you answer critics' claims that fusion is simply an attempt to "cash in" on the pop charts?

KEY TERMS & KEY PEOPLE

acid jazz	groove	Jaco Pastorius
bossa nova	Herbie Hancock	progressive rock (prog rock)
Gary Burton	Headhunters	psychedelic rock
clavinet	Jimi Hendrix	Return to Forever
Chick Corea	hip hop	sampling
Larry Coryell	jump blues	session player
The Crusaders	Lifetime	sideman
Cubop	Mahavishnu Orchestra	slap bass
Miles Davis	mambo	synthesizer
Al Di Meola	MC; MCing	vamp
flamenco	John McLaughlin	Weather Report
freestyle	Pat Metheny	Tony Williams
funk	Joni Mitchell	Josef (Joe) Zawinul
fusion jazz	modal jazz	

Latin Jazz

From Chapter 10 of *Discover Jazz*. First Edition. John Edward Hasse, Tad Lathrop. Copyright © 2012 by Pearson Education, Inc. All rights reserved.

Latin Jazz

by Isabelle Leymarie, Tad Lathrop, and John Edward Hasse

TAKE NOTE

- How did Afro-Cuban and Brazilian jazz draw on similar musical roots to create different musical styles?
- What native Cuban and Brazilian musical rhythms and musical instruments have influenced the development of Latin jazz?
- How did Latin music influence early jazz?
- Who were the key Cuban and Puerto Rican musicians in jazz history?
- What was the influence of Brazilian music on jazz?
- What other Caribbean music styles have had an influence on jazz?
- What are some more recent trends in Caribbean and Latin jazz?

HISTORICAL EVENTS

MUSICAL EVENTS

1898

The Spanish-American War results in the United States gaining control over Cuba and indefinite colonial authority over Puerto Rico, Guam, and the Philippines

PHOTO COURTESY DEPARTMENT OF DEFENSE.

1902

Cuba gains its independence from the United States

Mexican Revolution led by a variety of forces, including followers of Pancho Villa and Emiliano Zapata, leads to a period of turmoil, ending in 1917 with the adoption of a new Constitution

1910–17

PHOTO COURTESY GEORGE GRANTHAM BAIN COLLECTION/LIBRARY OF CONGRESS.

1914

United States opens the Panama Canal, connecting the Atlantic and Pacific oceans

Cuban habanera rhythm heard in W. C. Handy's hit *St. Louis Blues*

• The *maxixe* and tango dance crazes sweep the United States, thanks to such performers as Vernon and Irene Castle

1915

• U.S. Marines enter Haiti and remain there until 1934

1917

Puerto Ricans are granted U.S. citizenship, and begin to settle in New York City, bringing their music with them

1927

Cuban flutist Alberto Socarrás records *Shootin' the Pistol*, one of the first Latin jazz recordings

Rumba craze sweeps the United States

1930

A coup in Cuba puts the army in control under General Batista, who rules Cuba on and off over the next decades, until he is deposed in the Cuban Revolution of 1959

1933

1936

Duke Ellington's *Caravan* features Puerto Rican-born trombonist Juan Tizol

1940

Trumpeter and saxophonist Mario Bauzá and singer and maracas player Machito found the Afro-Cubans, the first major Latin jazz ensemble

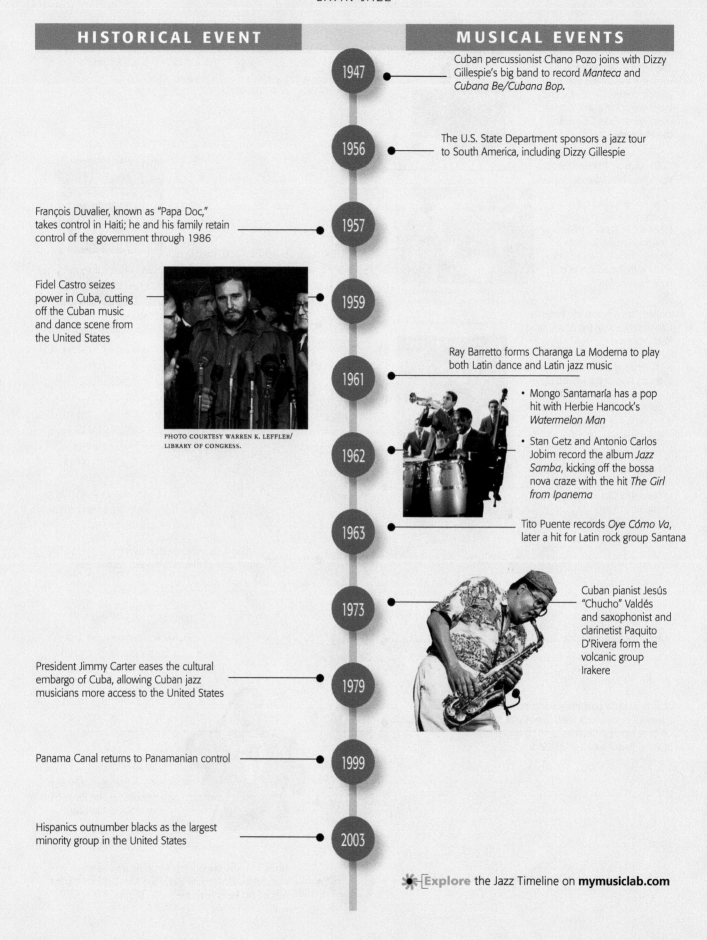

HISTORICAL EVENT		MUSICAL EVENTS
	1947	Cuban percussionist Chano Pozo joins with Dizzy Gillespie's big band to record *Manteca* and *Cubana Be/Cubana Bop.*
	1956	The U.S. State Department sponsors a jazz tour to South America, including Dizzy Gillespie
François Duvalier, known as "Papa Doc," takes control in Haiti; he and his family retain control of the government through 1986	**1957**	
Fidel Castro seizes power in Cuba, cutting off the Cuban music and dance scene from the United States	**1959**	
	1961	Ray Barretto forms Charanga La Moderna to play both Latin dance and Latin jazz music
	1962	• Mongo Santamaría has a pop hit with Herbie Hancock's *Watermelon Man* • Stan Getz and Antonio Carlos Jobim record the album *Jazz Samba*, kicking off the bossa nova craze with the hit *The Girl from Ipanema*
	1963	Tito Puente records *Oye Cómo Va*, later a hit for Latin rock group Santana
	1973	Cuban pianist Jesús "Chucho" Valdés and saxophonist and clarinetist Paquito D'Rivera form the volcanic group Irakere
President Jimmy Carter eases the cultural embargo of Cuba, allowing Cuban jazz musicians more access to the United States	**1979**	
Panama Canal returns to Panamanian control	**1999**	
Hispanics outnumber blacks as the largest minority group in the United States	**2003**	

PHOTO COURTESY WARREN K. LEFFLER/ LIBRARY OF CONGRESS.

✳ Explore the Jazz Timeline on **mymusiclab.com**

azz's richness can be attributed in part to its ability to assimilate and develop the most diverse musical influences. Eastern European folk melody, Indonesian gamelan, and Japanese scales are just a few of the sounds that over time have expanded the stylistic bounds of jazz. But no foreign influences on jazz have been more significant and pervasive than Latin American and Caribbean music. A key reason is that jazz and Latin and Caribbean music share African and European sources and are thus inherently compatible. The mixture of jazz and Latin music is, as Cuban singer and bandleader Machito aptly put it, "a marriage made in heaven." Latin jazz brings together the harmonic sophistication, instrumentation, and improvisational techniques of jazz with the complex polyrhythms and the percussion of Latin America and the Caribbean.

There is no single sound called Latin jazz. Rather, several different strains of Latin American and Caribbean music have seeped into the jazz playbook. These strains have brought jazz many intriguing "Latin" alternatives to jazz's standard instrumentation and swing rhythm.

Cuban jazz musician Paquito D'Rivera performing in 1991. PHOTO COURTESY DAVID REDFERN/REDFERNS/GETTY IMAGES.

One vital Latin-Caribbean strain (which has numerous variations) is Afro-Cuban. Characteristics such as syncopated bass lines and complex rhythms played on congas, bongos, *timbales*, *claves*, and maracas have marked Afro-Cuban styles as exciting settings for jazz improvisation, as evidenced in **Dizzy Gillespie**'s *Manteca* (CD II, Track 9/Download Track 33) and perhaps more familiarly in the recent popular music of guitarist Carlos Santana.

Another prominent Latin American influence is Brazilian. As rhythmically syncopated as Afro-Cuban, Brazilian jazz differs in some fundamental ways, especially in the **bossa nova** style, exemplified by **Antonio Carlos Jobim**'s *The Girl from Ipanema* (CD II, Track 10/Download Track 34). While Afro-Cuban is often extroverted, flashy, and "hot," Brazilian music can be soft, "cool," and bubbling with light syncopation, or it can be propulsive and densely textured as in the high-energy

---

bossa nova Portuguese for "new tendency"; a syncopated, sensuous musical style refined from the samba and introduced in the late 1950s in Rio de Janeiro, Brazil.

135

samba *baterias* (percussion groups) led by giant pounding *surdo* drums overlaid with intricately interlocking *agogôs* (bells), shakers, and other percussion.

Common Sources, Different Sounds

Afro-Cuban and Brazilian jazz have both similarities and differences. The similarity accounts for the ease with which Latin music blended with jazz: essential

---

samba (Portuguese, derived from the Bantu *"semba,"* meaning "navel") a Brazilian dance of Congo origin; percussive, propulsive music in $\frac{2}{4}$ time to accompany this dance; the symbol of the Rio carnival (called Carnaval).

bateria percussion section of a Brazilian *escola de samba*, famed for performances during Carnaval.

surdo (Portuguese) bass drum that keeps one of the fundamental rhythms in Brazilian samba; also the name of the rhythmic pattern played on the drum.

agogô (Portuguese) a double clapper-less bell beaten with a stick, used in Brazilian music.

---

parts of both music styles are traceable to the same African sources. The slave trade of the seventeenth through the nineteenth centuries brought millions of West Africans across the Atlantic Ocean to ports all along the eastern seaboard of the Americas—in Brazil, Cuba, Haiti, and the southern United States. In each location, the displaced Africans—who included the Yoruba and Abakuá from Nigeria, the Arará from Benin (formerly Dahomey), and Bantu groups (including Congos) from what is now Angola and the Democratic Republic of Congo—sustained their cultural and religious identities through practice of their traditional music and dance. But their music also melded with that of the host cultures. In Latin music, an African-derived emphasis on rhythm was filtered through mostly European-derived cultures—Spanish in the case of Afro-Cuban, Portuguese in the case of Brazilian—yielding contrasting styles that eventually crossed paths and mingled through the movement of peoples.

The slave trade of the seventeenth through nineteenth centuries brought millions of West Africans across the Atlantic Ocean to ports all along the eastern seaboard of the Americas—in Brazil, Cuba, Haiti, and the southern United States.

Issues

Music of Hope and Survival

How do Afro-Cuban and Brazilian musics reflect the troubled histories of the peoples who created them?

There's a key reason for Afro-Cuban music's fire and emotion and Afro-Brazilian music's passion and soulfulness. Both musics are descended from forms used to affirm identity in the face of violent uprooting and dislocation from native countries. Africans transplanted to points in Cuba and Brazil during the slave trade strove to preserve their social and religious traditions through music and dance. In Cuba, Yoruba slaves camouflaged their religious celebration to avoid persecution; behind a façade of Spanish Catholicism, slaves secretly invoked their own gods, called *orisha*, through the practices of song and dance and especially drumming. In Brazil, music helped slaves communicate their shared spirituality and native culture in an atmosphere of often violent subjugation. The same phenomenon took a slightly different form in the United States, where field workers ended their days with sung affirmations and prayers. Their songs evolved into the blues, an expression of vitality amid oppression that became a foundation of American popular music and jazz. Similarly, Cuban and Brazilian slave rhythm and song traditions integrated into Latin popular music over time, investing it with the depth of feeling and spirituality that slaves poured into the original music to affirm life in the face of impossible circumstances.

—*Tad Lathrop*

A Heritage of Rhythm and Percussion

Rhythm and percussion thrived in Latin American and Caribbean cultures, where drumming flourished and developed early on to a greater degree than in the United States. Stateside, during the pre–Civil War period, drums made by African Americans were systematically prohibited and destroyed. The white clergy viewed them as "devilish instruments" associated with "lewd" dancing, and slave owners feared that the slaves would use them to encode calls for rebellion. In the relatively more lenient and less puritanical Catholic countries of Latin America and the Caribbean, however, "black" drums and other percussion instruments were, although intermittently repressed, mostly tolerated.

Both social and religious activity and ritual played an important role in spreading African influences through Latin and Caribbean cultures. People of African descent often formed clubs and secret societies based on ethnic origin that helped preserve ancient traditions; and when organized under the aegis of Christian churches, these gave rise to syncretic religious cults (cults that combine native beliefs with elements of other religions, such as Christianity), such as *santería* in Cuba, *candomblé* in Brazil, and *vodun* in Haiti. Whether in secular or religious contexts, singing and dancing were (and remain today) accompanied by a vast array of drums and other percussion instruments.

Latin American percussion instruments. Top, from left to right: güiro, shekere. *Middle, from left to right:* caxixi, *frying pan* agogô *bells, standard* agogô *bells,* tamborim. *Front, from left to right:* maracas, double *ganza.* PHOTO COURTESY CHRIS STOCK/ LEBRECHT MUSIC & ARTS.

> ## TAKE NOTE
>
> - How did Afro-Cuban and Brazilian jazz draw on similar musical roots to create different musical styles?

Cuban Roots

Some of the most exciting sounds in jazz have come from Cuban-derived or influenced bands and musicians. Breakneck tempos and bravura instrumental solos over percolating multi-percussion blends—these and other characteristics have entertained audiences for decades in the bands of, among many others, Dizzy Gillespie, Machito, and Mongo Santamaría and, more recently, in the group **Irakere** and its alumnus **Paquito D'Rivera**. The widely known and enjoyed style *salsa* is derived in large measure from Cuban influences.

One source of the highly rhythmic and outgoing cast of Afro-Cuban music is the Spanish influence, invested with the passion of flamenco guitar and its dance propelled by the stomping of feet and the clicking of castanets. The other, perhaps key, reason for Cuban music's power is its rich African cultural heritage, well preserved throughout the island's history.

Prominent African influences in Cuba came from descendants of the Nigeria-originated Yoruba people, whose music and dance incorporated highly complex rhythms, call-and-response singing, and **batá** drums (three different-sized hand drums). The Yorubas' wide selection of intricate rhythm patterns (called **toques**) in combination with the low, middle, and high sounds produced by the different-sized drums, provided essential ingredients for Latin percussion of today. Additional influences came from the Nigeria-derived Abakuá sect and the Dahomey-descended Arará, who accompanied their dance music with batteries of drums, sticks, bells, and rattles. The Congo-originated Bantu people used large barrel drums from which evolved today's widely used congas.

These African influences mixed with Hispanic to yield core sounds and styles of popular Afro-Cuban music. In the 1800s there was the **canción** tradition—vocal music with guitar accompaniment—with its styles the romantic bolero and the earthier *guaracha*. A French influence entered from Haiti following the island's slave uprising of 1791: the **contradanza** (from French *contredanse*) became the favorite dance of Cubans, played on strings, woodwinds, brass, and percussion. It incorporated *clave* rhythms, and it generated the **danza** and the **danza habanera**—the latter being one of the first Cuban styles to travel to, and find popularity in, Europe

and the United States. A further permutation of danzas was the **danzón**—a light-classical dance music (generally using piano, flute, violin, and *timbales*) that for about a century prevailed as a favorite dance music in Cuba.

The rhythmic core of Afro-Cuban music is a pattern called the **clave**, typically (but not always) played on a pair of sticks called *claves*. The pattern commonly consists of two even beats followed by three beats the second of which is syncopated. This is called the 2-3 *clave*. Sometimes the reverse, 3-2, is used.

2-3 Clave

3-2 Clave

((•—Listen to these rhythms on **mymusiclab.com**

Linked in structure to patterns found in West African music, the *clave* carried over into Afro-Cuban dances including the rhythmically complex **rumba**, which developed in rural areas of Cuba in the mid-nineteenth century and later thrived in the cities of Havana and Matanza (before inciting a *rumba* craze in the United States in the 1930s). The *clave*'s distinctive three-plus-two structure—simplified, over time—provided a compelling anchor for ensembles

---

contradanza (Spanish) Cuban dance popular in the eighteenth century.

danza (Spanish) a nineteenth-century musical genre, using the *habanera* rhythm, derived from the *contradanza*, popular in Cuba in the eighteenth and nineteenth centuries; a predecessor to the *danzón*.

danza habanera a Cuban social dance in duple time and performed in a ballroom or on a stage; originating in the late nineteenth century, it became one of the first Cuban styles to become popular in the United States and Europe.

danzón (Spanish) a light classical dance accompaniment derived from the *danza* and originating in Cuba in the late nineteenth century.

clave (Spanish) a basic rhythmic pattern of Cuban and Puerto Rican music, played over two bars; the *clave* beat holds the band together. In Latin jazz, the *clave* is often implied, rather than stated by the *clave* sticks.

rumba (Spanish, "rhumba" in English) a music genre derived from the Cuban *son* and popularized in the 1930s; also a ballroom dance performed by both Latino and non-Latino audiences in the United States and in Europe.

---

batá (Yoruba) a set of three double-headed drums originally from the Yoruba people (present-day Nigeria and Benin) in West Africa typically used in *santería* ceremonies in Cuba.

toques (Spanish) drum rhythms in ritual Afro-Cuban music.

canción (Spanish) literally, "song": song style focusing mostly on lyrics/melody, with guitar accompaniment.

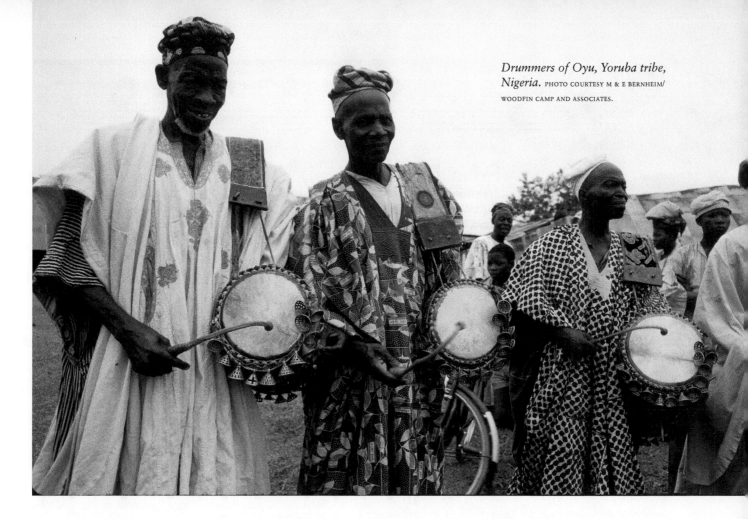

Drummers of Oyu, Yoruba tribe, Nigeria. PHOTO COURTESY M & E BERNHEIM/ WOODFIN CAMP AND ASSOCIATES.

of singers, ***tumba*** and ***quinto*** drums (later the names of, respectively, the lowest- and highest-pitched conga drums), and other miscellaneous percussion.

The *clave* was also a core element of ***son***, a derivation of the *canción*. Considered one of the more complete syntheses of Cuba's African and Spanish cultures, *son* originated in the late 1800s as a combination of Bantu-derived rhythm and the poetry of Spanish-descended farmers. In the 1920s *son* replaced the more polite *danzón* as Havana's most popular dance music.

Son's instrumentation and rhythmic structure prototyped those of later Latin ensembles: acoustic bass and conga drum on a rhythm called the ***tumbao*** (from *tumba*, meaning drum); *clave* sticks on the rhythm of the same name; bongos, maracas, and shakers playing additional patterns; a scraper called a ***güiro***; a guitarlike instrument called the ***tres*** plucking a repeating arpeggio cross-melody called a ***montuno***; and a rhythmically active singer. Later *son* groups added trumpet. A two-drum instrument called the *timbales*—used in *danzón* groups—became central in later Afro-Cuban groups.

Danzón may have been driven out of style in Havana by *son*, but it reemerged in a new form when some musicians added to it elements of different styles including trumpets playing vocal lines from *rumbas*, and beefed-up rhythm including the *tumbao*. The

((• **Listen** to a demonstration of Afro-Cuban rhythms on **mymusiclab.com**

---

tumba (Spanish) the largest and lowest-pitched of the conga drums; national dance of Santo Domingo in the nineteenth century.

quinto (Spanish) the smallest and highest-pitched of the conga drums, which in Cuban music usually improvises.

son (Spanish) a genre that emerged in the late nineteenth century in the rural areas of eastern Cuba. It developed as an urban type of music in Havana in the 1920s and became commercialized in the United States under the name *rumba* or *rhumba*. The *son* forms the backbone of salsa.

tumbao (Spanish, of African derivation) a rhythm pattern played by the conga and the string bass.

güiro (Taino—the original Amerindian language spoken in Cuba) a serrated, rasped gourd used in Puerto Rican and Cuban music.

tres (Spanish) a stringed instrument used in traditional Cuban and Puerto Rican music.

montuno (Spanish) an improvised section, in Cuban popular music and salsa; kind of contrapuntal accompaniment used in salsa and in Cuban music in general.

Style & Technique

Cuban Rhythms

 Listen to these rhythms on **mymusiclab.com**

Following an African tradition, the various instruments of the rhythm section in Cuban folk and popular music create polyrhythms anchored by a basic pattern called *clave*. This *clave* can be implied or stated by a pair of *clave* sticks. There are different types of *claves* according to the type of music played. The most common one is the so-called "2-3" or "*son*" *clave*, characteristic of a genre called *son*, which began growing in popularity in Cuba in the late 1920s.

2-3 *clave*:

The **timbales**, consisting of two snare drums mounted on a stand, play a pattern called **cáscara**. (**Tito Puente** is one of Latin jazz's most celebrated *timbaleros*.) The left hand usually keeps the *clave* while the right hand can improvise around the *cáscara*. In Latin jazz, *timbales* may be replaced by a set of trap drums, or both instruments may be employed simultaneously.

Example of *cáscara*:

Right hand:

Left hand:

name eventually given to this highly popular blend was **mambo**. And from it, as mambo bands took their sounds to the United States and elsewhere, emerged big band mambo, *cha-cha-chá*, and salsa.

Brazilian Roots

With a land mass that covers nearly half of South America and a population ranked fifth largest in the world, Brazil dominates its continent. Brazilian

---

timbales   (Spanish) a drum set with two tuneable snare drums with different pitches, two cow bells, a cymbal or cymbals, and sometimes a woodblock; typically played with two sticks; developed in Cuba, inspired by the European tympani; used in Cuban music and in salsa music.

cáscara   (Spanish) a rhythmic pattern played on *timbales*.

mambo   (Bantu) a highly syncopated instrumental genre created by Cuban bandleader Pérez Prado and first performed by him in Mexico; a dance style highly popular in the 1950s that was a precursor to salsa.

culture—especially its musical culture—is richly developed and has global reach. As in Cuba, African-derived traditions thrive in Brazil, which has its own vast array of rhythms and percussion instruments. These are used to accompany a panoply of traditional events and local performances—including Carnaval sambas, cult ceremonies of African origin, and spontaneous street-corner jam sessions—that to this day feed into the broad spectrum of styles, from folk to rock to pop, that make up the Brazilian musical mix.

Accounting for why Africa-derived musical ideas developed differently in Brazil than in Cuba starts with the impact of Brazil's Portuguese culture. The colonization of Brazil by the Portuguese from about 1500 forward brought some distinctive characteristics and practices: a language considered to be one of the most lyrical and musical in the world; a sense of poignancy, soulfulness, and longing that would inform song lyrics; favored instruments including flute, guitar, clarinet, violin, accordion, piano, drums, triangle, tambourine; an appreciation for complex, syncopated rhythms; a celebration called the *entrudo*, which would be the

The conga and the bass both play patterns called *tumbaos*.

Example of *tumbao*:

On certain sections, especially during other instruments' solos, the piano (as well as the guitar, the vibes, the *tres*—a stringed instrument used in traditional Cuban and Puerto Rican music—and violins) may play patterns called *montunos*.

Example of *montuno*:

The bongos, the maracas, the *güiro*, the **shekere** (a big shaken gourd with a mesh of beads), the **campana** (cowbell) and other percussion instruments each play their own patterns.

Cuba has produced many musical genres. In the 1930s, jazz incorporated elements of the *rumba*; in the late 1940s and 1950s, Cubop mostly used mambo, *cha-cha-chá*, and bolero rhythms; and in the late 1970s, Cuban jazzmen experimented with a new genre called *songo*. Latin jazz has also delved into traditional secular and sacred Afro-Cuban rhythms, one well-known example of which is Mongo Santamaría's *Afro Blue* (1959), with its $\frac{6}{8}$ time feel (although for convenience's sake, it's written in $\frac{3}{4}$):

—Isabelle Leymarie

prototype of the later Carnaval tradition that would nurture so much Brazilian music; and, last but not least, a tolerance for African culture that permitted deep comingling of traditions.

Early on, the **lundu**, a kind of circle dance brought by Bantu slaves, entered Portuguese society as a song style with guitar accompaniment and gained wide popularity. Notably, the *lundu* and other Afro-Brazilian dances included a movement called the **umbigada** in which couples bump navels as an invitation to the dance—the pulse of which some contend is directly related to the samba.

It's the samba, perhaps more than any other musical style, that stands as the centerpiece of Afro-Brazilian music. Its distinctive $\frac{2}{4}$ rhythm, pounded out on giant *surdo* drums, anchors a dense, intricate, and thrilling matrix of interlocking rhythms played on numerous different African-derived percussion instruments: **repique** (**repinique**, medium-sized drum), **caixa** (smaller drum), *agogô* (double bell hit with a stick), **cuíca** (friction drum), **reco-reco** (scraper, derived from

shekere (Yoruba) a rattle consisting of a large gourd with beads held, by a mesh net, on the outside, instead of on the inside as in *maracas*; shaken in rhythm and struck with the palm of the hand; of West African origin.

campana (Spanish) a cowbell, played with a stick as a percussion instrument; used in Afro-Cuban and salsa music; also called *cencerro*.

lundu (Bantu) song and dance with Angolan roots, brought to Brazil by slaves in the eighteenth century; an ancestor to various urban Brazilian song forms.

umbigada (Portuguese) a movement in Afro-Brazilian dances during which the dancer touches navels with another dancer as an invitation to dance.

repique (repinique) (Portuguese) a two-headed tenor drum; played in Brazilian samba.

caixa (Portuguese) a Brazilian snare drum.

cuíca (Portuguese) a Brazilian friction drum used often in samba music.

reco-reco (Portuguese) a Brazilian scraper made of bamboo or metal.

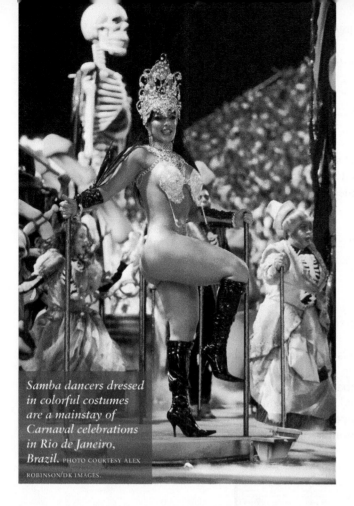

Samba dancers dressed in colorful costumes are a mainstay of Carnaval celebrations in Rio de Janeiro, Brazil. PHOTO COURTESY ALEX ROBINSON/DK IMAGES.

original Brazilian Indians), *shekere*, **tamborim** (small tambourine without jingles), and **pandeiro** (similar to the tambourine).

Samba developed in Rio de Janeiro in the early 1900s with the influx of immigrants from the Afro-Brazilian population of Bahia to the coastal north. At informal social gatherings and jam sessions the samba was forged with influences from the *lundu* and several other precursors: the **maxixe**, a lively exuberant dancehall style born in Rio around 1880, mixing *lundu*, the Argentinian tango, Cuban *habanera*, and polka; and the **marcha**, an uptempo $\frac{2}{4}$ rhythm like the samba, derived about 1899 from the tango and *habanera*. Over time, different strains of samba emerged, and samba expanded from its

---

tamborim (Portuguese) a small, jingle-less tambourine played with a single or double stick, used in Brazilian music.

pandeiro (Portuguese) a Brazilian percussion instrument similar to the tambourine.

maxixe (Portuguese) a Brazilian couples dance, originating around 1870, with elements of the polka and the Brazilian tango. It became popular in the United States and in Europe at the turn of the twentieth century.

marcha (Spanish) a march.

---

roots as an expressive outlet for the underclass to a widely disseminated (via the newly invented radio) and highly popular national trend.

Starting in the late 1920s, Rio became the home of **escolas de samba**—samba schools that doubled as social clubs, in which their thousands of members would prepare samba performances for the annual competitive Carnaval samba parade. During the parades, watched by tens of thousands, the school's *baterias* (percussion ensembles of several hundred strong) would thrill audiences with highly synchronized rhythms supporting several thousand singers–vying against other *escolas* for highest ranking. The tradition continues to this day.

Early interaction with U.S. jazz helped Brazilian music evolve from samba to what would become Brazil's best-known musical export. As early as 1946 vocalist Dick Farney (with his hit *Copacabana*) and, a few years later, singer and pianist Johnny Alf—both Brazilians who were exposed to North American jazz—began signaling the coming of a new style of Brazilian music with jazz inflections. Further developments came in 1953, when the Brazilian guitarist Laurindo Almeida recorded in the United States the album *Laurindo Almeida Quartet Featuring Bud Shank* (reissued in 1961 as *Brazilliance*), an amalgam of Almeida's knowledge of the samba and saxophonist Shank's expertise in jazz. Almeida and Shank further pursued their experiments in "jazz samba," as they termed it, with *Holiday in Brazil* (1958) and *Latin Contrasts* (1959).

From 1955 to 1961, new artistic movements flourished in Brazil under the liberal government

---

escola de samba Brazilian organization or club where samba is practiced for performance in Carnaval and other events.

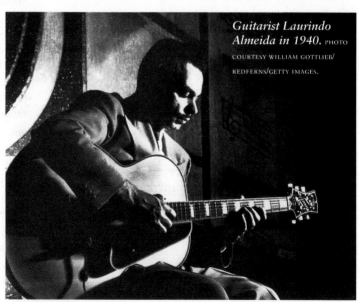

Guitarist Laurindo Almeida in 1940. PHOTO COURTESY WILLIAM GOTTLIEB/REDFERNS/GETTY IMAGES.

Style & Technique

Brazilian Rhythms

((•— Listen to these rhythms on **mymusiclab.com**

Brazil boasts a wealth of rhythms and musical genres.

The samba, which began to develop in Rio de Janeiro at the beginning of the twentieth century, is an ebullient $\frac{2}{4}$ style. Good examples of jazz sambas are Luiz Bonfá's *Samba de Orfeu* (1959) and Dizzy Gillespie's *Winter Samba* (1966). In a jazz samba, the bass may play the following pattern:

while the piano and the guitar may "comp" (accompany with chords) in the following way:

The piano defers to guitar, which is the main chordal accompanying instrument in Brazilian rhythm section; typically, the guitarist picks with the fingers and plays the bass line independently with the thumb—and the thumb is often doubled by the *surdo*.

The bossa nova, created in Rio de Janeiro in the late 1950s and adopted by jazz musicians in the early 1960s, is a medium-tempo $\frac{4}{4}$ style characterized by an offbeat pulse. Some of the most famous bossa novas in jazz include Kenny Dorham's *Blue Bossa*, Lee Morgan's *Ceora*, and Antonio Carlos Jobim's *The Girl from Ipanema*, *Corcovado*, *Wave*, *How Insensitive*, *Triste*, *Meditation*, *Desafinado*, *No More Blues*, and *Once I Loved*. The piano and the guitar play variants of the following basic rhythm:

To add color, percussionists such as **Airto Moreira** have also used such small instruments as the *agogô* and the *cuíca*.

Agogô rhythm:

Cuíca rhythm:

—Isabelle Leymarie

of President Juscelino Kubitschek, and this burst of creativity extended to the local music. In Rio, a group of Brazilian musicians became increasingly drawn to jazz—and there were plenty of visiting U.S. musicians to fuel their interest, from Dizzy Gillespie (on a 1956 State Department-sponsored tour) to guitarists **Charlie Byrd** and Jim Hall to singer Ella Fitzgerald. The jazz-inclined Brazilian musicians, whose members notably included a composer named Antonio Carlos Jobim, began holding jam sessions in 1956 in a handful of clubs in the Copacabana neighborhood of Rio de Janeiro. From their creative interactions emerged a style that modernized and toned down the samba, adding sophisticated and intricate chord progressions and rhythmic accompaniment—often on guitar—that hovered always slightly ahead of the pulse, in syncopation to it. Compared to the more propulsive, extroverted samba (not to mention fiery Cuban rhythms), this Brazilian music was airier, more subdued, more intimate and cerebral. As it caught on, it acquired the label bossa nova—literally, the "new tendency."

The bossa nova was officially launched by guitarist and singer João Gilberto's recordings of Antonio Carlos Jobim's *Desafinado* (1958) and *Chega de Saudade* (1959), and then by Marcel Camus's 1959 film *Black Orpheus* (*Orfeu Negro* in Portuguese), which featured such classics-to-be as Luiz Bonfá's *Manha de Carnaval* and Jobim's *A Felicidade*.

In Brazil's two largest cities—Rio de Janeiro and São Paulo—a host of musicians and singers established their credentials performing the bossa nova. Many of these musicians would become well-known beyond Brazil's borders. They included pianists Sérgio Mendes, who offered his own brand of jazz samba; Eumir Deodato, who wrote arrangements for Frank Sinatra and Tony Bennett; and guitarist Baden Powell, with his exciting mixture of Afro-Brazilian, jazz, and classical strains.

After the decline of the bossa nova, a new generation of highly creative musicians emerged in Brazil. Starting in the mid 1960s a genre called **MPB**—for *música popular brasileira*—encompassed the work of diverse singer-songwriters who pulled freely from many sources, including bossa nova, jazz, rock, reggae, and music from all parts of Brazil, to frame their personal musical visions and lyrics. Especially notable were Milton Nascimento, whose high-pitched voice enhances the haunting quality of many of his compositions, including *Ponta de Areia* (from the Wayne Shorter album *Native Dancer*, 1974). That song was also recorded by the singer Elis Regina, whose vibrato-free, sometimes soaring vocal approach somehow embodied the Brazilian quality of *saudade*—longing, nostalgia, and yearning—for a brief period of acclaim until her death in 1982.

The creative environs of Brazil produced so many notable and distinctive musicians that a balanced and meaningful accounting is not possible in a short narrative. Still, there are standouts including the singer-songwriters Gilberto Gil and Caetano Veloso, who spearheaded the iconoclastic **Tropicália** movement with mixes of everything from traditional Bahian rhythm to rock and roll—spawning associated efforts in other art forms. Pianist-singer Ivan Lins, singer-songwriter Chico Buarque, and singer-guitarist-composer Jorge Ben have added their own distinct colors to Brazilian music.

A purely instrumental tradition existed in Brazil as well, including **choro**, which emerged in Rio de Janeiro in the late nineteenth century. An improvisational form predating jazz, *choro* involved soloing over European harmonies with Afro-Brazilian syncopation, typically on flute accompanied by guitar and the four-stringed *cavaquinho* in early *choro*. *Choro*, with an ever-expanding selection of instruments, remained an important part of the Brazilian music playbook over the years. Among those who employed it in the 1970s was the composer and multi-instrumentalist **Hermeto Pascoal**—while also exploring a virtually limitless array of other musical possibilities. Not widely known outside of Brazil, Pascoal acquired a reputation as a musician's musician in his country. Whether writing for standard instruments or nonstandard ones (toys, pots, pans), pursuing such experiments as writing a song a day for a year, or penning such notable compositions as the *choro/baião Bebe* (1973) and the *Missa Dos Escravos* (*Slaves Mass*, 1977), Pascoal proved a musical innovator unlike anyone else, although his

Herman Pascoal playing a button accordion, 2000. PHOTO COURTESY LEON MORRIS/REDFERNS/GETTY IMAGES.

MPB (*música popular brasileira*) post–bossa nova Brazilian urban popular music, combining elements from different genres.

Tropicália an experimental, style-mixing arts movement—with a strong musical component—of late 1960s Brazil.

choro (Portuguese) a type of Brazilian popular music, improvised and usually instrumental, that originated prior to jazz.

Style & Technique

Comparing Aspects of North American, Afro-Cuban, and Afro-Brazilian Jazz

Among the differences between Afro-Cuban and Afro-Brazilian jazz styles—as well as their antecedents—are their different approaches to the role of the bass and bass drum. Brazilian samba has the *surdo* (bass drum) and acoustic or electric bass *anchoring* the rhythm, emphasizing the main beats in $\frac{2}{4}$ time. Cuban music, on the other hand, has the conga and bass playing offbeats, *destabilizing* the core rhythm. The two feelings are substantially different. The following chart shows other differences—of the most general kind—between Afro-Cuban, Afro-Brazilian, and North American jazz. All three have complexities that extend far beyond these summaries.

—*Tad Lathrop*

	NORTH AMERICAN	AFRO-CUBAN	AFRO-BRAZILIAN
Heritages	African, French, English, Italian, German, Mexican, Cuban	African, Spanish, French	African, Portuguese
Root styles	blues, ragtime, marches	*son, danzón, contradanza, habanera, rumba*	*lundu, maxixe, marchá, choro,* samba
Developed styles	swing, bebop, cool jazz, mainstream, Latin jazz, Brazilian jazz	mambo, *cha-cha-chá*, bolero, salsa, *songo*	samba, bossa nova, MPB
Character	widely varied in expression, based on musicians' personal styles	"hot," brash, extroverted	*samba:* powerful, propulsive, infectious *bossa nova:* "cool," light, sensual, subtle, gentle
Rhythmic core (bass)	walking bass	*tumbao*	*surdo*
Main accompaniment instrument	primarily piano	primarily piano	primarily guitar
Rhythm matrix	even, four-to-the-bar pulse accented with syncopation	syncopated *tumbao* bass line, *clave* 3-2 or 2-3, *montuno,* cyclical maracas, cross-rhythms	*surdo* and bass anchoring the beat, cross-rhythms on accompanying percussion and guitar
Typical rhythm instruments	drum set	conga, bongo, *timbales, claves* (sticks), maracas, cowbell, *güiro* (scraper), *shekere* (shaker)	*surdo* (bass drum), *repique* (tom tom), *caixa* (snare drum), conga, *agogô* (bell hit with stick), *ganza* (shaker), *cuíca* (friction drum), *tamborim, reco-reco* (scraper), *berimbau* (stringed bow), whistle

propensity for experimentation brings to mind such stateside iconoclasts as Sun Ra and Frank Zappa.

Pascoal had many musical associates, among whom one standout is the multi-percussionist, singer, and occasional bandleader Airto Moreira. A master of playing arrays of popping, twinkling, chiming, fluttering, whistling, rasping, slapping, hiccupping, and pattering instruments—not to mention the standard drum set—as one ambience-creating percussion tool, Moreira was at the forefront of a trend started in the 1970s in which Brazilian multi-percussionists were employed by jazz bands in the United States to add dimension and color to the sound. This trend was just one of the several major intersection points of jazz and Brazilian music during the twentieth century and into the twenty-first.

> **TAKE NOTE**
>
> - What native Cuban and Brazilian musical rhythms and musical instruments have influenced the development of Latin Jazz?

Early Latin Influences on Jazz

The Cuban *habanera* song and dance form, an antecedent of the popular *danzón* style, found popularity in California by the late nineteenth century, brought there by Mexican composer Miguel Arévalo. The brass band of the Mexican Eighth Cavalry Regiment performed various Latin tunes, among them *danzas* of Cuban origin, in New Orleans in 1884. (One of

African Americans dancing and singing the bamboula, New Orleans LA (ca. 1790–1800).

THE BAMBOULA.

the band's members introduced the saxophone to the Crescent City.) In addition, Cuban rhythms may have been brought to Louisiana by members of New Orleans's Onward Brass Band, who were reportedly among U.S. troops who fought in Cuba for its independence from Spain in 1898.

Habanera rhythm.

(((●—[Listen to this rhythm on **mymusiclab.com**

When jazz erupted onto the New Orleans music scene, the city had a bustling Latin and Caribbean population comprising, in part, Mexicans, Cubans, freed slaves from Santo Domingo, and settlers from Martinique and Guadeloupe. The city's music reflected their varied traditions. Creole balls featured **quadrilles** (square dances of French origin), **mazookas** (a Creolized version of mazurkas, still danced today in some Caribbean islands), and Cuban *danzas* and *habaneras*, all of which enjoyed great popularity. Voodoo rhythms from Haiti pulsated through black neighborhoods, while drums accompanied the *bamboula* and the

kalinda dances—both of Congo origin—when they were performed in the city's famed Congo Square. The New Orleans composer Louis Moreau Gottschalk, whose work foretold ragtime and jazz, drew freely from these dance rhythms for such works as *Bamboula—Danse de Nègre* (ca. 1846). And some black Louisiana folk songs sung in *patois* (a dialectal mixture of French and African words and turns of phrases)—*Missié Banjo*, for example—were infused with such Caribbean strains as the calypso or the beguine.

The New Orleans–born pianist-composer "Jelly Roll" Morton, who claimed to be the creator of jazz, considered what he called "the Latin tinge" a foremost ingredient of this emerging musical gumbo. This Latin tinge can be heard in ragtime instrumentals such as Jess Pickett's *The Dream Rag* (evidently from the 1890s) and *Tiger Rag* (1917; see "Jazz Classics: *Tiger Rag*," page 52), in Morton's *New Orleans Joys* (1923) and *Mama Nita* (1924), and especially in W.C. Handy's famed *St. Louis Blues* (1914; see "Jazz Classics: *St. Louis Blues*," page 39), with its *habanera*-based second section. These all share a bass line, called **"Spanish" (or "tango" bass)**, which resembles that of the *danza* or of the Argentinian tango. (Similarities between the Cuban *danza* and the Argentinian tango were not coincidental. The *danza* and *danza habanera* had derived from the French *contredanse*, which in Haiti—before it was brought to Cuba around 1791 and changed to the

---

quadrille (French) a square dance of French origin for two couples; a piece of music to accompany quadrille dancing.

mazooka (Creole) a Creolized version of the mazurka (a Polish folk dance in triple meter), still danced today in the French Caribbean islands of Martinique and Guadeloupe.

"Spanish" (or "tango" bass) a bass line containing syncopated figures, typically in *habanera* rhythm. The term was used in the early twentieth century to describe syncopated bass lines of certain rags, blues, and jazz pieces.

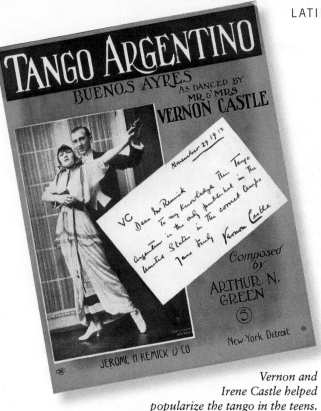

Vernon and Irene Castle helped popularize the tango in the teens.
COURTESY BENCAR ARCHIVES.

jazz. The band was nicknamed the "Hellfighters" because of their dedicated service in World War I as a colored U.S. regiment serving in France. They helped popularize proto-jazz in France during and after World War I.

Latin and Caribbean influences continued to be strongly felt in New Orleans. Tyers's *Panama* became a favorite of New Orleans brass bands, although they often dropped its *habanera* rhythm; and several Latin musicians performed in early New Orleans jazz bands.

Puerto Ricans, after being granted U.S. citizenship in 1917, migrated in increasing numbers to New York, where they first settled mostly in East Harlem. Their neighborhood, soon to be known as El Barrio, became a hub of musical activity and an incubator for many musical careers. The Puerto Rican trombonist **Juan Tizol** emigrated in 1920 to the United States. As a member of Duke Ellington's orchestra, Tizol began in the 1930s to introduce Latin-inflected compositions into Ellington's repertoire, among them *Conga Brava*, *Moon over Cuba*, and two of the most popular jazz standards, *Caravan* (1936) and *Perdido* (1942). (One day in 1936, Ellington remembered,

contradanza—had acquired an African tinge that came to be known as tango bass. In addition, Cuban sailors brought rhythms from their island to Argentina's Buenos Aires around 1850, and many Cuban musicians performed there in the late nineteenth and early twentieth centuries. Beyond this cross-fertilizing, Cuban popular music and Argentinian tango both have African roots in common.)

Latin and Caribbean elements also found their way into New York's pre-jazz music in such pieces as the *Cuban Cake Walk* (1901), performed by "Tim" Brymn, leader of the famed Clef Club Orchestra. Also in New York, the pianist and arranger William H. Tyers, who collaborated with the African American bandleaders James Reese Europe and Will Marion Cook, wrote several pieces influenced by Latin music: the tango-*maxixe Maori* (1908) and the tango *Panama* (1911)—both of which were recorded by Duke Ellington in 1928—and the Cuban dance *Trocha* (1913). Around 1915, the Brazilian *maxixe* (also known as "Brazilian tango" and the Argentinian tango became wildly popular in the United States.

In 1917, James Reese Europe recruited 15 Puerto Rican musicians—among them the famed composer Rafael Hernández—for his 369th U.S. Infantry Military Band, who performed highly syncopated material that forecast the coming of

Juan Tizol, valve trombone player of Duke Ellington's orchestra at the Hurricane cabaret, 1943. PHOTO COURTESY GORDON PARKS/LIBRARY OF CONRGESS.

Jazz Classics

Caravan

Ellington first recorded *Caravan* in 1936, with a septet, but the best-known version is the track he recorded a year later with his big band of 16 musicians. From drummer Sonny Greer's dramatic opening percussion effects to the final unresolved chord, this classic recording of *Caravan* paints an intriguing picture of some distant and exotic place. Its serpentine melody conjures an image of a Middle Eastern snake-charmer's trick, or a camel caravan undulating across the rolling sand dunes; yet at the same time, Tizol's inflections also bespeak his Latin American roots. *Caravan* is one of the Ellington orchestra's first efforts to incorporate influences from other cultures into its music.

Caravan is the single most-recorded Latin jazz composition. It is also the most-recorded composition with Duke Ellington's name on it. The Duke Ellington Orchestra made 191 recordings of *Caravan*, and other jazz musicians recorded it nearly 1,500 times. It has been recorded by a wide variety of musicians, ranging from Ella Fitzgerald, Chet Atkins, the Carpenters, and Phish, to the Latin artists Candido, Tito Puente, and Pérez Prado. It is included in the movies *Chocolat, Ocean's Eleven,* and *Ocean's Thirteen;* the Woody Allen films *Alice* and *Sweet and Lowdown;* and the television programs *The O.C.* and *The Simpsons.*

COURTESY JOHN EDWARD HASSE.

—*John Edward Hasse*

Tizol "came up with [part of *Caravan*]. See, it wasn't in tempo, he stood [and played it] sort of *ad lib.* He played it, [the] first ten bars, we took it and worked out the rest of it.")

Watch the video of *Caravan* by Duke Ellington on **mymusiclab.com**

TAKE NOTE

• How did Latin music influence early jazz?

Cuban Music and Jazz

Cuba's proximity to the United States contributed to the mixing of their musical cultures. Only 90 miles separate the two countries, and for many years a steady stream of people traveled between the island and the United States. By the early 1920s American jazz had reached Cuba and was spreading throughout the island nation; several North American musicians formed jazz groups in Havana. Conversely, Cuban big bands such as the Lecuona Cuban Boys—most of them influenced by Fletcher Henderson's arrangements—gained first local then international exposure.

Musical exchanges between the United States and Cuba intensified over the years. During the 1920s, North American record companies took a growing interest in Latin music, especially Cuban music, and offered contracts to several bands. As a result, two Cuban rhythms—the *son* (commercialized under the name *rumba* or, in English, rhumba), and the **conga** (a Carnival rhythm of Congo origin, brought to the United States by the Cuban singer and actor Desi Arnaz)—became popular across the country. These rhythms aroused the interest of jazz musicians such as Sidney Bechet and Willie "The Lion" Smith (who together recorded *Rose Rhumba* and *Baba Rhumba*), and Cab Calloway (*Doin' the Rhumba* and *The Congo Conga*).

Then, in the 1930s, Cuban music took the United States by storm. The Cuban flutist Alberto Socarrás, who moved to Harlem in 1927, helped to establish it in the United States. From 1937 to 1940 Socarrás performed at the famous New York nightspot the Cotton Club, opposite Duke Ellington, Cab Calloway,

---

conga a dance of the Cuban carnival, which gained popularity in the United States in the 1930s and 1940s; a rhythm of Congo origin, it features a heavy fourth beat.

A CLOSER LOOK

Cuban percussionist Machito and his orchestra, the Afro-Cubans, created some of the earliest Latin jazz. The band came into prominence in the 1940s as the Afro-Cuban style was gaining popularity through the bands of Xavier Cugat and Pérez Prado. Machito, with his brother-in-law **Mario Bauzá**, melded the *clave*-based rhythmic patterns of Cuban dance music with the dense instrumental textures of jazz big bands, with exciting bop solos thrown in

✳ Explore on **mymusiclab.com**

((•─ **Hear** a tribute to Machito and the Afro-Cubans by Bobby Sanabria on **mymusiclab.com**

for good measure. An irresistible combination, it propelled the Afro-Cubans to a career that lasted decades.

—*Jeff Rupert*

The Congas

The rhythm section in Afro-Cuban music, with its inclusion of several percussionists, reflects a West African heritage more than does the typical jazz band rhythm section. The conga player pictured is Carlos Vidal, who played with Machito and several important jazz bands including Stan Kenton's. Other important conga players associated with Machito were Cándido Camero and Patato Valdés. Just as in the West African tradition, Afro-Cuban drummers or percussionists take turns playing ostinato (repeated) figures and soloing.

The Bongos

Bongos, along with congas, *claves*, and cowbell, add to the variety of percussion sounds in Latin jazz. José Mangual, Sr., is seen here playing the bongos.

The Drum Set

Drums in Latin jazz are often supplemented with *timbales* (usually two free-standing drums with a cymbal or cowbell, played standing). Ubaldo "Uba" Nieto, Puerto Rican *timbale* player, is seen here playing the drumset.

The Bass

The bass part in Afro-Cuban music differs from the walking bass line known in jazz. It is more syncopated as it joins with percussion in a rhythm pattern referred to as the *tumbao*. The bass's rhythmic interaction with the percussion section is crucial to the feel of Afro-Cuban jazz.

PHOTO COURTESY FRANK DRIGGS COLLECTION.

Mario Bauzá • Trumpet

Cuban-born Mario Bauzá originally played clarinet, and switched to trumpet. As musical director for Machito's Afro-Cubans, he brought the influences of Dizzy Gillespie, Cab Calloway, Stan Kenton, and other jazz bandleaders to a cross-pollination of jazz and Afro-Cuban music. Bauzá came to the United States in 1930, and soon became a member of Chick Webb's band, one of the most prominent swing big bands in New York at the time. With the Afro-Cubans, he and his brother-in-law Machito introduced Latin music to the New York City jazz scene, influencing Dizzy Gillespie and Charlie Parker, among others. Bauzá was also responsible for bringing percussionist Tito Puente into prominence by hiring him as a member of Machito's Afro-Cubans.

Machito • Maracas and Bandleader

Machito (Frank Grillo) was a singer as well as a bandleader and percussionist. Raised in Cuba, he played music there professionally before moving to New York and establishing a presence in the Latin music scene. His founding of the Afro-Cubans cemented his place in jazz history, and he led the band through several eras and musical trends—such as salsa—that he helped create. Machito was also featured with non-Latin bands that capitalized on the mambo (a kind of Afro-Cuban beat, and a dance) craze of the 1950s and 1960s.

and Louis Armstrong, creating a stir. At different times in his career and according to the venues where he performed, Socarrás led several jazz-oriented Latin ensembles—among them the Afro-Cuban Rumbas, who appeared to acclaim at the Apollo Theater and at the Savoy Ballroom in Harlem—and helped break down racial barriers in previously segregated U.S. clubs. (Socarrás is also known for making what were probably the first jazz flute solos on record—on *Shootin' the Pistol* in 1927, and *Have You Ever Felt That Way*, 1929.)

Cuban music and jazz began to merge more completely in the early 1940s, with the creation in New York of the Afro-Cubans, the seminal big band founded by the Cuban-born trumpeter and saxophonist Mario Bauzá and his brother-in-law, singer and maracas player **Machito (Frank Grillo Gutiérrez)**. A well-schooled instrumentalist, Bauzá had played with some of the best ensembles in Havana and, after moving to New York in 1930, with popular U.S. bandleaders Chick Webb and Cab Calloway. Machito had sung with some of the top *son* groups in Havana. Comprising both Latin and jazz musicians, Bauzá's and Machito's ensemble—in which Bauzá served as

musical director while Machito fronted the orchestra—combined the riffs and the brass and reed sections of jazz with authentic Afro-Cuban percussion and rhythms. At first, some black Americans—eager to dissociate themselves from the image of a "primitive and savage" Africa that the hand-held drums conjured in the minds of many whites—professed shock at the band's powerful percussion, completely new in jazz at the time. Nevertheless, many were soon won over by the Afro-Cubans' irresistible rhythms and eventually became ardent fans.

Bauzá's *Tanga* (1943; *JTSA* Disc 2/Track 22), a head arrangement influenced by Duke Ellington's "jungle" style of growling brass instruments, launched what came to be called **Cubop** (*Cuban* plus *bebop*). Cubop laid down a high-energy, multi-layered mix of sounds, with fluid, bebop-style melody lines played over *montunos*—brief yet intricate countermelodic vamps typically played on piano—unfolding against complex rhythmic textures. The Afro-Cubans brought

---

Cubop   from "Cuban" plus "bebop"; Afro-Latin-flavored bebop, pioneered in the 1940s by Cuban trumpeter-arranger Mario Bauzá.

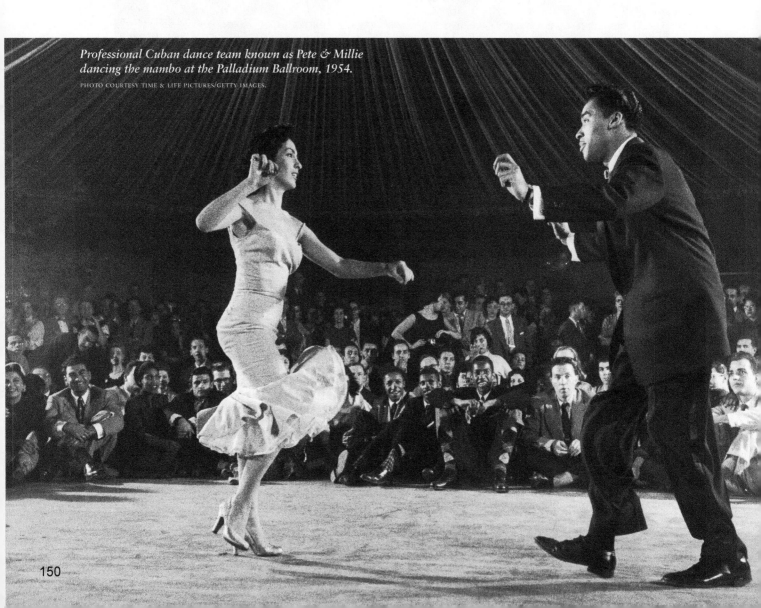

Professional Cuban dance team known as Pete & Millie dancing the mambo at the Palladium Ballroom, 1954.
PHOTO COURTESY TIME & LIFE PICTURES/GETTY IMAGES.

this recipe to their memorable rendition of *Tanga* at Carnegie Hall in 1949, a concert whose star power—with Charlie Parker, Duke Ellington, and Lester Young on hand—evidenced the growing popularity of the Latin strain in jazz.

The flowering of Cubop in the late 1940s and early 1950s coincided with crazes for the the big band mambo and the *cha-cha-chá*, two styles created by the Cuban musicians (Dámaso) Pérez Prado and Enrique Jorrín, respectively. Top Latin bands battled it out and the best dancers strutted their stuff at New York City's famed Palladium Ballroom, the "temple of the mambo." Located on Broadway, the Palladium was also a haunt for Dizzy Gillespie and other jazzmen, who performed just around the corner in the 52nd Street clubs (and was a hangout for such celebrities as actor Marlon Brando, who occasionally enjoyed trying his hand on the conga drums). The proximity of the Palladium Ballroom and 52nd Street nightclubs contributed to the cross-fertilization of Latin music and bebop.

Over the years, Gillespie, saxophonists Cannonball Adderley, Johnny Griffin, Dexter Gordon, and countless other jazzmen all performed and/or recorded with the Afro-Cubans. The longest-running Latin band in the United States, the Afro-Cubans lasted until Machito's death in 1984. They inspired many other orchestras in the United States, including those of Stan Kenton, Tito Puente, and Tito Rodríguez, as well as various aggregations in Cuba. Kenton recorded *Machito* (1947) as a tribute to the singer and bandleader, and borrowed part of the Afro-Cubans' rhythm section, including Machito himself on maracas, for his rendition of *The Peanut Vendor* (1947), which became his best-selling work.

The classically trained Cuban-born composer and arranger "Chico" (Arturo) O'Farrill imparted brilliance and sophistication to the Afro-Cubans, with arrangements that offered greater harmonic complexity than the more traditional approaches of the band's other arrangers. O'Farrill's *Afro-Cuban Jazz Suite* (1951), performed by the Afro-Cubans, guest-starred saxophonist Flip Phillips, powerhouse drummer Buddy Rich, and most notably Charlie Parker, who breezed with stunning ease through the complex Latin rhythms. O'Farrill led his own ensemble in the 1950s; worked with Dizzy Gillespie, Count Basie, and others post-1965; recorded with Gillespie and Machito in 1975 (*Afro-Cuban Jazz Moods*); and in the late 1990s recorded *Pure Emotion* (1995) and *Heart of a Legend* (1998–99). Over the course of his career, O'Farrill wrote and arranged for bandleaders as diverse as Benny Goodman, Lionel Hampton, and rocker David Bowie, among many others.

The appeal of Cuban music to jazz musicians was at least threefold: The energy and thrill of multiple percussion instruments playing complex rhythms induces a desire to move and dance. Cuban music also makes

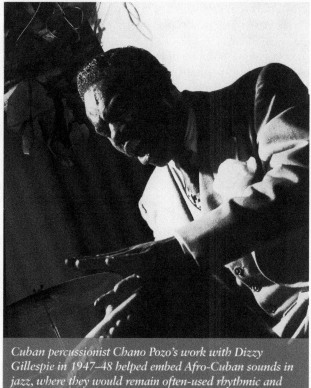

Cuban percussionist Chano Pozo's work with Dizzy Gillespie in 1947–48 helped embed Afro-Cuban sounds in jazz, where they would remain often-used rhythmic and melodic ingredients. PHOTO COURTESY © HERMAN LEONARD PHOTOGRAPHY LLC.

frequent use of breaks, an effective device that helps spice up and propel songs. In addition, the simple harmonic structure of many Cuban tunes allows soloists to "stretch out" without overly worrying about chord changes, thus providing another source of excitement.

A large number of U.S. jazzmen took to Latin music: Duke Ellington recorded *The Peanut Vendor* (1931), Louis Armstrong *La Cucaracha* (1935) and *Mexican Swing* (1938), Artie Shaw *Frenesí* (1940), and Jimmy Dorsey *Aquellos Ojos Verdes* (under the name *Green Eyes*, 1941). But it was Dizzy Gillespie who was became the first North American bandleader to fuse bebop and Afro-Cuban rhythms. A close friend of Bauzá's since their joint tenure with Cab Calloway, Gillespie had become acquainted with the *clave* during his stint in Harlem with flutist Alberto Socarrás. In 1947, on Bauzá's recommendation, Gillespie hired into his big band the outstanding **conguero** (conga player) Luciano "Chano" Pozo, freshly arrived in New York from Havana. Pozo introduced hand-held drums into a U.S. jazz ensemble for the first time, as well as sacred Afro-Cuban chants and the rhythms of the ***rumba brava*** (a

---

conguero (Spanish) a player of the conga drum.
rumba brava (Spanish) refers to several Cuban traditional vocal and instrumental genres of Congo derivation, among them the *guaguancó,* the *columbia,* and the *yambú.* The *rumba brava,* also danced, is different from the ballroom *rumba.*

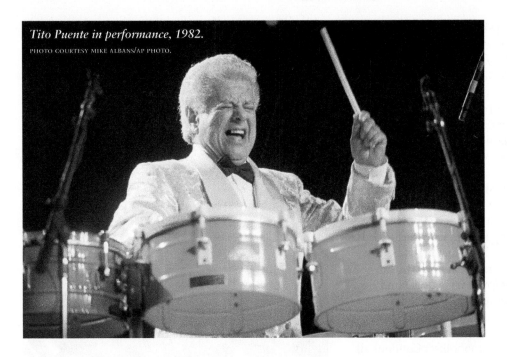
Tito Puente in performance, 1982.
PHOTO COURTESY MIKE ALBANS/AP PHOTO.

James Moody as well as with Latin musicians. But Pozo's career was cut short when, on December 2, 1948, he was shot down in a bar in Harlem. His impact on jazz, however, proved long-lasting. After Pozo's death, Gillespie later recruited a string of percussionists, and the conga drum and the bongo became mainstays of many jazz and dance ensembles, from singer-pianist Nat "King" Cole's 1950s trio to trumpeter Roy Hargrove's 1990s group Crisol.

By the 1960s, big bands that featured Latin jazz had given way to more intimate ensembles—called "combos" at the time in both jazz and Latin music—that usually consisted of piano, vibes or guitar, bass, bongos, and flute. Most representative of this era were the combos formed by Cuban percussionist **Mongo Santamaría**, American vibraphonist Cal Tjader, British pianist George Shearing, and percussionists Tito Puente and **Ray Barretto**, both Nuyoricans (Puerto Ricans from New York). Groups led by U.S. musicians generally accentuated the jazz side, while those led by Latinos leaned more toward a Latin feel. Santamaría's group served as an incubator for such talented newcomers (and future headliners) as pianists Herbie Hancock and **Chick Corea**. Hancock brought Santamaría his freshly penned *Watermelon Man*—a catchy, funky blues-like piece—which Santamaría recorded in 1962 to become the *conguero*'s first hit.

A *timbalero*, vibraphonist, and highly prolific composer and arranger with hundreds of recordings under his name, Tito Puente—known as "El Rey" (The King)—popularized the *timbales* in the United States, as well as the flute in Latin jazz. Born in East Harlem in 1923, he grew up listening to both jazz and Latin music, and he studied piano, organ, trap drums, vibes, *timbales*, conga, and composition. He began to play professionally at the age of 14. At 18, in 1941, he worked six months with the Afro-Cubans, and later he led both dance-oriented Latin big bands and smaller, more experimental Latin jazz ensembles. Two of his most famous compositions are *Ran Kan Kan* (1949) and *Oye Cómo Va* (1963), the latter recorded

musical genre of Congo and Spanish origin). It took a while, however, to fine-tune things. Pozo didn't immediately fit the bebop mold, and, conversely, Gillespie and his bandmates needed a certain amount of coaching before they could adapt to the exacting idiosyncrasies of Afro-Cuban music. "Chano taught us all multirhythm; we learned from the master," reminisced Gillespie. "On the bus, he'd give me a drum, [bassist] Al McKibbon a drum, and he'd take a drum. Another guy would have a cowbell, and he'd give everybody a rhythm. We'd see how all the rhythms tied into one another, and everybody was playing something different."

Pozo's pyrotechnics tested the mettle of Gillespie and his men. The band soon made history though, with *Manteca* (1947), *Cubana Be/Cubana Bop* (also 1947), *Tin Tin Deo*, and other compositions. The fiery *Manteca*, with its introduction and A and A' sections based on authentic Cuban vamps (*tumbaos*, see "Cuban Rhythms,")—peppered with Gillespie's shouts of "*Manteca!*"—and with its contrasting, jazzier bridge, was a novelty. Even more revolutionary was Gillespie's and upcoming composer George Russell's *Cubana Be/Cubana Bop*, with its advanced modal colors, and its middle section, on which Pozo let loose on conga and chanted ritual Yoruba chants.

The Gillespie band's February 1948 concerts at the Salle Pleyel in Paris turned the city on its ear. Audiences were stunned and Gillespie even witnessed a fistfight between the advocates of old-time jazz, whom modernists derisively nicknamed "moldy figs," and the fans of bebop, who were in turn dubbed "sour grapes."

Back in the United States, after his European tour with Gillespie, Pozo recorded with tenor saxophonist

((•— **Hear** a tribute to Tito Puente on **mymusiclab.com** by rock guitarist Carlos Santana in 1970. The tunes can notably be heard on an album representative of Puente's Latin jazz work, *El Rey* (1984), which also includes the jazz standard *Autumn Leaves*, as well as John Coltrane's *Equinox* and *Giant Steps*.

Like Puente, Ray Barretto, a powerful *conguero*, cultivated both jazz and Latin music. Born in Brooklyn in 1929, Barretto discovered the conga drum while stationed in Munich with the U.S. Army when he heard a record of Chano Pozo with Dizzy Gillespie. Back in New York, he participated in jazz jam sessions in Harlem. As a sideman, he performed and recorded with countless jazz musicians, ranging from pianist Red Garland and saxophonist Eddie "Lockjaw" Davis to Dizzy Gillespie and Herbie Hancock. In 1957, he replaced Mongo Santamaría in Tito Puente's orchestra, and then worked four years with Cal Tjader. In 1961 Barretto formed his own Latin group, called Charanga La Moderna, and he gradually shifted from Latin dance music, scoring a hit in 1963 with the catchy *El Watusi*, to Latin jazz. In the 1990s, his New World Spirit band included an eclectic mix of young musicians, from the Columbian pianist Héctor Martignon to the Japanese drummer Satoshi Takeishi (they can be heard on Barretto's album *Taboo*, 1994).

Another Nuyorican, pianist **Eddie Palmieri**, brought a somewhat different sound to Latin music in the early 1960s with his band La Perfecta. It was known as "the band with the crazy roaring elephants," due to its use of a trombone section instead of the more standard trumpets. Palmieri, who had studied *timbales* as a youth in addition to piano, went on to explore various fusions of Latin music with North American rhythm and blues, soul, funk, and jazz over a career that spanned more than 50 years. His 2007 *Sympatico* earned a Grammy Award for Best Latin Jazz Album, an accolade that was seconded by the Jazz Journalists Association.

The free exchange of musicians and musical ideas between Cuba and the United States—which had culturally enriched both countries—came to a halt in 1960, when Washington severed its ties with Havana after Fidel Castro nationalized all U.S. property. In the early 1960s, following the Cuban Revolution, Cuban government officials first looked upon jazz as "degenerate American music," but they eventually changed their views and new artists began to emerge. In 1973, pianist Jesús

Mongo Santamaría in performance (ca. 1960). PHOTO COURTESY BOB WILLOUGHBY/ REDFERNS/GETTY IMAGES.

"Chucho" Valdés and saxophonist and clarinetist Paquito D'Rivera formed the volcanic group Irakere (from a Yoruba word meaning "forest"). With its impressive array of percussion and bravura-style solos, Irakere gave a new impulse to Cuban jazz and rapidly became the most famous band in its country. Amid its battery of percussion the group made use of the *batá*—the set of three double-headed drums of Yoruba origin that had been such an early foundation in the development of Afro-Cuban music. The *batá*, then a novelty in jazz, gradually became more widespread in Cuban popular music.

In 1977, American jazz masters Dizzy Gillespie and **Stan Getz** performed in Havana, and "discovered" Irakere. When in 1979 President Jimmy Carter eased up on the cultural embargo on Cuba, Irakere was able to book a tour in the United States. The tour—the first performances of a Cuban jazz band in the United States in 20 years—earned huge acclaim, and their debut Columbia album earned them a Grammy Award in 1980.

In 1980, more than 100,000 Cubans defected from their country to the United States; their numbers included clarinetist D'Rivera and drummer Ignacio Berroa, who brought a new shot of Cuban energy to the States. Trumpeter **Arturo Sandoval**, also from Irakere, defected 10 years

Listening Guide

(((•━━ **Listen** to *Manteca* by Dizzy Gillespie and His Orchestra on **mymusiclab.com**
CD II, Track 9/Download Track 33

MANTECA • DIZZY GILLESPIE AND HIS ORCHESTRA

Music: Chano Pozo and Dizzy Gillespie, 1947. Personnel: Dizzy Gillespie, Dave Burns, Elmon Wright, Jr., Benny Bailey (trumpet); "Bill" (William) Shepherd, Ted Kelly (trombone); John Brown, Howard Johnson (alto saxophone); Joe Gayles, George "Big Nick" Nicholas (tenor saxophone); Cecil Payne (baritone saxophone); John Lewis (piano); Al McKibbon (bass); Kenny Clarke (drums); Luciano "Chano" Pozo (conga). Recorded December 22, 1947, in New York. Timing: 2:58.

Overview

Manteca (meaning "grease" but also "marijuana" in Cuban slang) is one of Cubop's most significant compositions. The tune, which had its public premiere December 27, 1947, at Town Hall in New York City, became a major hit for Gillespie and a staple of his repertoire until the end of his career. In 1948, *Manteca* also stunned listeners at the Salle Pleyel, in Paris, as well as at the Pasadena Civic Auditorium in California.

Key Features

- *Manteca* is fascinating for its jubilant mood, high energy, and contrast between the initial vamps and the "head"—based on traditional Cuban rhythm patterns called *tumbaos*—and the bridge, played with a straight-ahead $\frac{4}{4}$ jazz feel. The enjoyment shared between the musicians is palpable and infectious.
- Form: Initial vamps are followed by a melody in ABA' form: a 16-bar A section based on a B-flat *tumbao* (with saxophone chorus) and ending with a different rhythm pattern on the last two bars; a 16-bar swing bridge (with trumpet improvisation); and a 16-bar A' in B-flat, followed by a repetition of the initial vamps.
- Standard big-band instrumentation: Sections of trumpets, trombones, and saxophones, and a rhythm section of piano, bass, and drums, plus the addition—new in bebop at the time—of congas.
- Melody and harmony: The initial vamps and the A section stem from conga rhythms created by **Chano Pozo,** while the jazzy and very fluid bridge was composed by Gillespie with the help of saxophonist Bill Graham and arranger Walter "Gil" Fuller. The arrangement was ghostwritten by **Chico O'Farrill,** who used it again in his *Manteca Suite,* recorded by Dizzy Gillespie's Orchestra in 1954. O'Farrill again produced an excellent version of *Manteca* on *Heart of a Legend* (1999).
- Arrangement: The skillful arrangement creates a crescendo and decrescendo of intensity with several climaxes (at the end of the A and A' sections and during Gillespie's brief but highly charged solos). The Latin A and A' sections herald the rhythm of the mambo—a genre that would become highly popular in the United States in the early 1950s. The shifting textures of the riffs and the contrasts between the different sections sustain the sense of excitement throughout the piece.
- Rhythm: The introduction of the conga in jazz initially created a stir but the instrument soon became a fixture of many other jazz ensembles. Playing *tumbaos* also was a novelty for bass players. At first, bassist Al McKibbon had trouble mastering the new rhythm, but said that "*Manteca* really opened my eyes and mind and heart and everything." The conga, however, plods and feels somewhat unnecessary on the bridge. Gillespie often wished Pozo would refrain from playing on this section, but Pozo was a headstrong man who liked to have his way.

Paquito D'Rivera's role in the Cuban group Irakere brought him to the United States, where he remained to forge his own Latin-bop sound. PHOTO COURTESY ANDY FREEBERG.

- Stylistic variety: The orchestra led by Gillespie in the late 1940s was a revolutionary one and the first bebop big band in the history of jazz. Kenny Clarke, who played on this date, also pioneered bebop, creating a whole new way of distributing accents on his drums. There is nonetheless a marked difference between Gillespie's dazzling lines and Nicholas's tenor solo, which is still rooted in the swing style of the 1940s.

—*Isabelle Leymarie*

TIME	SECTION	MELODY/INSTRUMENTATION
0:00	INITIAL VAMP	Bass and conga enter with a B-flat *tumbao* while Gillespie shouts "Manteca!"
0:08	SECOND VAMP PLAYED OVER THE FIRST ONE	Baritone sax joins in with a different B-flat vamp which, superimposed on the first one, creates interesting polyrhythms.
0:18		Brass joins in with riffs while Gillespie improvises.
0:29–0:31		Short and powerful *tutti* riff.
0:32	INITIAL VAMP	Return to the bass-and-conga *tumbao*.
0:38	A (16 BARS)	Melody stated in call-and-response form by the reeds and the brass.
1:00	BRIDGE (16 BARS)	Bridge: First eight bars stated by the reeds against brass riffs while the conga adapts to the jazz feel.
1:12		Second eight bars of the bridge stated by Gillespie.
1:22	A'	Same as A section.
1:33	INITIAL VAMP	Initial bass-and-conga *tumbao*.
1:37		Baritone sax joins in.
1:39		Reeds join in.
1:42		Short and powerful *tutti* riff.
1:48	SOLO (VAR. OF A)	Tenor saxman "Big Nick" Nicholas plays a solo against riffs on the A section, briefly quoting *Blue Moon*.
2:10	BRIDGE	First eight bars stated by the brass with countermelodies by the reeds.
2:21		Second eight bars stated by Gillespie, who improvises around the melody.
2:32	A'	A' section stated by the reeds the brass and punctuated by a resounding "Manteca!"
2:43	SECOND VAMP	B-flat vamp by brass and reeds with shout of "Manteca!"
2:52	INITIAL VAMP	Initial *tumbao* by bass and conga.
3:03	END	Short final drums accent by Kenny Clarke.

later. D'Rivera and Sandoval both enjoyed fruitful and long-lasting careers in the United States, first joining Gillespie's United Nations Orchestra, established in 1990, and playing on countless record dates as both sidemen and leaders. (In 2000, Sandoval's life and defection were portrayed in the Home Box Office television docudrama *For Love or Country: The Arturo Sandoval Story,* and in 2005, D'Rivera became the first Latin jazz artist to earn a prestigious Jazz Masters Award from the National Endowment for the Arts.) These exiles were later joined by pianist Gonzalo Rubalcaba, whom Dizzy Gillespie had discovered while in Cuba in 1985, and who moved to Miami in 1997, proving himself one of the more interesting young pianists in jazz.

Beginning in the 1970s and 1980s, in New York, young Puerto Rican Nuyoricans such as Jerry and Andy Gonzalez and their Fort Apache Band, as well as pianist Hilton Ruiz and trumpeter Charlie Sepúlveda, created brawny, highly charged sounds that crackled with the city's electricity.

California also eagerly embraced Latin jazz, from the mambo orchestras of Pérez Prado and René Touzet in the 1950s to the boogaloo and funky Latin jazz of percussionist Willie Bobo in the 1960s, on to more recent sounds. In New Orleans, a Latin and Caribbean lilt continued to mark the styles of many mid-to-late-twentieth-century New Orleans musicians,

---

tutti (Italian) all; played by an entire ensemble.

Listening Guide

(((•── **Listen** to *Airegin* by Tito Puente on
mymusiclab.com
CD II, Track 8/Download Track 32

AIREGIN • TITO PUENTE

Music: Sonny Rollins, 1954. Arrangement: Brian Murphy and Tito Puente, 1989. Personnel: Robbie Kwock, David "Piro" Rodriguez (trumpet); Mary Fettig, Mitch Frohman (saxophone); Sam Burtis (trombone); Sonny Bravo (piano); Bobby Rodriguez (bass); Jose Madera (congas); Johnny Rodriguez (bongos); Rebeca Mauleón (synthesizer); Tito Puente (*timbales*); John Santos (*shekere*, bongos). Recorded July 31–August 1, 1989, in San Francisco. First issue: *Goza Mi Timbal* (Concord Picante CCD-4399), 1990. Timing: 4:11.

Overview

Tito Puente's version of Sonny Rollins's mainstream jazz standard *Airegin* (Nigeria spelled backwards) "cooks" as only Latin-energized jazz can. Here, the melody and improvised solos burn over a percolating, mambo-flavored brew of interlocking rhythms. Congas, bongos, *timbales* and the syncopated *tumbao* bass line—interlaced by the piano's catchy *montuno* (repeating countermelody)—complete the Afro-Cuban-derived recipe.

The A-B-A-C form of the melody departs from the standard 32-bar length (8+8+8+8) by adding an extra four bars to the B section. The resulting 36-bar form, 8+12+8+8, provides the structure for each solo chorus.

This track and others from Tito Puente's Grammy Award–winning 1990 album *Goza Mi Timbal* are considered some of the finest examples of mainstream jazz tunes fused with Latin rhythm.

—*Tad Lathrop*

TIME	SECTION	INSTRUMENTATION	MELODY
0:00	INTRO	Rhythm section	The rhythm section (percussion, bass, piano) introduces the tune with a syncopated *clave* pattern, climaxing to an abrupt stop.
0:09	CHORUS 1, A	Band	Trumpets and saxes lead into the melody (answered by trombone at 0:11 and 0:15). It is a ricocheting bop-style phrase (in minor key) played twice, low and high. 8 bars.
0:17	B		Long notes cycle smoothly through major keys descending in half steps. 12 bars.
0:31	A		As in the first A, the rhythm section drops out dramatically for the first and fifth measures. 8 bars.
0:39	C		Variation on B. 8 bars. Percussion marks the ending, and leads into Chorus 2.
0:48	CHORUS 2, AB	Trumpet solo, first half	As trumpet begins soloing, the rhythm section up-shifts to an exciting, propulsive groove—a traditional Afro-Cuban rhythm matrix of off-beat bass *tumbao*, *clave* variations by the *timbales*, and piano *montuno*.
1:10	A	Trumpet solo, second half	Sharp contrast as trumpet sustains a rapid **tremolo** (using a technique called triple tonguing). The *montuno* on piano becomes more audible.
1:18	C		Trumpet shifts the tremolo to ultra-fast riffs over the C section.
1:27	CHORUS 3, ABA	Trombone solo	As trombone enters, the rhythm continues to cook. The trombone solo moves rhythmically—playing off the underlying groove—as it outlines the chord changes of sections A, B, A.
1:58	C		Solo ends in continuous double-time phrases.
2:07	CHORUS 4, ABAC	Sax solo	Saxophone solos through sections A and B, with the same rhythmic feel as the trombone. The solo briefly doubles speed at 2:21. On the second A section and into C, the feel stays much the same as the sax hurtles forward over bubbling percussion.
2:46	CHORUS 5A	Horn unison	Horns all join in a new melody—three punchy unison riffs through section A, ending with two "hits."
2:55	B	Percussion solo	Percussion solos feverishly through the 12 bars of B.
3:08	A	Horns unison	Horns replay their melody over the second A section.
3:16	C	Percussion solo	More fiery solo percussion over section C (6 bars instead of the usual 8).
3:23	CHORUS 6, ABAC	Band	Head: The full band reprises the main melody, minus the last 2 bars.
4:00	CODA	Band	The tune's percussive 8-bar intro is repeated, this time with saxophone soloing freely until all end together in bar 9.

among them the rhythm and blues pianists "Professor Longhair" (Henry Roeland Byrd), Fats Domino, Allen Toussaint, James Booker, and Dr. John; drummers Vernell Fournier, Ed Blackwell, and Idris Muhammad; and the rollicking Dirty Dozen Brass Band. Finally, Latin jazz, which had largely disappeared from New Orleans since the days of Jelly Roll Morton, returned to the Crescent City in 1998, when the fiery Los Hombres Calientes was founded by percussionist Bill Summers, trumpeter Irvin Mayfield, and drummer Jason Marsalis. This band used Latin rhythms, but Summers, Mayfield, and Marsalis came from the jazz tradition and improvised more in a modern jazz style.

Many of Brazilian guitarist Antonio Carlos Jobim's compositions—including One-Note Samba, Triste, Corcovado, Desafinado, *and* Meditation—*have become cornerstones of the standard jazz repertory.* PHOTO COURTESY GENE LEES/DOWN BEAT ARCHIVES.

> ### TAKE NOTE
>
> - Who were the key Cuban and Puerto Rican musicians in jazz history?

Brazilian Music and Jazz

It didn't take long for Afro-Brazilian and jazz sensibilities, once exposed to each other, to bond into a sophisticated and sensuous musical hybrid quite distinct from Afro-Cuban and other flavors of Latin jazz. There were two moments in particular when Brazil and jazz reached their highest heights of interaction: the bossa nova infusion during the 1950s and the samba-fusion movement of the 1970s and 1980s.

Among the American musicians who tuned in to the bossa nova was Dizzy Gillespie. He received a recording of Antonio Carlos Jobim's *Desafinado* from Argentine pianist-arranger **Lalo Schifrin**, and he took in more bossa nova, enthusiastically, during a trip to Brazil in 1961. That same year, other U.S. jazz musicians including guitarist Charlie Byrd, trumpeter Kenny Dorham, flutist Herbie Mann, and saxophonist Zoot Sims made their own visits to Brazil and fell in love with this new genre. Byrd, back in the United States, introduced his friend saxophonist Stan Getz to the new sounds, and the two paired up to record an album. Their *Jazz Samba* (1962), which featured Jobim's *Desafinado* and *Samba de Uma Nota Só (One Note Samba)*, became a bestseller. In the same year, Herbie Mann issued *Do the Bossa with Herbie Mann*, and he and trumpeter Kenny Dorham flew to Brazil to record with pianist

Sérgio Mendes's Sexteto Bossa Rio. On November 21, 1962, a momentous bossa nova concert—featuring Jobim, **Luiz Bonfá**, and many others—was held at Carnegie Hall. The event attracted an overflow crowd, drew dozens of reporters, and brought into the audience such illustrious musicians as Gillespie, Miles Davis, pianist Erroll Garner, and singer Tony Bennett.

The popularity of bossa nova in the United States soon soared. In 1963, Stan Getz recorded Jobim's *The Girl from Ipanema* with Jobim on piano, João Gilberto on guitar and vocals, and Gilberto's wife Astrud on vocals. A year later its parent LP, *Getz/Gilberto*, became hugely successful (and it remains one of the most

Getz and Gilberto at the time of their major hits. PHOTO COURTESY FRANK DRIGGS COLLECTION.

---

tremolo   dynamic effect achieved by rapid alternation of a note's loudness levels.

Listening Guide

CD II, Track 10/Download Track 34

THE GIRL FROM IPANEMA (ORIGINAL TITLE: GARÔTA DE IPANEMA) •
STAN GETZ AND JOAO GILBERTO

Music: Antonio Carlos Jobim, 1962. Portuguese lyrics: Vinícius de Moraes. English lyrics: Norman Gimbel. Personnel: Stan Getz (tenor saxophone); João Gilberto (vocals and guitar); Astrud Gilberto (vocals); Antonio Carlos Jobim (piano); Tommy Williams (bass); Milton Banana (drums). Recorded March 18, 1963, in New York. First issue: *Getz/Gilberto* (Verve V6-8545), 1964. Timing: 5:22.

Overview

For many all over the world, *The Girl from Ipanema* is the epitome of the bossa nova, if not of Brazilian music in general. The song was inspired by a beautiful, real-life woman who used to pass everyday by the Veloso—Jobim and lyricist Vinícius de Moraes's favorite bar in Rio de Janeiro—on her way to the beach. (De Moraes collaborated on many songs with Jobim, bringing a literacy and intelligence to the words that complement the subtlety of the music.) Jobim first recorded it in Brazil shortly before this 1963 New York session, supervised by producer Creed Taylor. Astrud Gilberto—João's wife—had only come to the studio to be with her husband, but Getz convinced her to sing the lyrics in English. While crooners and usually powerful vocalists

were the norm in jazz, *The Girl from Ipanema* introduced a new nonchalant way of singing *sotto voce*, almost as if in a whisper. Verve, the record company, didn't believe in the commercial potential of the album and waited until 1964 before releasing it. When it finally was released, it earned three Grammy Awards and became a bestseller.

Key Features

- With its syncopated rhythm and relaxed atmosphere, *The Girl from Ipanema* perfectly exemplifies the charm of the bossa nova, a $\frac{4}{4}$ genre quite different from the more ebullient $\frac{2}{4}$ samba from which it claims to be derived.
- Form: ABA: 16-bar A section, 16-bar bridge, 8-bar A (with Getz improvising on the whole form). This could also be described as AABA: the 16-bar A section really consists of an 8-bar melody, repeated. The listening chart highlights that substructure. (The B section's length, 16 bars, is unusual. In standard AABA form the B section is 8 bars.)
- Mood: The general mood is graceful and subdued. Both João and Astrud Gilberto sing softly—Astrud with what has

been described as a "little girl's voice." Jobim plays unobtrusive filigree lines under her and Getz, and when stating the theme, uses sparse but highly efficient chords. Getz blows with tender lyricism and, like Jobim, never intrudes on Astrud Gilberto's singing. The whole song gives a feeling of poise and utmost elegance, and the lyrics (both in Portuguese and in English) fit the melody perfectly.
- Rhythm: The syncopated interlocking of the bass, the guitar, the piano, and the drums is particular to the bossa nova. Its essence is in the steady beat of the bass overlaid with guitar chords played slightly ahead of or behind the beat.
- Harmony: Like many other compositions by Jobim, *The Girl from Ipanema* is harmonically very interesting. It modulates up a half step on the bridge, whose first 12 bars are characterized by an unusual chord progression and quarter-note triplets, which create a dreamy, languid atmosphere. Yet the tune is catchy and easy to remember, and has since given rise to countless cover versions.

—Isabelle Leymarie

popular jazz albums of all time). While some Brazilian musicians dismissed Getz's reading of the bossa nova as inauthentic, the album nonetheless contributed to the enduring popularity of Brazilian music in jazz circles. As for Jobim, a classically trained pianist and composer as well as a guitarist and vocalist, he made history as the figure most associated with jazz bossa nova, the composer of many exceptional pieces, a remarkable number of which have become jazz standards.

Bossa nova's rhythm, its chromatic melodies, and its intriguing harmonies provided jazz musicians a new direction—an alternative setting to the swing-based rhythms and blues-tinged melodies of mainstream jazz. The rhythm, in particular, provided

Astrud Gilberto sang on the memorable recording of The Girl from Ipanema, *accompanied by her husband, Brazilian singer-guitarist João Gilberto.* PHOTO COURTESY JAN PERSSON/REDFERNS/GETTY IMAGES.

TIME	FORM	MELODY	INSTRUMENTATION
0:00	INTRODUCTION (FOUR BAR)	João Gilberto, humming.	Guitar.
0:07	A, FIRST HALF	Gilberto sings the song in Portuguese.	
0:22	A, SECOND HALF		
0:24			Bass and the drums enter lightly—almost inaudibly—under Gilberto.
0:36	B (BRIDGE)		
0:42			Jobim comes in on piano under Gilberto on the fourth bar.
1:06	A	Gilberto returns to the A section.	
1:21	SECOND VERSE, A FIRST HALF	Astrud Gilberto enters, singing in English.	Guitar, bass, and drums.
1:36	A, SECOND HALF		
1:50	B		
1:56			Jobim comes in on piano under Astrud Gilberto on the fourth bar.
2:20	A	Astrud Gilberto returns to the A section.	Guitar, bass, and drums.
2:35	A, FIRST HALF	Getz states the melody.	Saxophone, backed by the rhythm section minus the melody.
2:49	A, SECOND HALF	Getz improvises on the second eight bars of the A.	
3:03			Jobim (piano) comes in under Getz on the last bar before the bridge.
3:04	B	Getz solos on the bridge, embroidering the melody.	
3:33	A	Getz finishes his chorus.	
3:48	A, FIRST HALF	Jobim states the melody with very rhythmic chords.	Piano.
4:03	A, SECOND HALF		
4:17	B	Astrud Gilberto comes in on the bridge, singing it in English. The song fades out with a repeat of the words "but she doesn't see."	Guitar, bass, and drums, while Getz on saxophone plays countermelodies.

a fundamental shift in feel. In swing, the rhythmic undercurrent of soloing can be described as "swing" eighth notes, played with a dash of emphasis on the offbeats. But with bossa nova, the soloist's feel is of evenly spaced eighth notes, even though the band's rhythm may be highly syncopated. With the "swing" removed and with a stricter rhythm, the soloist's accents may stand out more, emphasizing rhythmic expressiveness.

As this rhythmic style took a permanent place in the jazz repertoire, a second wave of Brazilian influence brought a more overt rhythmic physicality and broader array of percussion color—more samba than bossa nova—into the mainstream jazz repertoire. Chief among the conduits were the Brazilians Airto

Moreira and his wife, singer Flora Purim, and U.S. musicians Chick Corea and Pat Metheny, who more than other jazzmen spread the samba sound through the jazz community and beyond.

Lured by jazz, many Brazilian musicians settled in the United States. Multi-percussionist Airto Moreira, among them, soon found work with no less than Miles Davis. Through his playing on the seminal fusion album *Bitches Brew* (1969) and five other Davis albums, Moreira's colorful arrays of percussion sounds caught the ears of associated musicians.

Two years earlier than *Bitches Brew*, an album titled *Duster* (1967) by Boston-based vibraphonist Gary Burton, offered some of the non-swing, straight-eighth-note rhythms of bossa nova but with electronics and a bit more force. And in 1969, an album by a young pianist named Chick Corea became a must-listen-to "find" among musicians. That disc, *Now He Sings, Now He Sobs* (1969), explored innovative harmonies in an acoustic-piano trio format but was also notable for the samba and bossa nova rhythms that seemed to propel Corea to extraordinary heights of expression. (Corea also had Cuban sounds in his ear, having earlier played in the combo of conga player Mongo Santamaría.)

Corea (who had played on Miles Davis's *Bitches Brew*) connected with Moreira as well as Flora Purim, and with other musicians they made some of the earliest full integrations of samba and jazz on two 1972 albums by the group Return to Forever. The track *Spain*, with its pro-tracted and exciting samba-flavored solo section, became a touchstone for musicians who wanted to display their "chops" while enjoying the sojourn into impassioned, Spanish-tinged melody.

Moreira and Purim, meanwhile, applied themselves to their own group, Fingers, that displayed a fuller range of Brazilian rhythmic possibilities to U.S. audiences and musicians. Moving from banks of multi-percussion to a seat at the drum kit, Moreira powered sets of tunes that left little doubt about how exciting and eclectic an Afro-Brazilian and jazz mix could be. An album, *Fingers* (1972), cap-tured some of that variety and excitement.

Not surprisingly, Moreira turned up on another seminal meeting of jazz and Afro-Brazilian music, Wayne Shorter's 1974 recording *Native Dancer*, featuring Brazilian singer-songwriter Milton Nascimento. An analysis of the opening track, Nascimento's haunting *Ponta de Areia*, could paint it as a musical portrayal of two cultures first encoun-tering each other hesitatingly, then coming together joyously. At any rate, the album stands to this day as one of the main markers in the road to fully realized Brazilian jazz.

There was only one Airto, but there was increasing demand for what he did. Other multi-percussionists moved into the market, leaving color-ful imprints of their own on a wide variety of jazz bands. Dom Um Romão—whose recording *Spirit of the Times* (1973, with U.S. guitarist Joe Beck) broke new ground in the building of tougher, grittier Afro-Brazilian jazz constructions—joined the fusion group Weather Report. Guilherme Franco, Naná

Airto Moreira rode into jazz on the 1970s Brazilian-percussion wave. PHOTO COURTESY INSTITUTE FOR JAZZ STUDIES, RUTGERS UNIVERSITY.

Vasconcelos, and a host of others provided jazzmen such as Keith Jarrett, McCoy Tyner, and Pat Metheny their own beds of percolating percussion over which to express new ideas.

Guitarist Pat Metheny deeply absorbed the Afro-Brazilian feel and developed it into a distinctively airy, colorful, and obliquely accented mix that coalesced beautifully on the 1978 recording *The Pat Metheny Group*. Two tracks from that set, *Phase Dance* and *San Lorenzo*, pointed to a hybrid of subtly Brazil-tinted jazz with rock and even country music. Years later, on the 1994 recording *First Circle*, Metheny took the same blend to less surprising but at times equally soaring heights, with Afro-Brazilian percussion fea-tured near front and center.

From that 1970s heyday, the wave of Afro-Brazilian percussion and rhythm swept further through jazz. It sometimes emerged as soft support for easy-listening "smooth jazz" and at others times provided a robust, audience-pleasing break from otherwise straight-ahead jazz sets, but it always exemplified the successful blend of jazz with genres outside its immediate stylistic vicinity.

- What was the influence of Brazilian music on jazz?

More Sounds from the Caribbean

Afro-Cuban and Afro-Brazilian sounds may dominate the Latin-Caribbean-jazz connection, but they are not the end of the story. The Caribbean islands host an intricate mosaic of cultures and languages, and their rich music reflects their diversity. Trinidad, for example, produced the **calypso** (first called *kaiso*), a carnival genre that spread to other islands as well as to the United States during the 1950s. Calypso, with its playful rhythms, offbeat phrasings, and cheerful melodies, was popularized stateside by a wide range of singers, including the Andrew Sisters, Ella Fitzgerald, and Harry Belafonte. Jazz musicians took to calypso as well. One of the most notable examples of calypso-infused jazz is Sonny Rollins's now-standard *St. Thomas* (1956; *JTSA* Disc 3/Track 12).

Latin artists who contributed to the spread of calypso include Tito Puente (*Calypso Mambo* and *Calypso Blues*, both from the early 1950s) and Mongo Santamaría (*Afro Lypso*, 1964). In 1976, Trinidadian steel-drummer Othello Molineaux introduced the **pans (steel drums)** into jazz, an instrument later taken up in the United States by Andy Narell.

Two foremost exponents of Caribbean jazz have been Jamaican: guitarist Ernest Ranglin (*Grooving*, 2001), and pianist Monty Alexander, whose repertoire often includes calypsos as well as reggae (the albums *Stir It Up: The Music of Bob Marley*, 1998, and *Jazz Calypso*, 2004).

The French-speaking Caribbean islands (Martinique, Guadeloupe, and Haiti) have created their own dance rhythms, among them the *biguine* (known as "beguine" in English), a medium-tempo genre somewhat akin to the calypso. In the late 1920s,

biguine orchestras, called "jazz" in Guadeloupe and Martinique, adopted the instrumentation of New Orleans jazz bands (clarinet, trombone, banjo, drums). Clarinetist Alexandre Stellio, from Martinique, adapted a rag as a *biguine* under the title *Serpent Maigre* ("lean snake," 1929) and popularized the *biguine* in France. In the early 1930s, Cole Porter heard the *biguine* and was inspired to write the song *Begin the Beguine* (1935), a major hit for bandleader Artie Shaw in 1938 and a jazz standard thereafter. More recently, pianists such as Mario Canonge (from Martinique) and Alain-Jean Marie (from Guadeloupe) recorded vibrant and compelling *biguine*-jazz albums such as, respectively, *Retour aux Sources* (1991) and *Biguine Reflections* (2000).

Saxophonist and flutist Jacques Schwarz-Bart and trumpeter Franck Nicolas, both from Guadeloupe, injected into their progressive jazz the stirring rhythms of *gwo ka*—a genre deriving from the drum music played by Guadeloupe maroons during colonial times to communicate with each other, and which, on the island, has since been revived as a symbol of cultural pride and resilience. Their work can be heard on *Soné Ka-La* (2006), and *Jazz Ka Philosophy* (2002), respectively.

- What other Caribbean music styles have had an influence on jazz?

Later Trends in Latin and Caribbean Jazz

Over the years, many talented artists from all over the globe have been drawn to Latin and Caribbean jazz. Lalo Schifrin, an Argentinian pianist, composer, and arranger, became a leading film and television composer—he wrote the theme for the TV series *Mission Impossible* (in $\frac{5}{4}$ time, 1966)—while playing jazz alongside some of the music's top stars. They included Dizzy Gillespie, to whose band Schifrin contributed a percussion-laden composition, the *Gillespiana Suite* (1960). Tenor saxophonist Gato Barbieri, an alumnus of Schifrin's band and a fellow Argentinean, purveyed a distinctively aggressive jazz sax sound while capturing the nostalgia of the Argentine *pampa* on such recordings as *El Pampero* (1971) and *Caliente* (1977).

Puerto Rican saxophonist David Sánchez delved into the robust *bomba*, an African-derived genre from the northern coast of Puerto Rico, on his album *Sketches of Dreams* (1995). His fellow countryman trombonist William Cepeda explored the hybrid *plena* on *Afrorican Jazz* (1998). Panamanian pianist

---

calypso (originally called *kaiso*) a music and dance tradition originally from Trinidad that, during the 1950s, spread to other Caribbean islands and the United States.

pan (steel drum) a musical instrument made from a large empty oil drum that has been tuned; originally from Trinidad.

biguine (French) a medium-tempo dance-based music originally from the French Caribbean; rhythmically similar to the calypso; "beguine" in English.

Gato Barbieri playing at Chicago's Viva Latin Jazz festival in 2005. PHOTO COURTESY MICHAEL JACKSON.

Latin and Caribbean jazz seems to be evolving towards an increased eclecticism and syncretism. Like Lalo Schifrin, the American pianist Clare Fischer composed and arranged Cuban- and Brazilian-inflected material (*Morning, Pensativa, Poinciana*) as well as straight-ahead jazz. Clarinetist Paquito D'Rivera, pianist Danilo Pérez, and saxophonist David Sánchez, to name only a few, proved equally at ease with modern jazz and with *rumbas*, sambas, *guaguancós*, and other Latin rhythms. In the United States and the Caribbean, groups such as the Caribbean Jazz Ensemble and the West Indies Jazz Band offered compelling syntheses of various West Indian genres. British saxophonist Courtney Pine, of Jamaican descent, incorporated jazz, Indian, African, and Caribbean strains (*To the Eyes of Creation*, 1992). Some artists have injected individual tunes with more than one kind of Latin rhythm. Two examples of this, both moving from Brazilian samba to Cuban *montuno* patterns, are vibraphonist Jay Hoggard's *São Pablo* (on his album *Rain Forest*, 1980) and Clare Fischer's *João* (on Gary Burton's *For Hamp, Red, Bags, and Cal*, 2000).

From its origins in Cuba, Latin jazz remains a *lingua franca* for many musicians all over the globe. As is true of the United States, Latin America and the Caribbean have proven to be an inexhaustible wellspring of musical ideas and a fertile seedbed of talent. Fed by and successfully incorporating myriad musical influences from different corners of the Americas, while exerting its own pervasive influence, the music these countries produce is in a state of constant evolution and seems poised to remain among the most vital artistic languages in years to come.

Danilo Pérez skillfully reworked the music of his native land in such tunes as *Panama Libre* (1992), *Panama Blues* (1998), and *Cosa Linda* (also 1998), bringing to them an adventurous approach to harmony and dynamics.

U.S. jazzmen have also turned toward Latin horizons beyond Cuba, Brazil, and the Caribbean. Bassist-composer Charles Mingus looked toward Mexico with the album *New Tijuana Moods* (recorded in 1957), and Colombia with *Cumbia & Jazz Fusion* (1976–77). Duke Ellington revealed inspiration from points south with his compositions *The Virgin Islands Suite* (1965, with a calypso movement), *The Latin American Suite* (1968), and his 1956 album *A Drum Is a Woman*, a fantasy history of jazz that featured three percussionists.

TAKE NOTE

- What are some more recent trends in Caribbean and Latin Jazz?

Explore Jazz Classics and Key Recordings on **mymusiclab.com**

- How did Afro-Cuban and Brazilian jazz draw on similar musical roots to create different musical styles?

Essential elements of both Afro-Cuban and Brazilian jazz are traceable to the same African sources. In each area, the displaced Africans sustained their cultural and religious identities through practice of their traditional music and dance. But their music also melded with that of the host cultures. In Latin jazz, an African-derived emphasis on rhythm was filtered through mostly European-derived cultures—Spanish in the case of Afro-Cuban, Portuguese in the case of Brazilian—yielding contrasting styles that eventually crossed paths and mingled through the movement of peoples.

- What native Cuban and Brazilian musical rhythms and musical instruments have influenced the development of Latin Jazz?

Dance rhythms from both Cuba and Brazil were the major influences on Latin jazz, along with a wide variety of native percussion instruments that were incorporated into their bands. Important Afro-Cuban styles influencing jazz included *son*, *rumba*, *habanera*, and mambo. In the United States these yielded *rumba*, big band mambo, *cha-cha-chá,* and Cubop. Important Afro-Brazilian styles influencing jazz included *maxixe* (Brazilian tango), samba, and bossa nova.

- How did Latin music influence early jazz?

Several popular Latin dances came to the United States and were adapted by early jazz musicians. The Cuban *danza* and the Argentinian tango contributed to the "Latin tinge" that Jelly Roll Morton and others recognized as a vital part of New Orleans jazz. The Brazilian *maxixe* (also known as the "Brazilian tango") and the Argentinian tango became wildly popular in the United States around 1915, influencing early jazz performers in New York City.

- Who were the key Cuban and Puerto Rican musicians in jazz history?

The Cuban flutist Alberto Socarrás, who moved to Harlem in 1927, was among the first musicians to wed jazz with Latin rhythms. The Afro-Cubans, led by percussionist Machito and trumpeter and saxophonist Mario Bauzá, were the first successful Latin big band playing in New York, beginning in the 1940s. In the late 1940s, Dizzy Gillespie became the first North American bandleader to fuse bebop and Afro-Cuban rhythms when he hired the *conguero* (conga player) Chano Pozo. During the 1960s, the combos formed by Cuban percussionist Mongo Santamaría, and Nuyorican (Puerto Rican New Yorker) percussionists Tito Puente and Ray Barretto and pianist Eddie Palmieri helped further popularize the music. After the Cuban revolution of 1959, the interchange slowed somewhat, but picked up momentum in the 1970s–1980s, thanks to the work of artists like pianist "Chucho" Valdés and saxophonist and clarinetist Paquito D'Rivera.

- What was the influence of Brazilian music on jazz?

Bossa nova and samba were the two key Brazilian dance rhythms that were wed with jazz. The bossa nova craze was launched by the hit recording *The Girl from Ipanema* by saxophonist Stan Getz and Brazilian musicians pianist/composer Antonio Carlos Jobim, guitar player/vocalist João Gilberto, and vocalist Astrud Gilberto. In the 1970s and 1980s, jazz samba-fusion was very popular. Chief among the conduits were the Brazilians Airto Moreira and his wife, singer Flora Purim, and U.S. musicians Chick Corea and Pat Metheny, who more than other jazzmen spread the samba sound through the jazz community and beyond.

- What other Caribbean music styles have had an influence on jazz?

The calypso, a Trinidadian carnival genre, spread to the United States in the 1950s. A notable example of its use in jazz is the Sonny Rollins standard *St. Thomas.* The French-speaking Caribbean islands (Martinique, Guadeloupe, and Haiti) have created their own dance rhythms, among them the *biguine* (known as "beguine" in English), a medium-tempo genre somewhat akin to the calypso.

- What are some more recent trends in Caribbean and Latin Jazz?

Latin and Caribbean jazz seems to be evolving towards an increased eclecticism and syncretism. Some have explored more regional folk rhythms, such as the Puerto Rican *bomba* or the *gwoka* rhythm of the Guadeloupe maroons. Others have freely combined rhythms from different cultures to create something entirely new. Still others, like saxophonist Paquito D'Rivera, pianist Danilo Pérez, and saxophonist David Sánchez, to name only a few, proved equally at ease with modern jazz and purely Latin music.

DISCUSSION QUESTIONS

1. Discuss some of the music you have heard that has elements of Latin traditions. Describe the feeling and the rhythm.

2. North American jazz, Afro-Cuban jazz, and Afro-Brazilian jazz are traceable to African origins. What developmental factors account for their differences?

3. Name some of the U.S. jazz musicians who helped popularize Latin elements at different points in the twentieth century. What do you think attracted them to the Latin elements?

4. Have you had any experience in dancing or watching Latin steps such as the *salsa*, *tango*, or *samba*? How do these steps differ from other steps you know?

5. Why do you think that despite Mexico's much larger population, Cuban and Puerto Rican jazz musicians have had much more overall exposure and influence in the United States?

6. The chapter mentions that such U.S. jazz musicians as Dizzy Gillespie were sent by the State Department to perform in Latin America as goodwill cultural ambassadors. Present arguments for why such tours are, or are not, a worthy use of taxpayer money.

7. After listening to *Manteca* and *The Girl from Ipanema*, compare them in terms of the moods and feelings they convey. Explore the cultural origins of any differences you perceive.

8. Discuss characteristics of Brazilian music that have been absorbed into jazz. Can you think of jazz standards (evergreens) that have a Brazilian flavor?

KEY TERMS & KEY PEOPLE

Ray Barretto	Dizzy Gillespie	Chano Pozo
Mario Bauzá	Irakere	Tito Puente
Luiz Bonfá	Antonio Carlos Jobim	*rumba*
bossa nova	Machito (Frank Grillo Gutiérrez)	samba
Charlie Byrd		Arturo Sandoval
calypso	mambo	Mongo Santamaria
clave	*montuno*	Lalo Schifrin
conga	Airto Moreira	*son*
Chick Corea	Chico O'Farrill	*surdo*
Cubop	Eddie Palmieri	Juan Tizol
Paquito D'Rivera	pan (steel drum)	*timbales*
Stan Getz	Hermeto Pascoal	*tumbao*

Jazz Forward

Jazz Forward

by José Antonio Bowen

TAKE NOTE

- How has mainstream acoustic jazz continued to flourish and develop?

- How has the avant-garde jazz movement of the 1960s and 1970s evolved and who are some of its key performers?

- How have some musicians begun to rethink the definition of jazz beyond the classic division between mainstream and avant-garde?

- Who are some of today's leading vocalists and vocal groups, and what roles do they play on the current jazz scene?

HISTORICAL EVENTS

MUSICAL EVENTS

1975 — Ornette Coleman's Prime Time band debuts its "free funk" musical style

1976 — Saxophonists David Murray, Hamiet Bluiett, Oliver Lake, and Julius Hemphill form the World Saxophone Quartet to explore free jazz music

President Reagan elected, moving the country to the right — 1980

1981 — Wynton Marsalis makes his first world tour at age 20 as trumpeter with the VSOP quartet

1984 — Alto sax player Steve Coleman forms the M-Base collective to explore wedding hip-hop and funk rhythms with jazz

Iran-Contra Affair shows United States secretly sold weapons to Iran to fund fighting rebels in Central America — 1986

Composer/saxophone player John Zorn forms the punk-jazz group Naked City with guitarist Bill Frisell and keyboardist Wayne Horvitz

1987

Berlin Wall falls, leading to the reunification of East and West Germany, as the Iron Curtain crumbles — 1988 — Jazz at Lincoln Center Orchestra debuts

1989

PHOTO COURTESY CARDAF/SHUTTERSTOCK.

1990 — Smithsonian Jazz Masterworks Orchestra established

Bill Clinton elected President, bringing Democrats back to power — 1992

1997 — Wynton Marsalis's *Blood on the Fields* is awarded a Pulitzer Prize, the first for a jazz composition

Clinton impeached for having sex with a White House intern; he is eventually acquitted — 1999

• "9/11": United States attacked by Al Qaeda and the World Trade Center is destroyed — 2001

• Apple launches iPod player and digital music-listening revolution

2002 — The Smithsonian Institution launches the first national Jazz Appreciation Month (celebrated each April)

United States invades Iraq, toppling dictator Saddam Hussein — 2003

2004 — Jazz at Lincoln Center opens its own facility on New York's Columbus Circle, featuring three performance halls

U.S. economy crashes — 2008

Barack Obama becomes first African American president of the United States — 2009

❋ Explore the Jazz Timeline on **mymusiclab.com**

PHOTO COURTESY ALAN FREED/SHUTTERSTOCK.

azz has always been a music of fusion and change: many of its players welcome new influences and actively seek innovation. But at the same time, because musical sounds are evanescent and musical styles constantly evolve, cultures must work to preserve the music of the past. So in jazz, the creation of new work has been accompanied by preservation of the old.

In the 1930s, swing bands powered ahead as preservationists looked back to earlier styles from New Orleans. In the 1960s, as experimental sounds echoed through Greenwich Village, vintage Dixieland jazz could be heard as well. In the 1970s, just as jazz-rock fusion was gaining momentum, a flood of new acoustic jazz records appeared.

Change *and* preservation: that's the way it has been with jazz since the music's early years, and the combination continues into the present. Change has occurred along several interacting paths: fusing with surrounding styles, experimenting with the very foundations of jazz construction, and interacting with world cultures.

The tendency for jazz to fuse with other styles of music has been a theme from the beginning. Jazz was born a hybrid. In New Orleans, jazz was fashioned from European brass band music, African drumming, Delta blues, Missouri ragtime, old hymns, Spanish rhythms, and popular Tin Pan Alley songs.

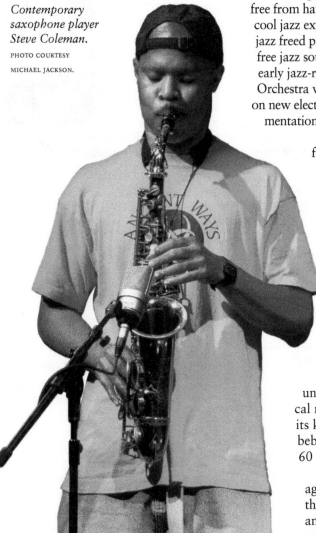

Contemporary saxophone player Steve Coleman.
PHOTO COURTESY MICHAEL JACKSON.

In each new style, jazz's emphasis on spontaneous improvisation led to a search for greater freedom. The beboppers wanted to play longer solos, free from having to follow the melody of popular songs, while players of cool jazz experimented with new textures and time signatures. Modal jazz freed players from having to follow chord changes, and players of free jazz sought sonic, harmonic, formal, and rhythmic freedom. The early jazz-rock fusion of Miles Davis, Weather Report, and Mahavishnu Orchestra was really a continuation of free jazz with an added emphasis on new electronic sounds, collective improvisation, and constant experimentation with rhythm, grooves, and meter.

The introduction of world music influences also brought forth new innovations in jazz. Latin jazz was inspired by the hope to reconnect more directly with African rhythm and be free of some of the European binary (march) rhythms of traditional swing. The new rhythms and scales of Indian music also offered freedom from Western conventions. Players from the United States and around the world fused jazz with native or ethnic musics in the continuing desire to find something new. These new fusions all involved improvisation over a rhythmic or harmonic repeating pattern, shareable across styles and cultures, so the basic language of jazz became a sort of new *lingua franca* for music making.

All of this occurred with remarkable speed, which brings up another constant theme in jazz: the unprecedented pace of change. Some eras of Western classical music lasted for longer than a century. But jazz generated its key historic styles—from New Orleans to big band swing, bebop, cool, hard bop, avant-garde, and fusion—in about 60 years. This pace continues as jazz evolves.

Balancing the "preservation" part of the jazz equation against the imperatives of change—maintaining the best of the old even as innovators invent the new—created debate and controversy about jazz and its definition. New Orleans revivalists argued against beboppers about the true nature of jazz. Mainstream purists denounced fusion as a sellout. Even when a revival movement appeared in jazz, it was usually accompanied by an alternative approach and a fresh battle over the definition of jazz.

Five broad phenomena that propelled jazz through its initial development continued to do so as jazz reached the end of its first century and entered its second:

1. Fusings: Jazz musicians sought to fuse jazz with an increasing diversity of other musical cultures and sounds, and players continued to interact with popular music grooves, techniques, and repertoire.
2. Neotraditional movement: In reaction to the experimentation of the avant-garde and jazz-rock fusion, a **neotraditional** movement arose—centering on trumpeter **Wynton Marsalis**—who sought to return jazz to its blues roots, while elevating the importance of key performer/composers such as Louis Armstrong and Duke Ellington.
3. Quest for the new: At the same time, an army of experimental and avant-garde players maintained their quest for change and new forms of freedom. The variety of these paths meant that the sound of jazz continued to diversify: any two jazz performances of the early twenty-first century were likely to be more different than ever before.
4. Accelerating change: The pace of change didn't let up: the tendency of jazz to fuse and morph accelerated in the jazz of the 1980s and beyond.
5. Redefining jazz: A group of jazz revivalists challenged the jazz practices of exploration with a new definition of jazz. This movement stoked controversy about the definition of jazz in the twenty-first century. The question became, "If all of these different sounds can be jazz, then what is jazz?"

The Continuing Life of Mainstream Acoustic Jazz

What jazz *was*, in its mainstream form, never disappeared. While jazz-rock fusion brought new attention to jazz in the

1970s, the core jazz approach—based on bop and swing—expanded during the same period. In 1970 and after, every jazz style ever created was still being played, and it was still possible to hear many of the legends who had created these styles: Louis Armstrong, Duke Ellington, Count Basie, Benny Goodman, Dizzy Gillespie, Ella Fitzgerald, Sarah Vaughan, Art Blakey, Charles Mingus, and Dave Brubeck were all still performing. Other players who had moved to Europe, such as Dexter Gordon and Stan Getz, returned to live in the United States and began recording again.

While the major record companies largely abandoned jazz for rock during the 1960s, several new companies appeared in the 1970s to keep the jazz tradition alive. In 1973, Norman Granz, who had earlier established Verve Records, founded Pablo Records and built an extraordinary roster of legendary jazz performers. Another label, Concord Records, was started in California by Carl Jefferson in the same year to record seasoned West Coast players.

Formal jazz education also focused primarily on core jazz principles associated with the mainstream. The initial rise of jazz education came in the 1970s. High school jazz bands and many university programs were founded, while a handful of educators—among them Jamey Aebersold, David Baker, and Jerry Coker—published educational materials that became standard. While every aspiring bass player knew the bass line from Herbie Hancock's *Chameleon* and every trumpet player wanted to be Maynard Ferguson playing *Gonna Fly Now* (the theme from the 1976 film

Dexter Gordon enjoyed renewed acclaim late in his career. PHOTO COURTESY ANDY FREEBERG.

neotraditional jazz mainstream jazz as preserved and practiced by some jazz musicians in the 1990s, most notably Wynton Marsalis.

History & Culture

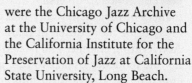

David Baker, musical and artistic director of the Smithsonian Jazz Masterworks Orchestra. PHOTO COURTESY THE SMITHSONIAN INSTITUTION.

Institutional Jazz Programs

It is perhaps ironic that jazz—noted for its outside-the-mainstream, anti-establishment ethos—has gained a great deal of support from public and private institutions over the last few decades.

Some wondered whether institutional involvement would change the music for the worse. But the arguments for such support were compelling: to preserve the growing history of jazz, to give jazz a stronger economic footing, to present it as a music equal in value to any other, and to help it reach new audiences.

Among the first institutions to embrace jazz were Tulane University in New Orleans and Hunter College in New York, each of which set up a jazz archive in the 1950s. (Hunter's Institute of Jazz Studies moved in 1966 to Rutgers University in Newark, New Jersey.) In 1971, the Smithsonian Institution in Washington, DC, established a presence in jazz that grew to be the world's most comprehensive set of jazz programs, including collections of memorabilia, artifacts, and oral histories, and the production of exhibitions, recordings, books, educational material, symposia, concerts, and radio and multimedia programs. The Smithsonian Jazz Masterworks Orchestra, founded in 1990 under the batons of David Baker and Gunther Schuller, plays the riches of the jazz repertory in the nation's capital and on national and international tours.

In the 1980s and 1990s, a number of other institutions got into the act.

Founded in 1986, the Washington-based Thelonious Monk Institute for Jazz has focused on nurturing young jazz performers, while the Kennedy Center, under advisor Billy Taylor, presented an ambitious series of concerts and school programs. The Library of Congress undertook a program of commissions to jazz composers. New York's Jazz at Lincoln Center, under the artistic direction of the charismatic Wynton Marsalis, developed its widely touring Jazz at Lincoln Center Orchestra in 1988, as well as the Essentially Ellington high school band contest (begun in 1995), a radio series, and lecture and film programs. In 2004, Jazz at Lincoln Center opened a new facility at Columbus Circle with three impressive performance halls, and as of 2011 offered 450 events per year in New York City and elsewhere. Carnegie Hall established its Carnegie Hall Jazz Band under trumpeter Jon Faddis in 1992 (although the band folded due to budget cuts in 2003), while the Brooklyn Academy of Music launched a cutting-edge performance series under clarinetist **Don Byron**.

Efforts began elsewhere in the United States to create jazz repertory orchestras and homes for jazz performance series and jazz archives. Among the latter were the Chicago Jazz Archive at the University of Chicago and the California Institute for the Preservation of Jazz at California State University, Long Beach.

The National Endowment for the Arts, founded in 1965, provided a modest stream of grants over the years for jazz and each year from 1982 to 2012, honored a series of distinguished musicians as NEA Jazz Masters. In the 1990s, three foundations stepped in to raise the ante: the Doris Duke Charitable Foundation; the Louis Armstrong Educational Foundation; and the largest jazz philanthropic donor of the twentieth century, the Lila Wallace-Reader's Digest Fund, whose grants included $7.5 million to the Smithsonian for a 10-year initiative of jazz programs and $6.9 million to National Public Radio.

European institutions include the National Jazz Archive in Amsterdam; the Norsk Jazzarkiv in Oslo; the Institute for Jazz Research in Graz, Austria; and the Jazz-Institut at Darmstadt, Germany.

—*John Edward Hasse*

Rocky), all of the new educational bands, programs, and materials were based on bebop as the essential style. Jazz-rock fusion might be on the radio, but acoustic jazz was in every classroom.

The presence of acoustic jazz hardly diminished in the 1980s. Trumpeter Clark Terry remained active as did saxophonists Phil Woods, Stan Getz, Dexter Gordon, and Sonny Rollins. There were also several important reunions of classic groups. Starting in 1981, the Modern Jazz Quartet reunited for regular concerts (with the same lineup they had maintained since 1955) and continued recording until 1993. Pianist Oscar Peterson also reunited with guitarist Herb Ellis and bassist Ray Brown, and the Heath Brothers (saxophonist Jimmy, bassist Percy, and drummer Albert "Tootie") went back on the road.

For an art form steeped in an aesthetic of change, it is hardly surprising that the history of jazz is dominated by young radicals reinventing the music of their elders. So jazz (like rock) has remained a challenge for older players. Do you play your old hits and abandon the fire of change that motivated you from the beginning, or do you continue to seek freedom and spontaneity even if it means reinventing your own style? For years Dave Brubeck avoided playing *Take Five*, but by the 1990s, he gave in and began including it at every concert. An exception, Miles Davis remarkably reinvented himself and jazz in surprising new ways throughout his career.

While producer Norman Granz introduced recordings of the "Great American Songbook" with Ella Fitzgerald and Oscar Peterson in the 1950s, jazz musicians in the 1960s and 1970s were keen on recording their own material. In the 1980s, however, collections of standards again became a mainstay for jazz players. This return to a format that once drew criticism for being populist and conservative occurred in the rock world, too: In 1983, rock singer Linda Ronstadt's album *What's New*, with arrangements by Frank Sinatra's arranger Nelson Riddle, proved the existence of a large audience for collections of standards; a host of aging rockers followed in her footsteps. Jazz singers, who had been interpreting standards all along, enjoyed growing audiences for their shows and recordings.

Through the 1980s and 1990s, the issues remained much the same for mainstream jazz musicians: the style and repertoire were established and were reinforced by both a graying audience and jazz schools. Most older musicians simply continued to play the same tunes in much the same style, and several found renewed success in the guise of "old masters."

Stan Getz, after popular success with the bossa nova in the 1960s and experiments with Chick Corea in the 1970s, returned in the late 1980s to his favorite ballads with a deepened sound and commitment to make some of his greatest recordings—with a quartet that included pianist Kenny Barron, bassist Rufus Reid, and drummer Victor Lewis. Saxophonist Joe Henderson, pianist Andrew Hill, and trombonist J. J. Johnson all returned to major labels and to critical success. Saxophonist Sonny Rollins continued to be as edgy and as popular as ever. On September 18, 2007, the 76-year-old Rollins returned to Carnegie Hall, 50 years after his debut there, to play with both his regular sextet and the 82-year-old (and equally young-sounding) drummer Roy Haynes.

Art Blakey was another powerful keeper of the flame. Like Miles Davis, Blakey also liked to hire young musicians, but Blakey continued to train them in his own thunderous style of hard bop. After the celebrated editions of his **Jazz Messengers** of the late 1950s (*Moanin'*; JTSA Disc 4/Track 1) and early 1960s (*One by One*; JTSA Disc 5/Track 1), the group made fewer recordings through the 1970s until Wynton and **Branford Marsalis** joined the band in 1980.

Watch the video *Build A New World* by Art Blakey and the Jazz Messengers on **mymusiclab.com**

Veteran bassist Ray Brown.
PHOTO COURTESY PAUL J HOEFFLER/DOWN BEAT ARCHIVES.

History & Culture

In 1993, the Smithsonian produced a traveling exhibition of its Duke Ellington holdings. COURTESY SMITHSONIAN INSTITUTION TRAVELING EXHIBITION SERVICE.

Hall of Famer Lionel Hampton performing in New York City (ca. 1946). PHOTO COURTESY WILLIAM P. GOTTLIEB/WILLIAM P. GOTTLIEB COLLECTION/LIBRARY OF CONGRESS PRINTS & PHOTOGRAPHS DIVISION.

Jazz Museums

The need for the preservation of jazz history has propelled several major museums and institutions to collect jazz materials over the last half-century, and more new museums open from time to time.

In the East, Louis Armstrong's house (3456 107th Street in Queens, New York City) is open to visitors, and a selection of his memorabilia is on display at Queens College, which houses the Louis Armstrong Archives. In Manhattan, Jazz at Lincoln Center offers a small "Hall of Fame" display and periodic exhibits of photographs. Uptown, the National Jazz Museum in Harlem, until a regular museum is built, maintains a small visitors' center and organizes weekly public programs such as panel discussions and lectures.

Beginning in 1988, the Smithsonian Institution's National Museum of American History has displayed some of its national jazz treasures, which include the vast, 200,000-page Ellington archive as well as Dizzy Gillespie's angled-bell trumpet; the clarinets of Benny Goodman and Artie Shaw; the drum sets of Buddy Rich and Gene Krupa; the band "library" of Jimmie Lunceford; John Coltrane's manuscript for *A Love Supreme*; artifacts from Miles Davis, Thelonious Monk, Herbie Hancock, and Tito Puente; photographs by Herman Leonard and William Claxton; 350 films; and papers of Ella Fitzgerald and the Apollo Theater. In nearby Baltimore, the Eubie Blake National Jazz Institute offers exhibits on this Baltimore-born ragtime and popular music composer/performer, along with Chick Webb, Cab Calloway, and Billie Holiday.

The South has a growing number of jazz sites. The Louisiana State Museum, in New Orleans, maintains a continuing exhibition on New Orleans jazz, while the city-owned Louis Armstrong Park features statues of hometown heroes Armstrong and Sidney Bechet. Also in the Crescent City, the New Orleans Jazz National Historical Park has rehabilitated Perseverance Hall near the old Congo Square and operates a visitors center in the French Quarter providing information, walking tours, demonstrations, and educational performances. In Florence, Alabama, the W. C. Handy birthplace (602 West College Street) is open to visitors, while the Alabama Jazz Hall of Fame, in Birmingham, honors 200 native sons and daughters, including Erskine Hawkins, Lionel Hampton, and Dinah Washington.

In the Midwest, the library at Indiana University in Bloomington features a Hoagy Carmichael room, displaying his jazz- and song-related memorabilia. In St. Louis, you can tour the restored Scott Joplin House State Historic Site (2658 Delmar). In Kansas City, Missouri, the handsome American Jazz Museum, in the historic 18th and Vine District, offers memorabilia of local musicians and has a performance space.

Out West, there is a Glenn Miller exhibit, chockablock with memorabilia, at his alma mater, the University of Colorado in Boulder.

—*John Edward Hasse*

Wynton Marsalis and the Hard Bop Revival

Despite all of the wonderful music being made by these old masters, it took an articulate young man from New Orleans to make mainstream acoustic jazz fashionable again. With a distinguished jazz pianist as a father, a childhood in the Baptist church, and a classical music education that included the Tanglewood Music Center and the Juilliard School of Music, Wynton Marsalis had the perfect pedigree to become the spokesman for a new jazz age.

Recognition came quickly. Marsalis had barely arrived at Juilliard in 1978 before he was playing with Blakey (in 1980), with whom he stayed for only a year before leaving at the age of 20 to tour the United States and Japan with the former Miles Davis rhythm section comprising pianist Herbie Hancock, bassist Ron Carter, and drummer Tony Williams. In 1982 he signed with Columbia Records and soon became the first musician to win Grammy Awards for both classical and jazz albums in the same year.

Marsalis's first quintet featured his brother Branford, drummer Jeff "Tain" Watts, and pianist Kenny Kirkland. His early groups were eclectic and carefully constructed, but they had mixed success. Indications of a personal style were evident on the album *Black Codes (from the Underground)* (1985), which featured changing time signatures and unusual phrase lengths. However, its absence of the names of the other musicians on the album cover—unusual in jazz—invited speculation about Marsalis's collegiality. When Branford and Kirkland left the band to tour with rock singer-composer Sting, Marsalis became publically angry. Controversy came slowly to Marsalis, but calling out his brother for playing "some [expletive] that's being called jazz" made it clear that Marsalis was already on a crusade to define jazz.

Three months later Marsalis formed a new group, retaining drummer Watts and bassist Robert Leslie Hurst III from the previous group and adding the remarkable blind pianist Marcus Roberts, who walked in with all of Marsalis's earlier material memorized. *J Mood* (1985) and *Marsalis Standard Time Vol. 1* (1986) followed quickly, and while the structures, texture, and meters were still complex, the finicky virtuosity of the earlier albums now seemed better reconciled with the imperfections of improvisation and the lyricism of his melodic style. Then in December 1989, Marsalis made his last recording in this style: "I knew

👁 **Watch** the video of *Well, You Needn't* by VSOP on **mymusiclab.com**

Drummer/bandleader Art Blakey in 1992.
PHOTO COURTESY MARC MARNIE/REDFERNS/GETTY IMAGES.

that when I did that album *[Live] at Blues Alley*," he said, "that I wasn't going to make another record in that type of style—all those really complex rhythms, playing fast, wild."

Over the next two years, Marsalis's thinking, life, and music would undergo a remarkable transformation. First, he quit classical music: "I found there was not enough time for me to pay respects to the unarguable greatness of European music or jazz. . . . The time I spent bludgeoning Haydn could have been devoted to learning how to swing and reaching a functional appreciation of the blues." Second, he became deeply interested in early jazz, especially the music of Louis Armstrong and Duke Ellington. In 1988 he agreed to become the chair of a new task force to perpetuate New Orleans music. Third, he came to see the blues as fundamental not just as music, but as the social and ritualistic cornerstone of the black experience in America. In this he was influenced by his growing relationship with critic Stanley Crouch and by Albert Murray's book *Stomping the Blues*. The Marsalis-Crouch-Murray position became an increasingly

A CLOSER LOOK

The talented Marsalis clan has matched the prominence of such other jazz families as the Boswell Sisters (Connie, Martha, and Vet), the Jones brothers (Hank, Elvin, and Thad), the Montgomery brothers (Wes, Monk, and Buddy), and the Heath brothers (Jimmy, Percy, and Tootie). After Wynton Marsalis gained fame in the 1980s, national attention eventually turned to

✳ Explore on **mymusiclab.com**

the sources of his talent. A New Orleans upbringing proved to be part of it, but so did the influential presence of a musical father, Ellis. The father and four brothers, as a family, won a National Endowment for the Arts Jazz Masters Award in 2011.

Ellis Marsalis • Piano

The patriarch of the family, Ellis Marsalis is a well-known jazz pianist and educator. He nurtured the careers of many New Orleans jazz musicians, including his own children.

Branford Marsalis • Soprano Saxophone

Branford has had the most eclectic career of any of the Marsalis offspring. Besides performing in his brother's first quintet from 1981 to 1985, he gained recognition for his work with the pop singer Sting and as leader of the *Tonight Show* television band from 1992 to 1995. During the first decade of the twenty-first century, he performed primarily with classical ensembles and focused on composition.

Jason Marsalis • Drums

Jason is considerably younger than his other musician brothers. He has developed a distinct style as a drummer based on his training in classical and Brazilian percussion. In 2001, he made his first recordings on the vibraphone.

PHOTO COURTESY JACK VARTOOGIAN/FRONT ROW PICTURES.

Wynton Marsalis • Trumpet

Wynton, the best known of the Marsalis clan, burst onto the jazz scene in the early 1980s and drew accolades as the next great trumpet player. Winning Grammy Awards for both classical and jazz trumpet performance in 1983, Marsalis became a leader of the neotraditional jazz movement. He became known for his criticism of jazz-rock and fusion, and especially of Miles Davis, whom he felt had turned his back on jazz. Marsalis was named the founding Artistic Director of Jazz at Lincoln Center in 2004.

Delfeayo Marsalis • Trombone

Delfeayo is better known as a record producer than as an active trombonist, but he does perform and record both with his family and his own groups. He has also scored music for television, the off-Broadway stage, and ballet.

prescriptive lament that jazz needed to return to its (somewhat romanticized) roots in the blues.

All of these influences can immediately be heard in *The Majesty of the Blues* (1989) and in the three-volume *Soul Gestures in Southern Blue* (1991). The classical tone, intricate meter shifts, and complex modern harmonies of the previous albums are replaced with growling and muted trumpet, slow deep grooves, and a wide variety of blues, a form that hardly appears in his early work. The reorientation toward New Orleans is completed with some clarinet, "tailgate" style trombone, and even some banjo playing.

While it was significant that Marsalis had changed his style, a fourth change in his life was much more significant for the future of jazz. In the summer of 1987, already perhaps more famous and influential than any previous jazz player, the 26-year-old Marsalis became the co-founder of the first jazz series at Lincoln Center in New York: Classical Jazz. This acceptance of jazz into the institutions of high art was welcomed, but

the idea of jazz as an institution seemed paradoxical. As artistic director of Jazz at Lincoln Center, Marsalis soon led an empire with competitions, commissions, a big band, a national education program, and, eventually, its own concert venues. Unlike previous jazz musicians whose influence was limited to the response to their music, Marsalis was now an institution himself, and his new vision of jazz became public policy. He gave frequent interviews, had his own national TV and radio programs, and wrote articles, letters, and books. His programming (initially only black artists, but excluding the then-living Miles Davis) became the subject of comment and controversy.

Marsalis's criticism of Miles Davis, if Marsalis were solely a musician, would have been controversial but ultimately just gossip. But as the head of the premier national jazz institution, Marsalis had an impact on who got heard. "Did some people lose some gigs because I don't like their style of music?" he asked. "Maybe that's true, maybe that's false, I don't know.

History & Culture

The Big Band Revival

After the swing era, the costs of maintaining big bands became prohibitive and the primary focus of jazz shifted to smaller units. Yet the big band sound continued to thrill, and over the years a variety of orchestras kept the unique big band experience alive.

The classic big band sound, with its accent on swing and its adherence to smooth ensemble lines, remained an important jazz niche and the focus of preservation-oriented jazz enterprises. Incarnations of the orchestras of Duke Ellington, Count Basie, Glenn Miller, and other swing bandleaders maintained demanding schedules performing in towns and cities across the United States and elsewhere. Repertory orchestras—purveying historic sounds and revitalizing traditions—emerged in the form of the Jazz at Lincoln Center Orchestra, the Smithsonian

Jazz Masterworks Orchestra, and city-based units such as the Chicago Jazz Orchestra and outfits in New Orleans, Dallas, Columbus, Seattle, and elsewhere.

College and high school jazz education provided a platform for continuation of the big band tradition. University bands, such as the University of Wisconsin-Madison Big Band, remained standard formats for jazz study and performance.

More experimental big bands emerged alongside the classic ones. Through the second half of the twentieth century and into the twenty-first, some big bands absorbed elements from classical, rock, and other types of music to create a new kind of swing that was more suited for listening than dancing. Bandleaders such as pianists Carla Bley, Toshiko Akiyoshi, and McCoy Tyner; bassists Charlie

Hear Maria Schneider discuss her piece *Concert in the Garden* on **mymusiclab.com**

Haden and William Parker; saxophonist **David Murray**; and composer Maria Schneider were among the better-known exponents of this newer approach. Influences on these innovators ranged from Basie and Ellington to Gil Evans and Charles Mingus. Indeed, the Mingus Big Band, a unit dedicated to its namesake's work, attracted a devoted following for its surprising and energetic sounds.

Other notable big bands included the Vanguard Jazz Orchestra, which began life as a band co-led by trumpeter Thad Jones and drummer Mel Lewis, and the Sun Ra Arkestra, which carried on the name of its visionary pianist-bandleader.

—*Calvin Wilson and Tad Lathrop*

But that's not controversial to me." But with this public persona and his ability to program his personal version of classic jazz, Marsalis set the terms for a new debate about the definition and future of jazz. This has made him perhaps the most important figure in jazz of the time, but also the most polarizing.

Still only in his thirties, but with a new septet and the new Jazz at Lincoln Center Orchestra at his disposal, in the early 1990s Marsalis turned his musical attention toward composition. Inspired by Ellington, Marsalis created postmodern epic journeys that mixed earlier jazz styles. *Citi Movement* (1993) is a 21-movement, two-hour suite written as

music for *Griot New York*, a modern ballet created by Garth Fagan (later a Tony Award winner for his choreography of Broadway's *The Lion King*). The movement *Down the Avenue* has a steady swing feel but is still a study in contrasts and references to the history of jazz. One minute the band plays almost a parody of 1930s dance-hall music, but then an edgy bop saxophone solo floats through, alternating with some New Orleans clarinet and growling trombone. The equally successful and lengthy *In This House, On This Morning* (1994) followed. While improvisation is still featured and the blues and the sounds of New Orleans made up the raw materials, Marsalis's music became increasingly intricate and composed. This period culminated in his three-hour oratorio *Blood on the Fields*, which, in 1997, became the first jazz composition to win the Pulitzer Prize in Music.

((•● **Hear** a profile of Wynton Marsalis on **mymusiclab.com**

Listening Guide

((•● **Listen** to *Down the Avenue* by Wynton Marsalis Septet on **mymusiclab.com** CD II, Track 14/Download Track 38

DOWN THE AVENUE • WYNTON MARSALIS SEPTET

Music: Wynton Marsalis. Personnel: Wynton Marsalis (trumpet); Todd Williams (tenor saxophone); Wessell Anderson (alto saxophone); Wycliffe Gordon (trombone); Reginald Veal (bass); Herlin Riley (drums); Eric Reed (piano). Recorded July 27–28, 1992, in New York City. First issue: *Citi Movement (Griot New York)*, Columbia C2K 53324, 1993. Timing: 4:45.

Overview

Down the Avenue is the fourth of 21 movements from *Citi Movement*, one of the many extended works written by Wynton Marsalis in the 1990s after he turned his attention to the blues, his New Orleans roots, and the music of Duke Ellington (who also wrote suites). Marsalis would go on to compose even longer suites for even larger forces,

including the Pulitzer Prize–winning three-hour oratorio *Blood on the Fields* for his Jazz at Lincoln Center Orchestra, but *Citi Movement* is a more tightly constructed work for his working septet of the time. Its seamless mix of improvisation and composition across a variety of older styles simultaneously looks both forward and backward, while the relaxed but driving swing would be a model for any era.

Key Features

- The composition juxtaposes rhythmic feels and styles of different jazz eras. These self-conscious references to older styles were a hallmark of postmodernism in art but a new occurrence in jazz.
- Even the two parts of each chorus (A and B) seem from different

eras: A is twice as long and modal, while the B is a traditional harmonic sequence.
- While there is a basic A (16 bars) + B (8 bars) form to each chorus, the piece does not follow the typical head arrangement of bebop. Instead, the short solos and pre-arranged material are often mixed in the same chorus to blur the boundary between improvisation and composition.
- The "melody" first occurs as a "background" behind a tenor sax solo, thus also blurring the lines between background and foreground. In retrospect the first A is an introduction and the second A (0:20) is the opening statement of the theme.

—*José Antonio Bowen*

While Marsalis was looking toward the jazz past for inspiration, his brother Branford turned his attention to improvisation in a wide range of contexts, along the way becoming one of the most underrated big brothers in musical history. After playing with jazz veterans such as Dizzy Gillespie and Miles Davis, Branford explored collaborations with rock performers Sting, Tina Turner, and the Grateful Dead. He led the Tonight Show Band on NBC television, formed the hip-hop inspired band Buckshot LeFonque, and pursued greater freedom and flexibility in his solos in a piano-less trio with drummer Jeff "Tain" Watts and bassist Rob Hurst—the rhythm section he had left in his brother's band in 1985. Rarely has a single musician explored such diverse areas of music.

Branford and Wynton were among four brothers—the others being Jason and Delfeayo—who followed in the footsteps of musician father Ellis Marsalis, Jr. Pianist Ellis exerted a powerful influence as one of the relatively few New Orleans locals to specialize in mainstream styles instead of traditional New Orleans jazz. His own recordings feature elegant playing and a deep appreciation of swing. Jason, as a drummer, and Delfeayo, as a trombonist and producer, also established themselves as excellent professional musicians. In 2011, all five were given the prestigious NEA (National Endowment for the Arts) Jazz Masters Award—an unprecedented family honor.

TAKE NOTE

- How has mainstream acoustic jazz continued to flourish and develop?

TIME	SECTION	MELODY/INSTRUMENTATION
0:00	A (16 BARS)	The movement begins with a tenor sax solo over backgrounds from the other horns and a solid swing foundation with four beats to the bar.
0:20	A (16 BARS)	The solo continues, but the "background" horn line now starts to sound like a melody.
0:40	B (8 BARS)	The horns play quiet, long tones, acting like the piano, while the bass solos, changing the rhythmic feel.
0:51	A (16 BARS)	Both the tenor sax solo and the horn "background" return as in the previous A section.
1:12	B (8 BARS)	The quiet bridge returns, but this time with a piano solo over a two-beat feel from bass and a dainty riff from the band as "background." For a moment, we seem to be in an elegant 1930s ballroom with a swing band.
1:22	A+B (16 + 8 BARS)	A trumpet solos with only the rhythm section as background.
1:54	A (16 BARS)	An alto sax solo competes with the band "background" that is led this time by the soprano saxophone and seems to be an inverted (upside-down) and harmonized (multiple notes at once) version of the earlier "background."
2:15	B (8 BARS)	The trombone and soprano sax solo together in a reminiscence of old New Orleans.
2:25	A+ B (16+8 BARS)	The piano solos with only the rhythm section as background.
2:56	A (16 BARS)	The "upside-down" version of the "background" is heard alone, played by the entire band with no soloing.
3:16	B (8 BARS)	The alto sax gets to finish his solo chorus (started at 1:54, but interrupted at 2:15) while the band plays a background of quiet long tones.
3:27	C (20 BARS)	A new double-time section begins with call-and-response falls (that sound like simulated whistles or car horns) from the brass at twice the speed in the rhythm section.
3:40	C' (10 BARS/ 20 BARS IN DOUBLE-TIME)	Stop time: the drums and bass stop playing time and only play the "hits" with the horns. The C' section is the same length as C, but the feel of the speed is cut in half again.
3:54	A (16 BARS)	The piano solos over the "background" as it appeared in the beginning (0:20), and it is now clear this is the "melody" of the piece.
4:14	B (8 BARS)	The piano and bass solo over the quiet bridge with the "dainty riff" in the band from the second chorus, but the drums stay in the four-to-a-bar pulse.
4:25	½ A (8 BARS)	We hear the first half only of the inverted and harmonized "melody" from the band.
4:35	POSTSCRIPT	The band alone (without the rhythm section) adds a slower short postscript.

Avant-Garde Jazz Continues to Grow

Left out by Marsalis at Lincoln Center, avant-garde jazz and free improvisation continued to thrive further "downtown" in Manhattan lofts such as the Ladies' Fort and Studio Rivbea, and in clubs such as 8BC, the Knitting Factory, and Tonic. While Marsalis was busy raising money to build a new kind of exclusive jazz house, these clubs celebrated experimental music of all kinds, from the free improvisation of Terry Riley, Pauline Oliveros, and **John Zorn** and the performance art of Laurie Anderson to the minimalism of La Monte Young and Steve Reich. Experimental jazz, rock, punk, and no-wave bands shared the stage with classical and conceptual artists. The Kitchen, initially a venue for video art, was soon a place where the music from Philip Glass, Rocco Di Pietro, and Brian Eno could interact with other art forms. Instead of trying to limit what jazz could be, these "new music" artists were interested in expanding and fusing jazz with other experimental musics.

While hardly old, many of the pioneers of free jazz were now elder statesmen of this alternative jazz culture. After playing in lofts in the early 1970s, free-jazz

innovator **Ornette Coleman**'s response to rock and fusion was to add multiple electronic guitars to his new band, **Prime Time**, to create a music some called "free funk." Their first album, *Dancing in Your Head* (1975), was typically eclectic and included traditional musicians from Jajouka, Morocco. Once again, Coleman was prescient: this simultaneous fusion of jazz with both world and rock influences would become common in the twenty-first century.

Coleman's interest in the electric guitar led to performances with Jerry Garcia (of the jam-rock group the Grateful Dead) and a **Pat Metheny** collaboration (*Song X*, 1985) that became *Down Beat*'s Record of the Year. Classical commissions and further public recognition followed. Coleman brought his original quartet back together with—and in contrast with—Prime Time for the double album *In All Languages* (1987) and the Tufts University commission *DNA Meets E=MC²*, which Coleman described as a duel between the acoustic (natural) and the electric (atomic) forces of the universe. In the 1990s, Prime Time experimented with dancers, video, and even an appearance from French philosopher Jacques Derrida. With the first Guggenheim Fellowship awarded to any jazz musician and a Pulitzer Prize for *Sound Grammar* (2007), Coleman continues in his seventies to perform alternatives to the Marsalis jazz orthodoxy.

Cecil Taylor was also awarded a Guggenheim and continued to perform and record for solo piano (*For Olim*, 1986), with his Feel Trio of the 1990s with bassist William Parker and drummer Tony Oxley, and for some even larger big-band projects. Pianist and composer **Anthony Braxton**, who joined the Association for Advancement of Creative Musicians (AACM) in 1966 and later taught at Wesleyan University, also continued as one of the most prolific and rapacious musicians in history, recording more than 100 albums as he attempted to rework the entire musical tradition.

Coleman, Taylor, and Braxton all embraced both jazz improvisation and classical composition. While they shared rejection by the jazz establishment, their awards—all have won MacArthur Fellowships (informally referred to as "genius" awards)—testify to their welcome by the academy. It was an unexpected paradox of the 1980s that both the most traditional jazz (Marsalis) and most experimental (Coleman, Taylor, and Braxton) would find different sorts of institutional acceptance and in radically different venues.

Free jazz appeared to have a new proponent in the person of reedman David Murray, who had been influenced by saxophonists Archie

Ornette Coleman, 2000. PHOTO COURTESY ANDREW LEPLEY/REDFERNS/GETTY IMAGES.

Exploratory saxophonist and big band leader David Murray performing at the 2002 New Orleans Jazz and Heritage Festival. PHOTO COURTESY LEON MORRIS/REDFERNS/ GETTY IMAGES.

Shepp and Albert Ayler. Playing both tenor sax and bass clarinet, Murray expanded sonic possibilities by playing higher notes and with blistering speed and circular breathing. Murray continued playing in a wide variety of styles and influences, but by the 1980s Murray, guitarist Bill Frisell, and the George Adams-Don Pullen Quartet were all trying to make free jazz swing again.

Murray typified this new approach to connecting an improvisational world without musical borders back to the bop mainstream. Murray was voracious in his musical appetites, leading the David Murray Octet (whose Mingus-like recordings for the Black Saint label seemed both formal and reckless at the same time), an experimental big band conducted by cornetist-composer Lawrence D. "Butch" Morris, and his own driving quartet with pianist John Hicks. In 1977, he joined with saxophonists Hamiet Bluiett, Oliver Lake, and Julius Hemphill to form the **World Saxophone Quartet**. Working without a rhythm section, they combined this new interest in classical avant-garde composition with the solo saxophone recitals of the 1970s and the spirit of New Orleans's collective improvisation. On *Steppin'*, swing, free funk, and open meter all flow seamlessly together, integrating what is composed and what is improvised. (Listen to *Steppin'* by World Saxophone Quartet, *JTSA* Disc 6/Track 6.)

Other "new music" artists were equally interested in expanding jazz and experimental music. A haunting and unusual sound characterized the guitar playing of Bill Frisell, and he issued eclectic recordings on ECM Records with saxophonist Joe Lovano, trumpeter Kenny Wheeler, and drummer Paul Motian. A more volcanic approach to free jazz was kept alive by saxophonists Tim Berne and David Ware. For all of these avant-garde jazz musicians, categories of music disappeared. The trend away from strict compartmentalization of styles continues today. Electric or acoustic, classical or jazz, European or African—it is all ground for experimentation and improvisation.

New Collectives and Ethnic Jazz

The compactness of New York has always encouraged cross-pollination and collaboration, and during the 1980s two new downtown collectives emerged: **Steve Coleman's M-Base**—whose track *The Glide Was in the Ride* (*JTSA* Disc 6/Track 7) mixes the jazz tradition with experimentation—and the circle of musicians around John Zorn.

John Zorn

Like others in the new music movement, Zorn drew upon a tremendous array of non-jazz influences. As a record store clerk by day, he listened to all sorts of music and sounds: cartoon soundtracks, punk rock, klezmer music, duck calls, and the classical composers

Hear an interview with John Zorn about his group Masada on **mymusiclab.com**

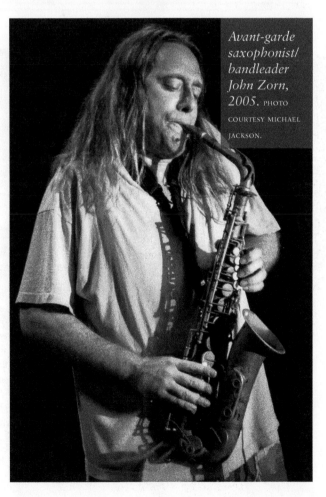

Avant-garde saxophonist/ bandleader John Zorn, 2005. PHOTO COURTESY MICHAEL JACKSON.

Webern, Cage, Stockhausen, and Philip Glass. After hearing an Anthony Braxton record, he switched from piano to alto saxophone and studied the music of avant-garde saxophonists Albert Ayler, John Coltrane, and Pharoah Sanders.

His hardcore punk rock group, Naked City (1987–93), with Bill Frisell and keyboardist Wayne Horvitz, thrived on short bursts of intense music with "jump cuts" to radically different sounds and back again. Like these musical "jump cuts," Zorn's career has moved rapidly from one style to another. His first experimental compositions were called "game pieces" (most important was *Cobra* from 1984) that used rules and cues to guide a group improvisation. After years of self-produced albums, *The Big Gundown* (1985) brought together much of the downtown scene in a series of radical reworkings of the "spaghetti Western" film scores of Ennio Morricone. Zorn would

go on to score for films and the concert hall, but he is best known for his klezmer jazz **Masada** groups (1994–2007).

Jump cuts, and the influence of Ornette Coleman, can also be heard in the acoustic version of Masada, with trumpeter **Dave Douglas**, bassist Greg Cohen, and drummer Joey Baron. *Kilayim* (JTSA Disc 6/Track 13), for example, is based on one of Zorn's many new themes using Jewish modes, but what begins as a punk bar mitzvah band soon slams into a short blast of free jazz interspersed with screeching horns. Masada also appeared as a string trio and in an electric version.

While his music was hailed as a new form of jazz (called "thrash jazz" by some), Zorn himself questioned labels. "The term 'jazz,' per se," he asserted, "is meaningless to me in a certain way. Musicians don't think in terms of boxes." (His stance echoed an earlier one of

Style & Technique

Are Solos a Key Element in Jazz?

A debate arose in the 1990s over the role of improvisation and soloing versus composition in jazz. Is jazz primarily an art form based on the work of the composer, or are the individual performers' improvised solos the most important element in the music?

Wynton Marsalis took the position that jazz is fundamentally a *composed* art form and that the discipline of its tradition was essential. Marsalis's position was influenced by his belief that jazz had been unfairly lumped together with other forms of popular music. Jazz, he argued, is a highly structured musical form, and it requires years of training to achieve excellence in its performance. In the provocatively titled "What Jazz Is—and Isn't" (*New York Times*, July 31, 1988),

Keith Jarrett became noted for long solo piano improvisations—marked by his ecstatic utterances and expressive physicality—and for adventuresome but accessible small-band music. PHOTO COURTESY JAZZSIGN/LEBRECHT MUSIC & ARTS.

Marsalis proposed that pop musicians were simply riding on the coattails of jazz's reputation when they claimed to be performing a kind of jazz-rock fusion. Marsalis attacked rock and pop musics' lack of sophistication in their melodies and harmonies, contrasting them with the richness of the work of classic jazz composers such as Ellington.

In Marsalis's view, it is heroic to preserve what is truly great about jazz music. Marsalis saw Miles Davis's move to fusion not as a continuation of a tradition of jazz experimentation, but as a commercial sellout. He felt Davis—along with the record companies and promoters of jazz rock—were trying to cash in on jazz's artistic cachet. Marsalis's criticism of the avant-garde (from the late Coltrane and Ornette Coleman to the Art Ensemble of Chicago and

Duke Ellington, who resisted labels and categories.) This attitude was typical among the downtown musicians who were trying to forge something completely new. Speaking in general about the 1980s and 1990s new music scene in New York, Zorn wrote that "the music explicitly and violently resists the classifications that these so-called thinkers have so desperately tried to impose on it: from the ludicrous *comprovisation* to the ambiguous *postmodernism* to the meaningless *totalism*."

In 1995, Zorn founded the record label Tzadik to record "the best in avant garde and experimental music, presenting a worldwide community of musician-composers who find it difficult or impossible to release their music through conventional channels." While not all of the musicians on the label (or even in Masada) were Jewish, Zorn's recording series, Radical Jewish Culture, identifies the character of much of the music and a new emphasis on ethnic jazz.

In the same way that players from Norway or South Africa had tried to give the international language of jazz a local accent (a phenomenon sometimes called *glocalization*), downtown players such as trumpeter Steven Bernstein and cellist Erik Friedlander, and the band Hasidic New Wave, experimented with mixing free jazz with klezmer, a jazz-like folk music created by Eastern European Jews but now reborn in New York City. Other mixtures emerged, based on players' ethnicities: percussionist Roberto Juan Rodriguez and eclectic guitarist Marc Ribot mixed Cuban jazz with klezmer. This interest in making jazz reflect the player's culture can also be

collective improvisation spontaneous composition performed simultaneously by members of an ensemble.

the World Saxophone Quartet) was to argue that it was not jazz.

While free jazz might appear to be uninterested in swing and the blues, it can also be seen as a pure form of **collective improvisation**, where, as in the original New Orleans jazz, multiple people improvised simultaneously. So the jazz world was stunned when Marsalis attacked the idea of solos and improvisation as central to jazz in a *Jazz Times* interview:

I think there is going to be an end to the old style of jamming on the bandstand that was really initiated during Charlie Parker's time. Historically, that was never a part of jazz music, not in the beginning . . . solos didn't come into fashion until Louis Armstrong and didn't become ingrained into jazz until the bebop thing came along. So I think there will be more emphasis put on presentation and composition as opposed to just soloing, which is a really boring and predictable way of presenting music.

A few months later, critic Ben Ratliff made use of this quote in an equally controversial article, "The Solo Retreats from the Spotlight in Jazz," that appeared in the May 28, 2000, *New York Times*. One of the many passionate letters printed by the *Times* in response included this one from pianist **Keith Jarrett**:

May I ask whose soloing Mr. Marsalis is referring to? And may I ask Mr. Ratliff what he thinks jazz actually is, if not those few precious exploding moments? And what does he think genius is? Those exploding moments can hold more sustenance than all the "jazz literature" (whatever that is) ever written. Look at Duke's band: how does his written music sound now, without those monster soloists-improvisers? Dry, lifeless, institutional. It is personal narrative we're losing, personal awareness: players with something to say. If that thread is broken (and it may well be), we're not going to write our way into the jazz future without important improvisatory voices, because

the narrative that is jazz will have died. The spirit of jazz is the spirit of personal freedom, only spontaneous individual acts. Jazz needs these acts of freedom to reconfirm itself in every era. It is in the player's art, not the writer's. There is no future if there is no present.

Duke Ellington is a key figure for both Jarrett and Marsalis. For Marsalis, Ellington's role as composer was the guiding force behind the band's unique sound, while the individual soloists were carrying out Ellington's vision in their performances. For Jarrett, however, it is the spontaneity and creativity of those solos that gives the music life and makes it jazz.

While new jazz has often raised questions about the old definitions of jazz, this more theoretical discourse about the nature of jazz indicates that indeed jazz has matured as an art; it has been around long enough to have a theory about itself. SOURCE: BILL MILKOWSKI, "WYNTON MARSALIS: ONE FUTURE, TWO VIEWS," *JAZZTIMES*, MARCH 2000; KEITH JARRETT, LETTER TO THE EDITOR, *NEW YORK TIMES*, JUNE 11, 2000.

—José Antonio Bowen

seen in the movement to create Asian American jazz ensembles, and even in Wynton Marsalis's emphasis on the importance of preserving the African American roots of jazz.

In addition to his work (as the non-Jewish member) with Masada, trumpeter Dave Douglas led both acoustic and electric bands and proved equally at ease with turntables, the progressive Dutch drummer Han Bennink, or celebrating the music of Mary Lou Williams (*Soul on Soul*, 2000). He considered John Coltrane, Igor Stravinsky, and Stevie Wonder to be his primary influences.

Issues

Jazz and Race Revisited

How have issues of race and class continued to play a role in jazz today?

Jazz lovers have always taken pride in the fact that jazz musicians have long been leaders in breaking down racial barriers. Long before the public would accept it, or the government would demand it, jazz musicians were integrating bands. By the 1960s and 1970s, jazz fans had come to expect racially integrated groups. At the same time, the idea that jazz was a black music became an important symbol for the Civil Rights and Black Power movements. In his influential book *Blues People: Negro Music in White America* (1963), LeRoi Jones (later known as Amiri Baraka) argued that the history of African American music was the history of African Americans coming to recognize the vitality and emotional validity of their own culture. Jazz didn't just have soul, it *was* soul. His story of a unique and vital folk music constantly fending off dilution from American popular music became a cornerstone for a new argument about race in jazz.

By the early 1980s, the tide seemed to be turning when Billy Taylor in *Jazz Piano: A Jazz History* (1982) argued that jazz had moved beyond African American music to become *Jazz: America's Classical Music*, the title adopted by Grover Sales for his 1984 book. It was a surprise then, when race again emerged as a topic in jazz after Wynton Marsalis began presenting concerts honoring only black musicians with the almost exclusively black Jazz at Lincoln Center Orchestra. Marsalis wrote, "People who invent something are always best at doing it, at least until other folks figure out what it is." Jazz writers James Lincoln Collier, in *Jazz, The American Theme Song* (1993), and Gene Lees, in *Cats of Any Color* (1994), responded that there was now reverse racism in jazz. Collier and Marsalis exchanged heated words in the *New York Times Book Review* and even held a public debate at Lincoln Center.

When in 1999 Richard Sudhalter published an exhaustive, scholarly 890-page book, *Lost Chords: White Musicians and Their Contribution to Jazz, 1915–1945* that argued that white and black musicians had both contributed to jazz "often defying the racial and social norms of their time to create a music whose graces reflected the combined effort," he was loudly and publicly denounced by some.

Another flashpoint came in April 2003 with a column in *Jazz Times* magazine by Stanley Crouch called "Putting the White Man in Charge." Crouch criticized white jazz critics for praising white artists "as an antidote to too much authority from the dark side of the tracks" and for trying to destroy a "Negro aesthetic" based upon the blues and swing. He singled out white "downtown" trumpeter Dave Douglas (*Down Beat*'s Trumpeter of the Year that year), writing that he "is far from being a bad musician, but he knows he should keep as much distance as possible between himself and [black] trumpet players like Wallace Roney, Terence Blanchard, and Nicholas Payton." Crouch was fired the next month.

For some, jazz has been a multicultural democratic space: a model environment where musicians of any race—"cats of any color," in Louis Armstrong's words—can play together. As jazz has become more global in the last 30 years, however, definitions rooted in the African American experience and the blues have become both more prominent and more controversial. World jazz musicians, like Jan Garbarek, readily admit that the blues isn't their tradition, and instead attempt to create a "native version" of jazz that is authentic to their own tradition. While the argument about the history and origins of jazz seems to have died down, future critics, players, and historians will need to determine how much of the past remains essential for future jazz cultures.

—*José Antonio Bowen*

Listening Guide

THE GLIDE WAS IN THE RIDE • STEVE COLEMAN GROUP

Music: Geri Allen. Personnel: Steve Coleman (alto saxophone); Geri Allen (piano); Lonnie Plaxico (bass); Marvin "Smitty" Smith (drums); collective vocal. Recorded March 1985, in New York City. First issue: *Motherland Pulse*, JMT 852 001. Timing: 4:03.

Overview

Both the rhythmic audacity and the collective voice of hip-hop were important influences for the musicians that Steve Coleman gathered in New York in the early 1980s under the banner of M-Base. Coleman insisted, however, that this was not a musical style, and indeed the pieces on this first album present a wide array of different approaches to improvisation. M-Base was also a community and Coleman emphasized the Chicago background of the musicians and the New Orleans rhythmic feel of the music. As with previous generations of jazz saxophonists, Coleman had an instantly recognizable sound and style, and his music relates clearly to the jazz tradition while also being both experimental and newly urban.

Key Features

- The familiar instrumentation is that of an acoustic jazz quartet, but the band strives to avoid familiar ways of playing and is comfortable with pop recording techniques of vocal overdubbing and an electronic fade of the band.
- Like much black popular music of the 1970s and 1980s, the bass line is a key element of both melody and rhythm—part of the composition's essence.
- The drummer establishes a relatively square rock pattern in four, but the bass line moves across the groove, creating an unconventional rhythm pattern where the bass is silent on the downbeat.
- The structure of the piece feels organic, with a saxophone melody followed by a unison bass, piano, and saxophone melody occurring only between the two solos.
- Improvisation is collective and structured; the improvisations and the melodies all relate to the opening bass line's juxtaposition of angularity and linear flow.
- The piece ends with a collective vocal chant (or "rap") satire of advertisement copy: "Before you take that final fall, if you do nothing else at all, tell the standbys on the side, the glide was in the ride."

—*José Antonio Bowen*

TIME	FORM	MELODY/INSTRUMENTATION
0:00	INTRODUCTION	The drums set up a quasi rock groove while the bass plays across the bar to set up an unusual rhythmic feel.
0:11		The piano joins and Steve Coleman begins his saxophone solo playing a series of related figures, also playing across the bar to further unsettle the rhythmic feel.
0:43	A	The saxophone introduces a new melody (A) and then continues to solo.
1:00		Five jabs from the piano across the time disturb the rhythmic pattern.
1:07	A	The saxophone again plays the A melody.
1:16	B	The bass, piano, and saxophone play a unison melody (B). It happens four times, with the saxophone making additions and further improvisations in each iteration.
1:45	PIANO SOLO	Geri Allen begins her piano solo with a series of one-handed, bop-ish runs, connecting the angularity of the melodies to bebop jazz.
2:05		The piano introduces some two-hand chords and unison figures.
2:22		The piano plays more vigorously and in the groove with two hands.
2:36		The piano and bass return to their opening figures.
2:46	A	The saxophone enters again with the A melody.
2:57		The piano returns to fast solo runs while the saxophone continues to experiment with the A rhythm.
3:08	B	The unison bass, piano, and saxophone B melody returns.
3:27		The band fades but continues with B, while an overdubbed group vocal chant/rap begins.
3:40		The band continues to play with B as the music fades out.

A musician of broad interests, clarinetist Don Byron ventured into klezmer, classical, salsa, rock, and jazz. PHOTO COURTESY DAVID REDFERN/REDFERNS/ GETTY IMAGES.

(1992), and *Def Trance Beat (Modalities of Rhythm)* (1995), Coleman updated the sound of Miles Davis's 1970s ensembles and Ornette Coleman's Prime Time band, making a persuasive case that the dance ethic that won jazz its following in the swing era still survived. All that was necessary was that it reflect contemporary styles.

Coleman had developed a strong straight-ahead bop technique before setting out on his own path, having performed in the Thad Jones-Mel Lewis big band and recorded with bassist Dave Holland. In turn, the M-Base movement exerted an influence on a generation of jazz performers who, while mindful of the music traditions, were also open to a multitude of ways to express themselves. Over the years, that spirit of exploration remained intact as Osby and Allen continued to push the limits of bop, Wilson helped to bring a broader audience to jazz singing, and Coleman remained open to a world of musical possibilities.

After graduating from the New England Conservatory, Don Byron helped revive the clarinet as an important jazz instrument, while also working as an important collaborator in many downtown projects and serving as artistic director of jazz for the Brooklyn Academy of Music (1996–99). He shared his interest in classical, klezmer, and hip-hop with the Philadelphia pianist Uri Caine. While both recorded albums of reworked classical music, Caine (often with Byron as a sideman) demonstrated notable fearlessness in reworking Bach, Beethoven, Mahler, and Wagner. He proved equally arresting playing a Fender Rhodes electric piano and a Hammond B-3 organ on *The Philadelphia Experiment* (2000) with Ahmir Thompson (drummer from the hip-hop band the Roots) and bassist Christian McBride. The album offers a world where jazz avant-gardist Sun Ra grooves next to Motown singer Marvin Gaye.

> **TAKE NOTE**
>
> - How has the avant-garde jazz movement of the 1960s and 1970s evolved and who are some of its key performers?

Reenvisioning Jazz

While some musicians preserved a conception of jazz that reached its zenith with bebop and its offshoots, and while others opened the doors of jazz to welcome far-flung styles, there were musicians (in addition to John Zorn) who set about completely rethinking jazz—in some cases to a point at which the term "jazz" perhaps became archaic. To some, "jazz"

In the 1980s, the neobop movement garnered most of the media attention, but not all jazz artists were involved in that trend. Based in Brooklyn, M-Base was spearheaded by alto saxophonist Steve Coleman, a Chicago native whose eclectic musical tastes were readily apparent in his compositions and performances.

M-Base stands for Macro-Basic Array of Structured Extemporization. In Coleman's music, that meant funk that swung, hip-hop that drew on bop, and street rhythms that made room for improvisation. The company he kept in the late 1980s was, in retrospect, exemplary: M-Base adherents included such end-of-the-twentieth-century stars as singer Cassandra Wilson, pianist Geri Allen, and alto saxophonist Greg Osby.

Although M-Base had no formal organization, its flagship was Coleman's group, Five Elements. On albums such as *Black Science* (1991), *Drop Kick* evoked a set of conditions, traditions, and practices that could impede artistic progress. Perhaps (for these musicians) the living legacy of jazz in the twenty-first century would be, simply, improvised music.

One of the thinkers whose work pointed toward a wide-ranging notion of improvised music, composer and pianist **Jason Moran**, emerged in the 1990s. Starting with the 1999 album *Soundtrack to Human Emotion*, Moran stood out as a voracious assimilator of whatever sounds he regarded as valuable, and a resourceful generator of ideas for producing new kinds of listening experiences. An alumnus of the Manhattan School of Music and a student of renowned'veteran jazz pianist (and Charles Mingus band member) Jaki Byard, Moran embraced the avant-garde, classicism, and populism along with jazz roots. His 2002 reworking of the 1930 James P. Johnson classic *You've Got to Be Modernistic* transformed it into a showcase for an improvising style that easily commingled stride-piano pyrotechnics with Cecil Taylor–style atonality. In *Planet Rock* (2002), Moran translated the 1982 raps of Afrika Bambaataa into piano melodies, generating an atonality based on direct human expression (in contrast to the mathematical, at times soulless, atonal formulations of twentieth-century art music) that he pursued further in later years. His 2010 track *Feedback, Pt. 2* juxtaposed ruminative, abstract piano chording with samples of feedback from rock guitarist Jimi Hendrix, generating a contrast in texture suggesting soft textile alternating with sand-paper or gravel.

Steve Turre, for many years a trombone-playing member of the *Saturday Night Live* band on network television, found musical sound in unlikely places—the cavities of sea shells. Focusing primarily on the conch, Turre amassed a collection of shells that he tuned to specific pitches, and used to evocative ends with his shell choir, the Sanctified Shells, and in other settings. A means rather than an end, shells simply expanded the palette—in which trombone remained central—from which Turre rendered audioscapes of vastly varied hue. Turre's blue-chip background playing with salsa and jazz figureheads—Art Blakey, Dizzy Gillespie, Max Roach, and Tito Puente among them—informed his expansive conception of what might be called "open source" improvised music. Within it, he could conjure expression of limitless range: from the primitive-sounding, "talking" melodicism of *Morning*, 1995, to the full-bodied, brash declamation of *Midnight Montuno (Descarga)*, 1993.

One of the highest-profile of the jazz musicians to emerge in the 1990s, pianist **Brad Mehldau** worked largely in a trio setting (with bass and drums) as he applied jazz, pop, and associated ideas to structures suitable for his improvisational inclinations. These ranged widely, from free improvisation with no readily apparent stylistic source other than Mehldau's imagination (*Paranoid Android*, 2002) to reconstructing pop songs as platforms for inventive melodic departures (*Dear Prudence*, 2002).

Even the 1990s-spawned jazz star most likely to inherit the mainstream mantle of "jazz giant," burly tenor saxophonist **Joe Lovano**, made his own case for expanding the bounds of jazz simply by virtue of the musicians he chose to play with. A veteran of the Woody Herman big band and the Thad Jones-Mel

((•—Hear a profile of Jason Moran on **mymusiclab.com**

Jason Moran at the Newport Jazz Festival, 2010. PHOTO COURTESY DOUGLAS MASON/ GETTY IMAGES.

Listening Guide

((•● **Listen** to *Planet Rock* by Jason Moran on **mymusiclab.com**
CD II, Track 16/Download Track 40

PLANET ROCK • JASON MORAN

Music: Afrika Bambaataa and Soulsonic Force, Arthur Baker, John Robie, 1982. Personnel: Jason Moran (piano; piano prepared with erasers, paper, paper clips, and clothespins; sound loops). Recorded: April 12, 2002, in New York. First issue: *Modernistic*, Blue Note 39838. Timing: 5:41.

Overview

Planet Rock, from Jason Moran's solo piano album *Modernistic* (2002), showcases several of the inclinations Moran brings to music: openness to and incorporation of a broad range of music traditions (in this case hip-hop and, indirectly, 1970s techno-pop); use of spoken word as a source of melody; interest in experimental jazz of the 1980s and 1990s, and affinity for twentieth-century atonal music. In *Planet Rock* we hear a clear departure from traditional notions of jazz (to the point where some might question calling it jazz), and we get a clear window into the boundary-defying thrust of Moran's thinking—the kind of thinking that moves music forward to new forms.

The original *Planet Rock* was a 1982 hit by "godfather of hip-hop" Afrika Bambaataa and Soulsonic Force. At the time the track was a dance-floor revelation, and it prototyped the soon-to-be-popular genres hip-hop and electronica, blending rap (rhythmically spoken) lyrics with electronic beats inspired by the German electro-pop band Kraftwerk, and **sampling** an eerie modal melody

from Kraftwerk's 1977 hit *Trans-Europe Express*.

For this version, Moran took on the task of translating most of those elements to piano—no small challenge. He achieved the goal by overdubbing several tracks, including "percussion" played on prepared piano and special effects produced by digitally manipulating recorded sound segments. "It was a matter of finding the connections between hip-hop and the piano-as-percussion-instrument, which I did via John Cage's prepared piano music," Moran recalled in 2007. "If I could put all that together, I thought, then *Planet Rock* could still work as a hip-hop piece, and not some jazzy version of it. It could still hold some of that drumbeat, it could still hold that bass line and I could play the lyrics."

Whether or not the track works as a hip-hop piece, the rap-derived melodies sound new, and conversely, they highlight the musicality of rapping.

Key Features

- Melody: Strikingly, Moran crafts "melodies" shaped by spoken word on the original hip-hop version of *Planet Rock*. It's an unorthodox technique for freeing melody from **tonality**, and Moran explores it further in a later tune, *Ringing My Phone* (2002), in which he "melodizes" recorded telephone conversations. In *Planet Rock* he also duplicates the repeated

melody (0:54) that Afrika Bambaataa borrowed from Kraftwerk in the 1982 original.
- Rhythm: Generated via piano "prepared" by inserting erasers, paper, paper clips, and clothespins on the strings, the rock-style rhythm is a steady mid-tempo $\frac{4}{4}$, accenting the first and anticipating the third of every four beats. The intensity changes during the tune, receding in volume at 2:21, returning at 4:50, and slowing at 5:14 through the fade.
- Style: Defying stylistic labels, Moran draws from hip-hop and self-developed techniques ("playing the lyrics") to concoct a mixture of atonal and modal free jazz with a rock-derived beat.
- Texture: Moran varies the texture with acoustic piano, percussive "prepared" piano, and recordings played backwards, providing an electronic swelling sound that opens the tune and recurs throughout.
- Form and structure: Three primary kinds of sections form the structural material: "verses," in which Moran is "playing the lyrics"; melodic interludes, featuring a modal melody (borrowed by Afrika Bambaataa from the band Kraftwerk); and a slower-paced melody (based on half notes) that supports Moran's improvisation.

—Tad Lathrop

Lewis Orchestra—both hard-core jazz ensembles—Lovano branched out over the years. Free jazz pianist-composer Carla Bley, third stream conceptualist Gunther Schuller, fusion guitarist John Scofield, and a trio featuring guitarist Bill Frisell and drummer Paul Motian, all drew on Lovano's saxophone sound and, in turn, he assimilated theirs. The results are audible in such open-sounding tracks as *Us Five* and *Wild Beauty*

on the 2009 album *Folk Art*, credited to Lovano and his band Us Five.

One of Us Five's members, **Esperanza Spalding**, emerged to great acclaim as a soloist in 2008 with a concept—conveyed through her full-throttle singing, bass playing, and arranging—of improvisational music that could venture anywhere (while favoring a Brazilian bent). Proof could be found in both the title

TIME	SECTION	MELODY
0:00	INTRO	Following an electronic swell (a recording played backwards), piano enters with a four-note blues figure, played twice.
0:05		Moran plays a more complicated figure. It is stated three times, with the third ending (0:16) on an octave crescendo.
0:17		An electronic beat enters (played on prepared piano in a pre-recorded take). A series of chordal swells (backwards recordings) ensue.
0:38	VERSE (8 BARS)	Moran picks out a melody as he simulates the phrasings of Afrika Bambaataa's rap. The melody has an imperfect, atonal quality and rhythmic variety.
0:54	MELODIC INTERLUDE (8 BARS)	A fixed melody (Kraftwerk's synth melody "sampled" by Bambaataa) interrupts the piano "rapping." It repeats in two different registers.
1:10	VERSE (8 BARS)	Moran returns to "rapping," with ever-changing rhythmic figures and notes that fall "outside" expected musical patterns.
1:26	MELODIC INTERLUDE (8 BARS)	The fixed melody is played again, twice.
1:42	VERSE (6 BARS)	Moran emphasizes two notes repeatedly and at 1:49 raises them a half step.
1:54	(8 BARS)	Ominous-sounding chords in call and response, low to high.
2:10	IMPROVISED CHORUS 1 (16 BARS)	Moran introduces a new melody built on half notes moving evenly in upward and downward directions. A swelling effect emanates from the piano notes.
2:42	IMPROVISED CHORUS 2 (16 BARS)	The half-note melody continues, morphing (2:50) into half-note accompaniment to improvising, which evolves into fractured, high-pitched shards of melody.
3:14	IMPROVISED CHORUS 3 (16 BARS)	Texture changes as the swelling half-note melody (via backward recording) returns to the foreground and the percussion backbeat drops out. Improvisation continues.
3:46	IMPROVISED CHORUS 4 (16 BARS)	The half-note melody continues, now without the "swelling" effect, and it morphs into chordal accompaniment under soloing.
3:56		Moran plays jabbing octaves.
4:07		Moran returns to tumbling single-note lines ending on repeated single notes.
4:18	INTERLUDE (16 BARS)	An interlude ensues, with piano maintaining a low-key rhythm . . .
4:32		. . . until a melody emerges, echoing the half-note melody from earlier.
4:42		A series of electronic swells similar to the opening of the tune is heard.
4:48		The backbeat becomes more pronounced.
4:51	MELODIC INTERLUDE (4 BARS)	The fixed melody returns, one time.
4:58	CODA (4 BARS)	High notes echo the fixed melody. Electronic swells mix with high piano notes.
5:07		The beat becomes spare and ambiguous.
5:13		Steady beat returns, but slower, as the piano fades with high chords and electronic chordal swells.

sampling (1) the use of a "sampled" section or piece of a preexisting recording in a new recording; (2) digitally recording a singer, instrument, or other sound to use as a "voice" in a synthesizer.

tonality relationship to a tonal center or key.

of her 2010 album *Chamber Music Society* and the music contained within.

TAKE NOTE

- How have some musicians begun to rethink the definition of jazz beyond the classic division between mainstream and avant-garde?

Vocal Jazz

The variety of approaches in vocal jazz in the second half of the century mirrored the expansion of instrumental jazz. Veterans Tony Bennett and Mel Tormé, along with such younger singers as Diane Schuur, Dianne Reeves, Karrin Allyson, Kevin Mahogany, and Jane Monheit, continued to sing the great American songbook. A quartet of veteran women singers—Betty

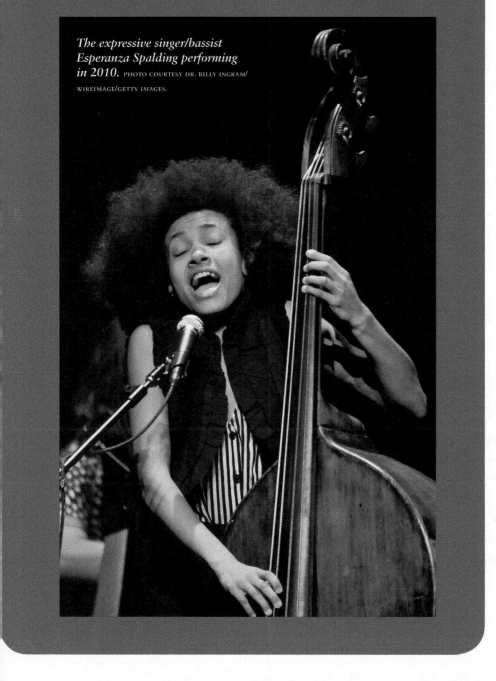

The expressive singer/bassist Esperanza Spalding performing in 2010. PHOTO COURTESY DR. BILLY INGRAM/ WIREIMAGE/GETTY IMAGES.

In the 1950s, Eddie Jefferson and Jon Hendricks put lyrics to recorded jazz solos and created vocalese, a technique that continues to find favor with male vocalists. From his debut in 1956, Mark Murphy forged a long and distinguished career scatting and singing vocalese, while Dave Frishberg made his name as a wordsmith best known for singing his own clever compositions including *I'm Just a Bill* (written for ABC Television's *Schoolhouse Rock*), *My Attorney Bernie*, and the widely sung *Peel Me a Grape*? With a string of critics' and readers' poll awards and a huge baritone voice, Kurt Elling continued in this tradition, singing standards, new compositions, and vocalese.

The internationalization of jazz extended to jazz singing. After successful stints in the 1970s in front of the Thad Jones-Mel Lewis Jazz Orchestra and on Broadway, the American singer Dee Dee Bridgewater moved to Paris in 1986 and returned to singing jazz. Her 2007 album *Red Earth* features a Malian band led by Cheick Tidiane Seck. Londoner Norma Winstone began singing jazz standards, but her wordless improvisations became an important part of the progressive ECM sound, especially as a unique new texture in Kenny Wheeler's big band on *Music for Large and Small Ensembles* (1990).

While jazz instrumentalists were drawn to rock fusions, jazz singers saw R&B or pop as more of a crossover point. Al Jarreau, for example, won a jazz Grammy award for his scat singing on the track *Take Five* from his album *Look to the Rainbow* (1977), which also reached number 49 on the pop charts. Nnenna Freelon moved easily back and forth from the classic jazz singing of Billie Holiday to the pop-soul of Stevie Wonder.

Cassandra Wilson managed to integrate her country, R&B, pop, and blues interests into jazz. After time with Ellis Marsalis in New Orleans, in Steve Coleman's M-Base, and touring with experimental altoist Henry Threadgill, Wilson launched a solo career with *Point of View* (1986). Initially, her progressive funk repertoire seemed at odds with her ability

Carter, Abbey Lincoln, Nancy Wilson, and Shirley Horn—all learned the importance of a unique style and sound. All three recreated old melodies in their own image. Tierney Sutton continued this tradition of rethinking standards and **scat singing**. Following in the footsteps of Horn and Nat "King" Cole, Diana Krall emerged as an accomplished pianist who could swing and phrase as well as any jazz singer on the scene.

scat singing   vocal improvisation, typically wordless; notable practitioners have included Louis Armstrong; the Boswell Sisters; Cab Calloway; Ella Fitzgerald; Eddie Jefferson; Lambert, Hendricks and Ross; and Dizzy Gillespie.

History & Culture

Vocal Groups

Jazz has always meant something different for vocalists: jazz singers needed to swing and have a unique sound, but most sang only as soloists in front of a big band, coming out occasionally to sing a song. All of that changed with the Boswell Sisters—Connee, Martha, and Vet—a trio who sang together in the 1930s and whose vocal harmony was widely imitated, most famously by the Andrew Sisters. Their dramatic reworking of pop tunes with tempo changes, improvised solos, and group scat singing were radical and innovative (listen to *Everybody Loves My Baby*, JTSA Disc 1/Track 17). Ella Fitzgerald was a huge fan and was deeply influenced by Connee. Big bands responded by adding even larger vocal groups, rather than just soloists, to their ensembles. The Modernaires joined Glenn Miller, and the Pied Pipers joined the Tommy Dorsey band to back up Frank Sinatra.

Then along came Eddie Jefferson, who sang note-for-note recreations of famous jazz solos. This technique was called *vocalese* and required the singer not only to memorize an instrumental solo but also to create lyrics. The greatest lyricist of this genre is Jon Hendricks, who along with Dave Lambert and British vocalist Annie Ross formed a new sort of jazz vocal group. The first Lambert, Hendricks and Ross LP was *Sing a Song of Basie* (1957), in which the group recreated complete arrangements from the Count Basie Band by singing all of the parts and adding lyrics. They did this using the new technique of **overdubbing**, a way to layer new parts on top of previously recorded parts using multitrack magnetic tape. For *The*

Swingers! (1959), they sang as a trio over a rhythm section, again singing versions of famous instrumental performances with lyrics by Hendricks, but now with increasingly modern arrangements by Lambert that featured tightly crafted individual vocal lines meshing together in dense clusters of sound.

This style of group vocal jazz became an important influence on 1950s and 1960s pop-oriented groups such as the Four Freshmen and doo-wop and R&B acts like the Drifters. The influences sometimes worked in both directions: One of the greatest arrangers of a cappella vocal jazz, Gene Puerling, came from a pop background, having founded the eclectic Hi-Lo's in 1953—they sang everything from barbershop quartet music to calypso. Puerling went on to lead the popular jazz vocal group Singers Unlimited.

Vocalese came to its peak with the Manhattan Transfer. After an aborted initial quintet (1969–71), bass Tim Hauser reformed a quartet with alto Janis Siegel, soprano Laurel Masse, and tenor Alan Paulin in 1972. They gained an early following in New York clubs and attracted the attention of Atlantic Records founder Ahmet Ertegun, who signed them to his label. The group's *Extensions* (1979) included a vocalese version of Weather Report's *Birdland* with lyrics by Jon Hendricks, which won a Grammy Award and remains a classic. The album is notable for its use of analog synthesizer backgrounds, but it also revived an interest (in both Europe and America) in close harmony singing and led to the creation of high school and college vocal jazz groups. This in turn led to a flourishing professional vocal jazz-group scene.

Darmon Meader, Peter Eldridge, Kim Nazarian, and Caprice Fox met at Ithaca College and formed the New York Voices with Sara Krieger in 1987. The New York Voices rejected vocalese for a new approach: they created their own arrangements of jazz standards and took improvised scat solos. (Meader is also an accomplished soloist on the saxophone.) Relentless rehearsal enabled them to swing as one voice.

Like instrumental jazz, group vocal jazz spread around the world and fused with other genres. Take 6 is a gospel-oriented a cappella sextet that formed at Oakwood College in Huntsville, Alabama, in 1980. Their brilliant 1988 debut album launched another revolution in college jazz singing that included a proliferation of "rockappella" groups. At the Royal Music Academy in Stockholm in 1984, the Real Group was inspired by **Bobby McFerrin** to create new versions of standards from *The Real Book* (the standard "fake book" collection of jazz lead sheets), while Vocal Sampling took male a cappella singing to Cuba. Zap Mama, a Belgium group of five mixed African European women, was led by Marie Daulne, who listened to blues and French music before returning to her native Congo to study traditional pygmy music and then sang in Brussels jazz cafés. The album *Zap Mama* (1991) may be an attempt to bridge Europe and Africa, but the improvisation over pygmy chants also feels like jazz coming home.

—*José Antonio Bowen*

---

overdubbing the practice of recording in synchronization with previously recorded material; used primarily in popular music to build layers of sound.

to channel Billie Holiday in standards, but ultimately her ability to unite disparate elements, especially new takes on familiar tunes, became as much a stylistic trademark as her deep smoky voice.

No singer, however, brought more innovation to vocal jazz than Bobby McFerrin. Eclectic in taste and influence, *The Voice* (1984) was a unique solo outing, with nothing but the sound of his voice. Jumping from low bass to falsetto, making sounds as he inhaled, overdubbing his own voice to create multiple parts, and mimicking other instruments, McFerrin added an arsenal of techniques and fresh ideas to jazz and singing. Some of his genius can be heard on his hit recording *Don't Worry Be Happy*.

TAKE NOTE

- Who are some of today's leading vocalists and vocal groups, and what role do they play on the current jazz scene?

Conclusion

Even fully matured, jazz continues to wrestle with its own identity. Is jazz now a classical and conservative art? Is it still a radical and experimental music making up its own rules as it goes along? Can it be both? For world musicians or Americans influenced by John

Jazz in the Marketplace

In the United States, jazz continues to have approximately the same share of recorded music sales as classical music (about 2 percent). Jazz, however, has always been a "catalog" seller, meaning that older music in the back catalog continues to sell for years. So while Miles Davis's *Kind of Blue* sold extremely well in its first year, it did not go "gold" (signifying 500,000 units shipped to retailers in the United States as certified by the Recording Industry Association of America [RIAA]) until 1993, then it went platinum (one million units) in 1997 and continued to sell, eventually going triple platinum (three million units) in 2002. *Kind of Blue* and Dave Brubeck's *Time Out* remain in the top 20 jazz albums sold each year.

Like the rest of American popular music, jazz began its commercial life on 78 records, which featured two songs, one on each side of the disc. Since the rise of the LP in the 1950s, however, jazz sales have been almost entirely in LP records or CDs. As music sales shift back

to singles via download sites such as iTunes—nearly 30 percent of all music sales were digital in 2010, according to the International Federation of the Phonographic Industry (IFPI)—will jazz do better or worse? At least one new Web site (jazz.com) has responded to this trend by reviewing and rating individual jazz singles (generally single tracks from longer CDs) again.

Jazz has always had obsessive fans. In fact, "discography" (the study of sound recordings) was started by jazz fans in the 1930s who recognized that different takes of a jazz performance were substantially different and consequently began to identify and catalog recordings of different performances. The Internet has allowed thousands of fans to create Web sites devoted to their favorite players and genres. There is more information on jazz available than ever before, and many Web sites also allow users to hear sound clips.

There has also been a huge expansion of summer jazz festivals, although as Wynton Marsalis pointed out, there has also been an

expansion of the range of music presented at them, and different festivals have taken on different repertoires and missions. Jazz festivals routinely include R&B, rock, smooth jazz, and other broadly popular styles as a way to expand their potential market. The annual New Orleans Jazz & Heritage Festival, for example, has hosted pop singers Billy Joel and Stevie Wonder, country musician Tim McGraw, rock singer Sheryl Crow, and many other non-jazz performers.

While the internal jazz community has been arguing about traditional versus experimental types of jazz, a different argument about the classification of jazz has been continuing in the commercial world. Saxophonist Kenny G claimed to be the best-selling jazz instrumentalist of all time (with more than 50 million records sold). Yet many jazz fans would classify Kenny G in the "easy listening" category, and "smooth jazz" as an instrumental category of R&B. Both Kenny G and smooth jazz are listed on the jazz charts.

—*José Antonio Bowen*

Zorn, jazz seems less a style and more a set of interests: improvisation, rhythm, exploration, and new fusions. Creative musicians today are applying these interests across a range of musical cultures and ideas: jazz can now be Asian or Jewish and electric or acoustic. At the same time, others see the importance of returning jazz to its African American roots and traditions and re-establishing boundaries for jazz.

But with all of this controversy at home (outside of the United States, this local debate is largely ignored), the basic language of jazz has become established as the *lingua franca* of modern music making. Around the world, melodic improvisation and even the names and recordings of the greatest performers in American jazz are commonly known. Jazz and its techniques have become the world's music.

Explore Key Recordings on **mymusiclab.com**

Bobby McFerrin's wide vocal range and ability to quickly shift between high and low registers enabled him to sing both melody and accompaniment.
PHOTO COURTESY MICHAEL WILDERMAN.

TAKE NOTE

- How has mainstream acoustic jazz continued to flourish and develop?

Mainstream jazz returned to fashion in the 1980s sparked by excitement surrounding trumpeter Wynton Marsalis. He would go on to mentor dozens of younger musicians, and shape the new Jazz at Lincoln Center as a highly visible home base for jazz. Jazz entered college curricula, music archives, and the repertoires of institutionally subsidized orchestras as an essential, still-evolving part of American cultural history.

- How has the avant-garde jazz movement of the 1960s and 1970s evolved and who are some of its key performers?

Downtown Manhattan lofts and clubs in the 1980s served as a home for a handful of experimenting musicians, including saxophonists David Murray and John Zorn, keyboardist Wayne Horvitz, and guitarist Bill Frisell.

- How have some musicians begun to rethink the definition of jazz beyond the classic division between mainstream and avant-garde?

Characteristic of jazz musicians later in the twentieth century was their ability and inclination to look back to bop for inspiration and to reach forward to new ideas. Notable in late-century jazz was a blurring, even a disintegration, of musical categories. Labels such as "jazz" and "rock" became decreasingly relevant.

- Who are some of today's leading vocalists and vocal groups, and what roles do they play on the current jazz scene?

Jazz singing has enjoyed a renaissance, with performers ranging from the inventive Bobby McFerrin, with his ability to sing percussion and bass accompaniment while also singing melody, to newcomers Kurt Elling, pianists/vocalists Diana Krall and Diane Schuur, Karrin Allyson, Jane Monheit, and Tierney Sutton.

DISCUSSION QUESTIONS

1. Before reading this chapter, which late-century jazz musicians were you most familiar with?

2. Discuss whether jazz of the 1990s and 2000s had any innovators with the originality and brilliance of Louis Armstrong, Charlie Parker, Duke Ellington, and John Coltrane.

3. Discuss what this chapter calls "an improvisational world without musical borders" and what it meant for jazz in the late twentieth century. Give examples.

4. Discuss institutional jazz programs. Do you feel that inserting jazz into institutions such as those discussed in this chapter has had any negative results for the music?

5. Identify some of the ways jazz singing in the late twentieth century differed from earlier kinds of jazz singing. Identify and compare leading singers of different jazz eras.

6. From what you've read and heard, do you feel jazz stopped evolving in the early twenty-first century? Or did it change so much that it was harder and harder to recognize?

7. Why do you think Wynton Marsalis has been a lightning rod for both praise and criticism?

8. There have been debates throughout the history of jazz about what constitutes "real" jazz—in the 1940s, swing versus bebop; in the 1960s, mainstream versus free jazz; in the 1970s, straight-ahead versus fusion; in the 1980s and beyond, acoustic/bop/straight-ahead versus everything else. Where do you stand in the latter debate?

KEY TERMS & KEY PEOPLE

Anthony Braxton
Don Byron
Ornette Coleman
Steve Coleman
collective improvisation
Dave Douglas
Keith Jarrett
Joe Lovano
Masada
M-Base

Branford Marsalis
Wynton Marsalis
Bobby McFerrin
Brad Mehldau
Pat Metheny
Jason Moran
David Murray
neotraditional jazz
overdubbing
Prime Time

sampling
scat singing
Esperanza Spalding
Cecil Taylor
tonality
Steve Turre
World Saxophone Quartet
John Zorn

Jazz Worldwide

by Kevin Whitehead

With contributions by E. Taylor Atkins ("Jazz in Asia and Oceania"); Mark Lomanno ("Jazz in the Middle East");
Cyril Moshkov ("Jazz in Eastern Europe"); and John Edward Hasse ("Jazz in Africa")

TAKE NOTE

- Who were the prominent musicians who brought jazz to Europe and how has a European jazz scene developed?
- What is the history of jazz in Asia and Oceania, and who are the vital figures creating original jazz music there?
- How did jazz develop in the Middle East, and who are some of the key players?
- Which musicians led the practice of jazz in Eastern Europe, and what were the characteristic styles?
- What styles of jazz are popular in Africa, and who are the dominant performers?
- How has global jazz continued to develop in the first decade of the twenty-first century?

From Chapter 11 of *Discover Jazz*. First Edition. John Edward Hasse, Tad Lathrop. Copyright © 2012 by Pearson Education, Inc. All rights reserved.

HISTORICAL EVENTS		MUSICAL EVENTS

1914 — Archduke Ferdinand of Austria is assassinated, launching World War I

1917 — Russian Revolution puts Vladimir Lenin and other Communists in power

1917 — James Reese Europe and his jazzy Hellfighters military band perform in Paris

1918 — • Clarinetist/tenor sax player Sidney Bechet among first jazz musicians to perform in Europe

1919 — Treaty of Versailles ends World War I

1919 — • Original Dixieland Jazz Band spends the year touring England

1921 — Mitchell's Jazz Kings first black jazz band to record in Europe

1922 — Mussolini takes power in Italy

1925 — *La Revue Nègre* opens in Paris, with clarinetist Sidney Bechet and singer Josephine Baker

1928–39 — African American Ada Smith ("Bricktop") operates her famous Paris nightclub where many jazz musicians performed

1933 — Adolph Hitler and Nazi party come to power in Germany

1933 — • Duke Ellington performs in Paris
• Solomon "Zulu Boy" Cele's Jazz Maniacs, a 16-piece band, forms in South Africa

1934 — Quintet of the Hot Club of France, with guitarist Django Reinhardt and violinist Stéphane Grappelli, debuts

1935 — The Nazis block Coleman Hawkins from touring Germany because they view jazz as "degenerate" music

1938 — English bandleader Ray Noble composes and records *Cherokee*, which becomes a jazz standard on both sides of the ocean

1939 — World War II begins with German invasion of Poland

1942 — Gandhi launches civil disobedience movement demanding Britain return India to self-rule

1945 — • Germany surrenders; Hitler commits suicide
• United Nations founded

1949 — Mao Zedung takes over as leader of China

1949 — Paris holds the Festivale International du Jazz with an array of important musicians

1952 — Elizabeth II crowned Queen of England

1952 — Oscar Peterson discovers Japanese pianist/composer Toshiko Akiyoshi while touring Japan, and arranges for her to record for Verve Records

HISTORICAL EVENT

MUSICAL EVENT

1955 — The Voice of America begins long-running *Music USA* worldwide radio broadcasts of jazz, eventually reaching 100 million listeners

Soviet Union launches first successful satellite, Sputnik — **1957**

In Africa, 17 nations are granted independence, including Nigeria and the former Belgian Congo — **1960** — In England, alto saxophonist Joe Harriott releases Europe's first free-jazz record: *Free Form*

Berlin Wall divides East and West Berlin — **1961**

Nelson Mandela, South African black leader, sentenced to life in prison for opposing apartheid — **1964**

Dutch drummer Han Bennink and Russian pianist Misha Mengelberg found the Instant Composer's Pool Orchestra to perform their own contemporary jazz works

Arab-Israeli War — **1967**

1968 — Egyptian drummer Salah Ragab forms the Cairo Jazz Band, among Egypt's first big bands

1969 — German jazz fan Manfred Eicher establishes the ECM label to promote contemporary jazz players from around the world

1974

Iran takes U.S. hostages — **1979**

South African pianist Abdullah Ibrahim records *Manenberg*, which becomes a symbol of resistance against apartheid

Mikhail Gorbachev calls for "Glasnost" in Soviet Union — **1985**

Soviet Union collapses — **1991**

1994

After fall of apartheid, Nelson Mandela elected president of South Africa — **1995** — French-Vietnamese guitarist Nguyên Lê, living in Paris, releases *Tales from Viêt-Nam*

Euro introduced as common currency of European nations — **1999**

2005 — Syrian Jazz Orchestra founded in Damascus, Syria

North Korea conducts first nuclear test — **2006**

Guitarist and vocalist Lionel Loueke, from Benin, combines African pop and jazz on his album *Karibu*

⁂ Explore the Jazz Timeline on **mymusiclab.com**

2008

950F 2009 NELSON MANDELA

RWANDA

COURTESY STAMPGIRL/SHUTTERSTOCK.

It's a rainy Sunday in December. The bassist Lelio Giannetto is at Palermo's airport on the Sicilian coast, where incoming flights are running late. He keeps looking at his watch.

Giannetto is an organizer of a three-day meeting—called "Dreamin' California"—of free improvisers from Sicily and the San Francisco Bay Area, that starts in a downtown theater tomorrow evening. Yesterday, he'd recorded with early arrival Tim Perkis, whose basic equipment is a laptop computer from which he coaxes abstract blurps and squeaks. Expected within the hour is Tom Nunn, who plays homemade instruments and has written a 300-page treatise on free improvisation, in which jazz is barely mentioned.

Tenor saxophonist Jan Garbarek brought distinctively Nordic elements to his jazz improvising. PHOTO COURTESY DAVID REDFERN/REDFERNS/GETTY IMAGES.

Think we're off the jazz map yet? Then ask Giannetto why he keeps checking the time. His answer is that he has a different kind of gig this afternoon, an hour or so away in the town of Salaparuta, with the Sicilian Jazz Dixielanders. In the nineteenth century, he explains, there was regular ship traffic between Salaparuta and New Orleans, a boat going out loaded with oranges and maybe a few hopeful immigrants and coming back full of cotton.

One couple who took the boat to New Orleans had a son who grew up to be Original Dixieland Jazz Band cornetist Nick LaRocca. All those Italians in old New Orleans were one reason opera was in the air, helping inspire Louis Armstrong's dramatic high-note endings.

The moral of the story is that you don't have to be American to see yourself in jazz. By the beginning of the twenty-first century, jazz was nearly everywhere, coming back around the bend just when you thought you'd left it. Colleges all over Europe were teaching it, wealthier European countries were subsidizing it. Even Beijing had launched an annual jazz festival, where musicians converged from the United States, Australia, Japan, Europe, and China itself—including the People's Liberation Army Big Band. But then, Shanghai had begun hosting itinerant jazz musicians as far back as 1926.

Jazz in Europe

The Early Years

Jazz went international early—no later than the fall of 1914, when the Original Creole Orchestra from New Orleans, including cornetist Freddie Keppard, toured western Canada for five weeks. They passed through again in 1916. The year after that, two homegrown Canadian jazz bands turned up, one in Vancouver and one in Hamilton, Ontario. Others quickly followed, in cities from Winnipeg to Montreal. (And Americans kept coming: pianist Jelly Roll Morton made Vancouver his base from mid-1919 through 1920.) In many ways, what happened in Canada set the pattern for jazz's reception in the rest of the world: the music was popular immediately, even if newspaper critics were hostile; musicians quickly attempted to do it themselves; a few African American musicians elected to stay around, because racial attitudes were less oppressive than in the United States; and many Canadian musicians got a good education listening to and playing with U.S. talent. As a practical matter, this meant working bands were racially integrated in Canada in the 1920s, much earlier than in the United States.

Jazz began crossing the oceans even before it turned up on records back home; for example, *Down Home Rag* was recorded in London in 1916 by the Versatile Four, an American vaudeville band then based in England. Their drummer, Charlie Johnson, was already swinging in a style based on military drumming.

In 1918, Australia's first jazz band was a smash hit in Sydney. In 1919, the Original Dixieland Jazz Band visited England and stayed a year. Around 1920, the Blue Band, from Holland, recorded in Berlin and London. Dutch colonials were playing jazz in Java by 1922; by 1926 they'd been joined by native Indonesians and itinerants from the Philippines.

The first great U.S. jazzman in Europe was clarinetist Sidney Bechet, who appeared in London in 1919 with Will Marion Cook's ragtimey Southern

The Original Dixieland Jazz Band, billed as "the creators of jazz" and the "sensation of America," played the Palladium and other London halls in 1919. They are shown here at London's Palais de Danse. PHOTO COURTESY FRANK DRIGGS COLLECTION.

197

Syncopated Orchestra. Swiss conductor Ernest Ansermet heard them often and wrote a now-famous review singling out Bechet as a harbinger of music that would sweep the world. Ansermet was astute enough to praise the quality of Bechet's blues at a time when Europeans may have had little knowledge of that style. When Cook's band broke up, its musicians scattered as far afield as Norway.

Back then, when the "jazz" label got pasted on nearly any music that moved, there was some confusion abroad about just what jazz was. Was its essence syncopation or improvisation? Was it futuristic noise music, or a novelty act with drummers doing tricks with sticks? Was it folk music or a more refined expression?

For that reason, American musicians on foreign soil were enormously important locally, even if little remembered back home. Take drummer Louis Mitchell, who in 1918 or 1919 took a jazz band to Paris and stayed over a decade. To quote John Szwed, jazz was "the shock to the system the French had been waiting for": modern, energetic, exotic. By 1922, composer Darius Milhaud was taking notes in Harlem nightspots, an influence you can hear on his *La Creation du Monde* (1923).

In Europe, black American musicians were suddenly in demand, and more than a few at home—encouraged by stories of racial tolerance told by black GIs returning from World War I—took the boat abroad. One pianist lured to Paris by an offer of $50 weekly was soon in London making $750 a week.

4ᵉ ANNÉE
NUMÉRO 22

PRIX : 4 FR.
(FOREIGN 5 FR.)

HOT

FRANK NEWTON

INTERNATIONAL REVIEW OF JAZZ MUSIC
REVUE INTERNATIONALE DE LA MUSIQUE DE JAZZ
DÉCEMBRE NOËL JANVIER

COURTESY FRANK DRIGGS COLLECTION.

When U.S. musicians left a local band, or a group showed up a few players short, locals began filling in. One such precocious French player was trombonist Leo Vauchant, born in 1904. Hearing Mitchell's band, he quickly grasped that improvisation was the point and soon figured out how to do it himself. In 1924 Vauchant began exchanging music lessons with symphonic composer Maurice Ravel, who wanted to know about jazz. Relying on his practical experience, Vauchant formulated loose guidelines for what worked or didn't, what was hip and what wasn't—an early glimmering of "jazz education" (but not the only one: jazz instruction books were sold in England by 1926, and by 1927 the Frankfurt conservatory was offering a jazz performance class). Surreal postscript: In 1931 Vauchant traveled to the States as a dance-band arranger. On one band's bus tour in Louisiana, he and a guitarist went out in a field during a rest stop to play impromptu blues for African American cotton pickers. By age 30 he'd glimpsed both jazz's intellectual future and its formative past.

By the mid-1920s, jazz records were being distributed overseas, and before long England and France (like the United States) had jazz critics. Pianist Claude Hopkins, in Paris to accompany singer Josephine Baker in 1925, found that local musicians had been studying the latest Armstrong sides: "Some of the European bands were so like Louis's band, you could hardly tell the difference. . . . The tone and the range weren't as good but the overall picture was pretty similar."

Still, for many outside the United States, these records posed more questions than they answered. Labels on 78s typically gave no or misleading information about who the players were, and when and where they recorded the disc—information necessary to fit fragmentary pieces of the jazz puzzle together. Thus were born the jazz discographers, tracking down dates and personnel, often by peppering visiting Americans with vexing questions about sessions long past. Over the years, many of jazz's most diligent discographers have come from outside the United States: France's Charles Delaunay whose 1936 *Hot Discography* was a stylistic model for many later examples; England's Brian Rust; Denmark's Jørgen Grunnet Jepsen; Belgium's Walter Bruyninckx; and Canada's Tom Lord.

The line dividing discographers and critics from active jazz promoters and producers was thin enough for several Europeans to cross, just as John Hammond did in the United States. Delaunay and French writer Hugues Panassié both produced numerous recording sessions; together, they directed the A&R program of the French label Swing. Critic Andre Hodeir played, arranged, and produced jazz, in addition to writing several noteworthy books on the subject.

History & Culture

Le Jazz Hot: Jazz in Paris between the World Wars

Jazz was born and raised in America, but in Paris between the wars it found its home away from home. Long a cosmopolitan city that encouraged personal and artistic freedom, the City of Light attracted hundreds of U.S. writers, painters, and classical and jazz musicians.

World War I jump-started Parisians' infatuation with syncopated music. In August of 1918, they discovered American Lt. James Reese Europe and his jazzy Hellfighters military band. Americans, thanks to their strong participation in the war, were loved by the French.

African Americans found a far more welcoming environment in Paris than in their native United States and drank in the greater freedom. When Mitchell's Jazz Kings recorded in Paris in December 1921, they made the first non-ragtime jazz disc by blacks in Europe. The St. Louis-born singer and dancer Josephine Baker achieved overwhelming success in *La Revue Nègre* (1925) and overnight became the darling of the French, while the African American singer Bricktop (Ada Smith) ran a highly successful nightclub in Paris (1928–39) where many top musicians performed. In 1920, Parisians had an opportunity to hear their first jazz artist of wide renown, Sidney Bechet, playing with Benny Peyton's Jazz Kings. In 1925, Bechet returned with *La Revue Nègre* and in 1928 played the nightclub Chez Florence, but then was expelled from the country for getting into a gunfight.

Bandleaders Paul Whiteman (1925) and Noble Sissle (1928) also played and made their marks in Paris, and at the end of the decade, many young, talented white Chicago musicians went to the city, among them Bud Freeman and drummer Dave Tough. France was also producing homegrown jazz musicians—the most important of the 1920s were trombonist Leon (Leo) Vauchant, trumpeter Philippe Brun, and pianist Stéphane Mougin, while the most outstanding orchestras were those of Ray Ventura and Grégor.

In the 1920s, jazz was terrifically in vogue, but in the early 1930s, the mass audience seemed to turn its back. Still, *Jazz Tango* magazine emerged in June 1930. And in 1932, a handful of amateurs established the Hot Club of France to offer concerts under the direction of critic Hugues Panassié and jazz activist and discographer Charles Delaunay. American records were widely distributed, and radio followed timidly.

In the first half of the 1930s, most young Parisian jazzmen were still works-in-progress. But their music took a flying leap thanks to their microscopic analyses of the best jazz recordings; live concerts (Duke Ellington in 1933 and 1939, Louis Armstrong in 1934); and jam sessions with leading American jazzmen. Europe's *crème de la crème* burst forth in 1934

DANCE·WITH·ME (DANSE·AVEC·MOI) BY SPENCER WILLIAMS. "REVU·NÉGRE" GRAND SPECTACLE. PLAYING·CHAMPS·ÉLYSÉE·MUSIC·HALL. NO ONE CAN LOVE ME DANCE·WITH·ME (DANSE·AVEC·MOI). PUBLISHED BY W.J. JOHNSON, 65 RUE DEMOURS, PARIS.

COURTESY FRANK DRIGGS COLLECTION.

with the Quintet of the Hot Club of France, centered around guitarist **Django Reinhardt** and violinist **Stéphane Grappelli**. Emerging around the Quintet were, among others, violinist Michel Warlop and saxophonists Alix Combelle and Andre Ekyan.

Thanks to Delaunay, the second half of the decade saw the debut in 1935 of the bilingual (French and English) magazine *Jazz Hot* (continuous, except for a wartime hiatus, until century's end) and in 1937 of the label Swing, which captured marvelous encounters between French jazz artists and visiting U.S. jazzmen.

In 1939, as the German army advanced into France, American musicians fled Paris; jazz would take a lower profile until after World War II.

—*Philippe Baudoin*

If European musicians at first emulated the Americans stylistically, by 1934 the seeds were planted for an alternative approach. That's when guitarist Django Reinhardt and violinist Stéphane Grappelli put together their Quintet of the Hot Club of France. Grappelli's violin, notably on *After You've Gone* and *Limehouse Blues* (both 1936), was as sweet, urbane, and sophisticated as Parisian café music. Reinhardt, a Belgian gypsy who couldn't read music and who had limited use of his fire-damaged fretting hand, proved a phenomenal jazz-guitar innovator. He had a stinging attack and improvised complex single-note lines broken up by a short series of charging chords that goosed the music forward—all rendered with distinctive flair (*Swing Guitars*, 1936, and *Minor Swing*, 1937). Traveling Americans who heard and played

with him related to it, even as they recognized that his harmonic and melodic vocabulary reflected his own roots at least as much as it echoed the blues.

Reinhardt was the model of the successful non-American jazz improviser. The Quintet inspired similar groups around the continent, and he belatedly spawned a raft of French or French-speaking pickers, including Raymond Boni, Philip Catherine, Boulou Ferre, Bireli Lagrene, and Belgium's electric-guitar wizard René Thomas. To date, no foreign-born jazz musician who didn't move to the United States has commanded nearly as much stateside attention or respect as Reinhardt.

(((•—[Hear] a profile of Django Reinhardt on **mymusiclab.com**

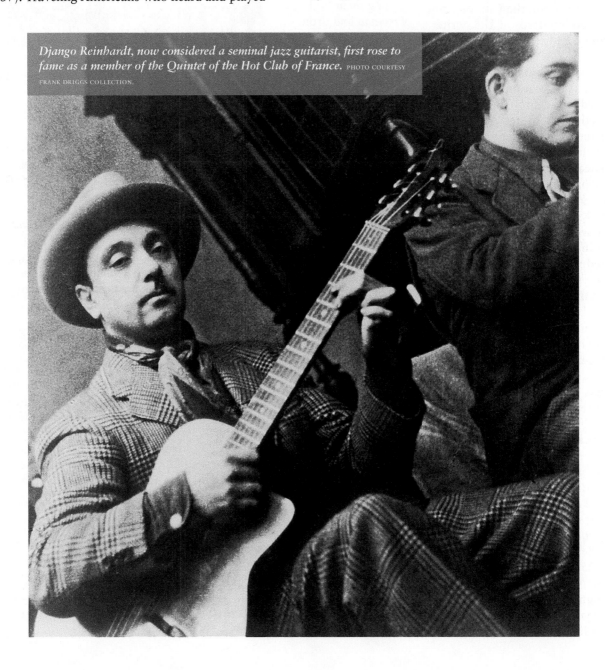

Django Reinhardt, now considered a seminal jazz guitarist, first rose to fame as a member of the Quintet of the Hot Club of France. PHOTO COURTESY FRANK DRIGGS COLLECTION.

Listening Guide

Listen to *Minor Swing* by Quintette du Hot Club de France on **mymusiclab.com**
CD II, Track 11/Download Track 35

MINOR SWING • QUINTETTE DU HOT CLUB DE FRANCE

Music: Stéphane Grappelli and Django Reinhardt, 1937. Personnel: Stéphane Grappelli (violin); Django Reinhardt, Joseph Reinhardt, Eugene Vees (guitar); Louis Vola (bass). Recorded November 25, 1937, in Paris. First issue: Swing 23. Timing: 3:17.

Overview

This café-style music is a prime example of the premier European jazz group of the 1930s, a Parisian string quintet featuring suave violinist Stéphane Grappelli and guitarist Django Reinhardt, the most admired non-American jazz musician of his time. Reinhardt was an influence on early electric guitarists such as Charlie Christian. Here he and Grappelli romp over a simple minor-chord progression, infusing their jazz with a European sensibility.

Key Features

- Reinhardt's punchy flat-picking and heavy vibrato immediately distinguish his sound. His right hand had been damaged in a fire, and he did most of his fretting with index and middle fingers only.
- A chunky two-beat rhythm feel predominates. Two strummed rhythm guitars lay down a strong "one *and* two *and*" syncopated feel typical of early jazz, over which the soloists freely place their accents.
- Form: A 16-bar melody, with the two similar halves separated by a two-bar break. Reinhardt and Grappelli solo in turn over another 16-bar template built on the same simple three- and four-note chords (A and D minor, E7). The closing 16-bar melody recalls but differs from the opening theme.

—Kevin Whitehead

TIME	STRUCTURE	MELODY
0:00	THEME	Guitar and violin state the theme, which does little more than outline the underlying chords of A minor and D minor. At 0:08, one (upward sliding) bass note fills a two-bar break, when the rest of the band falls silent. The (slap) bass returns with a descending run on the second break at 0:17.
0:20	GUITAR SOLO—CHORUS 1	Reinhardt jumps in on the end of the bass break with a diminished chord, then switches to mostly single-note lines, played with a flat pick. Note the symmetry of his first three phrases (all of which end on the keynote of A).
0:39	GUITAR SOLO—CHORUS 2	Reinhardt begins the chorus emphasizing a high E note, and concludes it with a skittering downward run (0:53) that lands on the keynote.
0:58	GUITAR SOLO—CHORUS 3	Notice Reinhardt's use of bluesy bent notes, as at 1:01 and 1:10. The chorus ends with a variation on the shapely phrase that introduced it.
1:17	GUITAR SOLO—CHORUS 4	Reinhardt begins with one of his signature moves—a flurry of wildly flailed chords, and ends the chorus with chord forms that emphasize the octave. (To manage these, he employed his damaged fingers, over which he had some limited control.) This dramatic climax paves the way for Grappelli's entrance.
1:36	VIOLIN SOLO—CHORUS 1	Grappelli—bowing the strings—like Reinhardt, elegantly wends his way through the underlying chords. But his phrasing and feeling are a little more relaxed than the guitarist's, a contrast that made them excellent partners. Note his slightly scratchy tone, which gives his lines more bite.
1:55	VIOLIN SOLO—CHORUS 2	The rhythm guitars (three, now that Reinhardt's joined them) really shine with their loudly accented strummed chords, as at 2:05. Just as Grappelli is about to enter his last chorus, someone—Reinhardt maybe—offers murmurs of encouragement, in English—jazz's universal language, "Yeah, man. Come on."
2:14	VIOLIN SOLO—CHORUS 3	Grappelli's slurred, high-pitched phrases starting at 2:24 effectively build tension, and lead him into his last chorus.
2:33	VIOLIN SOLO—CHORUS 4	Note the punctuating upward "rip" at 2:34. Syncopated, matching phrases from 2:43 on bring the solo to a climax.
2:51	CLOSING MELODY	The melody here outlines the chords as in the opening, with minor variations. But this time, the whole band is playing, which gives it greater urgency, and the E7 chord is outlined as well. The bass break at 2:58 echoes the one at 0:17. To finish, Grappelli plays a fast chromatic run, E down to E-flat and then up to A. The band responds with murmurs of approval at their having nailed the tune—contrived, but well deserved nonetheless.

Controversies

Naturally the music encountered resistance. Italians circulated an anti-jazz petition in 1923. One French composer explained that collective improvising was mathematically impossible. Swedish critics denounced Louis Armstrong when he visited in 1933.

In post-revolutionary Russia, folks had fiercely debated jazz's merits—even before they'd heard any jazz. Abroad as at home, there was always someone ready to argue what the music should or shouldn't be.

In 1926, two contradictory visions of jazz came to Russia. Bandleader **Sam Wooding**, criss-crossing Eurasia with the theatrical revue *Chocolate Kiddies*, championed Paul Whiteman's symphonic jazz. Drummer Benny Peyton's Jazz Kings, with Bechet on board, backed the hot alternative. Predictably, the music establishment backed the dead-end former approach, while grass-roots musicians supported the latter.

Jazz, like any art form, must be free to develop as it will; it does not take orders from the top. But in the Soviet Union, where the official line on any matter could reverse itself in an instant, jazz was a small boat on a high sea. For example, in 1934, a pro-jazz movie swept Russia. In 1936, the newspaper *Pravda* denounced jazz, then reversed itself, but sister paper *Izvestiia* continued the attacks. In 1937, some jazz musicians were hauled off to labor camps, or simply disappeared. In 1938, a sanitized, 43-piece State Jazz Orchestra was organized, its musicians paid twice the compensation of their classical counterparts—a grand if grim exception to the rule that jazzers always make less money. Hip audiences booed anyway. In 1939, subsidized regional swing orchestras cropped up. During World War II, army and navy jazz bands entertained the Russian troops.

In Germany, the situation was similarly tragic and absurd. The Nazis portrayed jazz as Jewish-Negro degeneracy—and declared syncopated music incompatible with marching—but because of existing trade agreements were obliged to allow in Armstrong records.

The Germans unwittingly helped the cause of European jazz in 1935. Coleman Hawkins, on tour in Western Europe as a featured guest with English leader Jack Hylton's band, was forbidden to enter Germany because he was African American. (Hylton continued on without him.) Stranded in Holland, Hawkins

The reception accorded Sam Wooding (seated, center) and his band in travels through Eurasia and South America in the 1920s wasn't matched in the United States, where the returning Wooding found that other pre–swing era bands had staked claim on domestic listeners. PHOTO COURTESY FRANK DRIGGS COLLECTION.

Trumpeter Buck Clayton (center) took his 14 Gentlemen of Harlem to the Canidrome club in Shanghai, China, in 1934. The band split up there; Clayton stayed on until he'd earned enough money to return to the States, where he joined Count Basie's band. PHOTO COURTESY FRANK DRIGGS COLLECTION.

worked and recorded with the capable swing band the Ramblers and with expatriate pianist Freddy Johnson, in Europe since 1928.

Johnson was one of a few American musicians locked up by the Germans in the early 1940s. After World War II, Valaida Snow—the most widely traveled jazz woman of the prewar years—would claim to have been held in a concentration camp; in fact she'd been detained by Danish authorities, possibly for her own protection. Before that, she'd traveled from Sweden to Shanghai and hit a lot of stops between. When her fellow trumpeter Buck Clayton spent two years in Shanghai in the mid-1930s—at the instigation of pianist Teddy Weatherford, who'd been bouncing around Asia for years, and would spend his final years playing in India—he found that Snow had taught some Shanghai chefs how to cook soul food.

Hawkins was naturally much in demand, and he stayed in Europe until 1939, playing with locals in Holland, France, Switzerland, England, and Scandinavia. That the father of the tenor saxophone

found European musicians acceptable colleagues gave them a strong psychological boost. He was impressed by Reinhardt; by his own French admirer, tenor saxophonist Alix Combelle; and by at least one chart the Ramblers brought him. Having him around also helped the Europeans see how a musician's life and art intertwine—how the choices made on the bandstand relate to the kind of day a musician's having, for example.

The War Years and After

In Germany even before World War II, and in occupied countries during it, musicians were encouraged to play good European music rather than "degenerate"jazz—never mind how bad the proposed alternatives sounded. The occupation government in Holland and at least one German district issued regulations for improvisers—riffing was limited or forbidden, plunger mutes and scat singing were off-limits, and other restrictions applied.

American tunes were outlawed, too, but musicians found ways around that. If the French lament

La Tristesse de St. Louis (*The Sadness of St. Louis*) sounded oddly like the Czech patriots' anthem *The Song of Resetovd Lhota* or the German *Das Lied vom Heiligen Ludwig* (*The Song of Saint Louis*) it's because all of them were *St. Louis Blues*.

Jazz continued to be played in Berlin itself. Germans put jazz into propaganda broadcasts aimed at the British, and vice versa. There was even a jazz band, known as the Ghetto Swingers, at the Czech Terezin concentration camp, and it's said there was one at Buchenwald. For some in Germany and occupied countries (as in the Soviet Union), jazz became a symbol of freedom and resistance; then and there as now and elsewhere, however, to be a jazz fan was no sure sign of liberal politics. There were jazz fans in SS uniforms too. In the long run, the war had much to do with the dissemination of jazz around the world. The United States' Armed Forces Radio played a conspicuous role in spreading jazz in Europe and Asia, both during and after the war. U.S. soldiers also played an important part. During wartime, they shared their **fake books**—informal sheet music—with Russian allies, who picked up on harmonic refinements they'd been missing. (But as the Cold War dawned, the Soviets flip-flopped again, confiscating saxophones in 1949.)

Postwar U.S. service folk in Germany and Japan gave the defeated powers a taste for the music. (U.S.-based radio broadcasts helped too.) In 1948, Takatoshi Kyogoku reported from Japan to *Down Beat* magazine that jazz had "swept over this country like wildfire since the end of the war." In Europe, homegrown musicians got work entertaining off-duty U.S. troops. One, German trombonist Albert Mangelsdorff, later developed a method of coaxing harmonies from his horn by playing one note and humming another, a technique now widely used by other trombonists; he may have been the most influential European jazz musician to follow Reinhardt.

There was a major jazz festival in Paris in 1949, with bebop players Charlie Parker, Miles Davis, Tadd Dameron, and Kenny Clarke among featured performers. After Sidney Bechet played at the festival, music stores reported a run on soprano saxophones. Bechet moved to France in 1951; he'd record there often through the 1950s (*Olympia Concert*, 1955, and *La Legende de Sidney Bechet*, 1949–58), and would become a national hero. The French—like the Italians, mindful of old New Orleans's cultural makeup—considered jazz part of their own cultural legacy.

In France, Bechet usually performed in traditional settings, but also with the Algerian-born piano modernist Martial Solal, whose manic inventions, hopping all over the keyboard, suggested Earl Hines's influence. In his long and productive career Solal recorded with such thoughtful Americans as altoist Lee Konitz (*Satori*, 1974, and *Four Keys*, 1979) and Dave Douglas (*Rue de Seine*, 2005) as well as a host of Europeans. His recording of *Neutralisme* (1999) with saxophonist Johnny Griffin (*JTSA* Disc 6/Track 15) is one example of his excellent accompanying work.

Along with tenor saxophonist Don Byas, Bechet was in the first wave of postwar expatriates who gravitated to Paris, Rome, Copenhagen, Amsterdam, and other cities where they could find work, respect, and the good life. By 1965 there were so many American jazz musicians in Paris, the French musicians' union complained the Yanks were getting all the good gigs.

Not that Americans there neglected their French colleagues. Drummer Kenny Clarke often played with bassist Pierre Michelot, sometimes backing temporary Parisian Bud Powell, as on the pianist's albums *Cookin' at Saint Germain* (1957–59) and *The Complete Essen Jazz Festival Concert* (1960). (Powell's experiences in Paris were part of the inspiration for *'Round Midnight*, 1986, one of several feature films focusing on jazz abroad.) For 12 years, Clarke also co-led a successful pan-European big band with Belgian pianist Francy Boland, heard on the albums *Two Originals* (1967–68) and *Three Latin Adventures* (1968).

When Miles Davis visited in 1957 to tour with Clarke, Michelot, pianist Rene Urtreger, and tenor saxophonist Barney Wilen, director Louis Malle asked Davis to score his film noir *Ascenseur pour L'Échafaud* (*Lift to the Scaffold*). Jazz soundtracks were then a French fad: John Lewis, Art Blakey, and Duke Ellington also did one each, respectively, *Sait-on Jamais* (*No Sun in Venice*) (1957), *Des Femmes Disparaissent* (*The Disappearing Women*) (1958), and *Paris Blues* (1961).

Blakey, by the way, was later quoted as saying about jazz, "It's American music, and no one else can play it." But that didn't stop him from hiring, over the years, such musicians as Russian trumpeter Valery Ponomarev, Australian saxophonist Dale Barlow, Nigerian bassist Essiet Essiet, or Japanese bassists Isao Suzuki and Yoshio Suzuki—or from recording in the 1950s with drummers from Senegal, Nigeria, and Jamaica.

Regional Conceptions of Jazz

The indigenous sounds of cultures worldwide have played an important role as source material for new, regional conceptions of jazz as well as thematic material for jazz played by Americans.

---

fake book a collection of printed music in a kind of musical shorthand, specifying only melody line, chord symbols, and lyrics—musicians have to fake the rest; used by many jazz musicians.

Issues

The German jazz band Weintraub's Syncopators (shown here in 1931) appeared in the 1930 film The Blue Angel, *which rising Nazi official Josef Goebbels denounced as "offal."* PHOTO COURTESY ULLSTEIN BILD/THE GRANGER COLLECTION, NYC.

Jazz under the Nazis

Why did the Nazi government (and other totalitarian regimes) object to jazz music?

To many Germans of the 1930s who subscribed to the notion of a superior Aryan race, jazz—because of its black origins and its loose, danceable rhythm—was widely considered to be counter to German moral and cultural standards. Thus, immediately after the Nazi takeover in March 1933, Germany's new rulers banned jazz from all radio programs on the grounds that it was a form of musical decadence. Josef Goebbels, the Third Reich's minister for public enlightening and propaganda, referred to jazz as "talentless and unimaginative juggling with notes"(a position that didn't prevent him from employing a jazz band, Charlie and His Orchestra, in propaganda broadcasts to North America and Great Britain).

In many ways jazz was the antithesis of Nazi regimentation and a symbolic threat to the regime's control. The authorities disliked it not only because they associated it with despised racial minorities, including Jews, but also because it emphasized freedom, spontaneity, and individualism.

Under Nazi rule, Jewish dance and jazz musicians were unable to pursue their professions and were forced to leave the country. (One emigre, Francis Wolff, launched a record company in the United States that would one day become almost synonymous with jazz: Blue Note.)

The German government discouraged the public from playing, listening, or dancing to jazz, but the ban was difficult to enforce. American jazz recordings were readily available until the United States entered the war in 1941. Afterward, until 1944, the German companies Odeon, Brunswick, and Imperial pressed hot jazz records for sale in neutral and occupied countries, but the discs found their way back into Germany and were unofficially available "under the counter."

Not surprisingly, jazz became a symbol of resistance. In order to fool informers and the secret police, jazz fans and musicians organized clandestine sessions, cut off telltale composers' names and song titles from sheet music, and misled the censors by disguising jazz standards under new names.

Despite the repressive climate, jazz enjoyed unprecedented popularity during the Nazi years, not only in such occupied countries as Norway, France, the Netherlands, and Czechoslovakia but also in Germany. And jazz musicians somehow continued to play and evolve. Some of Germany's finest jazzmen—including Kurt Hohenberger, Heinz Wehner, Freddie Brocksieper, Max Rumpf, Ernst Hollerhagen, Helmut Zacharias, and Benny de Weille—emerged, played, and recorded under Nazi rule. And their ranks were supplemented by such visiting foreign players as Kai Ewans, Fud Candrix, Teddy Stauffer, Thore Ehrling, Jean Omer, Eddie Tower, Cesare Galli, and Tullio Mobiglia.

By the time the war ended with the Nazis' defeat, jazz was in Germany to stay.

—Rainer E. Lotz

Sidney Bechet (right), one of the earliest U.S. jazz players in Europe (1919), spent his last years in France. PHOTO COURTESY DOWN BEAT ARCHIVES.

Sidney Bechet's tours in the 1920s had also taken him to Sweden, Spain, France, Italy, Hungary, Czechoslovakia, Greece, and Egypt; his biographer John Chilton said that later in life Bechet surprised listeners by playing various folk themes he'd heard in such places long ago; he was in the vanguard yet again, as interest in world music was beginning to build. In post–World War II Japan, there was a fad for jazzing up traditional themes. In 1951, Stan Getz, in Sweden with a local rhythm section, recorded a Swedish folk tune that became a jazz standard as *Dear Old Stockholm*. Within a few years, Sweden's celebrated baritone saxophonist **Lars Gullin** began recording original pieces with a folk flavor.

By now, foreign musicians had a good understanding of jazz as a reflection of the United States' cultural mix and of players' own experiences. It was inevitable that some would ask, "If U.S. jazz builds on indigenous materials like the blues, shouldn't our jazz reflect our culture and upbringing?"

With that question, jazz abroad began to grow up and out, beyond imitating American models. Not that outlanders didn't still look to the United States for new directions. Australians after World War II, for example, shadowed successive American trends—New Orleans revival, bop, cool, modal, free, and jazz and poetry—and produced the brilliant neo-bebopper,

lightning-quick alto saxophonist Bernie McGann. But they, too, were mindful of what they brought to the table: in 1964 there was even an Australian TV series called *Jazz Meets Folk*.

A regional conception of jazz was developing in England too, where the growth of jazz had been complicated by a decades-long protectionist blockade of U.S. talent—which didn't stop Americans from making English bandleader Ray Noble's *Cherokee* (1938) and its chord changes into jazz evergreens. The long-running feud between stateside and English musicians' unions had made it impossible for jazz musicians from either country to play the other, from 1935 to 1956—a crucial period in the States, encompassing the full flowering of the swing era and the birth and assimilation of bebop. The English scene lagged behind American developments, yet the ban also inspired a certain cocky, do-it-yourself attitude, heard in such period notables as trumpeter Nat Gonella. While the French continued to play with visiting Americans, the English made their own music.

That sense of independence bore fruit mostly in the years after the ban was lifted. In England, the folk-jazz connection was abetted by several factors: jazz musicians working in blues and folk-revival groups, several of which played Charles Mingus tunes; an influx of West Indians, including saxophonist

Joe Harriott and trumpeters Shake Keane and Harry Beckett, who brought island rhythms along; and the presence of black and white South Africans in exile, notably drummer Louis Moholo, pianist Chris McGregor, bassists Harry Miller and Johnny Dyani, trumpeter Mongezi Feza, and altoist Dudu Pukwana. The latter's "**township jazz**"—a blend of jazz sonorities, catchy tunes, and simple chord schemes (heard on *In the Townships*, 1973)—had a significant effect on the English jazz scene.

Curiously, polycultural South Africa remains the most jazz-oriented African country—a sign, perhaps, of the pronounced impact of European culture there. But that didn't stop such U.S. musicians as pianist Randy Weston, trumpeter Lester Bowie, multireedist Yusef Lateef, saxophonist Ornette Coleman, and drummers Max Roach and Ronald Shannon Jackson from going to various other African countries to play with local musicians or to investigate their music. And a number of U.S. musicians, including Weston, Lateef, Roach, and clarinetist John Carter, have deployed percussionists from North or West Africa on record as well.

The trend toward homegrown jazz styles really took off in the mid-1960s. Its Pied Piper and Johnny Appleseed was cornetist Don Cherry, one of several American modernists—among them, saxophonist Steve Lacy and pianist Mal Waldron—wandering Europe then, looking for work and partners. Cherry discovered Gato Barbieri, in Paris; sought out and studied with exiled South African pianist Dollar Brand, later called **Abdullah Ibrahim**, whose rolling polyrhythms—as on *African Piano* (1969) and *African River* (1989)—can suggest an African percussion choir; went to Milan to play with the remarkable pianist **Giorgio Gaslini** after reading about him in London; and spent many years off and on living and recording in Sweden, particularly inspiring musicians there. (Listen to Ibrahim's *Manenberg [Revisited]*, CD II, Track 12/Download Track 36.)

Where most previous Americans in Europe sought out, not always successfully, musicians who could play on American terms, Cherry encouraged Europeans to be themselves: he was an avatar of world music, writing compositions flavored by various south-of-the-equator cultures. From 1978 to 1984, he was in a fine co-op trio, Codona, with Brazil's Vasconcelos

and American sitarist and tabla player Colin Walcott, of the groundbreaking world-jazz group **Oregon**, a spinoff of Paul Winter's band.

After 1970, the Scandinavians got another boost from the German record label ECM, which favored quiet, almost meditative music adorned with atmospheric studio echo. ECM's northern discoveries included pianist Bobo Stenson—whose out-of-tempo intros leading up to playing over a steady pulse reflected his interest in the music of India—and tenor saxophonist **Jan Garbarek**, who had played with Cherry and with U.S. composer George Russell. Garbarek worked with Norwegian folk materials in all manner of settings—one album featured a Nordic wind harp—and his pinched, restrained sound has been much imitated. In the 1970s he was in pianist Keith Jarrett's "European quartet"with Swedish bassist Palle Danielsson and the graceful Norwegian drummer Jon Christensen.

"What I'm playing today—whatever it is—I'm playing because I once learned the language of jazz,"Garbarek said, "but we also have our own blues equivalents, our own folk music."This Nordic consciousness was taken even further by Kristian Blak, a pianist

Drummer Kenny Clarke, 1946. PHOTO COURTESY FRANK DRIGGS COLLECTION.

---

township jazz   jazz that originated in the black townships of South Africa, characterized by ostinatos.

from Denmark's remote Faroe Islands, who in 1984 recorded a jazz LP, *Concerto Grosso*, by his group Yggdrasil in a cave formed by the sea, to the accompaniment of crashing waves.

Other notable ethnic influences came from India, a country with no strong jazz tradition, but where improvisation is central to music making. Indian music was a full-blown fad in the 1960s: the Beatles and other rock bands adopted the **sitar** (a lute that features strings that are not directly played but vibrate "sympathetically" when other notes are plucked) and **tabla** (paired Indian drums); saxophonist John Coltrane recorded *India* (on *Live at the Village Vanguard*, 1961), albeit no more than a vague impression of droning Carnatic music; West Coast sax player Bud Shank recorded with sitar master **Ravi Shankar** on the album *Fire Night* (1962); British saxophonist Joe Harriott mixed jazz and Indian players in *Indo-Jazz Suite* (1966). In the 1970s, John Handy draped rhythmically supple alto saxophone improvisations over simplified Indian rhythmic cycles on the album *Karuna Supreme* (1975). Indian strings and percussion had been used for exotic color—as on some electric Miles Davis recordings from 1970—but India's contribution to the jazz vocabulary has been primarily rhythmic, its fiendishly complex additive rhythm patterns stimulating jazz much the way Latin rhythms have.

The most important figure in this connection was English guitarist John McLaughlin, with his strong feel for South Indian music and the blues, two traditions with the shared characteristics of string bending, floating pitches, and elaborations on basic compositional forms. His electric Mahavishnu Orchestras of the 1970s—which at various times included Czech keyboardist Jan Hammer and French violinist Jean-Luc Ponty—hinted at Indian influences on such albums as *The Inner Mounting Flame* (1971) and *Birds of Fire* (1972). (For an example of the Mahavishnu Orchestra's sound, listen to *Celestial Terrestrial Commuters* [*JTSA* Disc 5/Track 11].) The influences were more on the surface in McLaughlin's later acoustic group **Shakti**, which employed Indian violinist L. Shankar and percussionist Zakir Hussain and played fast and fiery jazz ragas. In the 1980s and 1990s, whippet-fast Indian hand-drummer Trilok Gurtu played with many Western musicians and groups, including Oregon and Jan Garbarek.

---

sitar   Indian stringed instrument consisting of a resonating gourd and a long neck supporting seven principal strings, plus 12 to 20 sympathetic strings.

tabla   a pair of drums of North India, played with the fingers, palms, and hands.

Experimental and Free Jazz in Europe and Beyond

Even nowadays, American soloists touring Europe sometimes encounter incompatible rhythm sections (although Stan Getz, who lived in Copenhagen from 1958 to 1961, found a compatible bassist in the U.S. expatriate Oscar Pettiford). In 1963 a strange album from Copenhagen rang in new changes from just such incompatibility: the rhythm section (which included bass prodigy **Niels-Henning Ørsted Pedersen**, who'd go on to work with pianist Oscar Peterson) played with a smooth sense of swing, but the visiting American seemed to be fighting the players all the way. That record, *My Name Is Albert Ayler*, announced the European debut of free jazz, which had even more profound consequences there than in the United States. If Americans could break free of their jazz past, so could Europeans. In England, alto saxophonist Joe Harriott had already made Europe's first free-jazz record—*Free Form* (1960)—on which he sometimes sounded strikingly (if coincidentally) like Ornette Coleman.

By the late 1960s numerous Western Europeans had declared that they no longer played jazz; rather, they were playing "European improvised music," employing scant if any predetermined material. It was a thoroughly transnational movement, with musicians crossing borders looking for like-minded souls. As English saxophonist Evan Parker put it, "It really was reassuring to know you weren't alone, you weren't crazy. Or if you were crazy there were other people who were just as crazy as you."

The major players came mostly from Germany (including saxophonist Peter Brötzmann, who personified his country's roaring high-energy take on the concept); England (where Parker and guitarist Derek Bailey helped define a quieter, more cooperative model); and Holland, where pianist Misha Mengelberg, drummer **Han Bennink**, and saxophonist Willem Breuker brought a sense of subversive fun to the music. A key contributor, Danish-Congolese saxophonist John Tchicai, had already made a dent in the United States, recording with Archie Shepp and with Coltrane on the latter's roiling album *Ascension* (1965).

That European movement eventually mushroomed into a worldwide circuit of free improvisers, many of whom recognized no kinship with jazz but (like Garbarek) wouldn't be doing what they did without its example. The Dutch model proved particularly attractive to some observers, because it embraced swing rhythm, while the German and English tended not to. The playing of Bennink—one of the heaviest swingers in or out of Europe, even while performing such visual stunts as bouncing his

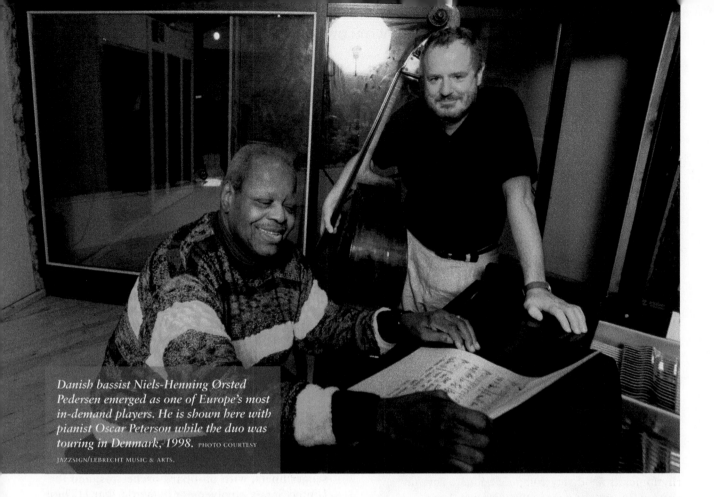

sticks off the floor—even harkened back to vaudeville drummers. (A theatrical side also popped out in the Lithuanian trio that personified the new, liberal Soviet jazz of the 1980s: keyboardist Vyacheslav Ganelin, saxophonist Vladimir Chekasin, and drummer Vladimir Tarasov.)

Mengelberg—born in Russia, of temporarily transplanted Dutch and German parents—composed music that reflected his conservatory training, a finely honed sense of the absurd, and an admiration of Thelonious Monk and pianist Herbie Nichols. (Monk loomed large on the European scene when he was overlooked in the United States; some pianists who bore his stamp included Germany's Alexander von Schlippenbach, Switzerland's Irene Schweizer, England's Stan Tracey, and Russian-born nomad Simon Nabatov.) For this writer at least, Mengelberg's (and Bennink's) ICP— the **Instant Composers Pool Orchestra** of eight to ten pieces—offered one of the world's finest mixes of jazz chops and conceptual smarts; the group could twist Ellington, Nichols, and Monk tunes into elegant pretzels, as the album *Bospaadje Konijnehol* (*Forest Path Rabbit Hole*) (1986–91) attests.

Italy produced more than its share of good jazz musicians, ready to play with visiting American soloists—Chet Baker recorded with many of them. And Italy had no shortage of lyrical horn players, the best known of whom was trumpeter Enrico Rava.

Still, in terms of developing a national jazz identity, Italy lagged behind Western Europe; chalk it up to national disorganization rather than lack of ambition. Giorgio Gaslini, in particular, tried about all there was to try: bop just after World War II, cool and free jazz, jazzed-up folk songs, and reconciliations of jazz and 12-tone music.

For a period in the 1990s Gaslini played piano in the Italian Instabile Orchestra, the first successful attempt to bridge the musical gap between the industrial North and the rural South. It brought in musician-composers from all over the boot and provided a setting in which a pan-Italian sound could discover itself. The group offered a rich mix, including Rava; multireedist Gianluigi Trovesi, who combined jazz and folk elements in a natural way; the manically comic trumpeter (and IIO founder) Pino Minafra; and elder statesman and squirrelly altoist Mario Schiano. He began free-improvising in 1960 and said later he didn't consider himself a jazz musician anymore. Why, then, did he remain so fond of playing such chestnuts as *Moonlight in Vermont* and *Lover Man*? "Nostalgia," he said.

Of all the European scenes, Italy may be the richest in untapped potential, not least because it stands at the crossroads of so many cultures that have their own rhythmic and melodic traditions. It's one to watch in the future.

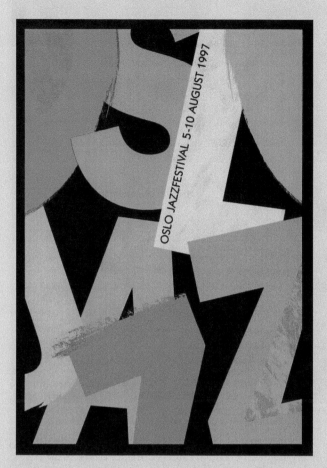

International jazz festivals offered audiences and musicians alike an idyllic alternative to cramped, smoky, noisy nightclubs. The hundreds of festivals presented every year— in such cities as Oslo, Paris, Berlin, and Edinburg—also added up to an important source of work for jazz bands.
COURTESY JOHN EDWARD HASSE.

As is Canada, the site of several pockets of independent jazz activity by late in the twentieth century. In Montreal—where Oscar Peterson came up before he arrived on the U.S. scene in 1949—an independent crop of French-speaking improvisers, such as saxophonist-flutist Jean Derome and electric guitarist René Lussier, were bringing Quebecois consciousness to improvised music's subversive/political aspect. In Toronto, the heart of the Canadian radio industry, and thus the center of big band activity, trombonist and arranger Rob McConnell led the best known. In Vancouver, such forward-looking improvisers as the percussive but lyrical pianist Paul Plimley and clarinetist François Houle helped keep things hopping. The influx of Asians into western Canada late in the century held the promise of spawning more

cross-cultural players, such as the Canadian-Chinese pianist from Toronto, Lee Pui Ming. Still, such cross-cultural contracts have been slow to develop in the new century, which is not to mention the many Canadian musicians—from high-note trumpeter Maynard Ferguson to neobop pianist Renee Rosnes, and the lyrical trumpet and flugelhorn player Ingrid Jensen—who made their mark in the States.

> **TAKE NOTE**
>
> • Who were the prominent musicians who brought jazz to Europe and how has a European jazz scene developed?

Jazz in Asia and Oceania

From its earliest days, jazz spread across the Atlantic, Pacific, and Indian Oceans with astonishing speed. Several factors helped speed its journey: new mass media (published sheet music and recordings); the European and American imperial presence in Asia and the Pacific islands; the growth of transoceanic tourism aboard passenger liners, with on-board orchestras; and the United States involvement in World War I. These conditions accelerated the movement of printed and recorded music and musicians, guaranteeing that jazz and its related dances would rapidly become worldwide forms of entertainment and expression.

Early Twentieth Century

The Philippines seems to have been the earliest site of jazz activity in Asia and Oceania; this may not be surprising, since it was a U.S. colony, yet the introduction and diffusion of jazz in the Philippine archipelago is not well documented. What we do know is that by the early 1920s, Filipino musicians were the most in-demand jazz musicians in Pacific Asia. Adept at "faking"(improvising mostly by ear), they earned a reputation second only to that of homegrown American talent, but Filipinos were in far greater supply. The dance halls, cabarets, movie theaters, and revues that began to appear in Shanghai, Osaka, Hong Kong, and Singapore in the years immediately after the Great War often featured Filipino jazz bands as headliners. The prominent Japanese saxophonist and composer Ryǒichi Hattori, who performed with a band called the Manila Red Hot Stompers in the mid-1920s, recalled that Filipino jazzmen were "weak readers" but blessed with intuitive musicality.

Post–World War I Years

In the interwar decades, several American musicians of African and European descent visited parts of Asia, although in smaller numbers than those who visited Europe. Pianist Teddy Weatherford performed extended engagements in China, the Dutch East Indies (now Indonesia), and India; he is remembered fondly for generously instructing Chinese, Indian, and Japanese musicians until his death in Kolkata in 1945. Prior to joining the Count Basie Orchestra in 1936, trumpeter Buck Clayton traveled the Pacific Asia circuit and lived it up in Shanghai, where he could afford to employ Chinese cooks and domestic servants. Singer Midge Williams and her three tap-dancing brothers went from a Shanghai engagement to Japan, where in 1934 she recorded with the Nippon Columbia Jazz Band and played a weeklong gig at Tokyo's famous Florida dance hall. The presence of these and other American-born musicians, coupled with the widespread availability of jazz recordings, meant that Asian jazz was often derivative of prevailing trends, techniques, and repertoire in the United States.

There were exceptions, however. Chinese musician Li Jinhui and Koichi Sugii of Japan composed, arranged, and recorded music that combined elements of jazz, show tunes, and East Asian folk melodies in the late 1920s and early 1930s. These strikingly successful experiments forecast more radical musical fusions later in the twentieth century. However, jazz was not always welcome in the region. Some Asian nationalists felt it was driving out native music. The Chinese communists took the party line that jazz was a bourgeois tactic to divert the oppressed masses from making revolution, dismissing Li's music as "pornographic." On the other hand, Sugii's recordings helped prolong jazz's presence in wartime Japan, despite ultranationalist, anti-American sentiments.

After World War II

Jazz swept through Asia with renewed vigor after the post–World War II dismantling of Europe's Asian empires. The expanded U.S. military commitment to the region during the Cold War brought thousands of soldier-musicians to the Pacific islands and East and Southeast Asia. More importantly, native talent was nurtured through expanded employment opportunities at and around U.S. military bases. Jazz also figured prominently in propaganda from both sides in the Cold War. The U.S. government sponsored radio broadcasts and tours by prominent American jazz artists from Pakistan to Japan, to demonstrate the virtues of American-style democracy and to

deflect criticism of Jim Crow racism. By contrast, Asian communists condemned jazz as an example of cultural imperialism. However, the music's status on the political spectrum was unpredictable: Australian leftists embraced jazz as a signifier of radical populism, but in resolutely anti-communist countries like South Korea, jazz remained controversial and emblematic of generational tensions.

Asia's most developed scene emerged in Japan, where listeners were as enamored of jazz as they were of other forms of Western music. There, however, image at times won out over content. Fans and even jazz magazines occasionally invented fanciful jazz-player histories unencumbered by the facts. One gets the feeling that Japanese jazz's best days are ahead—which is not to slight such accomplished individualists as big band composer Toshiko Akiyoshi, a resident of the States, whose penchant for flutes suggested her roots; pianist Yosuke Yamashita, who combined Japanese-sounding materials with a hard-edged attack; and Toshinori Kondo, a free-jazzer capable of blasting earthy trumpet lines like an old New Orleans hero.

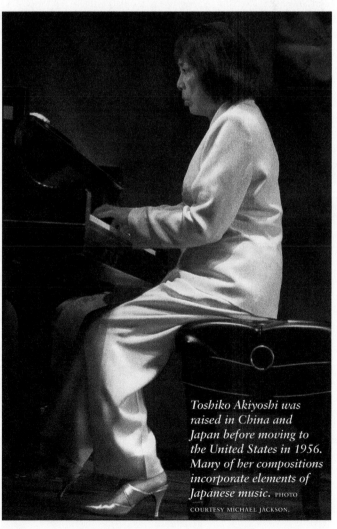

Toshiko Akiyoshi was raised in China and Japan before moving to the United States in 1956. Many of her compositions incorporate elements of Japanese music. PHOTO COURTESY MICHAEL JACKSON.

Late Twentieth Century

The last four decades of the twentieth century witnessed both the rise to international prominence of innovative Asian- and Oceanic-born jazz artists, and—despite the very different musical systems of Asia and the West—high-profile ventures to meld Asian classical and folk traditions with jazz. Since the 1950s, Japan has produced a slew of major artists, from bandleader-pianist Toshiko Akiyoshi and saxophonist Sadao Watanabe to guitarist Kazumi Watanabe and pianist Hiromi Uehara. Indian *tabla* drummers Trilok Gurtu and Zakir Hussain have earned esteem as jazz musicians through collaborations with Don Cherry, John McLaughlin, and Charles Lloyd. Filipina songstress

Charmaine Clamor and Chinese singer Coco Zhao have tackled what is arguably the single greatest challenge for non-native English speakers—jazz singing—and have also composed and performed credibly in Tagalog and Bisaya (Clamor) and Mandarin (Zhao). Although better known for his political role at home, the Thai monarch Bhumibol Adulyadej is also a jazz saxophonist and composer, whom Lionel Hampton praised as "the coolest king in the land."

Since the 1960s an "Asian tinge" has colored many jazz performances, frequently (if not always) involving collaborations with Asian musicians. Because many Asian musical traditions embrace extemporaneous performance, spontaneous dialogues with jazz musicians can be artistically fruitful. Joe Harriott and John Mayer

Listening Guide

((•· **Listen** to *Ting Ning* by Nguyên Lê on **mymusiclab.com**
CD II, Track 13/Download Track 37

TING NING • NGUYÊN LÊ

Music: Nguyên Lê/traditional. Personnel: Nguyên Lê (electric, acoustic, and fretless guitars; guitar synthesizer; computer and synths); Hao Nhiên (zither, *dan bau, sao* flute, *sapek* clappers); Paolo Fresu (trumpet); Simon Spang-Hanssen (saxophones and flutes); Michel Benita (acoustic bass); François Verly (percussion and keyboards); Trilok Gurtu (drums, percussion). Recorded October and November 1995 in Paris. First issue: *Tales from Viêt-Nam*, ACT 9225-2. Timing: 3:44.

Overview

From the rustic percussion and folk melodies of rural Vietnam to electric, effects-saturated guitar and jazz-tinged saxophone, *Ting Ning* takes the listener on an exotic mini-journey. The track exemplifies the fusion of jazz, rock, and world music at its most organic sounding. The leader, French-Vietnamese guitarist and producer Nguyên Lê, made many recordings of similarly style-mixing music in the 1990s and 2000s. He counts among his influences rock guitarist Jimi Hendrix,

the jazz-rock of Return to Forever and Mahavishnu Orchestra, and traditional jazz guitarists Wes Montgomery and Django Reinhardt. But where most others with similarly eclectic sources staked out comfortable positions in well-known musical zones, Lê built a multicultural soundscape of his own.

On *Ting Ning*, and its parent album *Tales from Viêt-Nam*, Lê mixed jazz players with Vietnamese traditional musicians to create "a journey back into my childhood, a return to lost roots."

Key Features

- Style: A mix of Vietnamese folk melodies, heavy-metal rock guitar, and jazz-tinged saxophone and drums.
- Colors: A blend and contrast of acoustic and electric—woody-sounding percussion mixed with acoustic flute, saxophone, and, later, electronically processed guitar. Textures evolve from the spare beginning to the densely textured climax.

- Rhythm and percussion: The band maintains a steady mid-tempo patter on rustic, acoustic instruments throughout, shifting up to double time (1:36) as the tune increases in excitement. The standard drum set, played by Trilok Gurtu, adds fullness and color to the rhythm sounds.
- Melodies shift among a Vietnamese-originated main melody with several variations (at 0:00, 0:15, and 0:36), a syncopated blues riff (2:01), and another syncopated riff that mixes blues with hint of the Vietnamese melody (2:32).
- Improvisation occurs most notably in the guitar toward the end of the piece (2:39). Lê uses the tune's melodic materials as the basis for screaming solo riffs.
- Form: The journey is from the spare, simple folk material to more contemporary jazz-rock fusion.

—*Tad Lathrop*

pioneered "Indo-jazz fusion," an effort later taken up by Nepalese-Bengali pianist Louis Banks and Goan saxophonist Braz Gonsalves, exploring the affinities between modal jazz and improvisatory practices of Hindustani *rāga*. Artists such as Alice Coltrane and Pharoah Sanders have composed and arranged with Asian instruments, modes, and motifs, creating music that has a deliberately mystical, meditative quality. On his 1961 album *In Fiesta*, Japanese drummer Hideo Shiraki seamlessly integrated Kinuko Shirane's fleet-fingered **koto** playing into his hard bop combo. Musicians of Chinese descent, such as Jon Jang, Fred Wei-han Ho, and Francis Wong, have created politicized "Afro-Asian" ensembles and compositions, sometimes integrating instruments such as the *erhu* (two-string fiddle) into their arrangements to a bluesy

effect. The American Voices Association sponsored the 2002 recording *Jazz Bridges Myanmar* incorporating the Burmese *pat waing* (tuned drum set) into jazz improvisations. Balinese composer I Nyoman Windha has written for **gamelan** ensembles with jazz quartet, while pianist Steve Suriajaya has done the same with Sundanese gamelan, creating richly layered pieces that illuminate the links between the *kotekan* (interlocking melody) and contrapuntal jazz aesthetics.

***

koto (Japanese) a Japanese zither (a stringed instrument) about six feet long typically with 13 silk strings.

gamelan Indonesian music, and set of instruments, notable for interlocking rhythms, microtones, repeating patterns, and metallophone-based sonorities.

TIME	FORM	MELODY/RHYTHM	INSTRUMENTATION
0:00	FOLK-LIKE MELODY	In a spare-sounding intro, a lively eight-bar melody is stated.	Flute duet with melodic percussion; cymbals provide accents.
0:14	FIRST VARIATION	Syncopated (uneven) rhythms in the melody interact with evenly spaced rhythms in the percussion.	Plus acoustic bass.
0:37	SECOND VARIATION	The texture thickens as saxophone enters, joining on a further variation of the melody, now shifted to a lower pitch area. Saxophone adds a "modern" tone to the previously rustic sound.	Plus saxophone.
0:50	THIRD VARIATION	The bass provides contrast with long, sustained notes. (Compare it with bassist Jaco Pastorius's work on *Birdland* (1:19; CD II, Track 5/Download Track 29).	The bass asserts itself, and drummer Trilok Gurtu fills in more.
1:05		Surprise! A tricky extra half-beat is inserted, shifting the melody slightly behind the established beat.	
1:18	FOURTH VARIATION	Texture thickens even more as a repetition of the melody is "doubled" in a higher register.	
1:35		A sustained stack of notes fades away as percussion continues. Rapid beats on hand drums and plucked eighth notes lead to drum-set improvisation.	
2:00	SYNCOPATED BLUES RIFF	A syncopated blues riff is played on saxophones.	Saxophones.
2:06		The riff ends on an offbeat and the notes sustain as drums maintain a propulsive, exciting groove for four bars.	
2:13	SYNCOPATED RIFF REPEATED	Saxophones repeat the syncopated blues riff.	Saxophones.
2:20		The riff ends again and notes sustain, as percussion continues grooving for eight bars.	
2:32	NEW MELODY	A new melody enters—a syncopated riff that mixes blues with elements of the main melody.	
2:39		Lê answers with a blistering set of bluesy guitar riffs spiced with extra "odd" notes.	Guitar.
2:45		The syncopated riff repeats, followed by more guitar improvisation.	
3:04	RETURN OF ORIGINAL FOLK MELODY	Echoes of the folk melody come in the form of full-band riffs. Guitar solos above the riffs and in response to them, with rapid phrases and howling high notes.	Full ensemble.
3:17		All join on final statement of melody ideas, leading to four closing accents.	

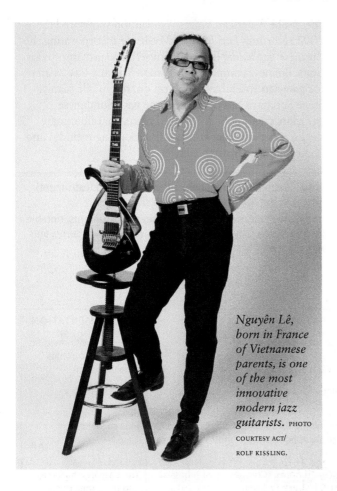

Nguyên Lê, born in France of Vietnamese parents, is one of the most innovative modern jazz guitarists. PHOTO COURTESY ACT/ ROLF KISSLING.

Twenty-First Century

In the early twenty-first century, most Asian and Oceanic metropolises boast respectable jazz scenes; even in communist China, there has been a revival of interest in Shanghai's former status as interwar Asia's jazz capital. And Asian musicians who are living far from their homelands have also made a large impact on the jazz world. These musicians don't always follow one musical path, but feel free to draw from various jazz styles. As just one example, French guitarist Nguyên Lê played in Orchestre National du Jazz, covered Jimi Hendrix tunes, and explored his cultural roots on *Tales from Viêt-Nam* (1996) with a cast including Italian trumpeter Paolo Fresu and drummers from India and England, Trilok Gurtu and Steve Argüelles.

 Watch a video of Nguyên Lê discussing how he composed *Ting Ning* on **mymusiclab.com**

TAKE NOTE

- What is the history of jazz in Asia and Oceania, and who are the vital figures creating original jazz music there?

Jazz in the Middle East

The term *Middle East* signifies not only a vast geographical region of the world stretching from Morocco to western India but also a diverse set of cultural constructs that derive from population migration, a variety of religious traditions (including Islam, Judaism, and Christianity), and shifting sociopolitical attitudes toward Western culture, including jazz music. Jazz in the Middle East has developed since at least the 1920s, incorporating and interpreting Western influences (through recordings and live performances) within local practices and styles of music, producing a rich and provocative milieu of sounds. Defining characteristics of jazz in the Middle East can be found most obviously in instrumentation, musical form/genre, and performance practices.

In the Middle East, some instruments are identified with particular cultures, while others retain a more pan-regional identity. Of the latter type, the **oud ('ūd)**, a **chordophone**, and **darbouka (dumbek)**, a goblet-shaped hand drum, are common in Middle Eastern jazz. Some instruments—the zither, for example—are shared among Middle Eastern cultures, although they vary locally in construction, performance practice, and repertoire.

Musical form and performance practice demonstrate the same dynamic range of pan-regional and culturally specific identities. Folk dances (such as the Bulgarian *horo*) composed in compound meters (groups of two and three beats, as in 3+2+2, or $\frac{7}{8}$) are common among Balkan cultures and have served as inspiration for many jazz compositions from this area. The **taksim (taqsīm)**, a solo instrumental improvisation found in Arab and Turkish music traditions, is another form that is frequently adapted to jazz contexts. Musicians also explore connections between musical systems, such as Middle Eastern melodic and rhythmic modes. The **maqam** is an Arabic or Turkish mode composed of tetrachords that forms the basis of melodic construction and improvisation. While these musical materials reference regional cultures, individual interpretations can vary greatly and transcend national and cultural borders.

***

oud ('ūd) (Arabic *al-'ūd*) a lute or chordophone common in Middle Eastern music.

chordophone a stringed instrument.

darbouka (dumbek) an Arabic goblet-shaped hand drum, common in Middle Eastern music.

taksim (taqsīm) a soloistic instrumental improvisation found in Arab and Turkish music traditions.

maqam (Arabic) an Arabic mode composed of tetrachords.

The Maghreb

The Maghreb, the region encompassing North Africa from Morocco to Libya, is said to include Andalucia, Spain, because of its history of multicultural influences, including the lasting influences of Sephardic Jewish and Muslim populations after their forced expulsion beginning in the fifteenth century. The legacy of Andalucia as a harmonious multicultural society continues to inspire musicians to explore the intersections of these cultures. Some of these influences (such as the highly punctuated and syncopated rhythmic patterns of *palmas* and *zapateo*, and melismatic vocal phrasing) can be heard in flamenco music, including the flamenco jazz of modern-day pianists Diego Amador (*Piano Jondo*, 2003) and Chano Dominguez (*New Flamenco Sound*, 2006). In the late twentieth and early twenty-first centuries Tunisian *oud* player Anouar Brahem (*Thimar*, 1998) and pianist Wajdi Cherif (*Jasmine*, 2006) both explored the intersections of Arab classical and Western European jazz traditions, shifting their emphasis among musical styles through collaboration with varied musicians.

The Mashriq

The Mashriq (the eastern coast of the Mediterranean, including Egypt) includes some well-established jazz cultures, especially in Israel and Egypt. Cairo, long regarded as a modern, cosmopolitan epicenter for music culture, hosts an annual jazz festival informed by a long history of local jazz performance. In the 1960s, Salah Ragab, a drummer, established several combos and a big band with which he recorded several albums, including collaborations with the American experimental bandleader Sun Ra (compiled in *The Sun Ra Arkestra Meets Salah Ragab in Egypt*, 1999).

Jewish cultures are active in countries around the world, and Israel serves as an epicenter of Jewish jazz music. Through institutionalized education and a vibrant festival scene, Israeli-born jazz musicians, such as bassists Avishai Cohen and Omer Avital, exhibit influences from the Middle Eastern, Western, and Eastern European branches of the Jewish diaspora. For example, Cohen's *Adama* (1998) includes *oud* and Middle Eastern melody and harmony. Oudist Marcel Khalife and vocalist Rima Khcheich, both of Lebanese descent, are internationally renowned musicians whose careers are bolstered by successful recordings and festival performances. Syrian Abdullah Chhadeh performs on **qānūn** (plucked zither) and fronts several projects that have garnered success among local jazz and international festival audiences.

Anouar Brahem, performing live onstage, playing the oud, 2007. PHOTO COURTESY PHILIP RYALLS/REDFERNS/GETTY IMAGES.

Anatolia and Caucasus

Anatolia and the Caucasus region, which encompasses the nations surrounded by the Black and Caspian Seas, includes Turkey, home of the Middle East's most established jazz culture. Percussionist Okay Temiz, among others, has achieved much success, often collaborating with musicians outside of Turkey; one of his best recordings is *Magnetic Band*

---

qānūn a Middle Eastern stringed instrument, like a plucked zither, with 72 to 75 strings.

Abdullah Chhadeh performs with his band, April 24, 2009, in Abu Dhabi. PHOTO COURTESY AFP/GETTY IMAGES.

in Finland 1995 (released in 2004). Jazz in Armenia traces its history back 70 years, and several organizations in Azerbaijan have recently founded a Web site (www.jazz.az) that celebrates local jazz culture, including the publication of an anthology that features Azerbaijani musicians.

Arabian Peninsula and Central Asia

The Arabian Peninsula and Central Asia (encompassing Iran, Pakistan, Afghanistan, and neighboring former Soviet republics) reveal relatively little information on their jazz cultures, partly due to changes in political environments within the last several decades. In Iran, however, jazz thrived in the 1960s, through recordings, television programs, and music festivals. Iraqi-American Amir ElSaffar performs both as a classical Iraqi singer and a trumpeter in the tradition of American jazz (*Two Rivers*, 2007). In 2010 he collaborated with Hafez Modirzadeh, an Iranian-American saxophonist and scholar/educator. The collaborative work of these artists demonstrates the potential for jazz to serve prescriptive, socially conscious goals by emphasizing mutual respect and peaceful commonality that rise above political or cultural conflicts.

Middle Eastern Influences on American Jazz

American jazz musicians have explored Middle Eastern music through jazz—both in collaboration with Middle Eastern musicians and in personal interpretations of the region. Randy Weston (*The Splendid Master Gnawa Musicians of Morocco*, 1995), Ornette Coleman (*Dancing in Your Head*, 2000), and Pharoah Sanders (*The Trance of Seven Colors*, 1994) all recorded with musicians from Morocco. In the 1960s, bassist Ahmed Abdul-Malik (*East Meets West*, 1960) and flautist Herbie Mann (*Impressions of the Middle East*, 1967) recorded jazz albums influenced by Middle Eastern music. The best known of these is Dave Brubeck's *Blue Rondo à la Turk* (1959; CD I, Track 21/Download Track 21) and Duke Ellington's *Far East Suite* (1966), inspired by his State Department tours of both the Middle East and Japan. (Listen to *Isfahan* from the *Far East Suite*, *JTSA* Disc 5/Track 7.) More recently, John Zorn and the musicians on his Tzadik record label have extended the sonic boundaries of Middle Eastern music and Euro-American jazz in recordings such as *Bar Kokhbar* (1996) and *Live at Tonic* (2001).

> **TAKE NOTE**
>
> • How did jazz develop in the Middle East, and who are some of the key players?

Jazz in Eastern Europe

In Eastern Europe, a region prone to political turmoil, bloody wars, and repression, jazz became an outlet for individual expression and a manifestation of artistic and personal freedom. Musically, jazz in Eastern Europe drew in varying measures from American jazz (filtered through the sensibilities of local players), a wide variety of native folk traditions (Jewish **klezmer**, Slavic folk songs, Gypsy dance music), and European classical music.

It was not until 1920–22 that the earliest accounts of jazz performances in Eastern Europe began to emerge. Some countries were visited by touring American musicians. In other countries, local enthusiasts listened to and tried to imitate early 78-rpm jazz records—most notably those of the Original Dixieland Jazz Band—imported (or smuggled) from the United States. In Russia, the first documented jazz performance took place in Moscow on October 1, 1922 (celebrated since 1982 as the

---

klezmer (Yiddish) traditional Eastern European Jewish music, which underwent a revival in the late-twentieth-century United States; such jazz musicians as John Zorn and Don Byron have sometimes blended klezmer with jazz.

birthday of Russian jazz). The band was local, led not by a musician but by a dancer. Valentin Parnakh, an innovator of European modern dance, and a poet and literature historian, had spent many years in Western Europe, where he fell in love with this exciting new music from beyond the ocean.

The first Russian jazz band to be recorded was pianist Alexander Tsfasman's, in 1928; within the next 10 years, the first Eastern European jazz recordings were made in Czechoslovakia, Poland, Romania, and other countries. Recordings contained either American standards, reproduced by local musicians with more or less accuracy, or dance tunes. Until the 1940s, the very word "jazz" for Eastern Europeans meant a certain type of band rather than a style of music (a band that, unlike a traditional brass band, included saxophones, a drum set, and, in many cases, violins and accordions along with the brass). Any modern danceable music, even with a strong influence from local folkloric traditions, was called "jazz" if it was played by a "jazz band." Soloists and vocalists could emulate the blues, or employ Eastern European sonorities (most notably derived from Jewish klezmer and local brands of Gypsy folk music), or simply stick to the melody without much improvisation; still, they were called "jazz musicians." Examples included the Czech dance bandleader Rudolf Antonín Dvorský, who would perform both jazz tunes and Czech folk songs, and the U.S.S.R. (Union of Soviet Socialist Republics)-based singer-actor Leonid Utyosov, whose State Jazz Orchestra of the Russian Soviet Federative Socialist Republic might play American jazz, klezmer, Gypsy romance songs, and Russian folk tunes during the same concert. German trumpet player Eddie Rosner, who emigrated to Poland after Hitler was elected Germany's chancellor in 1933, defected to the Soviet Union with his entire Polish band when Hitler's troops entered Poland in 1939; he gained wide popularity in the U.S.S.R. by adding local pop tunes and Polish songs translated into Russian to his repertoire of jazz standards.

Then, for more than a decade, World War II and subsequent political shifts across the subcontinent made it difficult for jazz to evolve there; its very survival was in question in the late 1940s. Jazz, although never officially banned, was depicted by the Communist authorities as "decadent bourgeois music" and went mostly underground. Even Utyosov's band, the most popular band in the Soviet Union, dropped the word "jazz" from its name and continued as the State Variety Orchestra. Eddie Rosner was arrested in 1946—officially for the "unauthorized attempt to cross the state border" (he tried to leave the U.S.S.R. for Poland without permission from the government)—and served a six-year term in Siberian labor camps (where he, not surprisingly, led a successful prison jazz band).

Change came in the mid- and late 1950s. Everywhere in Eastern Europe, new generations of musicians were turning toward jazz: they felt that the music, especially in its new styles of bebop, hard bop, and, later, free jazz, was the ultimate expression of personal creative freedom. Regional musicians tried to scale the new summits of jazz musicianship, mostly by picking up the music by ear from smuggled American vinyl records or from taped transmissions of the U.S. international short-wave radio service Voice of America. (Willis Conover, the VOA jazz host, became the general source of jazz information for thousands of musicians in Eastern Europe.) Slight liberalization of political regimes, first in the countries outside the Soviet Union and then within the U.S.S.R. itself, made it possible for musicians to emerge from the cultural underground to the mainstream of their countries' music scenes.

Poland

In Poland, the success of Krzysztof Komeda, a gifted jazz pianist and popular film score composer, opened the way for an entire generation of first-class jazz improvisors who were not only emulating the Americans but also trying to incorporate their own cultures' richest music traditions into their own, personal jazz voices. Two former members of the Komeda Quartet, saxophonist Zbigniew Namyslowski and trumpet player Tomasz Stanko, became the creative leaders of the Polish jazz scene (and the Eastern European scene in general) for the decades to follow. (Listen to Tomasz Stanko on *Suspended Night Variation VIII*, *JTSA*, Disc 6/ Track 16.) The present-day generation of musicians, including brilliant pianists Marcin Wasilewski and Leszek Mozdzer and saxophonist Adam Pieronczyk, keeps this legacy alive.

Czechoslovakia

In Czechoslovakia, similar processes were complicated by political upheaval in 1968; many jazz musicians emigrated to the West, which enriched American jazz with the likes of keyboardist Jan Hammer (who would join the fusion group Mahavishnu Orchestra), bassist George Mraz (born Jirí Mráz), and bassist Miroslav Vitous (an eventual member of Weather Report), but slowed down the evolution of local jazz scenes for almost two decades. Recently, musicians such as flautist Jirí Stivín and violinist/singer Iva Bittová have worked within a poly-stylistic idiom on the edges of jazz, avant-garde, and modern classical music.

Hungary

Hungarian jazz also suffered a substantial brain drain, as emigration from there was probably the easiest in the whole Eastern bloc; early émigrés such as guitarist Attila Zoller (who moved to Germany in 1948 and then made it big in New York in the 1960s) were followed by the likes of guitarist **Gábor Szabó** (who moved to the United States in the mid-1950s). More recently, however, a strong jazz scene enjoyed state support in Budapest, overseen by pianist and educator Károly Binder and influenced by Hungary's free-jazz patriarch, pianist György Szabados.

Romania

In Romania, although the local Communist regime was more hard-line than anywhere else in Eastern Europe, pianist Johnny Raducanu developed his local brand of jazz music, influenced by Romanian and Gypsy folk dance tunes, starting in the late 1950s, and his followers (pianist Ion Baciu, Jr., guitarist Ionut Dorobantu, and vocalist Teodora Enache, among others) kept the genre alive even in the worst years of the Ceausescu dictatorship in the 1980s.

Yugoslavia

Yugoslavia, although culturally part of Eastern Europe, never became part of the Warsaw Pact—the military alliance of Eastern European Communist countries. This enabled the 1971 launch (by an American company) of Eastern Europe's largest jazz festival, the Belgrade Newport Jazz Festival, in this federated country's capital in 1971. Twenty years later it was discontinued as the Balkan states entered a decade-long period of violence, civil wars, and the ultimate disintegration of Yugoslavia. In 2005, a group of enthusiasts in Belgrade revived the event under the name the Belgrade Jazz Festival.

Bulgaria

Bulgarian jazz, since its relatively late start in the 1960s, was always marked by incorporation of the complex, odd rhythmic patterns of local music into jazz improvisation; those rhythms became a trademark of pianist Milcho Leviev, who worked as a performer and arranger with the American trumpeter-bandleader Don Ellis and drummer Billy Cobham in the 1970s. (Leviev continued to influence the jazz scene in his native country by giving master classes in its capital, Sofia.) Most contemporary Bulgarian improvisers gravitate toward open concepts and cross-pollination of modern classical, Bulgarian folk, and avant-garde jazz music.

The Former Soviet Union (Union of Soviet Socialist Republics, or U.S.S.R.)

The jazz scene in the Soviet Union enjoyed a period of unexpectedly broad support from the state authorities following the 1960s and through the 1980s, as the Communist rulers felt that rock music was a more dangerous enemy of their ideology: jazz musicians, at least, did not sing protest songs, and they made the Soviet Union look good when they toured internationally. In Russia, the U.S.S.R.'s largest member republic, Moscow and Leningrad were the jazz centers, where several thousand professional musicians played in big bands, in combos, or solo, and practiced all existing jazz styles, from Dixieland and swing to free jazz, and from bebop to fusion.

Many Russians emigrated in the 1970s to 1990s. Some found success in the United States or in Europe. Some also returned to Russia: Leningrad-born saxophonist Igor Butman, active on the New York scene in the early 1990s, returned to run a successful jazz club, a superb big band, a record label, and a major jazz festival in Moscow. Several Russian musicians tried to be visible on the American scene without leaving their native land; they included Moscow-based saxophonist Oleg Kireyev, his fellow Muscovite pianist Ivan Farmakovsky, and St. Petersburg-based pianist Andrey Kondakov. As in other Eastern European countries, some Russian players opted to explore inter-genre possibilities; French horn virtuoso Arkady Shilkloper, active in both Europe and Russia, purveyed his own blend of jazz and modern classical music.

Other prominent jazz scenes in the former Soviet Union were Lithuanian, Estonian, Ukrainian, Armenian, and Azeri. While Azerbaijan is geographically in Asia, its jazz scene is well connected with Europe, where Azeri jazz superstar Aziza Mustafa Zadeh followed the steps of her father, the late pianist Vagif Mustafazadeh, who in the 1960s and 1970s pioneered the use of the native Azeri music style *mugam* in jazz improvisation. Jazz musicians in Armenia work in the same direction, incorporating the complex odd rhythms and ancient scales of Armenian music in jazz, most notably in the Armenian Navy Band (note the irony: Armenia is a landlocked country, and therefore has no navy!) led by American-born percussionist Arto Tunçboyaciyan, who in the 1990s moved to the land of his forefathers to explore his musical heritage.

The Ukraine

Many Ukrainian jazz performers during the period of 1990s economical instability moved to the United States, Europe, or Russia; still, the country offered a vibrant jazz scene, grouped around several strong jazz festivals in the capital of Kyiv and in Lviv, Odessa, Kharkiv, and Donetsk.

Estonia

Estonia, in its Soviet period, was the site of the Tallinn International Jazz Festival, which served as the meeting point for the entire Soviet jazz community in late 1960s. In independent Estonia, the festival flourished again, under the name Jazzkaar (Jazz Rainbow), now presenting musicians from all over the world, often in collaboration with strong local players (most notably, guitarist Jaak Sooäär).

Lithuania

Lithuania remains the country with one of the most original and well-evolved local brands of jazz in Eastern Europe, arguably ranking second after Poland. In the Lithuanian capital of Vilnius, in the early 1970s, three musicians from other Soviet locales began a collaboration that yielded a unique brand of free jazz—or "operative composition,"as they would call it. In 1986, as the Ganelin Trio, they became the first Soviet free-jazz band to tour the United States, garnering critical acclaim. Pianist Slava Ganelin left Vilnuis for Israel in 1987, but the other two, saxophonist Vladimir Chekasin and percussionist Vladimir Tarasov, still serve as Lithuanian jazz patriarchs, raising new generations of prolific improvisers with their unique individual voices.

TAKE NOTE

- Which musicians led the practice of jazz in Eastern Europe, and what were the characteristic styles?

Jazz in Africa

Jazz has deep roots in the music and culture of sub-Saharan Africa—most American slaves came from West Africa—and it was only a matter of time before the jazz impulse would reach and resonate in Africa. When it did, what happened varied widely in this large and diverse continent, which contains more countries—54—than any other.

Jazz spread primarily to urban areas in relatively better-developed countries. In the early years, jazz reached Africa through sheet music,

films, and especially phonograph recordings. For example, in the early 1930s, the Lagos (Nigeria) Police Band was listening to recordings of Louis Armstrong. In later years, radio, especially broadcasts on the Voice of America, helped spread the sound, as did occasional visits by American musicians. From 1956 to 1973, the U.S. State Department sponsored tours of such jazz musicians as Randy Weston, Woody Herman, Duke Ellington, and Dizzy Gillespie, which won many new fans for the music. Most of all, many Africans loved and still love Louis Armstrong, who toured about 30 cities across the continent, has been honored on the postage stamps of seven African nations, and remains the most popular American jazz musician in Africa.

South Africa

South Africa boasts the longest and by far strongest jazz tradition on the continent. Anthropologist David Coplan ascribes this to "similarities in the socio-historical experience of black Americans and South Africans, including rapid urbanization and industrialization and racial oppression . . . [and] the value of black American models for black South African urban cultural adaptation, identity, and resistance."

In the late 1910s and 1920s, slow boats from America brought not only cargo but also early jazz recordings. The music inspired black musicians in the segregated, impoverished townships and their speakeasies or *shebeens*, but the question of whether to absorb American musical elements sparked controversy in the local black press. Many performers imitated American styles, learning them from recordings, sheet music, or movies. In the 1930s, Solomon "Zulu Boy" Cele's Jazz Maniacs fused swing instrumentation, call and response between brass and reeds

Hugh Masekela performing in Chicago, 2005. PHOTO COURTESY MICHAEL JACKSON.

Listening Guide

((•— **Listen** to *Manenberg (Revisited)* by Abdullah Ibrahim on **mymusiclab.com**
CD II, Track 12/Download Track 36

MANENBERG (REVISITED) • ABDULLAH IBRAHIM

Music: Abdullah Ibrahim, 1974. Personnel: Carlos Ward (flute); Ricky Ford (tenor sax); Abdullah Ibrahim (piano); David Williams (bass); Ben Riley (drums). Recorded October 1985 in Englewood Cliffs, New Jersey. Original issue: *Water from an Ancient Well*, Black Hawk BKH50207. Timing: 6:12.

Overview

South African pianist Abdullah Ibrahim, known early in his career as Dollar Brand, grew up in the Manenberg section of segregated Cape Town surrounded by *kwela* music: peppy, melodically and harmonically simple major-key melodies originally played on pennywhistles (mass-produced metal flutes). His tune *Manenberg*, like other South African jazz, catches the flavor of *kwela*. This arrangement, for his New York band Ekaya, features an elaborate "solo" for melded flute and tenor sax, to offset the elementary tune.

Key Features

- The melody consists of two basic motifs over a recurring three-chord progression that anchors the entire piece. In Ibrahim's performances the number of repetitions has varied; the form as heard here is AAABBB.
- The scripted, unison "solo" for flute and tenor follows the same chords; there's no sense of a chorus structure or overall development. All the melodic and thematic material is derived from the F major scale, as if played on a pennywhistle.
- The long written episode is striking for what's absent. There are no blue notes, little fast virtuoso playing or variation in dynamics, no building to a climax or even a real ending. But it has the freshness and loose extemporized feel of real improvising. *Manenberg (Revisited)* has the timeless quality of folk art—as if its cycling motion could go on forever.
- Ekaya was an international band: three members were born outside the United States: Ibrahim, David Williams (from Trinidad), and Carlos Ward (Panama).

—*Kevin Whitehead*

TIME	SECTION	MELODY
0:00	INTRO/VAMP	A two-bar melodic figure (followed by two bars of gospel-like piano, rolling over the same chords) is played twice as an introductory vamp, at a stately pace. Note the **triplet**-like, skipping momentum of drummer Ben Riley, who uses brushes throughout. Bassist David Williams, the son of a calypso bass player, elaborates on and slides over the constant three-chord two-bar cycle. Note his inventive fills, at the ends of those cycles, in the entire performance.
		Throughout, Riley tends to go easy on the first beat of a $\frac{4}{4}$ measure, giving his drumming a Caribbean lilt. From 0:11, he sometimes plays his version of a reggae "one drop"—leaving out that first beat altogether.

(in the style of Fletcher Henderson; and *marabi*, a guitar or keyboard style of the slum yards, creating considerable excitement. By the 1940s, militant voices began advocating for the absorption of specifically *African* musical materials into jazz—a shift that would ultimately profoundly shape South African jazz. By the mid-1940s, bands such as the Harlem Swingsters began experimenting with fusing the cyclical harmonies of *marabi*, "a slow, heavy beat .. . and American swing," writes Chris Ballantine. "The result was nothing less than a new kind of jazz: its practitioners and supporters were eventually to call it African jazz, or *mbaqana*."

By the 1940s and 1950s, jazz groups large and small proliferated in cities and towns across the country. By the late 1950s, South African jazz was diverging in two directions: the *marabi*-oriented dance bands and a more overtly political, progressive style, inspired by the American avant-garde. The leading exponent of the progressive style was the Jazz Epistles—led by pianist Dollar Brand and featuring Hugh Masekela (trumpet), Jonas Gwangwa (trombone), and Kippie Moeketsi (reeds). They made one album (*Verse One*, 1959) before going into exile after the white racist government cracked down heavily in 1960. Other musicians joined the exodus including Brand's wife, singer Bea Benjamin, and white bandleader Chris McGregor, who organized a racially integrated band, the Blue Notes (*B My Dear*, 1964).

TIME	SECTION	MELODY
0:20	THEME A	Flute and tenor enter—voiced in unison throughout the performance (as if they're a single instrument). The A motif is the same as that introductory vamp, echoed here by piano, in classic call and response. Riley's "one drop" occurs at 0:21 and 0:25.
0:30	THEME A REPEATED	Flute and tenor sax continue to voice the melody.
0:40	THEME A REPEATED	Bass and drums subtly vary their accompaniment; otherwise, there is no development.
0:50	THEME B	The second figure is a slow, descending four-note run, with the first note repeated. It begins on the second beat of the bar. Piano then echoes the horns: more call and response.
1:00	THEME B REPEATED	As just heard, with response from imitative piano.
1:10	THEME B REPEATED	Note, again, the lack of development, of holding in place, reinforced by the verbatim call and response between winds and piano.
1:20	SCORED "SOLO" FOR HORNS	The horns begin by playing an answer to Theme B, as if moving into the next part of the melody—but the line proceeds without repetition. This "solo" continues for 100 bars (plus a two-bar **tag**). Its melody does not repeat itself, or make much overt reference to the opening themes, though it does rely on, and sometimes develops, small kernel phrases. The phrases are often linked by rhythmic imitation and variation, but the short sequences rarely run more than four bars.
		Minor subplots develop and disappear: a catchy, repeating figure will be introduced (as at 2:08 and 5:06) and dropped. At other times riffs will be spun out into longer, more complex variations (as from 3:22 to 3:47—with a false ending after the high note at 3:40 before the final phrase).
		Although there's no sense of overall development, Riley and Williams build tension by gradually accelerating the tempo very slightly, and with impromptu accents. Williams constantly varies his runs around the basic chords; Riley's brush slaps on snare drum get more emphatic. A two-bar tag (5:15) is squeezed in behind the (anticlimactic—almost cut off) end of the scored improvisation; note the loping, reggae-like feel of the rhythm trio.
5:20	PIANO VAMP (THEME A)	Piano vamps, as at the beginning of the performance (though with fewer repeats).
5:29	THEME A (HORNS)	In feel, the closing theme closely resembles the parallel sequence at 0:21.
5:38	THEME A REPEATED	As just heard.
5:48	THEME A REPEATED	Decelerating tempo signals an ending. Note how Riley's snare drum accents drill home the new tempo. We end with a rumble of cymbal rolls, piano tremolo chords, and bass thrumming the keynote.

During the decades of white oppression of black and colored (mixed-race) peoples, black and white musicians could not play on the same stage and a jam session might be broken up by the police. Jazz became a cry for freedom, which is why the authorities suppressed it and even forbade the public from listening to banned musicians. Converting to Islam in 1968, Dollar Brand became Abdullah Ibrahim and in 1974 penned *Manenberg*, named for one of the Cape Town townships where people settled after the government demolished the homes of 60,000 black people. *Manenberg* became an anthem for those resisting the government. In 1978, the exiled South African bassist Johnny Dyani recorded *Song for Biko*, for student leader Steven Biko, killed in 1977 while in police custody.

((●—Hear a profile of Abdullah Ibrahim on **mymusiclab.com**

triplet   three beats fit evenly into the time span of two, as in

tag   a phrase tagged on or added to the end of a chorus or, more commonly, a piece; the latter is formally known as a *coda*.

Against this backdrop, in 1983, at the University of KwaZulu-Natal in Durban, Darius Brubeck, son of the American pianist-composer, initiated the first degree-granting course in jazz studies offered by an African university. The fall of apartheid in the early 1990s brought new freedom for the music—lessening its political urgency, but also permitting the flowering of jazz radio programs, jazz recordings, jazz festivals (for example, the Cape Town International Jazz Festival, established in 1999), a training school for youth (Johnny Mekoa's Guateng Jazz Academy), and a South African Association for Jazz Education.

After fully free elections in 1994, some exiled musicians returned home, while longtime musicians made new recordings: "Big Voice" Jack Lerole improvised on the pennywhistle in *kwela*-style jazz on *Across Africa* (2003). New artists emerged, such as Moses Taiwa Molelekwa, who fused traditional and electronic instruments in *Genes and Spirits* and stacked alluring polyrhythms in *Ntatemoholo* (both from the album *Genes and Spirits*, 1998).

Ethiopia

If South African jazz sounds different than American jazz, Ethiopian jazz sounds even more exotic to American ears, because of its "oriental" or Arabic-sounding pentatonic scales. These Ethiopian scales figure prominently in the work of composer and multi-instrumentalist Mulatu Astatke, who worked with Duke Ellington and is "the father of Ethiojazz." His recording career runs from the 1960s (*Éthiopiques 4: Ethio Jazz & Musique Instrumentale, 1969–1974*) to 2010's *I Faram Gami I Faram*. Today, Ethiopia's capital, Addis Ababa, hosts a renewed jazz scene and even a nascent African School of Jazz.

Senegal

In Senegal, jazz became popular in the 1930s through recordings of U.S. and French musicians. During World War II, U.S. servicemen stationed there introduced American recordings, instruments, and dancing styles. After the War, the then-capital city Saint Louis became a center for jazz in West Africa, as bands playing New Orleans, swing, and bop styles became popular. In the 1950s and 1960s, Cuban and Latin styles took precedence. The Saint-Louis Jazz Festival, founded in 1990, pays homage to the city's one-time jazz prominence, and ranks as one of the most important in Africa. Intriguing new jazz, some incorporating indigenous sounds, is still heard in Senegal. The Senegalese saxophonist Abdoulaye N'Diaye has mixed *kora* and other African instruments with American ones, as on *Xarrit Sama* (2001).

South African pianist Abdullah Ibrahim (a.k.a. Dollar Brand) followed mid-1960s ventures into free jazz with a return to African musical ideas, yielding music of great harmonic and rhythmic variety and emotional depth. PHOTO COURTESY ANDY FREEBERG.

Other Locales

Elsewhere, jazz has made toeholds, and mixes with other kinds of music at venues such as Burkina Faso's Festival Jazz à Ouaga, established in 1992. By 2010, partly as a draw for tourists, jazz festivals were springing up in Angola, Mozambique, Cape Verde, and other countries.

In the United States, "jazz" has been a contested term; its meaning in Africa is often at least as variable as it is stateside, and can mean simply a band playing for social dancing. But however one defines it, American jazz has influenced a wide array of African musicians, from Ghanian Highlife and Congolese *rumba* bands, singers such as South Africa's Miriam

Ladysmith Black Mambazo performs Paul Simon's Under African Skies *at BAM on April 9, 2008, in New York City.* PHOTO COURTESY AMY SUSSMAN/GETTY IMAGES.

Makeba and Cape Verde's Cesaria Evora, to the South African choral group Ladysmith Black Mambazo, the Cameroon-born electric bassist Richard Bona, and the Afropop pioneer Fela Kuti.

TAKE NOTE

• What styles of jazz are popular in Africa, and who are the dominant performers?

Global Jazz in the Twenty-First Century

In the new century, jazz musicians and musicians inspired by it continued to come from all over the globe. Guitarist and vocalist Lionel Loueke, from Benin, played intricate rhythms that reflect African pop as well as jazz (the album *Karibu*, 2008). The Syrian Jazz Orchestra was founded in 2005—in the wake of a jazz festival in Damascus produced by the Swiss embassy—and involved Syrian, Dutch, German, and Greek musicians; the Brooklyn-based, Finland-born pianist Frank Carlberg has written music for them. The Israeli scene became productive enough to start exporting players to New York. In the late 1990s,

bassist Omer Avital led a sextet every week at the Greenwich Village club Smalls, and later employed his countryman Avishai Cohen on trumpet—not to be confused with the Israeli bassist Avishai Cohen. The trumpeter also worked with two of his émigré siblings in the band 3 Cohens, as on *Braid* (2007)— recorded as his clarinetist/saxophonist sister Anat was becoming a critical favorite.

By then jazz in Europe had become so vital the English critic Stuart Nicholson frequently made the case—as in his 2005 book *Is Jazz Dead? (Or Has It Moved to a New Address)*—that European jazz had taken the lead, the American variety, in his view, having fallen into a purely retrospective phase. But the musicians he touted as jazz's new European wave were steeped in American music: Norway's Nils Petter Molvaer's plaintive trumpet, electronics, and funk rhythms owe an obvious debt to 1970s and 1980s Miles Davis; the club/dance beats of Swedish pianist Esbjörn Svensson's trio E.S.T. (*Somewhere Else Before*, 2001) derived from techno and hip-hop—like the American group Medeski Martin & Wood that came before them. Indeed, it seemed Nicholson was unaware of progressive developments in New York, Chicago, and elsewhere, dismissing a scene across the Atlantic on the basis of incomplete information—the way some Americans, knowing no better, had written off jazz abroad.

European and American musicians maintained cordial relations however—particularly in Chicago, where Germans (Peter Brötzmann), Scandinavians (Swedish saxophonist Mats Gustafsson, Norwegian bassist Ingebrigt Haaker Flaten, and drummer Paal Nilssen-Love), Austrians (trumpeter Axel Dörner), and Dutch musicians (Misha Mengelberg and other members of his ICP) collaborated with local improvisers such as saxophonist Ken Vandermark. Gustafsson,

Vandermark, and Nilssen-Love all play in Brötzmann's multinational band based in Chicago on *Chicago Tentet at Molde 2007*.

✳️ Explore Key Recordings on **mymusiclab.com**

TAKE NOTE

- How has global jazz continued to develop in the first decade of the twenty-first century?

TAKE NOTE

- Who were the prominent musicians who brought jazz to Europe and how has a European jazz scene developed?

The first great U.S. jazzman in Europe was clarinetist Sidney Bechet, who first toured in 1919. By the mid-1920s, singer/dancer Josephine Baker achieved overwhelming success in Paris, where many top jazz musicians performed. In 1932, the Hot Club of France was established, which later in the decade became home to guitarist Django Reinhardt and violinist Stéphane Grappelli and their famed Quintet. In the 1930s, Louis Armstrong, Duke Ellington, and Coleman Hawkins performed extensively in Western Europe. However, under some of Europe's more repressive governments, such as the Nazis in Germany and the Communists in Russia, jazz was often viewed as "decadent" music and was seriously repressed. After World War II, regional styles developed by homegrown talent led to a blossoming of jazz across Europe.

- What is the history of jazz in Asia and Oceania, and who are the vital figures creating original jazz music there?

In the decades before World War II, a small number of jazz musicians toured in Asia and Oceania, and some homegrown music was also created. However, jazz swept through Asia with renewed vigor after World War II. While jazz remains controversial in some countries—such as China and Korea—in others it has become highly popular, notably Japan. Japan has produced many leading jazz performers, including big band composer Toshiko Akiyoshi; pianist Yosuke Yamashita; and trumpeter Toshinori Kondo. Since the 1960s, there have been various collaborations between Asian and American jazz players and new musical styles created by Americans of Asian descent. Asian

musicians who are living far from their homelands have also made a large impact on the jazz world, notably French–Vietnamese guitarist Nguyên Lê.

- How did jazz develop in the Middle East, and who are some of the key players?

American jazz musicians such as Dave Brubeck and Duke Ellington have explored Middle Eastern music through jazz—both in collaboration with Middle Eastern musicians and in personal interpretations of the region. While jazz is not widely performed in certain Arabic/Islamic countries where Western music is resisted, there are many jazz cultures in the region, including in Egypt, Israel, Turkey, and the Balkans. The Israeli Avishai Cohen, Turkey's Okay Temiz, and Iraqi-American Amir ElSaffar are among prominent Middle Eastern jazz players.

- Which musicians led the practice of jazz in Eastern Europe, and what were the characteristic styles?

In Eastern Europe, a region prone to political turmoil, jazz became an outlet for individual expression and a manifestation of artistic and personal freedom. Polish trumpeter Tomasz Stanko, Czech bassists George Mraz and Miroslav Vitous, Hungarian guitarists Attila Zoller and Gábor Szabó, and Lithuania's Ganelin Trio are among the more prominent Eastern European jazz players. Musically, jazz in Eastern Europe drew from American jazz, native folk traditions, and European classical music.

- What styles of jazz are popular in Africa, and who are the dominant performers?

While jazz has its roots in African music, it has developed most strongly in certain areas, notably South Africa, which has a tradition of jazz music that goes back to the 1920s. Under apartheid, jazz played a key role in expressing resistance to the regime, particularly in the work of such musicians as pianist Abdullah Ibrahim. In Ethiopia, Arabic-influenced music has been predominant, particularly in the work of composer and pianist Mulatu Astatke. Jazz has long been popular in Senegal, where saxophonist Abdoulaye N'Diaye has mixed *kora* and other African instruments with American ones.

• How has global jazz continued to develop in the first decade of the twenty-first century?

In the new century, jazz musicians and musicians inspired by it continued to come from all over the globe. Some critics even feel that the most innovative jazz being made today is occurring outside of the United States. Jazz continues to flourish globally, with a free interchange of ideas and styles occurring.

DISCUSSION QUESTIONS

1. What were some of the ways American jazz spread around the world?
2. Why would jazz be viewed as subversive by the German government during World War II and by Iron Curtain countries during the Cold War?
3. What aspects of life in Paris and other cities around Europe made those places attractive to American jazz musicians?
4. In jazz music that you have heard and can recall, identify musical elements—instruments, songs, rhythms—derived from countries other than the United States.
5. Identify some of the technological advances of the twentieth century that contributed to the spread of jazz worldwide.
6. In light of jazz's spread to many parts of the globe, do you think it is still American music? Whose music is it?

KEY TERMS & KEY PEOPLE

Han Bennink
chordophone
darbouka (dumbek)
fake book
gamelan
Jan Garbarek
Giorgio Gaslini
Stéphane Grappelli
Lars Gullin
Joe Harriott
Abdullah Ibrahim

Instant Composers Pool Orchestra
klezmer
koto
Nguyên Lê
maqam
Niels-Henning Ørsted Pedersen
oud ('ūd)
Oregon
qānūn

Django Reinhardt
Ravi Shankar
Shakti
sitar
Gábor Szabó
tabla
taksim (taqsūm)
township jazz
Sam Wooding

Index

Page references followed by "f" indicate illustrated figures or photographs; followed by "t" indicates a table.